Maths

for Key Stage 2

It's a Maths extravaganza from CGP!

This brilliant CGP book is bursting with Maths questions for 10-11 year olds. They're split into three difficulty levels to suit pupils of all abilities — with plenty of fun challenge pages added in for variety.

Every topic from the Year 6 Programme of Study is covered, and it's all perfectly matched to the latest National Curriculum!

What CGP is all about

Our sole aim here at CGP is to produce the highest quality books — carefully written, immaculately presented and jam-packed with helpful content.

Then we work our socks off to get them out to you — at the cheapest possible prices.

Year 6

Contents

Section 4 — Ratio and Proportion

Section 5 — Algebra

Section 6 — Measurement

Section 7 — Geometry

Section 8 — Statistics

Published by CGP

ISBN: 978 1 78294 799 8

Editors: Tom Carney, Joanna Daniels, Liam Dyer, Zoe Fenwick, Shaun Harrogate, Katya Parkes, Hannah Roscoe, Ben Train, Ruth Wilbourne, Dawn Wright

With thanks to Christopher Lindle, Simon Little, Maxine Petrie, Tina Ramsden, Glenn Rogers, Hayley Thompson and Karen Wells for the proofreading.
With thanks to Ana Pungartnik for the copyright research.

Printed by Elanders Ltd, Newcastle upon Tyne.
Clipart from Corel®
Cover image: © iStock.com/FrankRamspott

About This Book

This book covers every topic that you need to learn in Year 6 Maths.
We've packed it full of questions and made sure there is the right practice for everyone.

You'll find examples at the start of each topic. These are great reminders of how you might answer some of the questions on the topic.

Topics are each split into three Sets:

- **Set A** is perfect for getting to grips with the Year 6 topics.
- **Set B** is ideal practice if you're up to speed with the Year 6 topics.
- **Set C** offers an extra stretch if you're comfortable with the Year 6 topics.

Your teacher will let you know which Set you should work on.

At the end of each topic, the objective sums up the maths skills you've learnt. You can use the tick boxes to show how confident you feel about the topic.

Negative Numbers

You'll have seen negative numbers before, but now it's time to use them in lots of real life contexts.
If a problem seems difficult, draw a number line to keep track of how far past zero you've gone.

Example

Alan is digging up his buried treasure.
He is 18 m above sea level.
The treasure is 7 m below sea level.

How many metres will Alan have to dig in total?

Alan has to dig 18 m to reach sea level.

Then he has to dig 7 m further.

18 + 7 = **25 m.**

Set A

An anchor is –10 m under a boat.
The flag on the mast is 8 m above the boat.

1. What distance separates the anchor from the flag?

The anchor is lowered by 5 m and the flag is raised by 2 m.

2. What distance separates them now?

The diagram on the right shows a model volcano.
What is the distance between:

3. the flag and the diamond?
4. the top of the volcano and the bone?
5. the diamond and the top of the volcano?
6. the diamond and the bone?

Set B

A scientist slowly raises the temperature of an experiment. It starts at –18 °C, and warms up by 3 °C every 30 minutes.

What temperature will it be:

1. after two hours?
2. after three and a half hours?
3. after five hours?
4. after six and a half hours?

Look at the table on the right.

What is the difference in temperature between:

5. New York and Moscow?
6. London and Toronto?
7. Athens and the North Pole?
8. Sydney and Antarctica?
9. the North Pole and Antarctica?

Location	Temperature
North Pole	–34 °C
Moscow	–5 °C
London	11 °C
Toronto	–2 °C
New York	17 °C
Athens	23 °C
Sydney	29 °C
Antarctica	–48 °C

Set C

A submarine is at –450 m.
The ocean floor is at –800 m.

1. How far does the submarine have to dive to get to the ocean floor?

A plane flies overhead at 4200 m.

2. How far apart are the plane and the ocean floor?

Look at the table on the right.

What is the difference between the starting and cooked temperature:

3. of the chips?
4. of the garlic bread?
5. Which food had the greatest change in temperature?

Food	Starting Temp	Cooked Temp
Chips	–16 °C	180 °C
Fish fingers	–19 °C	210 °C
Pork chops	1 °C	170 °C
Garlic bread	–12 °C	160 °C
Sausages	2 °C	180 °C
Pizza	3 °C	200 °C

I know and can use negative numbers in context.

4 Section 1 — Number and Place Value

© CGP 2017 — not to be reproduced, including photocopying or scanning

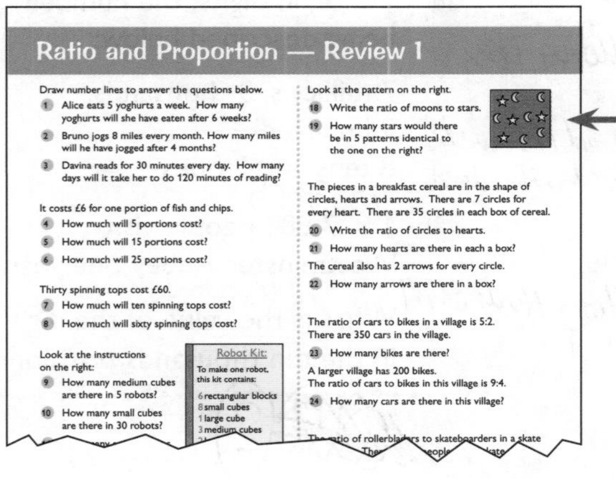

Ratio and Proportion — Review 1

Draw number lines to answer the questions below.

1. Alice eats 5 yoghurts a week. How many yoghurts will she have eaten after 6 weeks?
2. Bruno jogs 8 miles every month. How many miles will he have jogged after 4 months?
3. Davina reads for 30 minutes every day. How many days will it take her to do 120 minutes of reading?

It costs £6 for one portion of fish and chips.

4. How much will 5 portions cost?
5. How much will 15 portions cost?
6. How much will 25 portions cost?

Thirty spinning tops cost £60.

7. How much will ten spinning tops cost?
8. How much will sixty spinning tops cost?

Look at the instructions on the right:

9. How many medium cubes are there in 5 robots?
10. How many small cubes are there in 30 robots?

Robot Kit:
To make one robot, this kit contains:
6 rectangular blocks
8 small cubes
1 large cube
3 medium cubes

Look at the pattern on the right.

18. Write the ratio of moons to stars.
19. How many stars would there be in 5 patterns identical to the one on the right?

The pieces in a breakfast cereal are in the shape of circles, hearts and arrows. There are 7 circles for every heart. There are 35 circles in each box of cereal.

20. Write the ratio of circles to hearts.
21. How many hearts are there in each a box?

The cereal also has 2 arrows for every circle.

22. How many arrows are there in a box?

The ratio of cars to bikes in a village is 5:2.
There are 350 cars in the village.

23. How many bikes are there?

A larger village has 200 bikes.
The ratio of cars to bikes in this village is 9:4.

24. How many cars are there in this village?

The ratio of rollerbladers to skateboarders in a skate

After every few topics there's a **Review** page with even more practice questions — a perfect way to recap all of the topics you've learnt leading up to it.

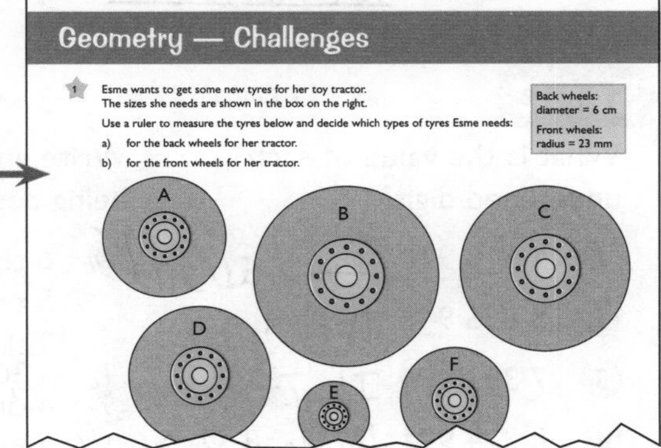

Geometry — Challenges

1. Esme wants to get some new tyres for her toy tractor.
The sizes she needs are shown in the box on the right.
Use a ruler to measure the tyres below and decide which types of tyres Esme needs:
a) for the back wheels for her tractor.
b) for the front wheels for her tractor.

Back wheels: diameter = 6 cm
Front wheels: radius = 23 mm

Each Section ends with some **Challenges**. These are a fun and interesting way to practise lots of the skills and topics you've covered in the Section.

They include loads of different questions and activities — you might have to draw, make shapes, work with other classmates, or create your own games!

The Answer Book for this Year 6 Textbook has answers to all the questions. It also includes a mapping of the Programme of Study, and a suggested Scheme of Work that teachers can follow throughout the year.

Free printable resources including blank coordinate grids can be found on our website:

www.cgpbooks.co.uk/KS2MathsResources

Place Value

Now you're in Year 6, it's time to wrestle with some really big numbers.
This year's new place value is millions, and it appears in numbers with seven digits or more.

Example

What is the value of the 6 in 6 835 120?

6	8	3	5	1	2	0
Millions	Hundred thousands	Ten thousands	Thousands	Hundreds	Tens	Ones

6 millions or **6 000 000**

Set A

What is the value of the:

1. 2 in 1 234 567?
2. 9 in 4 729 100?
3. 3 in 3 808 950?
4. 7 in 2 175 111?
5. 5 in 7 430 599?
6. 6 in 9 738 216?
7. 1 in 8 276 010?

Which digit is in the hundred thousands position of:

8. 9 122 974?
9. 8 793 241?

Which digit is in the millions position of:

10. 3 586 302?
11. 9 093 365?

Look at the number cards below.

4	8	1	2	7	3	5

Write the new number you make if you swap the:

12. millions and tens digits
13. hundred thousands and hundreds digits
14. ten thousands and ones digits

Set B

What is the value of each underlined digit?

1. $\underline{3}$ 058 338
2. 8 098 8$\underline{4}$7
3. 6 $\underline{6}$60 965
4. $\underline{2}$ 394 092
5. 3 45$\underline{7}$ 677
6. 1 8$\underline{5}$7 111

Look at the number 3 832 436.

7. Write the value of each three.
8. Write the value of each even digit.

Look at the number 7 731 896.

9. Write the value of each odd digit.

10. Write, in digits, the number being described below:
 7 millions, 3 thousands, 9 hundreds, 8 tens and 5 ones
11. 1 927 884 people visit Westminster Abbey one year. What is the value of the digit in the ten thousands position?

Set C

What is the value of each underlined digit?

1. 1 11$\underline{8}$ 935
2. 5 856 9$\underline{4}$9
3. 7 3$\underline{8}$3 474
4. 8 $\underline{7}$24 974
5. $\underline{3}$ 321 123
6. 9 902 20$\underline{9}$
7. 4 522 $\underline{7}$49

Write, in digits, the numbers being described below:

8. 6 tens, 3 millions, 5 ten thousands, 7 ones, 2 thousands and 4 hundreds
9. 4 ones, 7 thousands, 2 millions, 6 tens and 8 hundred thousands
10. 6 ten thousands, 8 ones, 4 hundreds, 8 millions and 6 hundred thousands

Look at the number cards below.

7	2	4	9	8	1	5

Use all seven cards to make:

11. the largest number you can.
12. the smallest number you can.
13. Write the largest seven-digit number you can think of.
14. How would you write ten million in digits?

I know the place value of the digits in a seven-digit number.      

Writing Numbers

Now it's time to make sure you can write large numbers using both digits and words.
Practise breaking big numbers down into each place value part and you should have no problems here.

Examples

Write five million, seven hundred and thirty-two thousand, nine hundred and eighty-one in digits.

5 000 000 + 700 000 + 30 000 + 2000 + 900 + 80 + 1 = **5 732 981**

Write 2 945 101 in words.
Two million, nine hundred and forty-five thousand, one hundred and one

Set A

Write in digits:

1. three hundred thousand
2. five hundred thousand, six hundred and seventeen
3. seven million
4. one million, two hundred thousand
5. six million and fifty-nine

Write in words:

6. 4 000 000
7. 9 900 000
8. 4 000 140
9. 3 504 400
10. 1 200 567
11. 8 045 800

12. There are two million, five hundred and ten thousand, four hundred and ninety different types of insect in the Amazon rainforest.
    Write this number in digits.
13. A rare painting is sold at an auction for £4 485 219.
    Write this amount in words.

Set B

Write in digits:

1. six million, nine hundred and seventy-three thousand, one hundred and forty-two
2. nine million, one hundred and twenty-nine thousand, seven hundred and ninety
3. three million, two hundred and twelve thousand, eight hundred and thirteen

Write in words:

4. 9 800 237
5. 4 735 400
6. Write each number below in words. Underline the even number.
   8 493 738
   1 493 729
   9 492 719

7. Write each number below in digits. Underline the odd number.

Six million, five hundred thousand and ninety-six
Eight million, six hundred thousand and twenty-four
Four million, five hundred thousand and sixty-three

Set C

Write in digits:

1. five million, eight hundred and forty-four thousand, eight hundred and sixty-two
2. nine million, two hundred and ninety-five thousand and ninety
3. seventeen million, six hundred and thirty-eight thousand and forty
4. thirty million, fifty-two thousand, one hundred and twelve

Write in words:

5. 7 304 494
6. 9 495 049
7. Write each number below in words. Underline the odd number.
   9 304 434
   8 348 491
   12 304 498

Write each city's population in digits.

8. Berlin: three million, six hundred and seventy-one thousand.
9. London: eight million, six hundred and seventy-three thousand, seven hundred and thirteen.

14 160 467 people live in Istanbul.

10. How would you write the population of Istanbul in words?

I can read and write very large numbers using digits or words.      

Negative Numbers

You'll have seen negative numbers before, but now it's time to use them in lots of real life contexts.
If a problem seems difficult, draw a number line to keep track of how far past zero you've gone.

Example

Alan is digging up his buried treasure.
He is 18 m above sea level.
The treasure is 7 m below sea level.

How many metres will Alan have to dig in total?

Alan has to dig 18 m to reach sea level.

Then he has to dig 7 m further.

18 + 7 = **25 m**.

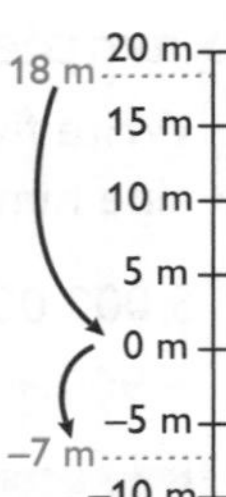

Set A

An anchor is –10 m under a boat.
The flag on the mast is 8 m above the boat.

1. What distance separates the anchor from the flag?

The anchor is lowered by 5 m and the flag is raised by 2 m.

2. What distance separates them now?

The diagram on the right shows a model volcano.
What is the distance between:

3. the flag and the diamond?
4. the top of the volcano and the bone?
5. the diamond and the top of the volcano?
6. the diamond and the bone?

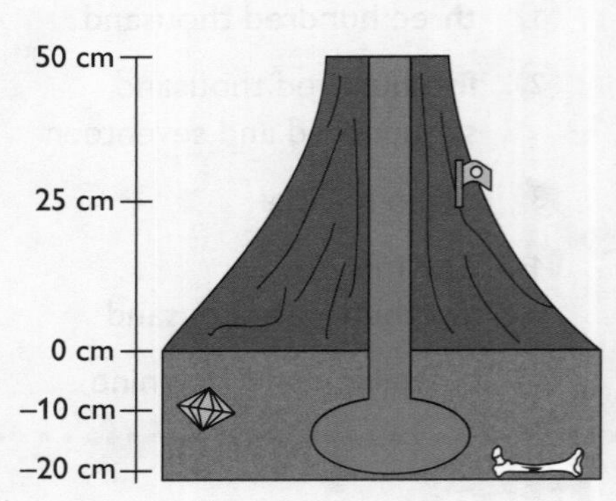

Set B

A scientist slowly raises the temperature of an experiment. It starts at –18 °C, and warms up by 3 °C every 30 minutes.

What temperature will it be:

1. after two hours?
2. after three and a half hours?
3. after five hours?
4. after six and a half hours?

Look at the table on the right.

What is the difference in temperature between:

5. New York and Moscow?
6. London and Toronto?
7. Athens and the North Pole?
8. Sydney and Antarctica?
9. the North Pole and Antarctica?

Location	Temperature
North Pole	–34 °C
Moscow	–5 °C
London	11 °C
Toronto	–2 °C
New York	17 °C
Athens	23 °C
Sydney	29 °C
Antarctica	–48 °C

Set C

A submarine is at –450 m.
The ocean floor is at –800 m.

1. How far does the submarine have to dive to get to the ocean floor?

A plane flies overhead at 4200 m.

2. How far apart are the plane and the ocean floor?

Look at the table on the right.

What is the difference between the starting and cooked temperature:

3. of the chips?
4. of the garlic bread?
5. Which food had the greatest change in temperature?

Food	Starting Temp	Cooked Temp
Chips	–16 °C	180 °C
Fish fingers	–19 °C	210 °C
Pork chops	1 °C	170 °C
Garlic bread	–12 °C	160 °C
Sausages	2 °C	180 °C
Pizza	3 °C	200 °C

I know and can use negative numbers in context.

Number and Place Value — Review 1

What is the value of the:

1. 7 in 4 876 294?
2. 3 in 3 958 012?
3. 2 in 5 942 931?
4. 6 in 9 034 867?
5. 9 in 1 847 429?
6. 5 in 8 392 541?
7. 3 in 7 348 920?
8. 1 in 4 271 932?

What is the value of each underlined digit?

9. 8 <u>9</u>36 576
10. 1 247 9<u>3</u>8
11. <u>6</u> 930 304
12. 8 1<u>7</u>8 935
13. 5 <u>6</u>47 010
14. 7 57<u>5</u> 481
15. 3 859 27<u>4</u>
16. 9 236 <u>8</u>52

Look at the number cards below.

6	2	3	5	8	9	1

What number do you make if you swap the:

17. tens and ten thousands digits?
18. millions and hundreds digits?
19. ones and hundred thousands digits?

Use all seven cards to make:

20. the largest number you can.
21. the smallest number you can.

Write, in digits, the numbers being described below:

22. 5 millions, 3 tens and 6 hundred thousands
23. 8 tens, 5 hundred thousands, 2 thousands, 6 millions, 3 ten thousands, 1 hundred
24. 2 hundreds, 7 millions, 8 hundred thousands, 2 ones, 4 thousands, 2 tens and 6 ten thousands
25. 4 ten thousands, 1 one, 6 hundreds, 9 millions, 7 thousands and 3 tens

Write in words:

26. 8 000 000
27. 7 800 000
28. 3 345 000
29. 2 630 700
30. 1 150 850
31. 8 053 500
32. 5 629 720
33. 4 830 273

Write in digits:

34. five million, seven hundred and thirty thousand, one hundred and six
35. nine million, four hundred and twenty-two thousand, five hundred and eighty-three
36. six million, nine hundred and fifty-four thousand, one hundred and seventy-three

A museum has three million and fifty thousand objects.

37. Write this number in digits.

In one year, the museum is given 300 000 more objects.

38. Write the new number of objects in words.

A country has two million and seventy-nine thousand, nine hundred and seventy-six people living there.

39. Write this number in digits.

One year 60 500 people move to other countries.

40. Write the new number of people in words.

41. Martha measured the temperature in her shed over the course of one day.
    - At 08:00 the temperature was –5.5 °C.
    - At 15:00 the temperature had risen by 8.5 °C.
    - At 21:00 the temperature had fallen by 4.9 °C.

    What was the temperature at 21:00?

Look at the bank balances below.

Name	Balance
Tia	£400
Rhys	–£230
Amir	–£560
Jalil	£600
Hana	£850

What is the difference between:

42. Rhys and Tia's balances?
43. Amir and Jalil's balances?
44. Hana and Amir's balances?
45. Jalil gives half of his money to Rhys. What is Rhys's balance now?

Top work finishing all of these questions — some numbers might be negative, but your attitude isn't!

Ordering Numbers

Putting massive numbers in order can seem like a tricky task, but there's really not much to it. Just compare each place value one at a time from left to right and Bob's your uncle.

Example

Which of these numbers is the largest?

<u>7</u> 632 904   <u>5</u> 942 813   <u>7</u> 635 649   <u>6</u> 941 395   Look at the first digit: 7 is the largest.

7 63<u>2</u> 904   7 63<u>5</u> 649   Both numbers have the same second and third digits.
Look at the fourth digit: 5 is the largest. So **7 635 649** is the largest number.

Set A

Which is larger:

1. 2 985 760 or 5 989 932?
2. 5 231 724 or 5 183 294?
3. 3 935 827 or 3 982 101?
4. 7 498 014 or 7 493 576?
5. 1 285 942 or 1 285 490?
6. 9 748 294 or 9 748 292?

Complete the gaps with < or >:

7. 4 752 528 ☐ 3 985 294
8. 8 929 371 ☐ 8 834 999
9. 7 433 914 ☐ 7 470 814
10. 6 385 123 ☐ 6 381 510
11. 3 049 908 ☐ 3 049 589
12. 9 669 849 ☐ 9 669 889

13. Order these numbers from smallest to largest:

3 234 596	5 750 519
4 731 984	4 582 834

14. Order these numbers from largest to smallest:

9 155 343	9 720 482
8 717 086	8 115 898

Set B

Which symbol, < or >, should go in each box below?

1. 5 860 482 ☐ 7 860 431
2. 4 396 379 ☐ 4 528 194
3. 3 237 376 ☐ 3 284 473
4. 2 283 597 ☐ 2 282 593
5. 2 492 349 ☐ 2 492 150
6. 6 094 180 ☐ 6 094 139

Find the largest number in each list:

7. 8 428 477, 9 458 106, 9 445 293, 9 429 877
8. 1 635 621, 1 639 788, 1 635 619, 1 637 909
9. 2 964 829, 2 966 273, 2 966 281, 2 966 311
10. 7 935 301, 7 935 344, 7 935 345, 7 935 351

Order these numbers from smallest to largest.

11.

3 199 334	3 007 641
3 761 490	4 491 916
4 097 518	3 688 909

12.

8 897 512	8 113 041
8 245 613	8 043 087
8 763 207	8 881 088

Set C

Find the third largest number in each list below.

1. 7 380 626, 8 274 389, 8 274 377, 7 379 802
2. 9 380 626, 8 274 389, 8 274 377, 9 379 802
3. 1 873 157, 1 876 855, 1 876 579, 1 739 732
4. 7 252 352, 7 239 696, 7 252 307, 7 252 391

Find all possible digits that make the statements below correct.

5. 3 489 ☐03 > 3 489 752
6. 5 388 330 > 5 ☐93 735
7. 9 697 850 < 9 69☐ 163
8. 1 7☐9 098 > 1 788 941
9. 3 570 336 < 3 5☐9 842
10. 6 707 8☐9 < 6 707 830
11. 3 397 528 > ☐ 397 528

Look at the table below.

Helicopter	Price
Blayd	£9 930 150
Chopp	£9 930 725
Flare	£9 936 145
Glorio	£9 906 605

Which helicopter:

12. is the third most expensive?
13. is the least expensive?

I can order and compare numbers up to 10 000 000.      

Rounding Numbers

Rounding makes numbers more manageable — it's really helpful when you're estimating things.
Now you're in Year 6, you'll need to be able to round pretty much any number that gets thrown at you...

Example

Round 4 633 976 to the nearest 1 000 000.

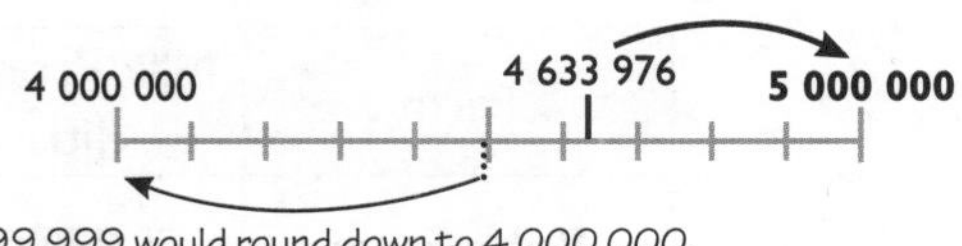

4 499 999 would round down to 4 000 000.

4 633 976 is between 4 000 000 and 5 000 000.

4 633 976 is more than 4 500 000, so round it up to **5 000 000**.

Set A

Round 931 273:

1. to the nearest 10
2. to the nearest 100
3. to the nearest 1000

Round 7 708 791:

4. to the nearest 100 000
5. to the nearest 1 000 000

Round to the nearest 1000:

6. 1 563 849
7. 2 697 093
8. 7 794 456

Round to the nearest 10 000:

9. 4 346 213
10. 8 507 008

Look at the box of numbers below.

6 579 418	6 575 034
6 568 932	6 564 989

11. Which number rounds to 6 570 000 when rounded to the nearest ten thousand?
12. Round the second smallest number in the box to the nearest one thousand.

Set B

Round 8 897 816:

1. to the nearest 1000
2. to the nearest 100
3. to the nearest 100 000

Round 3 047 398:

4. to the nearest 1 000 000
5. to the nearest 10 000

6. Norway has a population of 5 258 317.
   Round this number to the nearest 10, 100 and 10 000.
7. Look at this box of numbers:

5 259 799	5 269 995
5 269 997	5 269 993

Which numbers round to 5 270 000, to the nearest 10?

Is each number rounded to the nearest 100 000 or 10 000?

8. 2 764 031 ⟶ 2 800 000
9. 3 207 220 ⟶ 3 210 000
10. 4 311 258 ⟶ 4 310 000
11. 7 365 686 ⟶ 7 400 000
12. 1 788 359 ⟶ 1 790 000
13. 3 992 417 ⟶ 4 000 000

Set C

Round to the nearest 1000, 10 000 and 100 000:

1. 4 075 407
2. 2 218 240
3. 7 290 637

Round to the nearest 10, 100 and 1 000 000:

4. 3 029 650
5. 8 435 305

What power of 10 has each number below been rounded to?

6. 6 009 372 ⟶ 6 009 400
7. 9 794 120 ⟶ 9 800 000
8. 2 539 700 ⟶ 3 000 000
9. 9 720 109 ⟶ 9 720 110
10. 5 671 300 ⟶ 5 671 000
11. 7 477 810 ⟶ 7 480 000
12. 6 063 838 ⟶ 6 064 000

13. The distance around the Sun is 4 366 813 km.
    Round this number to the nearest 10, 100, 1000, 10 000, 100 000 and 1 000 000 km.
14. A lottery winner receives 2.5 million pounds (to the nearest £100 000).
    What is the largest whole number amount they could have won?

I can round numbers to any power of 10.

Solving Problems with Numbers

Now it's time to tie everything together with some real-life problems — who says maths isn't useful? Check out the examples below for a taste of the kinds of questions you might face... then get stuck in!

Examples

Look at the table on the right.

Which farm produced the most milk?

Farm	Milk Produced (litres)
Bob's Farm	7 077 241
Dairy Delights	8 571 811
Friesian Fantasy	8 643 160
Cow-belles	7 083 442

Look at the millions place value first:

7 077 241 litres   8 571 811 litres   8 643 160 litres   7 083 442 litres

8 is the largest.
Now look at the hundred thousands place value:

8 571 811 litres   8 643 160 litres

6 is the largest.
8 643 160 is the largest, so **Friesian Fantasy** produced the most milk.

Each farm rounds the amount of milk they produced to the nearest 10 000 litres.

Show that Bob's Farm and Cow-belles round to the same number.

Bob's Farm:

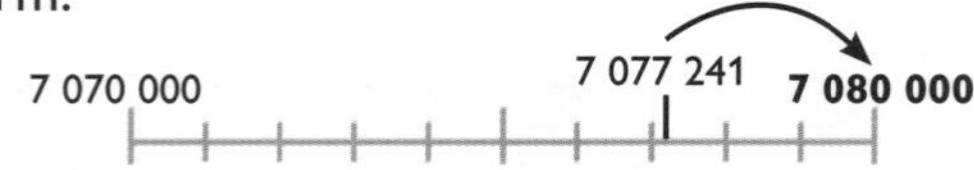

Cow-belles:

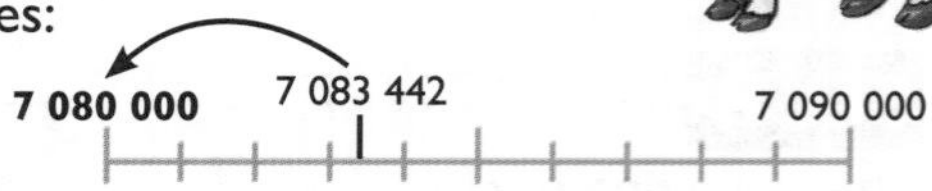

So Bob's Farm and Cow-belles both round their numbers to **7 080 000 litres**.

Set A

There are six ant colonies in a desert in Australia. The colonies have the following numbers of ants:

A: 3 345 181	D: 9 320 944
B: 8 292 499	E: 3 531 876
C: 8 866 906	F: 5 409 850

1 Which are the two largest colonies?

2 Which are the two smallest colonies?

3 How many ants are in colony B to the nearest 1000? Write your answer in words.

4 How many ants are in colony F to the nearest 10 000? Write your answer in words.

Leila goes to an old well which is at sea level (0 m). The bottom of the well is at –40 m. She drops coins into the well from different heights.

How far does a coin fall when Leila:

5 drops it from a building 5 m above the well?

6 drops it from a bridge 20 m above the well?

7 holds it 0.5 m into the well before dropping it?

Jack makes funny videos to share online. He gets £1 for every thousand people that watch a video.

How much does Jack get:

8 if 55 000 people watch a video?

9 if 780 000 people watch a video?

10 if 1 250 000 people watch a video?

The table below shows the scores of some friends after a game of golf.

Name	Score
Louisa	26
Kim	7
Alina	19
Larry	–2
Marcus	–8

What is the difference in score between:

11 Larry and Louisa?

12 Marcus and Kim?

13 Alina and Marcus?

Set B

A zoo asked 5 158 746 people in a country what their favourite zoo animal was.

1. The value of the 8 shows how many people said tiger. How many people said tiger?
2. The value of the 1 shows how many people said panda. How many people said panda?
3. The zoo asks another 1 430 000 people. What is the total number of people asked, to the nearest million?

Fran finds a note next to a safe:

> 2 hundreds, 4 hundred thousands,
> 9 thousands, 1 ten, 7 millions,
> 6 ones and 3 ten thousands.

4. Write the number on the note in digits.

The number, when rounded to the nearest 100 000 or 100, is the code to open the safe.

5. What two numbers could the code be?

Matthias the miner is at 25 m above sea level. The depth of some items are shown below:

Item	Depth
Diamond	–20 m
Vase	–25 m
Fossil	–50 m
Coin	–5 m
Armour	–17 m

6. Order the items, starting with the deepest.
7. What is the difference between the depth of the armour and the vase?
8. How far is Matthias from the diamond?

When he tried to dig down to the diamond, Matthias found the fossil instead.

9. How many metres past the diamond did he dig?

It takes 1 day to dig 5 m.

10. How long did it take to reach the fossil?

Set C

Riley is given the cards below by her teacher.

1	6	4	8	4	9	5

She must rearrange the cards to make the numbers described below.

Write the numbers Riley makes in words:

1. the largest possible number with the 9 in the thousands position.
2. the number that when rounded to the nearest 100 is 6 914 900.
3. the smallest possible number with the 8 in the millions position.

Three evil aliens test their freeze rays on people in different rooms. Once frozen, everyone warms up by 3 °C per hour. How long will it take someone to reach room temperature when:

4. Alien A freezes them at –5 °C in a 10 °C room?
5. Alien B freezes them at –100 °C in a 20 °C room?
6. Alien C freezes them at –200 °C in a –5 °C room?

Alien B sells his freeze ray for £7 936 850.

7. Write this amount to the nearest £1000, £100 000 and £1 000 000 in digits.

A bakery sells the following numbers of items:

Item	Number sold
Cupcakes	3 757 981
Banana bread	3 638 478
Cookies	3 753 232
Sausage rolls	3 840 377
Brownies	3 746 122

8. Order the items from worst to best-selling.
9. Round each number to the nearest 1 000 000 and add them together to estimate the total number of items sold.
10. Why is the estimate too high?

The bakery also sells 9 000 000 loaves (to the nearest million).

11. What is the largest and smallest number of loaves that the bakery could have sold?
12. A karate master practised his lotus kick 2 720 000 times in total. After every 20 000 kicks, he had finished training a student.

    How many students did the karate master train during his lifetime?

I can solve problems with numbers.

Number and Place Value — Review 2

Which is larger:

1. 7 201 796 or 1 396 840?
2. 4 362 783 or 4 362 896?
3. 2 420 980 or 2 426 749?
4. 3 735 375 or 3 753 753?

Which is smaller:

5. 5 961 675 or 5 899 750?
6. 7 167 683 or 7 156 947?
7. 8 258 552 or 8 266 204?
8. 9 688 932 or 9 688 929?

Complete the gaps with < or >:

9. 8 157 264 ☐ 8 098 301
10. 5 215 353 ☐ 5 251 535
11. 5 157 321 ☐ 5 155 890
12. 9 397 319 ☐ 9 397 348

13. Order the numbers below from largest to smallest.

4 649 116	4 755 104
4 638 052	4 644 371

14. Order the numbers below from smallest to largest.

5 573 452	5 501 819
5 234 596	5 525 178

Order the lists below from smallest to largest. Write the second biggest number in each list.

15. 2 786 490, 2 683 663, 2 641 225
16. 9 819 006, 9 810 916, 9 854 141
17. 7 602 114, 7 607 274, 7 602 420

Round 6 392 108 to the nearest:

18. 1000
19. 100
20. 100 000
21. 1 000 000

Round to the nearest 1 000 000:

22. 3 031 571
23. 1 944 441
24. 7 719 944
25. 6 047 797

Round to the nearest 10 000:

26. 6 589 514
27. 8 027 314
28. 1 180 015
29. 2 870 062

30. Which number below rounds to 7 500 000 when rounded to the nearest 100 000?

7 421 847	7 599 239	7 552 121
7 430 249	7 440 928	7 449 999
7 576 596	7 461 072	7 589 039

A football club spends £8 453 940 on new players.

31. Round this amount to the nearest £100, £1000 and £100 000.

The next year they spend four million pounds less.

32. Round the new amount to the nearest million.

33. A survey says there are 6 000 000 pigs in England, to the nearest million.

What are the largest and smallest possible numbers of pigs in England?

34. Sammy stands 58 m above sea level on a cliff. He drops a rock into the sea, which falls to –6 m.

How far does Sammy's rock travel in total?

35. The table below shows the temperature at 5 different beaches in summer and winter.

Beach	Summer	Winter	Change
A	15 °C	9 °C	6 °C
B	5 °C	–6 °C	°C
C	–10 °C	–20 °C	°C
D	22 °C	15 °C	°C
E	15 °C	–5 °C	°C

Copy and compete the column showing the change in temperature between summer and winter.

2 554 640 people visited Lisbon last year.

36. Write this number to the nearest 100 000 people.

The tourism board estimate that there will be 2 million more visitors in 5 years' time.

37. Write the estimate for the number of visitors to Lisbon in 5 years' time, in words.

You must be a well-rounded mathematician to see off these questions — well done!

Number and Place Value — Challenges

1 A pizzeria uses 7-digit order numbers to make their pizzas. Every pizza has tomato sauce and cheese, but the additional toppings needed are recorded using the place values below:

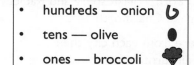

- millions — pepperoni
- hundred thousands — mushroom
- ten thousands — pepper
- thousands — sweetcorn
- hundreds — onion
- tens — olive
- ones — broccoli

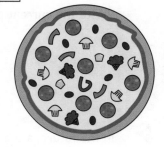

The pizza on the right has the order number: 8 532 173

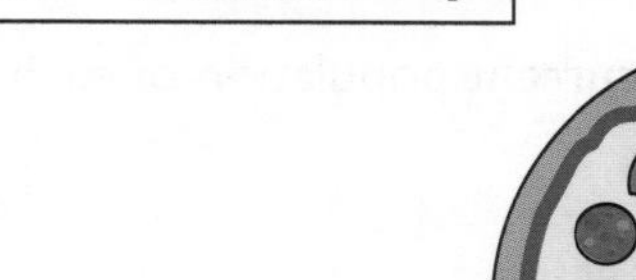

a) Draw pizzas for the following order numbers:

756 484 | 3 160 729 | 4 000 723

The pizzeria want to start making 'pudding pizzas'.

b) Think of seven ingredients (like jelly beans, chocolate...) and give each one a place value. Now find a partner and swap your new number menus over. Give each other two order numbers to draw.

2 In small groups, make two sets of number cards from 1 to 9 (make 18 cards in total). Now shuffle the cards and draw a card each until 7 cards have been drawn.

Using your cards, work together to make:

a) the smallest 7-digit number possible.

b) the largest 7-digit number possible.

c) the smallest even number possible.

d) the largest odd number possible.

3 To win the top prize on an Australian game show, a contestant has to correctly match the weights in milligrams (mg) below to the correct animal.

6 330 570 mg | 2 803 351 mg | 6 999 995 mg | 2 193 104 mg

Each animal has one hint to help the contestant work out its weight.

Koala

7 000 000 mg to the nearest 10 mg.

Platypus

2 200 000 mg to the nearest 100 000 mg.

Quoll

3 000 000 mg to the nearest million mg.

Echidna

This animal's weight has exactly 305 hundreds in it.

What is the correct weight of each animal?

Radiceville had so many people living there that many of them moved away to start three new cities.

- The population of Radiceville was 8 000 000.
- Half of Radiceville moved to make Williamsberg.
- Then half of both Williamsberg and Radiceville moved to make Challinorth.
- 200 000 more from each city then moved to Fairburntown.

Write the current population of each city in words and digits.

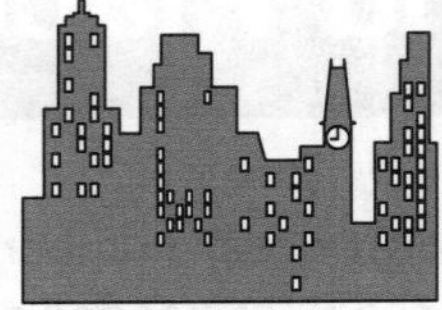
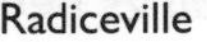
Radiceville

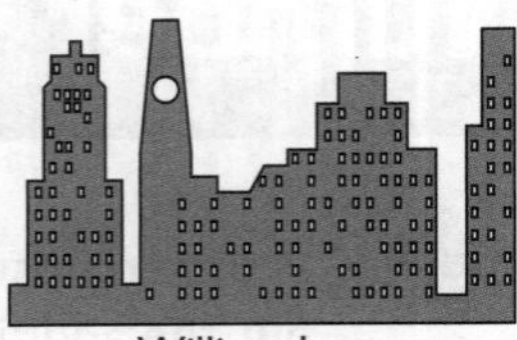
Williamsberg

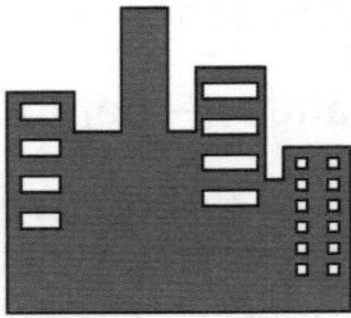
Challinorth

Fairburntown

In the future, a team of astronauts explores the galaxy looking for other planets to live on.

A planet whose average temperature is within 50 °C of 15 °C is safe for humans to live on. The planets discovered by the astronauts are shown in the table below.

a) List all of the planets that are safe for humans to live on.

b) What is the difference in temperature between Taplov and Blion?

c) What is the difference in temperature between Snabuta and Styria?

A star close to Mayvis dies, causing the planet's temperature to drop by 250 °C.

d) What is the new temperature of Mayvis?

e) Is Mayvis safe for humans to live on?

Planet	Average Temperature (°C)
Taplov	430
Styria	–30
Blion	–195
Mayvis	215
Snabuta	–60
Ocragua	65

Look at the codex below:

1	2	3	4	5	6	7	8	9	0

Use the codex to write the following numbers in words:

a)

c)  

b)

d) 

e) Which of these numbers can you make with the symbols in the box on the right?

- Two hundred and thirty thousand, eight hundred and ninety-three
- Four hundred and thirteen thousand, nine hundred and eight
- Nine hundred and forty-two thousand, one hundred and thirty-seven

Congrats on seeing off these challenges — it's hard work being a maths whiz...

Mental Addition

When you're adding numbers together in your head, it's really useful to know all about place value and partitioning. Have a look at the examples below to see how it's done.

Examples

What is 130 000 + 120 000?

130 000 has 130 thousands, and 120 000 has 120 thousands.

130 thousands + 120 thousands = 250 thousands.

So 130 000 + 120 000 = **250 000**

Work out 5 320 400 + 4 030 000.

5 320 400 + 4 000 000 + 30 000
= 9 320 400 + 30 000
= **9 350 400**

Set A

Work out:

1. 14 000 + 20 000
2. 53 000 + 40 000
3. 210 400 + 30 000
4. 461 000 + 500 000
5. 2 100 000 + 7 000 000
6. 6 480 000 + 2 000 000
7. 1 710 030 + 8 000 000

Work out:

8. 52 700 + 30 010
9. 360 000 + 410 000
10. 802 000 + 100 400
11. 700 500 + 280 000
12. 2 470 000 + 4 000 090
13. 5 430 000 + 2 050 000
14. 6 300 800 + 340 000

Find the missing number:

15. 24 000 + ☐ = 39 000
16. 10 560 + ☐ = 50 560
17. 320 420 + ☐ = 390 420
18. 3 000 400 + ☐ = 6 000 400
19. 3 640 000 + ☐ = 5 840 000
20. 1 450 000 + ☐ = 7 450 600
21. 5 520 000 + ☐ = 9 522 000

Set B

Work out:

1. 210 500 + 600 000
2. 700 250 + 200 000
3. 123 000 + 60 000
4. 3 170 000 + 3 000 000
5. 7 650 000 + 1 040 000
6. 4 250 000 + 3 700 000
7. 6 300 070 + 2 000 400

Work out:

8. 150 000 + 370 000
9. 426 000 + 290 000
10. 721 000 + 508 000
11. 5 804 030 + 1 000 070
12. 4 260 800 + 2 060 000
13. 3 505 000 + 2 800 000
14. 6 200 040 + 3 000 080

Find the missing number:

15. 170 300 + ☐ = 480 300
16. 628 200 + ☐ = 829 200
17. 750 000 + ☐ = 930 000
18. 4 380 500 + ☐ = 6 780 500
19. 2 350 800 + ☐ = 6 351 000
20. 6 190 000 + ☐ = 9 230 000
21. 1 136 000 + ☐ = 2 046 000

Set C

Work out:

1. 140 500 + 90 000
2. 600 370 + 700 000
3. 5 520 008 + 1 000 006
4. 6 850 000 + 2 200 000
5. 4 030 800 + 4 000 800
6. 1 765 000 + 8 090 000
7. 5 900 040 + 3 000 070

Work out:

8. 275 000 + 820 000
9. 616 000 + 703 000
10. 750 200 + 500 800
11. 4 700 030 + 800 006
12. 6 900 004 + 500 006
13. 4 200 135 + 2 900 000
14. 8 075 000 + 1 080 000

Find the missing number:

15. 607 200 + ☐ = 812 200
16. 285 000 + ☐ = 735 000
17. 510 010 + ☐ = 1 310 100
18. 3 005 900 + ☐ = 5 012 900
19. 7 300 640 + ☐ = 8 100 700
20. 4 853 617 + ☐ = 5 053 657
21. 1 043 755 + ☐ = 7 123 755

I can do mental addition with large numbers.      

Mental Subtraction

Now it's time to tackle mental subtraction. Just like mental addition, place values and partitioning are key when you're subtracting numbers in your head.

Examples

What is 380 600 – 40 000?

380 600 has 380 thousands, and 40 000 has 40 thousands.

380 thousands – 40 thousands = 340 thousands.

So 380 600 – 40 000 = **340 600**

Work out 4 700 060 – 3 000 040.

4 700 060 – 3 000 000 – 40
= 1 700 060 – 40
= **1 700 020**

Set A

Work out:

1. 90 000 – 40 000
2. 68 000 – 30 000
3. 476 000 – 50 000
4. 780 400 – 600 000
5. 4 800 000 – 600 000
6. 7 400 000 – 5 000 000
7. 9 625 000 – 2 000 000

Work out:

8. 85 000 – 52 000
9. 40 080 – 20 010
10. 375 000 – 120 000
11. 507 500 – 202 000
12. 3 500 700 – 2 000 100
13. 9 070 080 – 7 030 000
14. 6 940 000 – 330 000

Find the missing number:

15. 76 000 – ☐ = 26 000
16. 360 000 – ☐ = 350 000
17. 453 000 – ☐ = 250 000
18. 902 700 – ☐ = 302 500
19. 6 500 000 – ☐ = 6 300 000
20. 9 000 600 – ☐ = 5 000 100
21. 8 415 000 – ☐ = 1 405 000

Set B

Work out:

1. 430 000 – 200 000
2. 1 687 000 – 500 000
3. 379 000 – 80 000
4. 5 900 000 – 4 000 000
5. 2 327 000 – 400 000
6. 6 800 200 – 3 100 000
7. 8 050 900 – 2 000 400

Work out:

8. 920 000 – 70 000
9. 1 530 600 – 600 200
10. 6 400 030 – 900 000
11. 660 000 – 280 000
12. 345 000 – 160 000
13. 3 700 400 – 2 800 000
14. 7 325 000 – 6 000 400

Find the missing number:

15. 250 000 – ☐ = 140 000
16. 414 000 – ☐ = 214 000
17. 450 600 – ☐ = 250 500
18. 3 280 000 – ☐ = 2 780 000
19. 4 607 000 – ☐ = 807 000
20. 6 900 500 – ☐ = 6 400 450
21. 8 400 080 – ☐ = 2 500 080

Set C

Work out:

1. 460 000 – 80 000
2. 4 325 000 – 600 000
3. 2 460 200 – 500 200
4. 965 000 – 408 000
5. 5 610 700 – 2 000 180
6. 6 417 000 – 3 009 000
7. 9 705 000 – 4 800 000

Work out:

8. 400 000 – 42 000
9. 677 000 – 89 000
10. 165 000 – 86 000
11. 8 674 200 – 805 000
12. 2 351 000 – 509 000
13. 6 450 000 – 6 080 000
14. 8 000 750 – 8 000 060

Find the missing number:

15. 375 000 – ☐ = 285 000
16. 510 600 – ☐ = 270 600
17. 4 360 000 – ☐ = 3 660 000
18. 2 806 035 – ☐ = 1 897 035
19. 5 718 000 – ☐ = 658 000
20. 9 354 220 – ☐ = 8 484 220
21. 6 803 315 – ☐ = 794 314

I can do mental subtraction with large numbers.

Written Addition

When you're doing written addition, it's really important to make sure that all the numbers are lined up correctly. The same goes for decimals — make sure the decimal points are all in the same column.

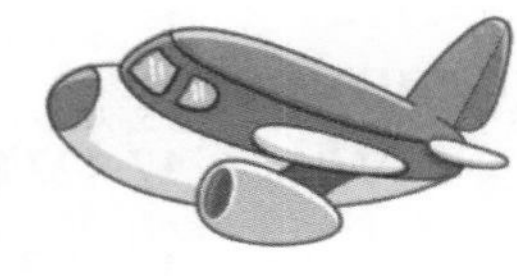

Examples

What is 215 368 + 574 613?

```
  2 1 5 3 6 8
+ 5 7 4 6 1 3
  7 8 9 9 8 1
          1
```

When she went on holiday, Freya flew 14 560.87 miles. Zach flew 21 267.05 miles when he went on holiday. How far did they travel in total?

```
  1 4 5 6 0 . 8 7
+ 2 1 2 6 7 . 0 5
  3 5 8 2 7 . 9 2  miles
      1       1
```

Set A

Work out:

1. 14645 + 28312
2. 827452 + 61737
3. 3402.7 + 1269.2

Work out:

4. 836207 + 142382
5. 2439.64 + 151.72
6. 1439124 + 4523814

Answer the following:

7. 38 741 + 23 232
8. 126 326 + 842 311
9. 698 435 + 181 443
10. 935 264 + 28 650
11. 4 416 327 + 2 380 256
12. 1 297 430 + 6 141 354
13. 2 348 140 + 5 026 258

Set B

Work out:

1. 362804 + 504179
2. 4857.62 + 3724.16
3. 8492.3 + 1272.46

Work out:

4. 5327404 + 2138168
5. 74241.76 + 22139.21
6. 3674.522 + 5270.169

Answer the following:

7. 7 382 404 + 1 286 218
8. 724 941.6 + 149 018.3
9. 3 427 894 + 6 520 750
10. 2 374 221 copies of the Daily News were sold in June. 3 912 072 were sold in July. How many were sold in total?

Set C

Answer the following:

1. 347 529 + 500 168
2. 7721.36 + 8524.9
3. 3 861 756 + 954 142
4. 5 428 616 + 3 742 070
5. 2 846 209 + 7 108 955
6. 568 747.2 + 216 235.4
7. 9743.306 + 194.898

Anita's shop sold 694 762 pots of blue paint last year. They also sold 470 156 pots of orange paint.

8. How many pots of paint did they sell in total?

This year they have sold 494 935 pots of orange paint.

9. How many pots of orange paint have they sold in total?

Here are the numbers of tickets sold by 3 football teams sold last year:

Hillcliff FC: 2 415 322
Treekirk FC: 1 972 468
Walltop Town: 2 540 269

Find the total tickets sold for:

10. Hillcliff FC and Treekirk FC
11. Walltop Town and Hillcliff FC
12. all 3 teams

I can use written addition.      

Written Subtraction

Now have a go at some written subtraction. Remember to make sure all your columns are in line before you start — and watch out for decimal points.

Examples

What is 17 427.8 – 6304.2?

```
   17427.8
 –  6304.2
   11123.6
```

Last month, Jill's bakery made 374 650 loaves.
Rav's bakery made 515 724.
How many more loaves did Rav's bakery make?

```
   4 11   6 12
   5  1 5 7  2 4
 – 3  7 4 6  5 0
   1  4 1 0  7 4
```

Set A

Work out:

1. 37895 – 23140
2. 359844 – 136691
3. 89265.7 – 76051.2

Work out:

4. 76945.2 – 50713
5. 2629866 – 1473614
6. 5274753 – 2166401

Answer the following:

7. 867 542 – 732 420
8. 943 829 – 510 387
9. 717 548 – 502 916
10. 8641.72 – 5126.42
11. 731 051.7 – 210 940.5
12. 6 747 638 – 4 322 914
13. 9 845 396 – 5 762 071

Set B

Work out:

1. 426357 – 302164
2. 517278 – 285116
3. 54392.72 – 23750.4

Work out:

4. 459612.6 – 292370.4
5. 6709326 – 5282074
6. 708693.2 – 124506.9

Answer the following:

7. 649 376.6 – 504 845.3
8. 9 074 056 – 7 150 941
9. 5 437 342 – 5 109 860
10. Last year a charity raised £84 317.10. This year it raised £597 332.52. How much more money did it raise this year?

Set C

Answer the following:

1. 946 279 – 382 048
2. 727 365 – 205 849
3. 347 509.7 – 213 156.2
4. 3 676 482 – 2 935 329
5. 4752.259 – 2935.064
6. 8 808 722 – 2 539 192
7. 89 327.51 – 4490.126

Find the number that is:

8. 49 560.42 less than 64 792.68
9. 3 642 573 less than 8 076 404
10. 62 851.26 less than 754 927.3
11. On one street, a house costs £492 337.84, and a flat costs £268 289.75. How much cheaper is the flat?

Here are some Saturday night TV viewing figures:

Starz: 7 856 395
Quizzi: 2 928 487
Newz: 715 479

12. How many more people watched Starz than Newz?
13. How many fewer people watched Quizzi than Starz?

I can use written subtraction.

Addition and Subtraction Problems

You know all about addition and subtraction now, so it's time to put those skills to the test.
Be careful though — think about whether you need to add or subtract before starting your calculation.

Examples

A yoghurt company sold £551 024 of blueberry yoghurt. They also sold £614 927 of vanilla yoghurt.

How much more did the company make from sales of vanilla yoghurt than blueberry yoghurt?

```
  5 11
  6 1 4 9 2 7
− 5 5 1 0 2 4
    6 3 9 0 3
```

So they made **£63 903** more from sales of vanilla.

A different company makes a vanilla yoghurt too. Their sales of vanilla yoghurt were £836 051.

In total, how much money do the two companies make from selling vanilla yoghurt?

```
    6 1 4 9 2 7
+   8 3 6 0 5 1
  1 4 5 0 9 7 8
    1
```

So the two companies made **£1 450 978** in total from sales of vanilla.

Set A

1. A sailor bought a new luxury boat for £548 752. It is now worth £103 210 less. How much is the luxury boat now worth?

Liz and Filip are taxi drivers. Since starting, Liz has driven 39 935 km. Filip has driven 40 060 km.

2. How far have Liz and Filip driven in total?
3. When Liz and Filip have driven a total of 280 000 km, they'll each get a new taxi. How much further do they have to drive until they get new taxis?

Sunnyhill Hotel had 235 420 guests last year. Glenside Hotel had 104 000 guests. Ribble View Inn had 80 020 guests.

4. How many more guests did Sunnyhill have than Glenside?
5. How many guests did Glenside and Ribble View have in total?
6. How many more guests did Sunnyhill have than Glenside and Ribble View combined?

Four players play a video game. Their scores are in the table below:

Team	Player	Score
Team 1	Jean	2 573 624
	Alain	3 000 009
Team 2	Kai	1 523 334
	Rose	4 001 000

7. What is Jean and Alain's total score?
8. What is Kai and Rose's total score?
9. Which team scored the most points? How many more points did they get than the other team?

A nature group is carrying out a forest survey. They count 3 217 354 birch trees, 2 000 070 pine trees and 1 202 204 ash trees.

10. How many fewer pine trees than birch trees did they count?
11. How many fewer ash trees did they count than pine and birch trees combined?
12. How many trees did they count in total?

Set B

A pop group is on a world tour. They performed for 415 654 people in July, 362 080 people in August, and 301 208 people in September.

1. How many people saw them in July and August in total?
2. The total number of tickets available for their shows in July and August was 882 942. How many tickets weren't sold?
3. In the three months, how many people went to their shows?

To make raspberry jam, a jam company uses 487 324.7 g of raspberries and 502 894.2 g of sugar every day.

4. How much do the ingredients weigh in total?
5. When the seeds are removed, the raspberries weigh 449 201.8 g. How much do the seeds weigh?
6. To make strawberry jam, they use the same weight of fruit, but 270 472.6 g less sugar. How much do the ingredients weigh in total?

A craft shop has 615 426 beads, 849 372 gold sequins, 518 102 silver sequins and 432 050 cm of lace in stock.

7. One customer buys 54 000 beads, and another buys 200 060. How many beads are left?
8. A delivery of 300 400 cm of lace arrives, but 132 420 cm is sent back because of damage. How much lace is now in the shop?
9. A customer needs a total of 1 574 826 gold and silver sequins. How many extra sequins will the shop need to buy?
10. The populations of different types of animals in a rainforest are shown below.

Mammals	362 564
Birds	640 000
Insects	7 890 530

Another 500 035 insects are released into the rainforest. How many more insects are there now than mammals and birds combined?

Set C

The table below shows the number of visitors to Madrid during three months.

May	300 700
June	834 200
July	1 940 000

1. How many more people visited Madrid in July than in May and June combined?

The number of visitors to Barcelona during the same three months was 9 135 865.

2. How many fewer visitors did Madrid have than Barcelona in these three months?
3. The number of visitors to Barcelona in June was 2 968 050 and in July was 4 672 800. How many people visited Barcelona in May?
4. In a TV dance competition, 3 847 324 people voted for the winner. Third place got 1 000 700 fewer votes than the winner. Second place got 352 940 more votes than third. How many people voted for second place?

Nandita thinks of a number.
She tells Conor that if she adds 484.639 to her number, the answer is 704.744.

5. Conor calculates that her number was 320.105. Show that his calculation is wrong.

Next, Conor thinks of a number.
He tells Nandita that when you subtract 1351.578 from his number, the answer is 2495.808.

6. Nandita works it out to be 3847.386. Show that her calculation is correct.

An estate made up of a mansion, barn, stables and land is worth £4 515 395. The land alone is worth £1 560 480 and the barn is worth £154 622.

7. The stables are worth £1 000 080 less than the difference between the land and barn. How much are the stables worth?
8. How much is the mansion worth?
9. The owner bought the mansion and land for a total of £345 100 less than their current value. What did the mansion and land cost in total?

I can solve multi-step problems using addition and subtraction.      

Calculations — Review 1

Work out the following in your head:

1 15 000 + 30 000
2 200 300 + 700 000
3 570 000 + 2 000 000
4 3 026 000 + 250 000
5 6 407 000 + 407 000
6 1 480 000 + 4 030 000
7 6 406 000 + 703 000
8 3 600 030 + 5 200 070
9 4 030 040 + 80 008
10 2 706 004 + 505 000

Work out the missing numbers in your head:

11 1 480 000 + ☐ = 3 580 000
12 465 000 + ☐ = 1 065 000
13 2 080 500 + ☐ = 2 170 500
14 8 304 710 + ☐ = 9 305 510
15 2 721 001 + ☐ = 3 630 010

Work out the following in your head:

16 55 000 – 13 000
17 690 700 – 60 500
18 8 300 000 – 2 000 000
19 7 600 000 – 3 200 000
20 1 300 000 – 800 000
21 8 950 000 – 270 000
22 6 700 500 – 400 060
23 5 322 100 – 3 800 000
24 3 688 000 – 1 090 000
25 3 658 200 – 60 050

Work out the missing numbers in your head:

26 1 080 000 – ☐ = 1 060 000
27 7 800 500 – ☐ = 6 800 000
28 5 406 060 – ☐ = 2 406 045
29 3 560 590 – ☐ = 2 390 590
30 2 876 941 – ☐ = 2 868 881

Work out:

31 $\begin{array}{r} 324706 \\ +\underline{464183} \end{array}$

32 $\begin{array}{r} 6642430 \\ +\underline{\ \ 749150} \end{array}$

33 $\begin{array}{r} 63215.07 \\ +\underline{51365.92} \end{array}$

34 $\begin{array}{r} 8315.358 \\ +\underline{8367.76\ \ } \end{array}$

Answer the following:

35 245 670 + 414 320
36 3 243 853 + 5 204 116
37 6127.38 + 3054.61
38 2 748 171 + 545 412
39 6 250 739 + 3 386 084
40 539 679.7 + 17 364.19
41 1 558 543 + 3 860 379
42 3 748 311 + 6 128 909
43 686 948 + 8 397 256
44 38 242.146 + 1757.96

Work out:

45 $\begin{array}{r} 792628 \\ -\underline{182103} \end{array}$

46 $\begin{array}{r} 4239620 \\ -\underline{1109170} \end{array}$

47 $\begin{array}{r} 92685.1\ \ \\ -\underline{40035.48} \end{array}$

48 $\begin{array}{r} 4154703 \\ -\underline{2607835} \end{array}$

Answer the following:

49 467 983 – 124 670
50 3 807 648 – 2 422 101
51 926 459.7 – 867 403.2
52 2 652 187 – 811 002
53 9 189 764 – 1 724 983
54 28 587.47 – 19 419.5
55 5 297 584 – 1 431 828
56 4 726 854 – 90 277
57 615 327.8 – 81 680.52
58 8 263 304 – 6 475 829

The table shows how many sweets a factory makes:

Jelly beans	3 152 000
Lollipops	800 300
Fizzy worms	2 301 400

59 How many fizzy worms and lollipops do they make in total?

60 How many sweets do they make in total?

61 How many more jelly beans do they make than the total number of fizzy worms and lollipops?

Three years ago, an airport with 3 terminals had 7 945 497 visitors. 4 627 512 visitors used Terminal 1, and 1 845 384 visitors used Terminal 2.

62 How many visitors used Terminal 3?

63 The number of visitors has increased by exactly 587 560 each year. How many visitors did the airport have this year?

Wow, that was a lot of tricky questions — well done for giving them a go!

Mental Multiplication

When it comes to mental multiplication, knowing your times tables comes in really handy. Also, try breaking up harder questions into simpler multiplications — that'll make mental multiplication questions a whole lot easier.

Examples

What is 70 × 8000?

<u>7</u>0 × <u>8</u>000 = **<u>56</u>0 000**

(<u>7</u> × <u>8</u> = <u>56</u>)

Break the number down to something easier, then add the zeros at the end.

Work out the answer to 620 × 5.

620 = 600 + 20

<u>6</u>00 × <u>5</u> = 3000

<u>2</u>0 × <u>5</u> = 100

So 620 × 5 = 3000 + 100 = **3100**

Set A

Work out:

1. 60 × 30
2. 4 × 500
3. 800 × 7
4. 3 × 3000
5. 20 × 4000
6. 90 × 7000
7. 60 × 5000

Find the missing values:

8. 730 × 8
   700 × ☐ = 5600, and
   30 × 8 = ☐, so
   730 × 8 = 5600 + ☐ = ☐
9. 290 × 3
   200 × ☐ = 600, and
   90 × 3 = ☐, so
   290 × 3 = 600 + ☐ = ☐

Calculate the following:

10. 230 × 5
11. 360 × 4
12. 608 × 6
13. 1010 × 3
14. 7300 × 4
15. 5200 × 6
16. 1700 × 7

Set B

Work out:

1. 90 × 40
2. 200 × 70
3. 300 × 110
4. 80 × 3000
5. 30 × 9000
6. 700 × 6000

Calculate the following:

7. 340 × 700
8. 2400 × 300
9. 950 × 800
10. 1070 × 12
11. 5006 × 90
12. 780 × 600

13. A factory prints 40 000 newspapers per hour. How many could it print in 60 hours?
14. Reggie can deliver 270 parcels in a day. How many could he deliver in 7 days?
15. A carrier bag costs 5p. How much would 904 carrier bags cost, in pence?

Set C

Work out:

1. 900 × 400
2. 7000 × 60
3. 30 × 5000
4. 80 × 9000
5. 1200 × 60
6. 1100 × 80

Calculate the following:

7. 4600 × 12
8. 903 × 800
9. 55 × 9000
10. 69 × 1100
11. 770 × 700
12. 9040 × 500

How many:

13. hours are there in a week?
14. minutes are there in a week?

15. Jen can walk to school in 690 seconds. How long would it take her to walk there 11 times?

I can do mental multiplication.      

Mental Division

Now it's time to tackle mental division. Knowing your times tables and breaking down harder calculations prove just as useful when you're dividing numbers in your head.

Examples

What is 5400 ÷ 9?

54 ÷ 9 = 6

5400 ÷ 9 = **600**

Work out the answer to 2200 ÷ 110.

22 ÷ 11 = 2

2200 ÷ 110 = **20**

Set A

Find the missing values:

1. 420 ÷ 7
   42 ÷ 7 = ☐
   420 ÷ 7 = ☐
2. 7700 ÷ 11
   77 ÷ 11 = ☐
   7700 ÷ 11 = ☐
3. 1080 ÷ 9
   108 ÷ ☐ = 12
   1080 ÷ 9 = ☐

Work out:

4. 360 ÷ 4
5. 550 ÷ 5
6. 4800 ÷ 8
7. 720 ÷ 90
8. 2400 ÷ 30
9. 1200 ÷ 20
10. 2800 ÷ 40

Work out:

11. 3200 ÷ 4
12. 1500 ÷ 5
13. 6300 ÷ 7
14. 9900 ÷ 11
15. 9900 ÷ 110
16. 4200 ÷ 60
17. 2100 ÷ 30

Set B

Work out:

1. 720 ÷ 8
2. 5400 ÷ 60
3. 77 000 ÷ 7
4. 48 000 ÷ 40
5. 81 000 ÷ 9
6. 1320 ÷ 12

Work out:

7. 540 ÷ 90
8. 8100 ÷ 90
9. 4200 ÷ 70
10. 96 000 ÷ 80
11. 84 000 ÷ 120
12. 960 000 ÷ 12

13. One week, Sofia read 2100 pages. She read the same number of pages each day. How many pages did she read each day?
14. Luis makes the same amount of jam each month. In a year he makes 7200 kg. How much jam does he make each month?

Set C

Work out:

1. 1200 ÷ 60
2. 3600 ÷ 40
3. 4200 ÷ 70
4. 1210 ÷ 110
5. 8400 ÷ 1200
6. 45 000 ÷ 900

Work out:

7. 63 000 ÷ 9
8. 48 000 ÷ 12
9. 840 000 ÷ 7
10. 88 000 ÷ 80
11. 360 000 ÷ 600
12. 5 400 000 ÷ 60

13. Ali bought plane tickets for himself and eleven of his friends. They cost him £10 800. How much was one ticket?
14. A chain is a unit of length equal to 11 fathoms. A fathom is 6 feet. How many chains make up 660 000 feet?

I can do mental division.

Mental Calculation Problems

Addition, subtraction, multiplication, division — you can do it all! These pages will let you practise using all those operations in your head. Remember to read the question carefully and think about what it's asking you to do.

Examples

Marc's stationery shop had 1 340 600 colouring pencils in stock. Last month, Marc sold 20 600 colouring pencils.

Marc then puts all the pencils into packs of 12.

How many packs of colouring pencils does he make?

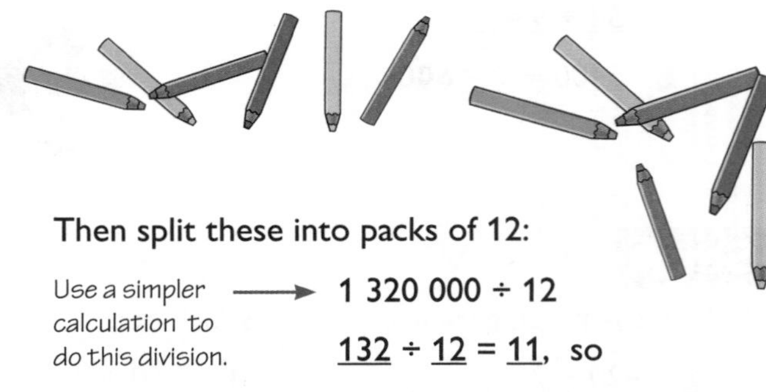

First, find how many pencils Marc has left:

Use partitioning to do this subtraction. → 1 340 600 – 20 600

1 340 600 – 20 000 – 600
= 1 320 600 – 600
= 1 320 000

Then split these into packs of 12:

Use a simpler calculation to do this division. → 1 320 000 ÷ 12

132 ÷ 12 = 11, so

1 320 000 ÷ 12 = 110 000

So Marc makes **110 000 packs** of pencils.

Hattie is a florist — she has 1460 bouquets of roses and 1140 bouquets of peonies. She sells each bouquet for £6.

How much money would she make if she sold them all?

1460 + 1140 = 2600 ← *You can use partitioning for this addition.*

2600 = 2000 + 600
2000 × 6 = 12 000, and 600 × 6 = 3600
So 2600 × 6 = 12 000 + 3600 = 15 600

So Hattie would make **£15 600**.

Set A

Euan bakes 2400 biscuits. He wants to decorate each biscuit with 4 sweets.

1. How many sweets will he need to decorate them all?
2. Euan puts the biscuits into boxes of 12. How many boxes does he make?

120 000 people flew from the UK to India in March and 520 000 people flew in April.

3. How many people flew to India in March and April in total?
4. Every person took one suitcase and one piece of hand luggage. How many bags did people take in total?
5. The number of people who flew to Japan is eight times smaller than the number who flew to India. How many people flew to Japan in those two months?

Watery Planet aquarium is home to 220 octopuses and 2700 angel fish.

6. An octopus has eight arms. How many arms do the octopuses in the aquarium have in total?
7. The angel fish are kept in tanks of 90. How many tanks of angel fish are there?
8. Watery Planet also has 292 000 seahorses. How many times more seahorses are there than octopuses and angel fish combined?

A new action film made £4 260 000 on its opening weekend. A new comedy made £3 050 000.

9. How much more money did the action film make than the comedy?
10. Each ticket cost £10. How many people went to see the two films in total?
11. In a survey, 7100 people said they loved the action film. Three times as many loved the comedy. How many people loved the comedy?

Set B

The table shows the cakes at a bake sale.

	Number of cakes	Slices per cake	Number of slices
Chocolate		8	1600
Carrot	230	6	
Fruit		12	1440

1. Copy and complete the table.
2. The other stalls at Fun Day raised £252 385. The bake sale raised £10 700. How much did the Fun Day raise in total?

252 465 people voted in a talent contest.

3. 160 000 of those were women. How many men voted?

4000 people under the age of 18 voted.
50 times as many people aged 18-35 voted.

4. How many people aged 18-35 voted?
5. How many people over the age of 35 voted?

Yas, Tom and Bella are playing a video game.

6. Yas scored 64 216 points. Tom scored 50 300 points. How many more points did Yas score than Tom?
7. Bella scored 72 000. She scored exactly the same number of points on each of the 9 levels. How many points did she score on each level?
8. On a game Tomas played, he noticed there were 2070 points available on 6 of the levels. How many points were available in total on those 6 levels?

A balloon shop has 9000 red balloons in stock. They have 12 times as many gold balloons.

9. How many gold balloons do they have in stock?
10. A customer buys 40 006 gold balloons. How many gold balloons does the shop have left?

Set C

There are 900 pupils at a school. Each pupil ran a lap of the school field for a sponsored event. A lap of the field is 1300 m.

1. What is the total distance run by the 900 pupils, in metres?

Each pupil raised £50 in sponsorship. There were also two donations — one of £12 030 and one of £7400.

2. What was the total amount raised by the event?

Hillcliff FC and Walltop Town are playing a football match. There are 34 340 people in the crowd. 5030 people are wearing Walltop Town shirts. 4 times as many people are wearing Hillcliff FC shirts.

3. How many people aren't wearing a Hillcliff FC or Walltop Town shirt?

13 200 people came to the match in minibuses. Minibuses seat 12 people.

4. How many minibuses did they need?

A company is making pizzas for a weekend film festival. 1330 guests are coming on Saturday and 2270 guests are coming on Sunday.

5. They use 40 g of mozzarella per guest. How many grams of mozzarella do they use in total?
6. They cut each pizza into 12 slices. There are exactly 4 slices per guest. How many pizzas have they made?

1 560 000 children and 1 140 000 adults visited Dizzy Heights theme park one year.

7. How many people visited in total that year?

Each visitor went on the roller coaster once. The roller coaster can carry 30 people at a time.

8. What is the smallest number of times the roller coaster could have run that year?

It costs £2 for a child to go on the roller coaster and £6 for an adult.

9. How much money did the theme park make from the roller coaster that year?

I can solve problems mentally involving all four operations.

Calculations — Review 2

Answer the following:

1 80 × 60
2 20 × 90
3 500 × 800
4 700 × 400
5 600 × 600
6 90 × 7000
7 30 × 8000
8 40 × 9000
9 800 × 700
10 70 × 5000
11 120 × 600
12 80 × 1100
13 11 × 1200
14 120 × 120

Find the missing values to complete the calculation:

15 520 × 6
500 × ☐ = 3000
20 × 6 = ☐
3000 + ☐ = ☐

16 840 × 9
800 × 9 = ☐
40 × ☐ = 360
☐ + 360 = ☐

Calculate the following:

17 130 × 4
18 270 × 3
19 180 × 5
20 620 × 6
21 370 × 4
22 550 × 70
23 6300 × 60
24 9400 × 80
25 7009 × 11
26 8500 × 90
27 4700 × 80
28 9800 × 12

29 There are 830 marbles in a bag. How many are there in 8 bags?

30 Oli needs 12 text books. Each book costs £36. How much will he spend?

31 There are 2400 raisins in a packet. How many raisins are there in 60 packets?

Answer the following:

32 540 ÷ 9
33 4800 ÷ 6
34 140 ÷ 20
35 550 ÷ 50
36 3600 ÷ 40
37 7200 ÷ 80
38 1320 ÷ 11
39 8400 ÷ 12
40 2700 ÷ 30
41 5600 ÷ 70
42 1440 ÷ 12
43 1210 ÷ 11
44 5600 ÷ 80
45 1080 ÷ 12

Find the missing values to complete the calculation:

46 5400 ÷ 6
54 ÷ ☐ = 9
5400 ÷ 6 = ☐

47 9600 ÷ 12
96 ÷ ☐ = 8
9600 ÷ 12 = ☐

Calculate the following:

48 15 000 ÷ 5
49 24 000 ÷ 4
50 180 000 ÷ 3
51 360 000 ÷ 6
52 32 000 ÷ 40
53 63 000 ÷ 70
54 48 000 ÷ 80
55 72 000 ÷ 90
56 640 000 ÷ 80
57 14 400 ÷ 120
58 88 000 ÷ 110
59 2 400 000 ÷ 120

60 Shaadi spent £360 on nine shirts. Each one cost the same amount. How much was one shirt?

61 12 identical bags of pasta weighed 4800 g. How much does one bag of pasta weigh?

Francis is working at a cafe.

62 On Monday, the cafe sold 10 574 cups of tea and 10 500 cups of coffee. How many cups of tea and coffee did they sell in total?

63 Francis is supposed to put 4 pieces of lettuce on every sandwich he makes. He has 4400 pieces of lettuce. How many sandwiches can he make?

64 Francis works for 6 hours a day and he is paid £10.20 an hour. How much does Francis earn in a day?

65 110 identical cans of lemonade have a volume of 33 000 ml. What is the volume of one can?

Deb and Ross are doing a sponsored cycle. Their route is 1320 miles and they aim to cycle at 12 miles an hour.

66 How many hours will it take for them to complete the journey?

They are aiming to raise £3500. Deb has been sponsored £940. Ross has been sponsored 3 times as much as Deb.

67 Show that they have raised more than their target.

Another set of questions completed — you're a mental multiplication and division pro!

Short Multiplication

Short multiplication is a written method you can use to multiply numbers.
Remember — always make sure the columns are properly lined up.

Examples

Use a formal written method to work out 4663 × 3.

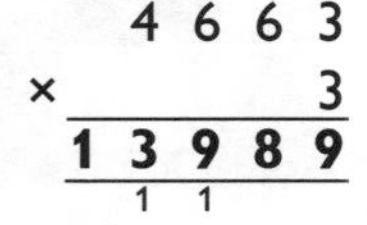

```
   4 6 6 3
×        3
 1 3 9 8 9
   1 1
```

Keep all columns lined up according to their place value.

Use a formal written method to work out 1256 × 6.

```
  1 2 5 6
×       6
  7 5 3 6
  1 3 3
```

Set A

Work out:

1.
```
  8 3 2
×     3
```

2.
```
  1 3 1 7
×       5
```

3.
```
  3 2 5 1
×       4
```

Work out:

4.
```
  4 0 7 3
×       3
```

5.
```
  3 2 1 4
×       6
```

6.
```
  5 1 2 6
×       4
```

Use short multiplication to work out:

7. 4261 × 5
8. 6315 × 4
9. 7042 × 5
10. A collector has four chairs, each worth £4236. How much are they worth in total?

Set B

Work out:

1.
```
  6 4 6 2
×       5
```

2.
```
  7 3 0 4
×       4
```

3.
```
  5 5 4 6
×       6
```

Use short multiplication to work out:

4. 4865 × 3
5. 5273 × 5
6. 2041 × 9
7. 5602 × 7
8. 4026 × 8
9. 3085 × 7
10. A theatre sells 3756 tickets each night for six nights. How many tickets have been sold in total on these six nights?
11. There are 1329 poppy seeds on a baguette. How many seeds are there on seven baguettes?

Set C

Work out:

1.
```
  8 4 7 3
×       5
```

2.
```
  4 3 2 7
×       7
```

3.
```
  9 2 0 6
×       8
```

What number is:

4. 9 times bigger than 3109?
5. 6 times bigger than 4260?
6. 7 times bigger than 7234?
7. 7511 times bigger than 4?
8. 8425 times bigger than 5?
9. 2973 times bigger than 7?

A train travels 6477 miles every year. How far does it travel:

10. in 7 years?
11. in 9 years?
12. A town has a population of 83 946. The nearest city is eight times bigger. What is the population of the city?

I can use short multiplication.

Long Multiplication

Long multiplication uses partitioning to make multiplying bigger numbers a lot less scary.

Example

Use long multiplication to work out the answer to 446 × 42.

$$\begin{array}{r} 4\,4\,6 \\ \times \quad 4\,2 \\ \hline 8\,9\,2 \\ 1\,7\,8\,4\,0 \\ \hline \mathbf{1\,8\,7\,3\,2} \end{array}$$

446 × 2 → 892

446 × 40 → 17840

446 × 42 = (446 × 2) + (446 × 40) → **18732**

Set A

Work out:

1. 265 × 23
2. 524 × 34
3. 363 × 41

Work out:

4. 1502 × 33
5. 3553 × 41
6. 4330 × 25

Use long multiplication to work out:

7. 464 × 21
8. 312 × 34
9. 416 × 42
10. 3113 times 24
11. 4224 multiplied by 51
12. 4103 multiplied by 35

Set B

Work out:

1. 572 × 37
2. 465 × 59
3. 624 × 45

Work out:

4. 3646 × 28
5. 2442 × 63
6. 5163 × 27

What is:

7. 736 times bigger than 54?
8. 562 multiplied by 61?
9. 4742 times bigger than 43?
10. 24 times bigger than 5174?
11. 3516 multiplied by 52?
12. 25 times 6739?

Set C

Work out:

1. 806 × 54
2. 7306 × 54
3. 9134 × 62

Work out:

4. 436 × 19
5. 728 × 93
6. 649 × 31
7. 9789 × 56
8. 4962 × 85
9. 7738 × 48
10. 3874 × 93

There are 454 grams in a pound. How many grams are there in:

11. 67 pounds?
12. 92 pounds?

There are 52 cards in a deck. How many cards are in:

13. 4847 decks?
14. 5383 decks?

I can use long multiplication.

Short Division

Short division is a written method that can help you divide bigger numbers. In Year 5, you saw how to divide by 1-digit numbers — now you'll use short division to divide by 2-digit numbers.

Examples

What is 9864 ÷ 12?

$$\begin{array}{r} \mathbf{8\ 2\ 2} \\ 12\overline{)9\ 8\ {}^{2}6\ {}^{2}4} \end{array}$$

Regan works for 1970 minutes each week.
Every task she does takes 13 minutes.
How many whole tasks can she do in a week?

$$\begin{array}{r} \mathbf{1\ 5\ 1\ r\ 7} \\ 13\overline{)1\ 9\ {}^{6}7\ {}^{2}0} \end{array}$$

If you get a remainder, you might need to round up or down, depending on the context of the question.

Regan can do **151** whole tasks.

Set A

Work out the following, writing any remainders as whole numbers:

1. $11\overline{)2\ 6\ 4}$
2. $12\overline{)1\ 5\ 6}$
3. $14\overline{)1\ 5\ 4}$
4. $16\overline{)1\ 9\ 2}$
5. $12\overline{)3\ 7\ 9}$
6. $15\overline{)3\ 5\ 5}$
7. $12\overline{)7\ 2\ 3\ 8}$
8. $11\overline{)3\ 6\ 4\ 6}$
9. Pablo has 817 seeds. How many seeds will he have left over if he shares them between 11 pots?
10. Annette has 5077 sequins. She makes hats and sews 25 sequins onto each hat. How many hats can she make?

Set B

Work out the following, writing any remainders as whole numbers:

1. $12\overline{)2\ 5\ 2}$
2. $11\overline{)9\ 5\ 7}$
3. $15\overline{)6\ 4\ 5}$
4. $25\overline{)8\ 2\ 5}$
5. $11\overline{)2\ 7\ 0\ 9}$
6. $12\overline{)1\ 9\ 8\ 8}$
7. $14\overline{)1\ 8\ 6\ 0}$
8. $23\overline{)3\ 0\ 4\ 2}$
9. A greengrocer has 475 apples. He sells them in bags of 13. How many whole bags can he fill?
10. A pop group wants to send a badge to each of the 8275 members of their fan club. Badges are sold in packs of 12. How many packs do they need?

Set C

Work out the following, writing any remainders as whole numbers:

1. $12\overline{)7\ 0\ 8}$
2. $11\overline{)7\ 1\ 9\ 4}$
3. $21\overline{)2\ 7\ 7\ 2}$
4. $15\overline{)5\ 4\ 4\ 5}$
5. $25\overline{)8\ 9\ 8\ 5}$
6. $23\overline{)5\ 3\ 1\ 9}$
7. $13\overline{)3\ 5\ 6\ 9}$
8. $18\overline{)1\ 0\ 6\ 0}$
9. A bakery has made 2852 bagels. They sell them in packs of 16. How many whole packs can they fill?
10. One week a ferry transported 4622 cars. The ferry can carry 28 cars at a time. What is the smallest number of journeys the ferry could have made?

I can use short division.

Long Division — 1

Long division is another way of dividing bigger numbers. It's set out in a similar way to short division, but your working out is written more clearly. Remember to keep your columns nice and tidy.

Examples

What is 924 ÷ 21?

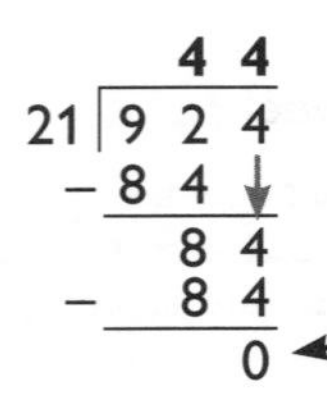

Stop when you get to zero, or less than what you're dividing by (which is 21 here).

924 ÷ 21 = **44**

What is 2010 ÷ 15?

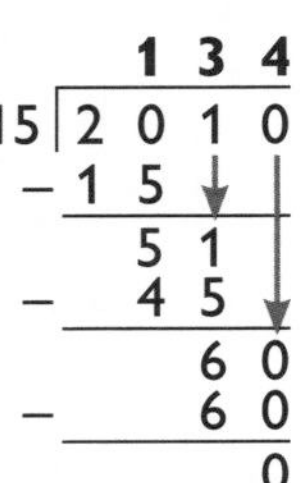

2010 ÷ 15 = **134**

Set A

Work out:

1. $11\overline{)4\,7\,3}$
2. $12\overline{)8\,8\,8}$
3. $15\overline{)9\,6\,0}$
4. $13\overline{)6\,3\,7}$

Work out:

5. $22\overline{)7\,0\,4}$
6. $25\overline{)6\,7\,5}$
7. $12\overline{)1\,8\,9\,6}$
8. $11\overline{)6\,5\,5\,6}$

Use long division to work out:

9. 903 ÷ 21
10. 432 ÷ 12
11. 812 ÷ 14
12. 767 ÷ 13
13. 4175 ÷ 25
14. 6974 ÷ 11

Set B

Work out:

1. $12\overline{)8\,0\,4}$
2. $16\overline{)6\,7\,2}$
3. $22\overline{)9\,0\,2}$
4. $25\overline{)9\,2\,5}$

Work out:

5. $11\overline{)6\,4\,1\,3}$
6. $13\overline{)4\,7\,3\,2}$
7. $24\overline{)3\,8\,1\,6}$
8. $21\overline{)2\,2\,8\,9}$

Use long division to work out:

9. 638 divided by 22
10. 952 divided by 28
11. 6328 divided by 14
12. 4788 divided by 21
13. 8892 divided by 26
14. 1386 divided by 33

Set C

Work out:

1. $15\overline{)4\,6\,3\,5}$
2. $23\overline{)3\,6\,5\,7}$
3. $29\overline{)3\,8\,8\,6}$
4. $17\overline{)9\,7\,4\,1}$

Work out:

5. 936 ÷ 18
6. 6762 ÷ 23
7. 9960 ÷ 24
8. 8848 ÷ 28
9. 1472 ÷ 32
10. 1274 ÷ 49

Doris wins £5712 at bingo. How much would each person get if she shares it equally between:

11. 14 grandchildren?
12. 16 nieces?
13. 17 nephews?
14. 28 friends?
15. 42 neighbours?

I can use long division.

Long Division — 2

You won't always end up with a zero at the bottom of your long division — you might find a remainder.

Example

Mandy has 4798 pens. She can fit 22 pens in a pencil case. Use long division to find how many pencil cases Mandy needs to fit all her pens in.

Do 4798 ÷ 22 using long division:

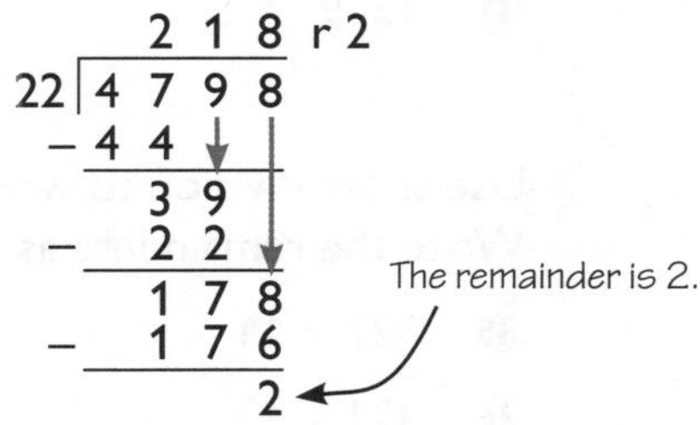

Mandy can fill 218 pencil cases, with 2 pens left over, so she'll need one more pencil case.

Mandy needs **219 pencil cases**.

Set A

Work out the following, writing remainders as whole numbers:

1. $15\overline{)679}$
2. $22\overline{)749}$
3. $11\overline{)654}$
4. $25\overline{)677}$
5. $12\overline{)580}$
6. $13\overline{)859}$
7. $21\overline{)2964}$
8. $15\overline{)2598}$

Work out the following, writing remainders as fractions:

9. 978 ÷ 12
10. 757 ÷ 21
11. 749 ÷ 14
12. Flo can fit 28 marbles in a bag. How many bags does she need for 3182 marbles?

Set B

Work out the following, writing remainders as whole numbers:

1. $12\overline{)818}$
2. $25\overline{)829}$
3. $14\overline{)800}$
4. $22\overline{)2492}$

Work out the following, writing remainders as fractions:

5. 2649 ÷ 21
6. 2568 ÷ 17
7. 4568 ÷ 16
8. 7503 ÷ 23
9. 1250 ÷ 39

10. Erica is making necklaces, with 18 beads on each one. She has 978 beads left. How many necklaces can she make?
11. Raheem needs 1496 plants. They are sold in trays of 21. How many trays will Raheem need to buy?

Set C

Work out the following, writing remainders as whole numbers:

1. $21\overline{)6658}$
2. $13\overline{)8549}$
3. $24\overline{)1466}$
4. $34\overline{)9665}$

Work out the following, writing remainders as fractions:

5. 8246 ÷ 16
6. 3840 ÷ 19
7. 6567 ÷ 17
8. 9429 ÷ 27
9. 2676 ÷ 35

10. A school needs to buy new cricket kits. They have £1012 to spend and kits cost £14. How many kits can they buy?
11. A bag of sweets contains 23 sweets. A headteacher needs 2188 sweets for her school. How many bags of sweets should she buy?

I am confident using long division.

Calculations — Review 3

Use short multiplication to work out:

1. 332×3
2. 2427×4
3. 3606×5
4. 4507×4
5. 5354×7
6. 2305×6

Use short multiplication to work out:

7. 6313 × 3
8. 5105 × 8
9. 3446 × 5
10. 4705 × 6
11. 3957 × 8
12. 8685 × 4

Use long multiplication to work out:

13. 332×24
14. 445×32
15. 245×44
16. 5443×62
17. 6234×53
18. 8709×85

Use long multiplication to work out:

19. 314 × 32
20. 526 × 45
21. 254 × 36
22. 6847 × 91
23. 5264 × 78
24. 7826 × 81

25. A gardener collects 6567 fallen leaves every day. How many does he collect in 5 days?

26. A salesman sold 8 cars for £8795 each. How much did the 8 cars cost in total?

27. A pen factory makes 4645 pens every day. How many do they make in 28 days?

28. There are 7189 parcels on a lorry. How many would there be on 87 lorries?

Use short division to work out:

29. $684 \div 12$
30. $891 \div 11$
31. $975 \div 15$
32. $3234 \div 14$
33. $1050 \div 25$
34. $1144 \div 22$

Use short division to work out the following. Write the remainders as whole numbers.

35. 927 ÷ 11
36. 421 ÷ 13
37. 615 ÷ 21
38. 8780 ÷ 12
39. 3576 ÷ 25
40. 7951 ÷ 22

41. 746 people arrive at a football tournament. They are split into teams of 11. How many full teams will there be?

Use long division to work out the following, writing any remainders as whole numbers:

42. $352 \div 16$
43. $967 \div 23$
44. $798 \div 14$
45. $2110 \div 17$
46. $6434 \div 19$
47. $1685 \div 31$

Use long division to work out the following, writing any remainders as fractions:

48. 704 ÷ 13
49. 858 ÷ 22
50. 920 ÷ 16
51. 9954 ÷ 14
52. 9209 ÷ 27
53. 2598 ÷ 41

54. An ice cream company has received an order for 336 tubs of ice cream. They can make 14 tubs per hour. How long will it take them to complete the order?

55. Apples come in crates of 22 apples. Clare needs 1080 apples. How many crates should she buy?

56. A rope factory makes 1324 m of rope every hour. The rope is sold in 23 m lengths. How many full lengths do they make every hour?

Looks like you've really got the hang of all this multiplication and division — fab work!

Common Factors

The factors of a number are the numbers that divide exactly into that number. Common factors are factors that are shared by two or more numbers. Have a go at finding common factors here — look out for prime numbers.

Example

Find all the common factors of 18 and 48.

The number 18 has factors 1, 2, 3, 6, 9 and 18.

The number 48 has factors 1, 2, 3, 4, 6, 8, 12, 16, 24 and 48.

The common factors of 18 and 48 are **1, 2, 3 and 6**.

Set A

1 Which of the numbers below have 9 as a factor?

29	54	108	63
71	99	18	

2 Which of the numbers below have 3 as a factor?

63	36	59	120
15	74	89	

Find a common factor (other than 1) of:

3 6 and 12

4 8 and 24

5 27 and 36

6 12 and 54

7 40 and 72

8 7 and 35

Find all the common factors of:

9 12 and 18

10 16 and 20

11 24 and 32

12 56 and 72

Find all the prime common factors of:

13 30 and 40

14 11 and 66

Set B

Find a common factor (above 2) of:

1 5 and 55

2 12 and 36

3 10 and 50

4 42 and 63

5 28 and 56

6 24 and 64

Find all the common factors of the following. Underline each prime common factor:

7 9 and 99

8 18 and 24

9 21 and 42

10 39 and 52

11 42 and 56

12 Marcel thinks of a number between 1 and 50. The common factors it has with 24 are: 1, 2, 3, 4, 6 and 12. What could Marcel's number be?

13 Lexi is thinking of two numbers between 1 and 50. Their common factors are: 1, 2, 7 and 14. List all the pairs of numbers that Lexi could be thinking of.

Set C

Find all the common factors of:

1 16 and 48

2 36 and 54

3 66 and 99

4 18 and 41

5 15 and 60

6 32 and 48

Find the highest common factor of:

7 9 and 63

8 16 and 40

9 11 and 88

10 24 and 56

11 36 and 144

12 66 and 110

13 17 is a prime number. Kit says that the only common factor of 17 and any other number will be 1. Explain why Kit is wrong.

14 Two numbers are "coprime" if their only common factor is 1. Which numbers from 1 to 10 are coprime with 18?

I understand and can identify common factors.

Common Multiples

All the numbers that appear in a number's times table are multiples or that number.
A common multiple of two numbers is a number that's a multiple of both — so appears in both times tables.

Examples

Find two common multiples of 4 and 5.

4 times table: 4, 8, 12, 16, 20, 24, 28, 32, 36, 40 ...

5 times table: 5, 10, 15, 20, 25, 30, 35, 40 ...

So **20** and **40** are common multiples 4 and 5.

What is the lowest common multiple of 4 and 5?

The smallest common multiple is **20**.

Set A

Find a common multiple of:

1. 3 and 6
2. 5 and 2
3. 5 and 7
4. 4 and 12
5. 6 and 8
6. 10 and 12

7. Find all the numbers below that are multiples of both 4 and 6:

36	54	60	12
24	40	28	

8. Find all the numbers below that are multiples of both 7 and 3:

21	14	77	54
36	63	42	

9. Find two common multiples of 5 and 8 between 1 and 100.
10. Find three common multiples of 4 and 12 between 20 and 50.
11. Find four common multiples of 9 and 3 between 10 and 50.

Set B

Find one common multiple between 20 and 40 of:

1. 4 and 10
2. 2 and 12
3. 7 and 14
4. 6 and 3
5. 5 and 7
6. 9 and 6

7. Find all the numbers below that are multiples of both 9 and 4:

81	108	27	36
52	90	72	

8. Find all the numbers below that are multiples of both 8 and 12:

36	24	96	48
80	72	64	

Find the lowest common multiple of:

9. 3 and 9
10. 4 and 6
11. 7 and 10
12. 9 and 12
13. 1 and 5 and 15
14. 2 and 6 and 11

Set C

Find a common multiple between 50 and 80 of:

1. 11 and 7
2. 4 and 8
3. 6 and 10
4. 3 and 12
5. 7 and 8
6. 8 and 12

Find the lowest common multiple of:

7. 3 and 7
8. 12 and 15
9. 6 and 8
10. 6 and 21
11. 2 and 5 and 7
12. 4 and 10 and 12

13. Think of two prime numbers and then find the lowest common multiple.

    Do this a few more times with different pairs of prime numbers.

    What do you notice about your answers?

I know and can identify common multiples.

BODMAS — 1

If there's more than one thing to do in a calculation, then there's a certain order in which you need to do each operation. This order is called BODMAS.

Example

BODMAS — **B**rackets, **D**ivision, **M**ultiplication, **A**ddition and **S**ubtraction

What is 12 × (6 + 3)?

BODMAS says to do the brackets first. ⟶ (6 + 3) = 9

12 × 9 = 108

So 12 × (6 + 3) = **108**

Set A

Find the missing numbers to complete the calculations:

1. 32 ÷ (8 – 4)
   = 32 ÷ ☐ = ☐
2. 12 – (5 + 2)
   = 12 – ☐ = ☐
3. (4 + 3) × 9
   = ☐ × 9 = ☐

Answer the following:

4. 42 – (20 + 2)
5. 45 ÷ (3 × 3)
6. 6 × (88 ÷ 11)
7. 60 ÷ (42 ÷ 7)
8. (13 – 7) × 3
9. (6 + 6) × 6

10. Dom thinks the answer to 8 × (7 – 3) is 53. Kelly thinks it's 32. Who is right?
11. Rav thinks the answer to 80 ÷ (10 ÷ 2) is 16. Todd thinks it's 4. Who is right?
12. Amy thinks the answer to (3 + 10) × 3 is 33. Suyin thinks it's 39. Who is right?

Set B

Answer the following:

1. 96 ÷ (8 + 4)
2. 346 – (3 + 7)
3. 60 ÷ (3 × 5)
4. 12 × (66 ÷ 6)
5. 150 ÷ (10 × 3)
6. (8 ÷ 2) × 25

Fill in the missing numbers:

7. ☐ – (2 × 8) = 4
8. 76 + (5 × ☐) = 96
9. ☐ ÷ (6 × 2) = 8
10. 5 × (☐ ÷ 9) = 35
11. 182 – (40 + 110) = ☐
12. 3 × (56 ÷ ☐) = 24

Write out the following using BODMAS rules:

13. First, add ten to fifteen. Then divide seventy-five by the result.
14. First, subtract ninety-one from a hundred. Multiply the result by three hundred.

Set C

Put brackets in these calculations to make them correct:

1. 14 + 4 × 4 = 72
2. 72 ÷ 87 – 79 = 9
3. 64 – 9 × 6 = 330
4. 10 × 15 – 10 = 50
5. 30 – 9 × 4 = 84
6. 50 ÷ 5 × 5 = 2

Fill in the missing numbers:

7. 72 ÷ (4 × 2) = ☐
8. ☐ + (11 × 4) = 261
9. 6 × (81 ÷ ☐) = 54
10. 108 ÷ (☐ – 28) = 12
11. 421 – (☐ ÷ 12) = 409
12. ☐ × (96 ÷ 8) = 132

Some of the following calculations are missing brackets. Add brackets where they're needed:

13. 48 ÷ 8 + 4 = 10
14. 5 × 7 + 5 = 60
15. 84 – 7 × 7 = 35
16. 4 × 16 ÷ 2 = 32
17. 144 ÷ 84 ÷ 7 = 12

I know how to use brackets.     

BODMAS — 2

After you've dealt with the brackets in a calculation, there's still an order in which you tackle the operations. Look back at BODMAS and follow that order. There are loads of calculations to have a go at on this page.

Examples

BODMAS — Brackets, Division, Multiplication, Addition and Subtraction

Work out 9 + 4 × 6 – (24 + 3).

9 + 4 × 6 – (24 + 3) = 9 + 4 × 6 – 27 ← 24 + 3 = 27
= 9 + 24 – 27 ← 4 × 6 = 24
= **6**

Work out 10 – 7 + 3.

10 – 7 + 3
= 3 + 3 ← When you have only addition and subtraction, you work from left to right — BODMAS says to do addition and subtraction together.
= **6**

Set A

Answer the following:

1. 5 + 7 – 6
2. 70 ÷ (16 – 6)
3. 3 × 20 – 17
4. 10 + 7 – 9
5. 4 × 8 – 3
6. (4 + 8) × 5

Fill in the missing numbers:

7. 5 × (15 – 7) = □
8. 20 – 12 + 7 = □
9. □ ÷ (53 – 43) = 6
10. □ – 6 × 2 = 5
11. 8 × 77 ÷ 11 = □
12. □ + 5 × 4 = 39

Charlie has £6. His mum gives him £12. Charlie then spends all of this money on 4 books, which all cost the same.

13. Write down the calculation you would do to find out how much each book was.
14. Work out the cost of each book.

Set B

Answer the following:

1. 33 ÷ (6 + 5)
2. 7 + 54 ÷ 9
3. 6 × 35 ÷ 7
4. 95 – 12 × 7
5. 8 + (12 – 5) × 6
6. (23 + 9) ÷ 4 – 2

Fill in the missing numbers:

7. □ + 5 – 10 = 12
8. □ ÷ (2 × 4) = 7
9. 15 ÷ 3 + □ = 24
10. 3 × 3 × 4 ÷ 2 = □
11. 29 + 14 – 7 × 2 = □
12. 34 – (7 + 5) × □ = 10

Last month, Scott spent £39 on 13 bus tickets to work. This month, he has travelled to work by bus 7 times.

13. Write down the calculation you would do to find out how much Scott spent this month.
14. Work out how much Scott spent this month on buses.

Set C

Fill in the missing numbers:

1. □ + 9 × 3 = 141
2. □ × 24 ÷ 12 = 16
3. 100 ÷ (25 – 20) = □
4. □ + 63 ÷ 7 = 83
5. 94 – 45 + 18 = □
6. (69 – 5) ÷ □ + 3 = 11
7. 27 + (□ + 8) × 10 = 137

Nina buys 6 packs of 15 balloons. Three balloons in each pack are damaged, so Nina can't use them. She decorates 9 rooms, each with the same number of balloons.

8. Write down the calculation you would do to find out how many balloons are in each room.

Then work out the answer.

Are the following true or false?

9. 77 + 132 ÷ 11 = 173 – 12 × 7
10. 8 – 3 + 5 × 6 = 8 – 1 × 3 + 2
11. 144 ÷ 12 ÷ 3 = (4 + 8) × 4 + 2 ÷ 2
12. 61 – (4 + 9) × 4 = (48 + 12) ÷ 15 + 5

I know what order to do operations.

Calculations — Review 4

Write down a common factor (other than 1) of:

1 6 and 18
2 4 and 20
3 3 and 36
4 24 and 88
5 16 and 64
6 32 and 56
7 64 and 88
8 22 and 110

Find all the common factors of:

9 14 and 42
10 24 and 48
11 5 and 45
12 72 and 88
13 24 and 96
14 36 and 66
15 30 and 75
16 12 and 73

Find the highest common factor of:

17 40 and 60
18 11 and 77
19 28 and 84
20 24 and 144
21 12 and 99
22 64 and 96

Gabby is picking pairs of numbers between 1 and 50. Use the information below to find the unknown numbers.

23 The common factors of the pair are 1, 2, 3, and 6. One of the numbers is 12, and the other number is smaller.

24 The common factors of the pair are 1, 3, 5 and 15. One of the numbers is 30, and the other number is bigger.

Find a common multiple of:

25 15 and 6
26 4 and 5
27 6 and 8
28 9 and 10
29 8 and 11
30 6 and 9
31 12 and 3
32 9 and 12

33 Find four common multiples of 4 and 6 between 1 and 50.

34 Find seven common multiples of 9 and 3 between 20 and 100.

35 Find three common multiples of 5 and 6 between 1 and 100.

36 Find all the numbers below that are multiples of both 6 and 8:

48	24	12	88	72	64

37 Find all the numbers below that are multiples of both 4 and 7:

56	24	77	28	35	84

Find the lowest common multiple of:

38 3 and 8
39 7 and 9
40 5 and 11
41 12 and 9
42 4 and 6 and 8
43 6 and 20 and 40

Answer the following:

44 $77 \div (8 + 3)$
45 $44 - (9 - 6)$
46 $(68 - 8) \times 4$
47 $11 \times (72 \div 9)$
48 $8 \times (132 \div 11)$
49 $(317 + 3) \div 4$
50 $(84 \div 2) \div 6$
51 $973 - (4 \times 8)$

Fill in the missing numbers:

52 $8 \times (6 - \square) = 8$
53 $\square - (99 + 1) = 28$
54 $44 \div (33 \div 3) = \square$
55 $54 \div (\square - 12) = 9$
56 $(65 + 5) \times 7 = \square$
57 $(\square - 240) \div 12 = 20$

58 Julian thinks the answer to 240 ÷ (60 ÷ 2) is 8. Erika thinks it's 2. Who is right?

Answer the following:

59 $8 + 2 - 6$
60 $8 - 2 + 6$
61 $9 + 4 \times 5$
62 $5 \times (87 - 75)$
63 $6 \times 54 \div 9$
64 $90 - 3 + 7 - 8$
65 $110 \div 11 \times 4 \times 2$
66 $324 - 84 \div 12$

Fill in the missing numbers:

67 $36 + 3 \times 4 = \square$
68 $\square - 5 \times 5 = 5$
69 $9 \times 56 \div \square = 63$
70 $14 - 3 + 28 = \square$
71 $5 \times 8 + 9 \times 2 = \square$
72 $\square - 4 \times 7 = 489$

73 A daffodil costs 38p and a tulip costs 45p. Jo has £7. She buys 7 daffodils. Write a calculation for how many tulips she can buy, and find the answer.

Well done on having a crack at these questions — good job!

Rounding Answers

Answers can be rounded to different degrees of accuracy — it doesn't always have to be powers of 10.

Example

Round 352 673 to the nearest 50.

When you're rounding to the nearest 50, you need to look at the tens and ones columns.

If the tens and ones are between 25 and 74, round to 50. If they're not, then round to the nearest 100.

HTh	TTh	Th	H	T	O
3	5	2	6	7	3

In 352 673, the tens and ones are 73. So you would round it down to **352 650**.

Set A

Round each answer to the nearest 100 and 1000:

1. 2431 × 3
2. 8668 ÷ 4
3. 9651 × 5
4. 54 624 + 45 270
5. 8 947 326 – 2 604 115

Round each answer to the nearest 50:

6. 12 415 + 46 322
7. 2442 ÷ 3
8. 68 268 – 42 017
9. 1852 × 6
10. 3724 × 26

There are 2 291 225 shells on one beach and 3 177 407 on another.

Round the total number of shells to:

11. the nearest 10 000
12. the nearest 100 000
13. the nearest 1 000 000

Set B

Round each answer to the nearest 20 and 50:

1. 7264 × 6
2. 4550 ÷ 14
3. 4348 × 57
4. 10 400 + 36 527
5. 9 468 206 – 1 256 513

Planet Barnot is 382 465 miles from Earth. Planet Snaffup is 798 372 miles further.

6. Find the distance between Earth and Snaffup.
7. Round this distance to the nearest 10, 20, 50, and 10 000 miles.

The population of Seaport is 5 078 281. The population of Frameford is 4 574 536.

8. Round the total population of the towns to the nearest 20 000.
9. Round the difference in the populations to the nearest 50 000.

Set C

Round each answer to the nearest 20 and 50:

1. 5641 × 38
2. 6 436 717 – 2 509 354
3. 6912 ÷ 12
4. 93 149 + 23 425
5. 703 796 – 274 307
6. 5 630 241 + 1 366 810

A manor had 986 714 visitors last year. A newspaper advert attracts 2500 more visitors per month this year.

7. How many visitors does the manor get in total this year?
8. Round this to the nearest 2000, 5000 and 500 000.

4 317 509 people watched a tennis final on TV. 2 568 095 watched online and 1 621 784 only saw the match highlights.

9. How many more watched on TV or online than watched the highlights? Round your answer to the nearest 200 000 and 500 000.

I can round answers to different degrees of accuracy.

Checking Calculations

It's important to be able to check your answers to calculations. A handy way to do this is by rounding and estimating. You can choose what to round to depending on the size of the numbers in the calculation.

Examples

In a survey, 1 647 379 said they prefer to go on holiday to a beach resort. 2 304 248 people said they would rather go to a mountain resort.

Estimate how many more people would rather go on a mountain holiday.

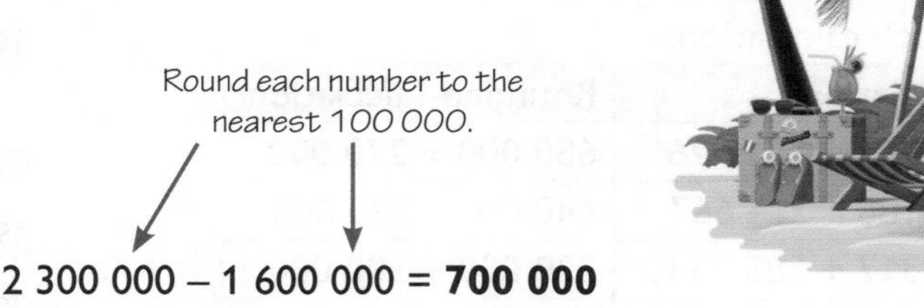

Round each number to the nearest 100 000.

2 300 000 – 1 600 000 = **700 000**

Estimate the answer to 375 982 + 416 054.

Round each number to the nearest 10 000.

380 000 + 420 000 = **800 000**

What is the difference between your estimated answer and the accurate answer?

```
   3 7 5 9 8 2
 + 4 1 6 0 5 4
   7 9 2 0 3 6
     1 1 1
```

800 000 – 792 036 = 7964

So the difference between the two answers is **7964.**

Set A

Write down a calculation you could use to check:

1. 51 911 + 64 892
2. 3342 ÷ 11
3. 24 096 + 646 039
4. 2452 × 12
5. 3 124 392 + 4 874 507
6. 6365 ÷ 19
7. 4549 × 21
8. 7 003 102 – 2 104 213

9. Match each calculation to a rounded calculation and an answer. The first has been done for you:

Calculation	Rounded calculation	Answer
486 311 + 196 450	750 000 – 220 000	690 000
746 337 – 219 462	490 000 + 200 000	640 000
8648 × 11	430 000 + 210 000	86 000
429 112 + 211 384	8600 × 10	530 000

Work out an estimate for the following calculations:

10. 3637 ÷ 12
11. 4 001 012 + 3 998 895
12. 349 707 – 124 488
13. 645 072 + 382 127
14. 5614 × 11
15. 8 601 371 – 3 107 520
16. 5967 ÷ 17
17. 7850 × 22

A toy shop has 575 874 blue building blocks. They also have 446 486 yellow and 483 152 green building blocks.

18. Estimate the total number of blocks they have.
19. Calculate the actual answer.

Set B

Write down a calculation you could use to check:

1 5476 × 19

2 946 111 – 427 006

3 429 125 + 782 035

4 8042 ÷ 18

5 6 639 848 – 2 113 230

6 987 892 + 496 859

7 7613 × 11

8 6838 ÷ 23

9 Sara has rounded to the nearest 10 000 incorrectly. Correct her rounding and estimate an answer for each calculation:

Calculation	Rounded calculation
686 954 + 271 926	680 000 + 270 000
442 186 – 214 667	440 000 – 220 000
326 317 + 585 934	330 000 + 580 000
942 650 – 125 789	940 000 – 120 000

10 Now work out another estimate for Sara's first calculation above by rounding to the nearest 1000.

11 Find the accurate answer to Sara's first calculation. Which of your two estimates is more accurate?

Write down an estimate and an accurate answer for the following:

12 8350 × 19

13 512 657 + 194 453

14 7615 × 28

15 1 310 456 – 1 207 624

16 8371 ÷ 11

17 176 899 – 145 012

18 647 515 + 396 984

Find an estimate for the following:

19 7 462 941 – 1 356 367

20 6766 ÷ 17

21 296 755 + 816 324

22 Find an accurate answer for each calculation, and work out the difference between your estimate and accurate answer.

Set C

Write down a calculation you could use to check:

1 742 859 – 308 716

2 5672 × 19

3 128 634 + 773 205

4 7832 ÷ 11

5 6 342 768 – 3 986 991

6 5364 ÷ 18

7 3068 × 21

8 864 398 – 213 404

In a month, a pilot is flying to all these destinations from Manchester. Here are the distances between Manchester and each location:

Los Angeles	8498 km
Sydney	16 986 km
Cape Town	9957 km
Buenos Aires	11 176 km

9 Estimate how much further away Sydney is than Los Angeles.

10 Estimate the total distance the pilot will fly to get from Manchester to each of the destinations.

11 Find the accurate answer. What is the difference between your estimate and the accurate answer?

Write down an estimate and an accurate answer for the following:

12 8073 ÷ 27

13 8 647 956 – 2 110 392

14 6548 × 18

15 668 986 + 380 027

16 4 285 336 + 5 490 624

17 9462 ÷ 19

18 746 510 – 218 309

19 Find estimates for the following by rounding to the nearest 10 000:

1 748 311 + 224 152

4 874 992 – 4 468 350

2 676 409 + 5 125 610

20 Now estimate the first calculation by rounding to the nearest 1000. Then find the accurate answer. Which of your two estimates is more accurate?

I can check calculations using estimation.      

Calculation Problems — 1

It's time to do some problems involving all four operations. Remember to read the question carefully and think about what steps and operations the problem involves.

Example

Last year, 9 255 450 people visited Hopeton Hall.
The table below shows the age groups that get half-price tickets, and how many tickets were sold last year. Everyone else pays full price, which is £1.

Age group	Number of tickets
0-17	2 694 396
65+	505 604

How much money did Hopeton Hall make from ticket sales last year?

Add the number of under 18s to the number of over 65s...

$$\begin{array}{r} 2\,6\,9\,4\,3\,9\,6 \\ +\quad 5\,0\,5\,6\,0\,4 \\ \hline 3\,2\,0\,0\,0\,0\,0 \\ \scriptstyle 1\,1\,1\,1\,1\,1 \end{array}$$

...and work out how much they paid:

So 3 200 000 people paid half-price.
They paid £3 200 000 ÷ 2:
$\underline{32} \div \underline{2} = \underline{16}$, so £$\underline{3\ 2}$00 000 ÷ $\underline{2}$ = £$\underline{1\ 6}$00 000

Work out how many people paid full price:

9 255 450 – 3 200 000 =
9 255 450 – 3 000 000 – 200 000 =
6 255 450 – 200 000 = 6 055 450
So they paid £6 055 450.

Finally, find the total:

6 055 450 + 1 600 000 =
6 055 450 + 1 000 000 + 600 000 =
7 055 450 + 600 000 = **7 655 450**

So in total, Hopeton Hall made **£7 655 450** from ticket sales.

Set A

The table below shows how many of each type of vegetable Farmer Jo grows per field.

Vegetable	Amount per field
Carrots	7245
Parsnips	5276
Pea plants	723 825

1. Farmer Jo needs 30 000 carrots — she has four carrot fields. Will she be able to grow enough?

2. In her parsnip field, 317 are rotten. The rest of them are put into bags of 11. How many bags can be filled?

3. In the pea field, 211 754 plants were eaten by insects. Farmer Jo planted another 645 154. How many pea plants does she have in total?

4. A school is being redecorated over summer. They order 441.43 m^2 green carpet and 440.57 m^2 blue carpet. The carpet is for 21 identical rooms. How big is each room?

5. Josh scores 1536 points out of 2400 after playing 12 levels of a video game. Each level is worth the same number of points. Josh scored the same number of points on each level.
   How many points did Josh miss on each level?

6. A hotel has 94 rooms. Each room sleeps between 1 and 4 guests. The incomplete table below shows the number of rooms of each size in the hotel.

Guests per room	Number of rooms
1	16
2	23
3	
4	46

How many guests can stay in the hotel?

Set B

1 A museum has 685 472 artefacts on show. They receive a donation of 125 478 artefacts, but then have to put 176 613 artefacts into storage.

How many artefacts are now on show at the museum?

Here are the populations of 4 cities:

Gregchester	2 423 165
Bondham	1 691 932
Millton	3 053 743
Westport	2 926 860

2 What is the total population of Millton, Westport and Gregchester?

3 Find the totals of the two most populated cities and the two least populated. What is the difference between these two totals?

4 In Bondham, 1 685 754 people are under 80. There are 4 times as many people 80 or over in Millton as there are in Bondham. How many people in Millton are 80 or over?

52 765 aliens are leaving Wardenia. There are only 48 823 seats on the spaceship. The aliens can attach extra pods onto the spaceship, which can carry 28 aliens each.

5 How many extra pods will they need to attach?

6 The passengers pay 8 564 352 ₩ (Wardenian dollars) in total. Fuel costs 100 ₩ for each passenger on the ship, and 10 ₩ for each in the pods. How much money is left after buying fuel?

The aliens all vote for where they want to go:

Earth	
Mars	7142
Jupiter	
Saturn	2480

Four times as many vote to visit Earth as those who vote for Mars and Saturn combined.

7 How many aliens vote to visit Earth?

8 How many aliens vote to visit Jupiter?

Set C

A construction site gets the following delivery:

Mortar	47 122.37 kg
Gravel	23 234.95 kg
Sand	8365 kg

1 They were expecting the delivery to total 81 000 kg. What is the mass of the missing material?

2 They need three times as much gravel as sand. How much more gravel do they need to get this amount?

18 355 people went to the cinema to see a spy film last weekend. 9589 went to see an animation film.

3 The tickets for the spy film cost £10 and for the animation tickets cost £5. How much money did the cinema make from the two films?

4 The number that saw a superhero film is 7 times as many as the difference between the numbers that saw the spy and animation films. How many people went to see the superhero film last weekend?

Here are some TV viewing figures for an athletics event:

Triathlon	2 236 376
Marathon	1 854 809
100 m Final	7 469 855

5 How many more people watched the 100 m final than watched the triathlon and marathon combined?

6 There were 124 000 people in the crowd at each event. How many people watched the three events in total, either there or on TV?

7 Half the triathlon TV viewers and a third of the 100 m final TV viewers were under 30. Estimate how many more viewers of the 100 m final than the triathlon were in this age group.

8 Sandeep has a 25.11 m piece of wire. He needs 97 shorter pieces, each 27 cm long. How much extra wire will Sandeep need so that he can make all 97 pieces?

I can solve multi-step calculation problems.

Calculation Problems — 2

You're an expert at these by now — so here are some more word problems to have a go at.

Examples

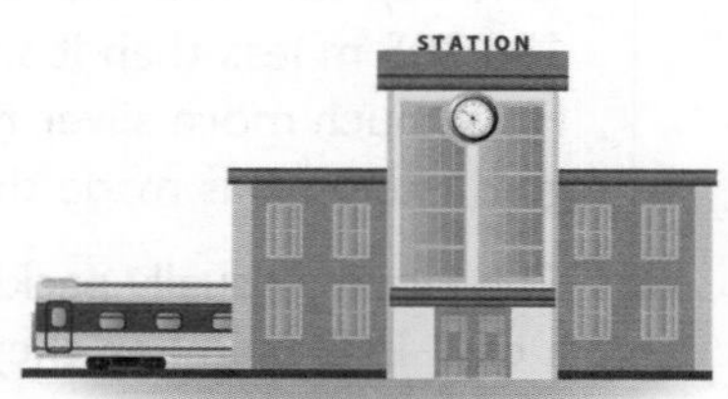

278 967 people were on trains arriving at Central station today.
42 856 people got off the train at Central station.
16 959 people got on the train at Central station.

How many people were on trains leaving Central station today?

Subtract the number that got off the train:

$$\begin{array}{r} 278967 \\ -\ 42856 \\ \hline 236111 \\ \hline \end{array}$$

Then add the number that got on the train:

$$\begin{array}{r} 236111 \\ +\ 16959 \\ \hline \mathbf{253070} \\ \hline {}_{1\,1\;\;1} \end{array}$$

So **253 070** were on trains leaving Central station.

Three coffee shops at Central station sold 8172 cups of coffee during the 12 hours they were open. If they all sold the same number of cups each hour, how many cups of coffee did each shop sell every hour?

Find the number of cups sold each hour in total.

$$\begin{array}{r} \mathbf{681} \\ 12\overline{)8172} \\ -\ 72 \\ \hline 97 \\ -\ 96 \\ \hline 12 \\ -\ 12 \\ \hline 0 \end{array}$$

Then work out how many that is at each coffee shop.

$$\begin{array}{r} \mathbf{227} \\ 3\overline{)6\,8\,{}^{2}1} \end{array}$$

So each coffee shop sold **227** cups of coffee per hour.

Set A

Chantel's new album sold 636 523 copies in its first week. In the second week 413 729 copies were sold. In the first two weeks, 296 970 of these sales were downloads.

1. How many of the copies sold in the first two weeks were not downloads?

In the third week, the album sold 185 600 more copies than in the second week.
In the fourth week, the album sold 174 900 fewer copies than in the third week.

2. How many copies were sold in the fourth week?

A shop had 2451 copies of the album in stock. When they sold out, they ordered twice this amount. But 1451 copies were missing from the delivery.

3. How many copies of the album were delivered to the shop?
4. They sold each copy for £8. How much do they make from this delivery?

Foodigo own twelve supermarkets.
Each week, the twelve shops sell a total of 1472 blocks of cheese, 1185 tins of tuna and 3576 chicken kievs.

5. They sell three times as many packets of ham as they do cheese and tuna combined. How many packets of ham do they sell each week?
6. Each store sells the same number of chicken kievs. How many chicken kievs does each store sell?

Foodigo needs to buy packaging. They buy boxes worth £21 376.80 and foil worth £65 263.15.
The packaging company give Foodigo a discount of £15 150.40.

7. How much does the order cost, after the discount?
8. They get 310 800 m of foil, in rolls of 100 m. The rolls are shared equally between the 12 stores. How many rolls does each store get?

Set B

A ribbon factory should produce 1 654 275 m of silver ribbon and 1 371 662 m of gold ribbon every day.

1. One day, the silver ribbon machine made 150 705 m less than it should have. How much more silver ribbon than gold ribbon was made that day?

2. The factory usually packs 134 crates of ribbon a day. In December, they have to pack 15 times as many crates as usual. How many crates do they pack in a week in December?

12 264 ate at Carlo's restaurants from Friday to Sunday. 10 178 of those people were there on Friday or Saturday. One seventh of the people eating there on Sunday didn't order dessert.

3. How many people ordered dessert on Sunday?

Carlo's use 3481 onions and 2864 peppers every day.

4. In one week, how many onions and peppers do Carlo's use altogether?

A town council have 214 small plant pots and 128 large plant pots. Small pots hold 16 plants and large pots hold 42 plants.

5. How many plants can the pots hold in total?

Plants cost 28p each.

6. What is the total cost of filling all the pots?

A holiday camp has 3658 guests. Each pays a £12 fee to visit a local castle. The holiday camp pays £26 923.50 for the coaches and tickets.

7. How much of the total fees will the holiday camp get to keep?

On Monday, 624 guests have signed up to go on the castle visit. On Tuesday, 475 guests are planning to go. The coaches will seat 21 people.

8. How many coaches will the camp need to book for Monday and Tuesday in total?

The castle does guided tours in groups of 40. Each tour lasts 20 minutes.

9. What will be the total running time of the tours on Monday?

Set C

A library bookcase has 8624 books, split equally across eight shelves — three shelves are non-fiction.

1. How many fiction books are on the bookcase?

847 632 people have membership cards for Landock Library. When another library closes, 1 045 204 people are invited to join Landock Library. Of those, 623 822 don't apply for membership.

2. How many people have membership to Landock Library now?

The library needs to get some more books. They order 14 842 travel guides and 26 527 biographies. They order 10 times as many crime novels as travel guides and biographies combined.

3. How many crime novels have they ordered?

4. A clothing company made £4 182 413 in October and £3 662 804 in November. £5 926 019 of sales in those two months were in the UK.

   In October and November, how much did they make from sales in other countries?

39 athletes are going to a tournament in America. Between them, the group have 2691 kg of kit, including their bags. They each take the same number of bags, each weighing 23 kg.

5. How many bags does each athlete take?

19 athletes want a seat near the front of the plane so they pay an extra £126 each.
13 athletes pay an extra £135 each for seats with more leg room.

6. How much extra do the athletes pay in total?

7. A comedy festival is taking place on Saturday. 7642 people applied for tickets, but there were only 4884 available. The comedy company decided to put on an extra night for those who didn't get tickets for Saturday.

   On the extra night, the company puts seats out in rows of 24. How many rows of seats will the company need to put out?

I am confident solving multi-step calculation problems.      

Calculations — Review 5

Round each answer to the nearest 10, 100 and 1000:

1. 2841 × 4
2. 26 453 + 61 244
3. 79 858 – 47 275
4. 3225 ÷ 5
5. 843 246 – 450 031
6. 2856 ÷ 3
7. 643 720 + 256 464
8. 4627 × 12

Round each answer to the nearest 20 and 50:

9. 264 372 + 453 273
10. 6692 ÷ 7
11. 9304 × 6
12. 914 371 – 460 159
13. 8512 ÷ 16
14. 836 422 + 457 261
15. 7 643 291 – 3 450 465
16. 214 × 36

17. A music video received 672 358 views on the first day it was uploaded online. The next day, it received another 844 053 views.

    Round the video's total number of views to the nearest 10 000 and 100 000.

Write down a calculation you could use to check:

18. 5684 × 23
19. 52 759 + 18 364
20. 687 526 – 404 385
21. 9779 ÷ 11
22. 3 487 506 – 2 145 290
23. 279 814 + 312 455
24. 6446 ÷ 22
25. 3249 × 74

Work out an estimate for the following calculations:

26. 274 305 – 121 286
27. 638 117 + 308 929
28. 4484 ÷ 19
29. 2537 × 63
30. 844 376 + 615 420
31. 4 748 866 – 1 651 372
32. 4950 × 28
33. 7342 ÷ 12

Write down an estimate and an accurate answer for the following:

34. 632 865 + 206 144
35. 1589 × 12
36. 7164 ÷ 18
37. 984 768 – 255 426
38. 2 652 910 + 7 350 765
39. 7247 × 29

40. A bakery makes 2794 brown rolls and 3110 white rolls. They make half as many croissants as white and brown rolls combined. How many croissants do they make?

41. The bakery receives an order for 2417 cupcakes. They have 20 trays that can hold 16 cupcakes, but all the other trays can only hold 12 cupcakes. How many trays of 12 will they need?

42. When they decorate the cupcakes, they put 7 chocolate swirls on 1450 cakes and 11 chocolate swirls on the other 967 cakes. In total, how many chocolate swirls will the bakery need to make to decorate all the cupcakes?

43. In an election, 2 690 319 people vote for the Dinner Party and 1 235 842 people vote for the Garden Party. In total, 9 216 552 people voted in the election. How many people voted for other parties?

44. There are 7248 tickets available for a music festival. Five eighths of the tickets are weekend passes. The rest of the tickets are day passes. How many day passes are available?

45. The festival has 34 zones on its campsite. 98 tents can be pitched in each campsite zone. The festival organisers are expecting there to be 5237 tents at the festival. How many more campsite zones will the festival organisers need to make?

46. A national park is 22 362.21 km^2. 10 753.65 km^2 is forest and 12.05 km^2 is water. How much of the national park is not water or forest?

47. There are 10 652 holiday cottages in the national park that sleep 4 people, 269 hotels that each sleep 86 people and 23 hostels that sleep 114 people. What is the maximum number of people that can stay in the national park's accommodation?

48. 4875 people signed up for a skiing lesson. There are 65 ski instructors and each one can lead a lesson for 15 students at a time. How many classes will each instructor have to do?

You're officially a calculations superstar! Well done!

Calculations — Challenges

1 For this game, you'll need to get into small groups.
You'll also need a dice and each person will need a counter.

- Each person rolls the dice and moves their counter along the grid by the number they have rolled.
- Each player has to then answer the calculation in the box they land in. Make a note of the answer.
- If you land on the start of a vine, climb the vine and move your counter forward to where the vine ends.
- If you land on a box where the end of a snake's tail is, slide down the snake and move your counter back to the head.
- After every player has crossed the finish line, add up all the answers you have collected during the game.
- The player with the smallest total wins.

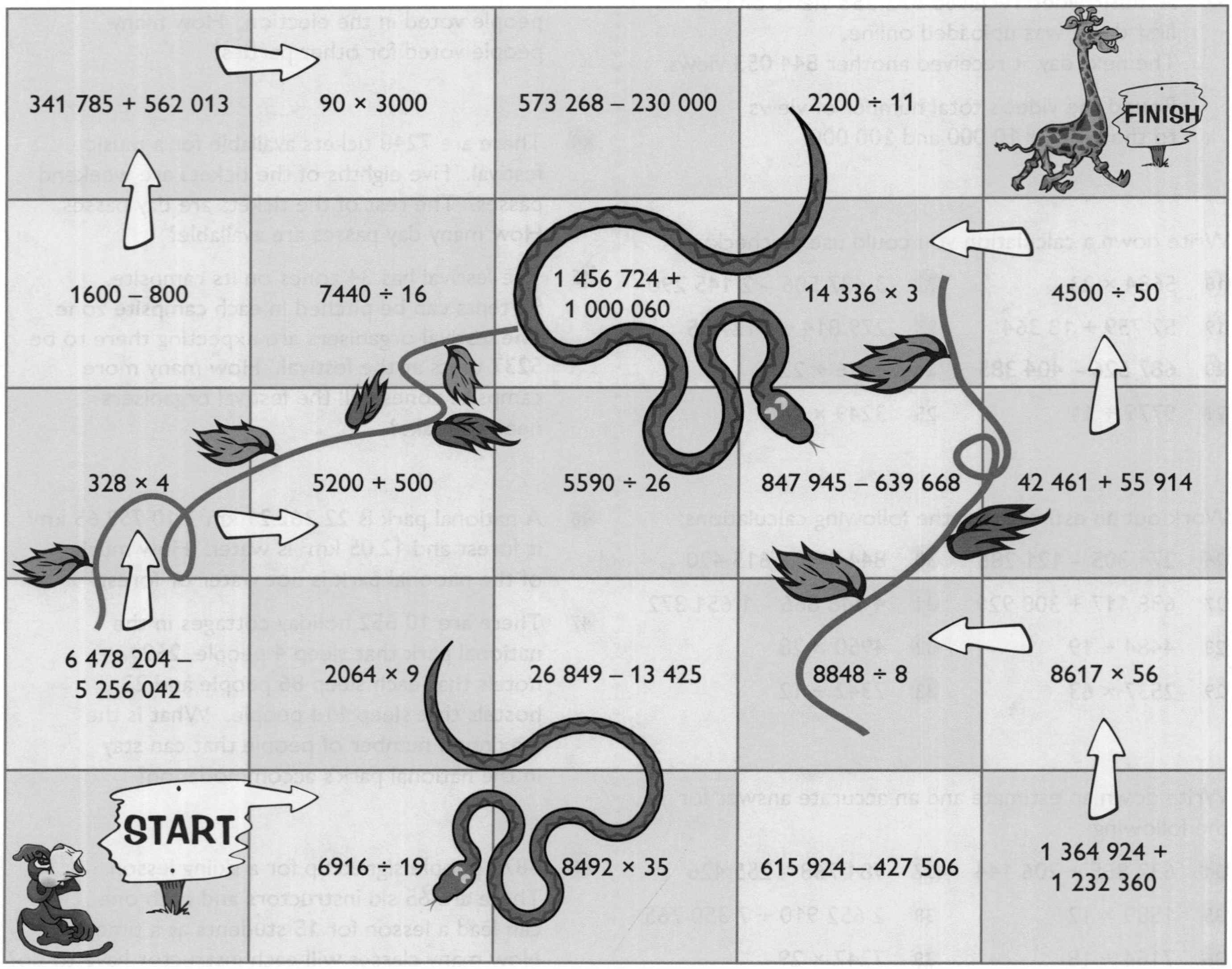

341 785 + 562 013	90 × 3000	573 268 – 230 000	2200 ÷ 11	FINISH
1600 – 800	7440 ÷ 16	1 456 724 + 1 000 060	14 336 × 3	4500 ÷ 50
328 × 4	5200 + 500	5590 ÷ 26	847 945 – 639 668	42 461 + 55 914
6 478 204 – 5 256 042	2064 × 9	26 849 – 13 425	8848 ÷ 8	8617 × 56
START	6916 ÷ 19	8492 × 35	615 924 – 427 506	1 364 924 + 1 232 360

2 Sienna has the answers to some calculations. The digits, operations and brackets from the calculations are all jumbled up in some envelopes.

Unscramble all the digits, operations and brackets in each calculation so that the answers Sienna has are correct.

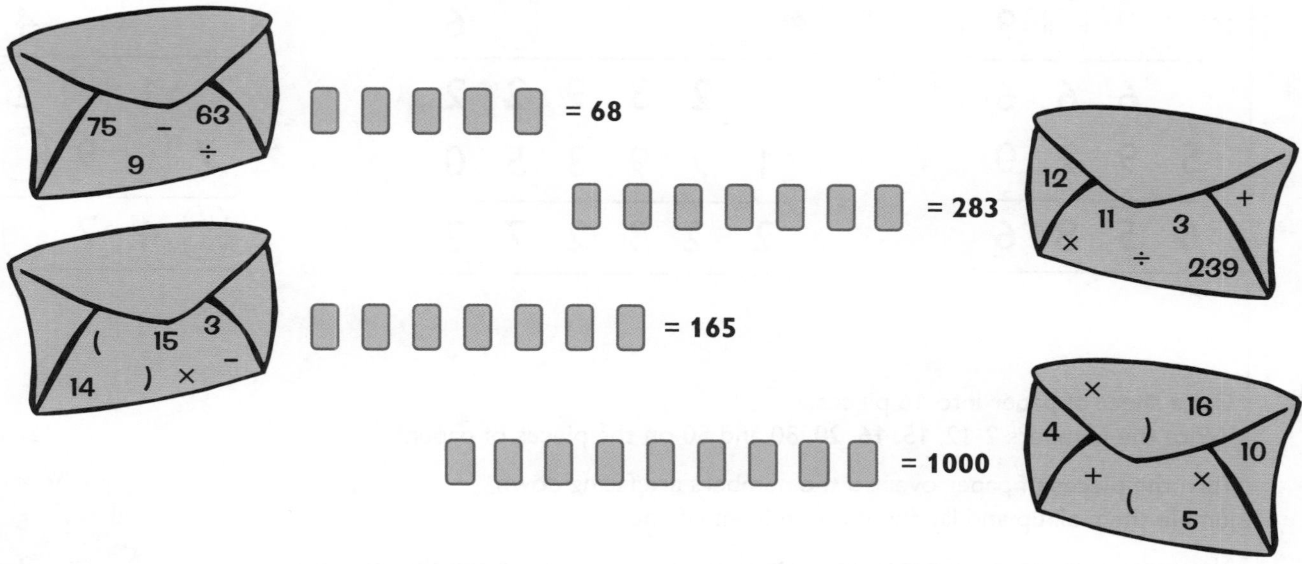

You'll need a partner for this challenge.

- The first player should ask the second player a multiplication question – up to 12 × 12.
- Once the second player has found the answer to the multiplication question, they should then ask the first player another multiplication question.
- After you've found both answers, jot them down and work together to find all the common factors they share.

Try this until you've found 5 pairs with 5 different amounts of common factors.

When you've found all those, repeat the challenge a few more times, finding the highest common factor of the two numbers you have.

Here's some information about a mountain range:

- To the nearest 10 000 m, the mountain range is 6 000 000 m long.
- To the nearest 1000 m, the tallest mountain in the range is 7000 m.
- To the nearest 50 m, the tallest mountain in the range is 7500 m.
- To the nearest 100 000, there were 7 400 000 visitors to the mountain range last year.

a) What's the longest and shortest length the mountain range could be?

b) What's the tallest and shortest height the tallest mountain could be?

c) What's the greatest and smallest number of visitors to the mountain range there could have been last year?

5 Find the missing numbers in each calculation below.

7 □	3 □ 8 7	□ 8 □ 3
× □ 9	× □ 6	× 4 □
6 6 6	2 3 9 2 2	1 □ 2 3
5 9 2 0	1 9 9 3 5 0	7 □ 9 □ □
6 5 8 6	2 2 3 2 7 2	□ 4 7 □ □

6 Cut a sheet of paper into 16 pieces.
Write the numbers 2-12, 15, 16, 20, 30 and 50 on the pieces of paper.

Turn the pieces of paper over so the numbers are facing down, jumble them all up and lay them out in front of you.

Now, pick two pieces of paper and turn them over so you can see the numbers:

- Can you find 5 common multiples of the two numbers?
- What is the lowest common multiple of your two numbers?

When you've done that with two pieces of paper five times, turn over three pieces of paper at a time and try to find the lowest common multiple of those numbers.

7 Captain Pinkfeather is looking at a treasure map. If he answers the calculations on the back of the map, the final answer will tell him how far away he is from the treasure, in millimetres.

a) Help him solve the calculations. The answer to each calculation will be the first missing number in the next calculation.

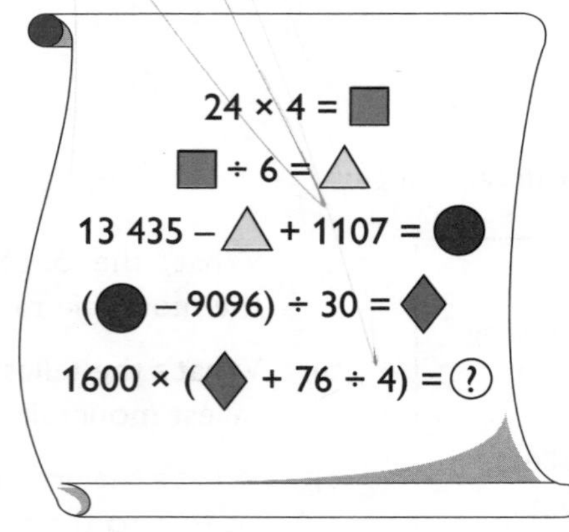

Hooray — Captain Pinkfeather found the treasure! Inside the chest, there's a crown worth £3 150 720, a jewel worth £2 241 060 and 9 rings that are each worth £9521.

b) In total, how much is the treasure worth?

Captain Pinkfeather accidentally drops 4 rings into the ocean.

c) How much is the treasure worth now?

Crikey, those calculations challenges were corkers!

Simplifying Fractions

To simplify a fraction you need to find an equivalent fraction that uses the smallest numbers possible.
For fraction questions, it's a good habit to give your answers as a simplified fraction.

Examples

Simplify these fractions:

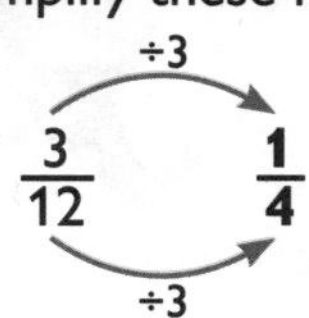

$\frac{3}{12} \xrightarrow{\div 3} \frac{1}{4}$

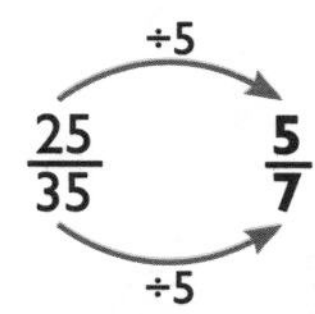

$\frac{25}{35} \xrightarrow{\div 5} \frac{5}{7}$

Divide the top and bottom by the biggest number which goes into both (the biggest common factor).

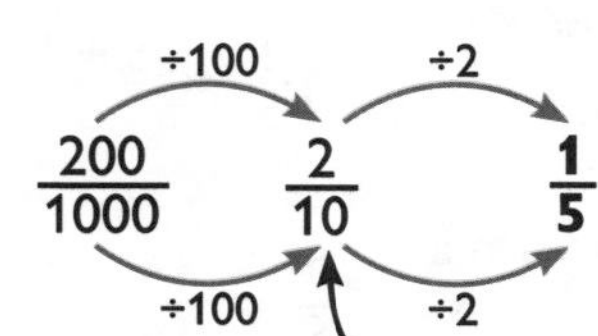

$\frac{200}{1000} \xrightarrow{\div 100} \frac{2}{10} \xrightarrow{\div 2} \frac{1}{5}$

This isn't a simplified fraction yet — divide the top and bottom until you can't find another equivalent fraction.

Set A

Use the fraction bars to help you simplify the fractions below.

1. $\frac{3}{6}$ 
2. $\frac{4}{12}$ 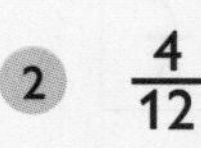 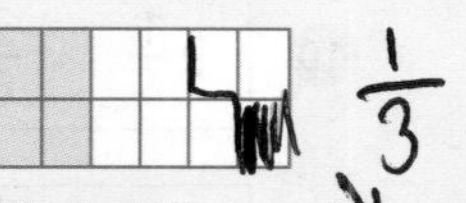
3. $\frac{6}{8}$ 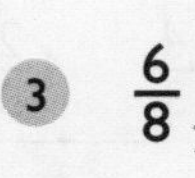 

Simplify these fractions:

4. $\frac{2}{4}$
5. $\frac{10}{40}$
6. $\frac{15}{20}$
7. $\frac{16}{24}$

8. Look at the fractions in the box below.

$\frac{3}{4}$	$\frac{5}{15}$	$\frac{5}{8}$
$\frac{9}{12}$	$\frac{2}{7}$	

Identify the fractions that can't be simplified.

Set B

Simplify these fractions:

1. $\frac{15}{45}$
2. $\frac{9}{36}$
3. $\frac{14}{35}$
4. $\frac{30}{36}$

Identify the fractions shown by the arrows below, giving your answers in their simplest forms.

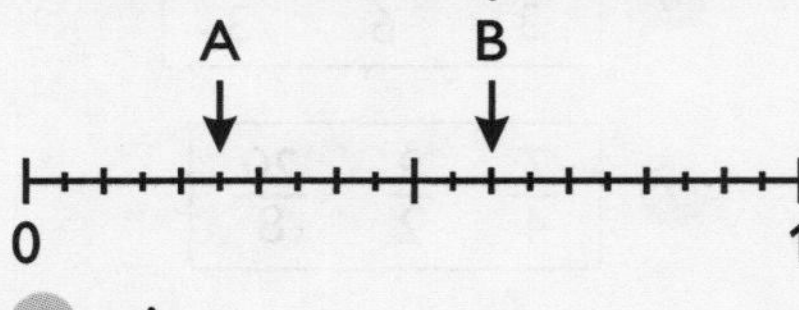

5. A
6. B

Look at the fractions in the box below.

$\frac{15}{18}$	$\frac{25}{30}$	$\frac{20}{30}$	$\frac{32}{40}$	$\frac{80}{100}$

Which fractions simplify to:

7. have a denominator of 3?
8. have a denominator of 5?

Set C

Each fraction below has been simplified. Find the missing numbers.

1. $\frac{\square}{8} \longrightarrow \frac{3}{4}$
2. $\frac{24}{36} \longrightarrow \frac{2}{\square}$
3. $\frac{30}{\square} \longrightarrow \frac{5}{9}$

Simplify these fractions:

4. $\frac{27}{45}$
5. $\frac{48}{72}$
6. $\frac{24}{88}$
7. $\frac{115}{200}$

8. Write a fraction, with a denominator of 20, that simplifies to $\frac{3}{4}$.

9. Reece says: "$\frac{45}{75}$ is equivalent to $\frac{120}{200}$". Simplify each fraction to show if he is correct.

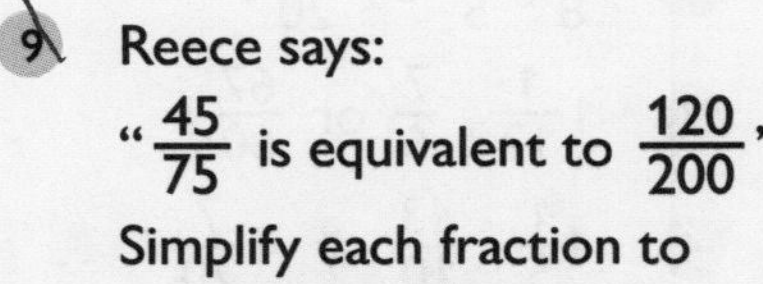

I can simplify fractions using common factors.

Ordering Fractions

You've ordered fractions before — this time, you'll come across fractions larger than one whole.

Example

Order these fractions, starting with the smallest: $\frac{9}{5}$ $\frac{17}{10}$ $1\frac{1}{5}$

Convert any mixed numbers into improper fractions: $1\frac{1}{5} = \frac{5+1}{5} = \frac{6}{5}$

Find equivalent fractions with a common denominator: $\frac{9}{5} = \frac{18}{10}$ $\frac{17}{10}$ $\frac{6}{5} = \frac{12}{10}$

So the correct order is: $1\frac{1}{5}$ $\frac{17}{10}$ $\frac{9}{5}$

Set A

Find the equivalent fractions and decide which is larger:

1. $\frac{1}{2} = \frac{\square}{10}$ or $\frac{3}{5} = \frac{\square}{10}$?
2. $\frac{15}{20} = \frac{\square}{4}$ or $\frac{8}{16} = \frac{\square}{4}$?
3. $\frac{2}{7} = \frac{\square}{21}$ or $\frac{1}{3} = \frac{\square}{21}$?
4. $\frac{30}{36} = \frac{\square}{6}$ or $\frac{28}{42} = \frac{\square}{6}$?

Which improper fraction is smaller:

5. $\frac{16}{10}$ or $\frac{11}{10}$?
6. $\frac{13}{8}$ or $\frac{9}{4}$?
7. $\frac{3}{2}$ or $\frac{50}{20}$?
8. $\frac{7}{5}$ or $\frac{18}{15}$?

Order the fractions below, starting with the smallest:

9. $\frac{7}{4}$ $\frac{11}{4}$ $1\frac{1}{4}$
10. $2\frac{1}{6}$ $1\frac{2}{6}$ $\frac{7}{6}$
11. $\frac{8}{3}$ $2\frac{1}{3}$ $\frac{4}{3}$ $1\frac{2}{3}$

Set B

Which fraction is smaller:

1. $\frac{1}{4}$ or $\frac{2}{7}$?
2. $\frac{5}{7}$ or $\frac{2}{3}$?
3. $1\frac{5}{9}$ or $\frac{15}{9}$?
4. $\frac{27}{12}$ or $2\frac{1}{12}$?
5. $\frac{2}{5}$ or $\frac{4}{11}$?

Find the smallest improper fraction in each list:

6. $\frac{13}{3}$ $\frac{10}{6}$ $\frac{7}{3}$
7. $\frac{7}{4}$ $\frac{9}{2}$ $\frac{20}{8}$
8. $\frac{6}{5}$ $\frac{25}{20}$ $\frac{5}{2}$

Order the fractions below, starting with the smallest:

9. $2\frac{1}{2}$ $\frac{7}{2}$ $\frac{6}{4}$
10. $\frac{24}{10}$ $\frac{11}{5}$ $3\frac{1}{5}$ $1\frac{3}{5}$
11. $\frac{11}{9}$ $1\frac{2}{3}$ $1\frac{5}{9}$ $\frac{7}{3}$

Set C

Which fraction is smallest:

1. $\frac{3}{5}$, $\frac{2}{6}$ or $\frac{7}{30}$?
2. $\frac{7}{8}$, $\frac{4}{5}$ or $\frac{17}{20}$?
3. $1\frac{1}{12}$, $\frac{7}{6}$ or $\frac{67}{60}$?
4. $4\frac{1}{5}$, $\frac{43}{10}$ or $4\frac{7}{20}$?
5. $\frac{19}{8}$, $\frac{29}{12}$ or $2\frac{2}{3}$?

Look at the improper fractions in the box below.

$\frac{8}{5}$ $\frac{12}{10}$ $\frac{55}{50}$ $\frac{28}{25}$

True or false?

6. $\frac{55}{50}$ is the smallest fraction.
7. Two fractions are smaller than $\frac{115}{100}$.

Three friends go jogging:

- Carlos jogs $3\frac{2}{3}$ km
- Felicia jogs $\frac{16}{9}$ km
- Rory jogs $\frac{47}{18}$ km

Who jogs:

8. the greatest distance?
9. the smallest distance?

I can order and compare any fractions.      

Adding Fractions — 1

As you've seen before, the trick to adding fractions is to make the denominators the same. When you've worked out an answer, do a quick check to see if you can simplify it.

Example

What is $3\frac{1}{3} + \frac{7}{6}$? Give your answer as a mixed number in its simplest form.

Write $3\frac{1}{3}$ as an improper fraction: $3\frac{1}{3} = \frac{10}{3} = \frac{20}{6}$ Then add: $\frac{20}{6} + \frac{7}{6} = \frac{27}{6}$

Write $\frac{27}{6}$ as a mixed number and simplify: $\frac{27}{6} = 4\frac{3}{6} = \mathbf{4\frac{1}{2}}$

Alternatively, you could turn $\frac{7}{6}$ into a mixed number, and then add the whole numbers and fractions separately.

Set A

Find the missing numbers:

1. $\frac{1}{2} + \frac{3}{10} = \frac{\square}{10} = \frac{\square}{5}$
2. $\frac{3}{8} + \frac{1}{24} = \frac{\square}{24} = \frac{\square}{12}$
3. $\frac{2}{15} + \frac{1}{5} = \frac{\square}{15} = \frac{\square}{3}$
4. $\frac{1}{12} + \frac{2}{3} = \frac{\square}{12} = \frac{\square}{4}$

Find the missing numbers:

5. $\frac{4}{3} + \frac{5}{6} = \frac{\square}{6}$
6. $\frac{7}{8} + \frac{5}{2} = \frac{\square}{8}$
7. $\frac{3}{5} + 1\frac{7}{20} = \frac{\square}{20}$
8. $2\frac{3}{8} + \frac{3}{16} = \frac{\square}{16}$

Find the missing numbers:

9. $1\frac{1}{3} + \frac{2}{6} = 1\frac{\square}{3}$
10. $1\frac{3}{5} + \frac{3}{10} = 1\frac{\square}{10}$
11. $2\frac{1}{2} + \frac{1}{12} = \square\frac{\square}{12}$
12. $1\frac{1}{8} + 1\frac{5}{16} = \square\frac{\square}{16}$

Set B

Work out, giving your answers in their simplest forms:

1. $\frac{1}{16} + \frac{1}{2}$
2. $\frac{1}{6} + \frac{7}{30}$
3. $\frac{3}{5} + \frac{1}{40}$
4. $\frac{14}{100} + \frac{3}{50} + \frac{4}{25}$

Work out, giving your answers as improper fractions:

5. $1\frac{4}{7} + \frac{1}{14}$
6. $1\frac{3}{5} + \frac{2}{15}$
7. $2\frac{8}{11} + \frac{5}{22}$
8. $1\frac{1}{5} + \frac{11}{25}$

Work out, giving your answers as mixed numbers:

9. $2\frac{3}{4} + \frac{1}{8}$
10. $1\frac{2}{9} + \frac{3}{18}$
11. $1\frac{7}{10} + 1\frac{1}{2}$
12. $2\frac{2}{3} + 1\frac{4}{9}$

Set C

Work out, giving your answers in their simplest forms:

1. $\frac{1}{8} + \frac{3}{8} + \frac{1}{4}$
2. $\frac{5}{12} + \frac{1}{6} + \frac{1}{12}$
3. $\frac{2}{5} + \frac{3}{10} + \frac{1}{20}$
4. $\frac{2}{9} + \frac{5}{18} + \frac{1}{3}$

Work out, giving your answers as improper fractions:

5. $1\frac{3}{10} + \frac{7}{20}$
6. $3\frac{1}{2} + 5\frac{3}{16}$
7. $2\frac{2}{15} + \frac{7}{150}$
8. $2\frac{7}{8} + 1\frac{7}{32}$

Find the missing numbers:

9. $\frac{15}{8} + \frac{\square}{4} = 4\frac{1}{8}$
10. $\frac{\square}{3} + \frac{9}{12} = 2\frac{5}{12}$
11. $\frac{\square}{21} + \frac{8}{7} = 1\frac{13}{21}$
12. $\frac{11}{6} + \frac{\square}{30} = 3\frac{1}{30}$

I can add fractions.

Adding Fractions — 2

These fractions won't add themselves — there's some more practice coming up.

Example

What is $\frac{3}{5} + \frac{3}{4}$?

Give your answer as a mixed number.

Find a common denominator and add together: $\frac{3}{5} = \frac{12}{20}$ and $\frac{3}{4} = \frac{15}{20}$

$\frac{12}{20} + \frac{15}{20} = \frac{27}{20}$

Convert to a mixed number: $\frac{27}{20} = \mathbf{1\frac{7}{20}}$

Set A

Find the missing numbers:

1. $\frac{1}{2} + \frac{1}{3} = \frac{\square}{6} + \frac{\square}{6} = \frac{\square}{6}$
2. $\frac{3}{4} + \frac{1}{5} = \frac{\square}{20} + \frac{\square}{20} = \frac{\square}{20}$
3. $\frac{1}{10} + \frac{2}{3} = \frac{\square}{30} + \frac{\square}{30} = \frac{\square}{30}$
4. $\frac{2}{9} + \frac{2}{5} = \frac{\square}{45} + \frac{\square}{45} = \frac{\square}{45}$

Find the missing numbers:

5. $\frac{3}{4} + \frac{1}{3} = \frac{\square}{12}$
6. $\frac{5}{6} + \frac{3}{8} = \frac{\square}{24}$
7. $1\frac{1}{2} + \frac{2}{9} = \frac{\square}{18}$
8. $1\frac{2}{7} + \frac{3}{5} = 1\frac{\square}{35}$

Work out, giving your answers in their simplest forms:

9. $\frac{4}{3} + \frac{1}{2}$
10. $\frac{1}{4} + \frac{1}{9}$
11. $\frac{2}{5} + \frac{1}{6}$
12. $\frac{1}{6} + \frac{3}{10}$

Set B

Work out, giving your answers in their simplest forms:

1. $\frac{1}{2} + \frac{1}{5}$
2. $\frac{2}{15} + \frac{7}{10}$
3. $\frac{5}{6} + \frac{1}{9}$
4. $\frac{1}{10} + \frac{1}{6} + \frac{2}{3}$

Work out, giving your answers as improper fractions:

5. $\frac{7}{8} + \frac{1}{3}$
6. $1\frac{1}{9} + \frac{3}{2}$
7. $2\frac{2}{5} + \frac{1}{12}$
8. $3\frac{1}{5} + \frac{1}{3}$

Work out, giving your answers as mixed numbers:

9. $\frac{7}{8} + \frac{7}{10}$
10. $1\frac{2}{5} + \frac{3}{4}$
11. $2\frac{1}{2} + \frac{7}{11}$
12. $3\frac{2}{3} + 1\frac{1}{2}$

Set C

Work out, giving your answers in their simplest forms:

1. $\frac{1}{3} + \frac{1}{3} + \frac{2}{5}$
2. $\frac{3}{8} + \frac{3}{10} + \frac{1}{8}$
3. $\frac{1}{12} + \frac{1}{6} + \frac{1}{5}$
4. $\frac{1}{4} + \frac{3}{10} + \frac{2}{5}$

Work out, giving your answers as improper fractions:

5. $1\frac{1}{3} + \frac{7}{20}$
6. $3\frac{7}{15} + 7\frac{1}{2}$
7. $4\frac{3}{8} + \frac{2}{3}$
8. $1\frac{1}{25} + 3\frac{1}{4}$

Find the missing numbers:

9. $\frac{5}{4} + \frac{\square}{3} = 1\frac{11}{12}$
10. $\frac{\square}{5} + \frac{5}{8} = 1\frac{9}{40}$
11. $\frac{\square}{2} + \frac{14}{9} = 4\frac{1}{18}$
12. $\frac{15}{8} + \frac{\square}{12} = 2\frac{19}{24}$

I am confident with adding fractions.     

Subtracting Fractions — 1

On to subtracting fractions now — check you understand the example before jumping in.

Example

What is $2\frac{1}{4} - \frac{5}{8}$? Give your answer as a mixed number.

Write $2\frac{1}{4}$ as an improper fraction: $2\frac{1}{4} = \frac{9}{4} = \frac{18}{8}$

Then subtract: $\frac{18}{8} - \frac{5}{8} = \frac{13}{8}$

Write $\frac{13}{8}$ as a mixed number: $\frac{13}{8} = \mathbf{1\frac{5}{8}}$

Set A

Find the missing numbers:

1. $\frac{1}{2} - \frac{1}{6} = \frac{\square}{6} = \frac{\square}{3}$
2. $\frac{1}{4} - \frac{1}{12} = \frac{\square}{12} = \frac{\square}{6}$
3. $\frac{11}{15} - \frac{1}{30} = \frac{\square}{30} = \frac{\square}{10}$
4. $\frac{37}{50} - \frac{7}{10} = \frac{\square}{50} = \frac{\square}{25}$

Find the missing numbers:

5. $\frac{15}{8} - \frac{3}{4} = \frac{\square}{8}$
6. $\frac{7}{5} - \frac{1}{10} = \frac{\square}{10}$
7. $1\frac{2}{3} - \frac{5}{9} = \frac{\square}{9}$
8. $2\frac{1}{2} - \frac{5}{12} = \frac{\square}{12}$

Find the missing numbers:

9. $\frac{7}{5} - \frac{3}{10} = 1\frac{\square}{10}$
10. $1\frac{3}{4} - \frac{5}{8} = 1\frac{\square}{8}$
11. $2\frac{2}{3} - \frac{1}{9} = \square\frac{\square}{9}$
12. $4\frac{7}{8} - 1\frac{5}{16} = \square\frac{\square}{16}$

Set B

Work out, giving your answers in their simplest forms:

1. $\frac{15}{16} - \frac{3}{4}$
2. $\frac{2}{5} - \frac{1}{15}$
3. $\frac{7}{4} - \frac{1}{2}$
4. $\frac{5}{7} - \frac{3}{14} - \frac{1}{28}$

Work out, giving your answers as improper fractions:

5. $1\frac{3}{4} - \frac{3}{8}$
6. $2\frac{4}{5} - \frac{11}{15}$
7. $2\frac{4}{11} - \frac{9}{22}$
8. $3\frac{1}{2} - \frac{7}{12}$

Work out, giving your answers as mixed numbers:

9. $3\frac{1}{2} - \frac{5}{16}$
10. $1\frac{7}{10} - \frac{11}{40}$
11. $2\frac{1}{6} - \frac{5}{12}$
12. $4\frac{1}{9} - 2\frac{1}{3}$

Set C

Work out, giving your answers in their simplest forms:

1. $\frac{3}{4} - \frac{1}{2} - \frac{1}{8}$
2. $\frac{9}{10} - \frac{3}{5} - \frac{1}{10}$
3. $\frac{11}{12} - \frac{1}{6} - \frac{1}{2}$
4. $\frac{4}{5} - \frac{1}{10} - \frac{3}{40}$

Work out, giving your answers as improper fractions:

5. $2\frac{2}{3} - \frac{8}{9}$
6. $6\frac{1}{4} - 3\frac{1}{36}$
7. $3\frac{4}{7} - \frac{17}{21}$
8. $9\frac{7}{8} - 5\frac{23}{40}$

Find the missing numbers:

9. $\frac{7}{3} - \frac{\square}{9} = 1\frac{7}{9}$
10. $\frac{\square}{2} - \frac{13}{16} = 1\frac{11}{16}$
11. $\frac{271}{100} - \frac{\square}{10} = 1\frac{41}{100}$
12. $\frac{\square}{12} - \frac{5}{6} = 3\frac{5}{12}$

I can subtract fractions.    

Subtracting Fractions — 2

There can be a lot to do before you even start subtracting fractions. It might help to convert any mixed numbers to improper fractions. Make sure you always get all the fractions over a common denominator too.

Example

What is $1\frac{1}{5} - \frac{1}{6}$?

Give your answer as an improper fraction.

Convert $1\frac{1}{5}$ into an improper fraction: $1\frac{1}{5} = \frac{6}{5}$

Find a common denominator then subtract: $\frac{6}{5} = \frac{36}{30}$ and $\frac{1}{6} = \frac{5}{30}$

$\frac{36}{30} - \frac{5}{30} = \mathbf{\frac{31}{30}}$

Set A

Find the missing numbers:

1. $\frac{3}{4} - \frac{1}{3} = \frac{\square}{12} - \frac{\square}{12} = \frac{\square}{12}$
2. $\frac{2}{3} - \frac{3}{5} = \frac{\square}{15} - \frac{\square}{15} = \frac{\square}{15}$
3. $\frac{8}{15} - \frac{3}{10} = \frac{\square}{30} - \frac{\square}{30} = \frac{\square}{30}$
4. $\frac{5}{7} - \frac{1}{4} = \frac{\square}{28} - \frac{\square}{28} = \frac{\square}{28}$

Find the missing numbers:

5. $\frac{10}{3} - \frac{1}{2} = \frac{\square}{6}$
6. $\frac{9}{4} - \frac{5}{6} = \frac{\square}{12}$
7. $2\frac{1}{3} - \frac{4}{5} = \frac{\square}{15}$
8. $1\frac{1}{6} - \frac{1}{5} = \frac{\square}{30}$

Work out, giving any answers bigger than 1 as mixed numbers:

9. $\frac{1}{2} - \frac{2}{5}$
10. $\frac{5}{7} - \frac{1}{3}$
11. $2\frac{4}{5} - \frac{1}{3}$
12. $1\frac{2}{3} - \frac{1}{4}$

Set B

Work out the following calculations:

1. $\frac{7}{12} - \frac{1}{8}$
2. $\frac{1}{4} - \frac{1}{11}$
3. $\frac{5}{6} - \frac{7}{20}$
4. $\frac{9}{10} - \frac{1}{4}$

Work out, giving your answers as improper fractions:

5. $2\frac{1}{6} - \frac{1}{9}$
6. $1\frac{10}{11} - \frac{1}{2}$
7. $1\frac{4}{5} - \frac{3}{8}$
8. $2\frac{1}{12} - \frac{3}{5}$

Work out, giving any answers bigger than 1 as mixed numbers:

9. $\frac{12}{5} - \frac{1}{6}$
10. $1\frac{7}{10} - \frac{1}{3}$
11. $1\frac{3}{8} - \frac{5}{12}$
12. $3\frac{1}{4} - 1\frac{4}{5}$

Set C

Work out the following calculations:

1. $\frac{2}{3} - \frac{1}{3} - \frac{1}{5}$
2. $\frac{3}{4} - \frac{2}{7} - \frac{1}{4}$
3. $\frac{1}{2} - \frac{1}{3} - \frac{1}{9}$
4. $\frac{9}{10} - \frac{3}{5} - \frac{1}{12}$

Work out, giving your answers as improper fractions:

5. $3\frac{4}{5} - \frac{2}{3}$
6. $2\frac{2}{9} - \frac{5}{6}$
7. $2\frac{1}{15} - \frac{3}{4}$
8. $3\frac{1}{6} - 1\frac{2}{7}$

Find the missing numbers:

9. $\frac{8}{3} - \frac{\square}{4} = 1\frac{5}{12}$
10. $\frac{\square}{6} - \frac{7}{10} = 1\frac{19}{30}$
11. $\frac{\square}{7} - \frac{3}{11} = 1\frac{23}{77}$
12. $\frac{7}{5} - \frac{\square}{12} = \frac{59}{60}$

I am confident with subtracting fractions.      

Fractions and Decimals — Review 1

Simplify the fractions below.
Use the fraction bars to help you.

1. $\frac{5}{10}$ 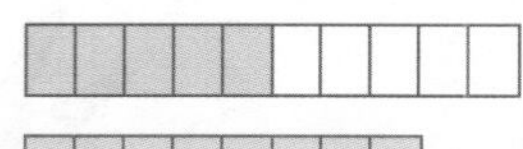
2. $\frac{12}{16}$ 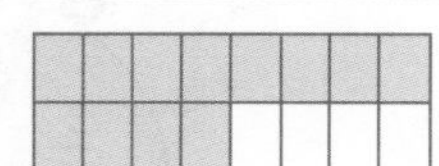

Simplify these fractions:

3. $\frac{2}{8}$
4. $\frac{10}{30}$
5. $\frac{10}{15}$
6. $\frac{12}{14}$
7. $\frac{22}{55}$
8. $\frac{40}{64}$

Which fraction is smaller:

9. $\frac{1}{3}$ or $\frac{3}{4}$?
10. $\frac{2}{5}$ or $\frac{1}{2}$?
11. $\frac{5}{6}$ or $\frac{3}{5}$?
12. $\frac{3}{8}$ or $\frac{1}{3}$?
13. $\frac{3}{7}$ or $\frac{5}{8}$?
14. $\frac{17}{20}$ or $\frac{14}{30}$?

Order the fractions below, starting with the largest:

15. $1\frac{1}{2}$ $\frac{5}{4}$ $\frac{13}{4}$
16. $\frac{8}{3}$ $\frac{17}{6}$ $1\frac{1}{6}$ $2\frac{1}{3}$
17. $\frac{10}{9}$ $\frac{4}{3}$ $2\frac{1}{5}$ $3\frac{2}{3}$

Work out, giving your answers as improper fractions:

18. $\frac{3}{2} + \frac{1}{8}$
19. $\frac{6}{5} + \frac{9}{10}$
20. $1\frac{1}{6} + \frac{5}{12}$
21. $2\frac{3}{4} + \frac{5}{8} + \frac{7}{16}$

Work out, giving your answers as mixed numbers:

22. $1\frac{3}{4} + \frac{5}{8}$
23. $2\frac{1}{6} + \frac{1}{18}$
24. $1\frac{2}{3} + 1\frac{1}{6}$
25. $3\frac{3}{5} + 1\frac{3}{20}$

Work out, giving your answers in their simplest forms:

26. $\frac{1}{2} + \frac{2}{5}$
27. $\frac{3}{5} + \frac{1}{6}$
28. $\frac{5}{6} + \frac{1}{10}$
29. $\frac{1}{20} + \frac{2}{15}$
30. $\frac{7}{30} + \frac{5}{12}$
31. $\frac{5}{11} + \frac{1}{10}$

Work out, giving your answers as mixed numbers:

32. $\frac{3}{2} + \frac{1}{3}$
33. $\frac{8}{5} + \frac{3}{4}$
34. $1\frac{3}{4} + \frac{5}{6}$
35. $2\frac{1}{6} + \frac{1}{11}$

Work out, giving your answers as improper fractions:

36. $\frac{13}{5} - \frac{3}{10}$
37. $\frac{10}{6} - \frac{13}{24}$
38. $2\frac{1}{4} - \frac{7}{12}$
39. $1\frac{4}{5} - \frac{3}{25}$

Work out, giving your answers as mixed numbers:

40. $\frac{12}{10} - \frac{3}{20}$
41. $\frac{11}{2} - \frac{3}{4}$
42. $2\frac{2}{5} - \frac{7}{10}$
43. $3\frac{1}{8} - \frac{9}{40} - \frac{1}{20}$

Work out the following calculations:

44. $\frac{1}{2} - \frac{1}{5}$
45. $\frac{9}{10} - \frac{6}{25}$
46. $\frac{5}{8} - \frac{5}{12}$
47. $\frac{7}{10} - \frac{1}{4}$
48. $\frac{5}{6} - \frac{11}{20}$
49. $\frac{4}{11} - \frac{3}{10}$

Work out, giving your answers as mixed numbers:

50. $\frac{7}{2} - \frac{1}{3}$
51. $\frac{5}{3} - \frac{1}{4}$
52. $2\frac{2}{5} - \frac{5}{6}$
53. $4\frac{1}{10} - \frac{2}{3}$

You showed off a load of great fraction skills there — good job!

Multiplying Fractions

Multiplying one fraction by another is a new skill for Year 6, but don't panic — see the example for how it's done.

Example

What is $\frac{1}{2} \times \frac{3}{5}$?

Multiply the top numbers.

$$\frac{1}{2} \times \frac{3}{5} = \frac{1 \times 3}{2 \times 5} = \frac{3}{10}$$

Multiply the bottom numbers.

Set A

Work out:

1. $\frac{1}{2} \times \frac{1}{3}$
2. $\frac{1}{6} \times \frac{1}{5}$
3. $\frac{1}{5} \times \frac{3}{4}$
4. $\frac{2}{3} \times \frac{2}{5}$
5. $\frac{4}{7} \times \frac{2}{3}$

Look at these number cards.

2	3	5	9

Pick numbers from the cards to complete each calculation.

6. $\frac{1}{\square} \times \frac{\square}{3} = \frac{2}{9}$
7. $\frac{1}{2} \times \frac{\square}{\square} = \frac{2}{10}$

Rewrite the calculations using fractions, and work out the answers:

8. one half multiplied by one half
9. one quarter multiplied by one third
10. two thirds multiplied by one fifth

Set B

Work out:

1. $\frac{1}{2} \times \frac{1}{8}$
2. $\frac{3}{10} \times \frac{1}{2}$
3. $\frac{5}{6} \times \frac{1}{3}$
4. $\frac{7}{10} \times \frac{3}{4}$
5. $\frac{2}{9} \times \frac{4}{5}$

Look at these number cards.

2	3	4	6	8

Pick numbers from the cards to complete each calculation.

6. $\frac{2}{\square} \times \frac{\square}{5} = \frac{8}{15}$
7. $\frac{\square}{5} \times \frac{5}{\square} = \frac{10}{40} = \frac{1}{\square}$

Work out, giving your answers in their simplest forms:

8. $\frac{1}{2} \times \frac{2}{5}$
9. $\frac{3}{5} \times \frac{1}{6}$
10. $\frac{4}{7} \times \frac{1}{8}$
11. $\frac{9}{10} \times \frac{2}{7}$

Set C

Work out, giving your answers in their simplest forms:

1. $\frac{2}{3} \times \frac{1}{4}$
2. $\frac{6}{7} \times \frac{7}{12}$
3. $\frac{1}{6} \times \frac{8}{11}$
4. $\frac{4}{9} \times \frac{5}{12}$

Are the following statements true or false?

5. $\frac{3}{4} \times \frac{1}{2} = \frac{4}{6}$
6. $\frac{3}{5} \times \frac{1}{9} = \frac{1}{15}$
7. $\frac{1}{3} \times \frac{3}{8} > \frac{5}{6} \times \frac{1}{4}$
8. $\frac{3}{5} \times \frac{3}{4} < \frac{1}{2} \times \frac{7}{10}$

Liane makes the three fraction cards below.

$\frac{1}{4}$	$\frac{2}{3}$	$\frac{1}{6}$

Which two fraction cards does she multiply to give the:

9. smallest answer?
10. largest answer?

I can multiply two fractions together.

Dividing Fractions

Dividing fractions by whole numbers is rather simple — just multiply the denominator by the whole number.

Examples

What is $\frac{1}{5} \div 2$?

$$\frac{1}{5} \div 2 = \frac{1}{10}$$

×2

Multiply the denominator by the whole number.

What is $\frac{3}{4} \div 3$?

$$\frac{3}{4} \div 3 = \frac{3}{12} = \frac{1}{4}$$

×3

Remember to simplify your answer if you can.

Set A

Work out:

1. $\frac{1}{2} \div 2$
2. $\frac{1}{3} \div 4$
3. $\frac{1}{5} \div 8$
4. $\frac{7}{10} \div 3$
5. $\frac{4}{5} \div 4$

Look at these number cards.

3	4	6	8

Pick numbers from the cards to complete each calculation.

6. $\frac{1}{7} \div \square = \frac{1}{21}$
7. $\frac{\square}{\square} \div 2 = \frac{3}{8}$

Are the following statements true or false?

8. $\frac{2}{5} \div 3 = \frac{6}{5}$
9. $\frac{4}{5} \div 2 = \frac{4}{10}$
10. $\frac{1}{2} \div 5 = \frac{1}{2} \times \frac{1}{5}$
11. $\frac{1}{2} \times \frac{1}{3} = \frac{1}{2} \div 2$

Set B

Work out:

1. $\frac{1}{12} \div 3$
2. $\frac{1}{10} \div 8$
3. $\frac{3}{4} \div 5$
4. $\frac{7}{8} \div 3$
5. $\frac{5}{9} \div 5$

Look at these number cards.

7	3	2	4	8

Pick numbers from the cards to complete each calculation.

6. $\frac{1}{\square} \div \square = \frac{1}{8}$
7. $\frac{\square}{\square} \div 2 = \frac{7}{16}$

Look at the rope below.

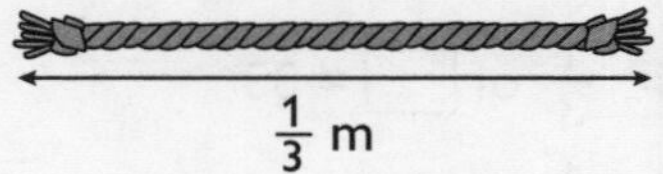

$\frac{1}{3}$ m

How long would each piece be if the rope was cut into:

8. two equal pieces?
9. five equal pieces?

Set C

Work out, giving your answers in their simplest forms:

1. $\frac{5}{12} \div 5$
2. $\frac{4}{5} \div 12$
3. $\frac{8}{12} \div 4$
4. $\frac{6}{7} \div 8$

Are the following statements true or false?

5. $\frac{2}{3} \div 8 = \frac{16}{24}$
6. $\frac{3}{5} \div 5 < \frac{7}{25}$
7. $\frac{5}{8} \times \frac{1}{2} > \frac{3}{4} \div 4$
8. $\frac{4}{5} \div 4 < \frac{3}{4} \div 3$

9. Bella has lots of toy cars. $\frac{4}{5}$ of her cars are red. She divides the red cars equally into six boxes.

   What fraction of all Bella's cars are in each box?

   Give your answer in its simplest form.

I can divide fractions by whole numbers.

Fractions of Amounts

These questions involve working backwards — you'll have to use your multiplication skills to find a whole thing from a given fraction of an amount.

Example

$\frac{1}{5}$ of the length of a snake is 60 cm.

How long is the whole snake?

$\frac{1}{5}$ of the whole length is 60 cm.

So the whole length is 5 times bigger than 60 cm.

5 × 60 = **300 cm**

Set A

Find the missing numbers:

1. $\frac{1}{2}$ of ☐ = 10
2. $\frac{1}{3}$ of ☐ = 12
3. $\frac{1}{10}$ of ☐ = 6
4. $\frac{1}{5}$ of ☐ = 5
5. $\frac{1}{4}$ of ☐ = 100

6. Look at the numbers below.

12	4	8

   Use each number once only to complete the statements:
   - $\frac{1}{4}$ of ☐ is equal to 3.
   - $\frac{1}{2}$ of ☐ is more than 3.
   - $\frac{1}{4}$ of ☐ is less than 3.

7. One sixth of the weight of a hamster is 7 g.

   What is the weight of the hamster?

8. One tenth of the height of a giraffe is 50 cm.

   What is the height of the giraffe?

Set B

Find the missing numbers:

1. $\frac{1}{2}$ of ☐ = 15
2. $\frac{1}{3}$ of ☐ = 33
3. $\frac{1}{4}$ of ☐ = 75
4. $\frac{2}{7}$ of ☐ = 6
5. $\frac{2}{9}$ of ☐ = 20

Rico has a stamp collection.
He tells Layla:
"$\frac{1}{12}$ of my stamps are triangles, and $\frac{1}{6}$ of my stamps are square."
How many stamps would Rico have in total, if Layla counts:

6. 11 triangular stamps?
7. 20 square stamps?

Sam is 9 years old.
One quarter of Miley's age is the same as Sam's age.

8. What is Miley's age?

Amir is 8 years old.
He says, "Two ninths of Miley's age is the same as my age."

9. Is he correct?
   Explain your answer.

Set C

Find the missing numbers:
(hint: simplify each fraction first)

1. $\frac{5}{10}$ of ☐ = 20
2. $\frac{3}{18}$ of ☐ = 12
3. $\frac{25}{100}$ of ☐ = 1
4. $\frac{8}{12}$ of ☐ = 16
5. $\frac{9}{15}$ of ☐ = 15

6. Anya is one twelfth of the height of the oak tree in her garden. Anya is 150 cm tall.

   What is the height of the oak tree?

7. Steve fills one sixth of a flask with 400 ml of water.

   What is the capacity of two flasks?

One half of a red pencil and one third of a yellow pencil are the same length.
The full length of the red pencil is 10 cm.

8. Work out the full length of the yellow pencil.

The red pencil is two fifths the length of a book.

9. What is the length of the book?

I can use fractions of amounts to find the whole amount.      

Multiplying and Dividing by Powers of 10

You should be familiar with tenths, hundredths and thousandths already. When multiplying or dividing a decimal by a power of 10, you just have to move the digits — left when multiplying and right when dividing.

Examples

Helena starts with £10.05 in her bank account.
At the end of the month, she has 300 times as much.

How much money is in her account now?

Multiply £10.05 by 100 first:

10.05 × 100 = £1005

Thousands	Hundreds	Tens	Ones		Tenths	Hundredths
0	0	1	0	.	0	5

(2 places, 1 place, 2 places, 1 place)

Then multiply by 3:

£10.05 × 300 = £1005 × 3 = **£3015**

Eric starts with 48.3 and divides it by a power of 10.
His new number has a 4 in the hundredths position.

What power of 10 did he divide by?

Remember that a power of 10 is a number that's a one followed by zeros — e.g. 10, 100, 1000, 10 000, etc.

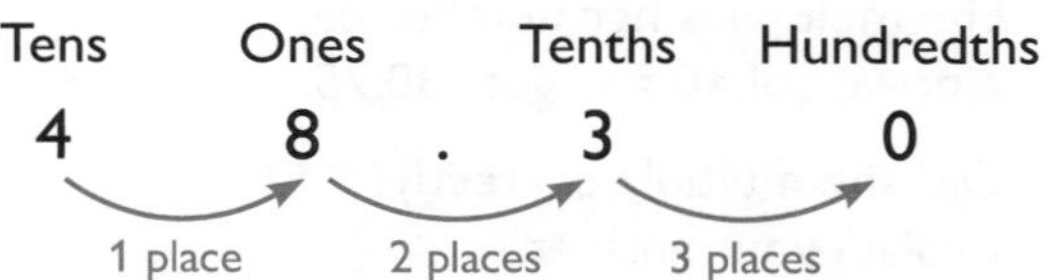

The 4 moves three places to the right, so he **divided by 1000**.

Set A

What is the value of each underlined digit after the multiplication?

1. $1\underline{2}.4 \times 10$
2. $0.3\underline{5} \times 100$
3. $4.30\underline{7} \times 1000$

What is the value of each underlined digit after the division?

4. $97\underline{5} \div 10$
5. $413\underline{9} \div 100$
6. $1\underline{5}36 \div 1000$

Look at the operations below.

× 100	÷ 100	÷ 1000	× 10

Choose the correct one to complete each of the following:

7. 32.8 ☐ = 328
8. 32.8 ☐ = 0.328
9. 32.8 ☐ = 3280

Find the missing numbers in the statements below:

10. 2.3 × 100 = 230, 230 × 2 = ☐
    So, 2.3 × 200 = ☐
11. 88 ÷ 2 = 44, 44 ÷ 10 = ☐
    So, 88 ÷ 20 = ☐

Fill in the missing numbers:

12. 5.2 × 10 = ☐, so 5.2 × 30 = ☐
13. 0.75 × 1000 = ☐, so 0.75 × 2000 = ☐
14. 16 ÷ 2 = ☐, so 16 ÷ 200 = ☐

Look at the numbers described below.

Number A 1 tenth and 2 thousandths

Number B 3 hundreds and 7 hundredths

Write, in digits:

15. Number A multiplied by 100.
16. Number B divided by 10.
17. The number 20 times larger than Number A.

Set B

What is the value of each underlined digit after the multiplication?

1. $3\underline{3}.45 \times 10$
2. $12.35\underline{9} \times 100$
3. $40.3\underline{1}7 \times 1000$

What is the value of each underlined digit after the division?

4. $21.\underline{4} \div 10$
5. $3\underline{3}4.8 \div 100$
6. $10\ 57\underline{6} \div 1000$

7. Tabitha starts with 0.375.

   She multiplies her number by a power of 10 and gets 30.75.

   Did she multiply correctly? Explain your answer.

Find the missing numbers in the statements below:

8. 4.12 × 10 = □, so 4.12 × 20 = □
9. 0.073 × 100 = □, so 0.073 × 300 = □
10. 3.105 × 1000 = □, so 3.105 × 2000 = □
11. 402 ÷ 2 = □, so 402 ÷ 20 = □
12. 86 ÷ 2 = □, so 86 ÷ 200 = □
13. 9006 ÷ 3 = □, so 9006 ÷ 3000 = □

Look at the amounts described below.

Amount A	**Amount B**
1 × £20 note	8 × £10 notes
8 × £1 coins	6 × £1 coins
4 × 10p coins	2 × 1p coins

Complete the sentences:

14. £2.84 is □ times smaller than Amount A.
15. £8602 is □ times larger than Amount B.

Set C

What is the value of each underlined digit after the multiplication?

1. $67.4\underline{9} \times 10$
2. $320.\underline{4}6 \times 100$
3. $119.00\underline{1} \times 1000$

What is the value of each underlined digit after the division?

4. $34\underline{7}.03 \div 10$
5. $278.\underline{9} \div 100$
6. $86\ 5\underline{3}6 \div 1000$

Work out:

7. 6010 ÷ 20
8. 13.15 × 300
9. 205 ÷ 5000
10. 0.038 × 2000

For the number machines below, describe the calculation used in each step.

11. 2.3 —?→ 0.23 —?→ 230
12. 391 —?→ 0.391 —?→ 3.91

Simon starts with the number below.

18 249

He makes a new number by doing a calculation with a power of 10.

He says, "The 8 is now in the ones position."

13. What calculation did he do?

He does a calculation on his new number with a power of 10.

He says, "The 4 is now in the ones position."

14. What number does he have now, and what calculation did he use?

I know the place value of numbers to three decimal places and can multiply and divide numbers by powers of 10.

Fractions and Decimals — Review 2

Work out:

1. $\frac{1}{2} \times \frac{1}{6}$
2. $\frac{1}{10} \times \frac{1}{4}$
3. $\frac{2}{3} \times \frac{1}{7}$
4. $\frac{3}{5} \times \frac{4}{5}$
5. $\frac{2}{11} \times \frac{3}{5}$
6. $\frac{5}{9} \times \frac{2}{3}$
7. $\frac{3}{8} \times \frac{7}{10}$
8. $\frac{4}{7} \times \frac{4}{9}$

What is:

9. one half multiplied by one quarter?
10. one third multiplied by one sixth?
11. one quarter multiplied by two fifths?
12. three quarters multiplied by seven tenths?
13. three fifths multiplied by two thirds?

Work out:

14. $\frac{1}{2} \div 3$
15. $\frac{1}{5} \div 6$
16. $\frac{3}{4} \div 10$
17. $\frac{7}{12} \div 2$
18. $\frac{9}{10} \div 5$
19. $\frac{1}{12} \div 6$
20. $\frac{2}{5} \div 2$
21. $\frac{11}{12} \div 11$

What is:

22. one quarter divided by two?
23. one tenth divided by five?
24. two thirds divided by three?
25. three fifths divided by eight?
26. nine elevenths divided by nine?

Find the missing numbers:

27. $\frac{1}{3}$ of $\square$ = 6
28. $\frac{1}{6}$ of $\square$ = 12
29. $\frac{1}{20}$ of $\square$ = 8
30. $\frac{1}{9}$ of $\square$ = 15
31. $\frac{1}{4}$ of $\square$ = 23
32. $\frac{2}{5}$ of $\square$ = 18
33. $\frac{6}{7}$ of $\square$ = 36
34. $\frac{11}{14}$ of $\square$ = 22

35. Farrah estimates that one sixth of a strawberry lace is 4 cm long.

    Write an estimate for the length of a whole strawberry lace.

36. Three fifths of the pupils in a school took part in a cross-country run.

    If 75 pupils took part in the run, how many pupils are there in the school?

What is the value of each underlined digit after the multiplication?

37. $4.2\underline{5} \times 10$
38. $0.\underline{1}29 \times 100$
39. $39.4\underline{5}8 \times 1000$
40. $0.02\underline{7} \times 10\,000$

What is the value of each underlined digit after the division?

41. $725.\underline{2} \div 10$
42. $121.\underline{3} \div 100$
43. $10\,\underline{8}06 \div 1000$
44. $60\,57\underline{5} \div 100$

Find the missing numbers in the statements below:

45. $80.6 \times 100 = \square$, so $80.6 \times 200 = \square$
46. $0.104 \times 1000 = \square$, so $0.104 \times 3000 = \square$
47. $98.4 \div 2 = \square$, so $98.4 \div 20 = \square$
48. $6240 \div 3 = \square$, so $6240 \div 300 = \square$

49. Each of the 200 employees in a company were given a £92.40 bonus one month. How much was given out in bonuses in total that month?

50. A model of the Eiffel Tower is 2000 times smaller than the real tower.

    The Eiffel Tower is 300 metres tall. How tall is the model tower?

Multiplying, dividing, decimals, fractions — you make it look so easy!

Multiplication with Decimals

Multiplying with decimals is just like regular multiplication — the only extra thing you've got to do is keep track of where the decimal point should go in your answer.

Examples

Work out 0.9 × 4

9 × 4 = 36

So 0.9 × 4 = **3.6**

0.9 is 10 times smaller than 9 so the answer is 10 times smaller too.

What is 2.84 × 16?

```
   2 8 4
 ×   1 6
 -------
 1 7 0 4
   5 2
 2 8 4 0
 -------
 4 5 4 4
 1
```

2.84 is 100 times smaller than 284 so the answer is 100 times smaller too.

So 2.84 × 16 = **45.44**

Set A

Work out:

1. 0.4 × 2
2. 0.2 × 9
3. 0.3 × 5
4. 0.9 × 8
5. 0.7 × 6
6. 0.5 × 11
7. 0.6 × 12

Find the missing values:

8. 67 × 4 = ☐
   So 6.7 × 4 = ☐
9. 134 × 6 = ☐
   So 13.4 × 6 = ☐
10. 8 × 7 = ☐
    So 0.08 × 7 = ☐
11. 73 × 9 = ☐
    So 0.73 × 9 = ☐

A carton of juice holds 0.7 litres. How many litres of juice do:

12. 3 cartons hold?
13. 12 cartons hold?

A pack of biscuits costs £1.60 and a bar of chocolate costs £0.68. What is the price of:

14. 8 packs of biscuits?
15. 7 bars of chocolate?

Set B

Work out:

1. 0.8 × 7
2. 1.2 × 4
3. 8.1 × 9
4. 0.04 × 3
5. 0.09 × 9
6. 0.21 × 8
7. 2.12 × 4

Use written multiplication to help you work out:

8. 8.4 × 3
9. 7.09 × 5
10. 5.34 × 8
11. 26.57 × 6
12. 8.88 × 19
13. 34.16 × 37

14. A train ticket costs £8.32. How much do 3 tickets cost?
15. A lap of the park is 1.69 miles. How many miles would 7 laps be?
16. A large bag of dog food weighs 4.57 kg. How much do 12 large bags of dog food weigh?

Set C

Work out:

1. 7.3 × 9
2. 0.42 × 3
3. 0.81 × 5
4. 3.22 × 8
5. 8.15 × 7
6. 14.27 × 4
7. 90.08 × 9

Use long multiplication to help you work out:

8. 5.6 × 12
9. 1.81 × 14
10. 2.44 × 15
11. 26.34 × 18
12. 18.01 × 34
13. 37.93 × 45

14. A tub can hold 34.35 litres of water. How much water can 7 tubs hold?
15. A textbook costs £16.79. Mrs Ford buys 16 textbooks. What is the total cost?
16. Kai needs 90 m of fence. He buys 23 sections of 3.92 m long fence. Will he have enough? Explain your answer.

I can multiply decimals by whole numbers.      

Division with Decimals — 1

When a number doesn't divide exactly into another number you get a remainder.
You can give the remainder as a decimal — have a look at these examples to see how it's done.

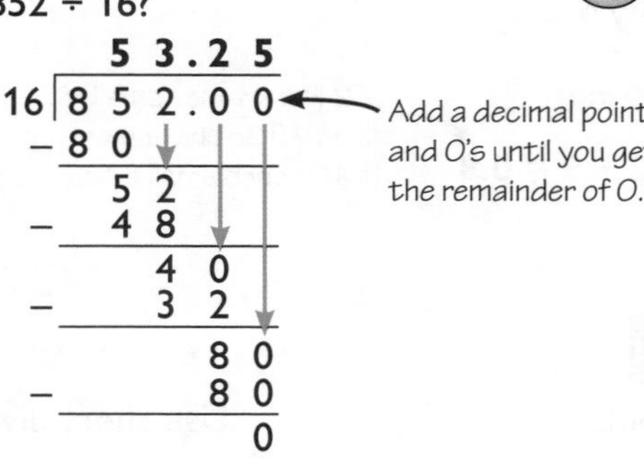

Examples

Work out 873 ÷ 6.

$$\begin{array}{r} 1\;4\;5.5 \\ 6\overline{)8\,{}^{2}7\,{}^{3}3.{}^{3}0} \end{array}$$

← Add a decimal point with a 0 after it — remember to put the decimal point in your answer too.

What is 852 ÷ 16?

$$\begin{array}{r} 5\;3.2\;5 \\ 16\overline{)8\;5\;2.0\;0} \\ -\;8\;0 \\ \hline 5\;2 \\ -\;4\;8 \\ \hline 4\;0 \\ -\;3\;2 \\ \hline 8\;0 \\ -\;8\;0 \\ \hline 0 \end{array}$$

← Add a decimal point and 0's until you get the remainder of 0.

Set A

Work out:

1. $5\overline{)47}$
2. $6\overline{)99}$
3. $4\overline{)86}$
4. $12\overline{)78}$

Work out:

5. $4\overline{)394}$
6. $8\overline{)852}$
7. $6\overline{)321}$
8. $4\overline{)657}$

Use short division to work out:

9. 703 ÷ 2
10. 432 ÷ 5
11. 473 ÷ 4
12. 684 ÷ 8
13. 819 ÷ 5
14. 570 ÷ 12

Set B

Work out:

1. $6\overline{)987}$
2. $5\overline{)588}$
3. $4\overline{)905}$
4. $8\overline{)758}$

Work out:

5. $15\overline{)39}$
6. $25\overline{)85}$
7. $20\overline{)898}$
8. $16\overline{)356}$

Use short division to work out:

9. 618 divided by 5
10. 230 divided by 8
11. 879 divided by 6
12. 987 divided by 12
13. 1874 divided by 5
14. 4854 divided by 12

Set C

Work out:

1. $5\overline{)463}$
2. $16\overline{)724}$
3. $15\overline{)3882}$
4. $12\overline{)6159}$

Work out:

5. 654 ÷ 8
6. 672 ÷ 25
7. 582 ÷ 24
8. 2883 ÷ 12
9. 6792 ÷ 15
10. 6426 ÷ 35

11. A charity auction raised £6879. The money was split equally between 4 charities. How much money did each charity get?

12. A petrol tanker contains 8244 litres of petrol. The petrol is shared equally between 15 tanks. How much petrol goes in each tank?

I can divide numbers to give decimals.

Division with Decimals — 2

You can use the methods of division you already know to divide decimals by whole numbers. Just like in decimal multiplication, you have to keep track of the decimal point in your answer.

Examples

Work out 7.2 ÷ 9.

72 ÷ 9 = 8

So 7.2 ÷ 9 = **0.8**

7.2 is 10 times smaller than 72 so the answer is 10 times smaller too.

A 5.44 m bamboo stick is cut into 16 equal sections. How long is each section?

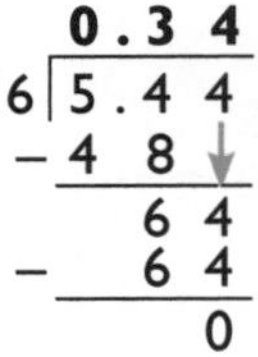

So each section is **0.34 m**.

Set A

Work out:

1. 2.4 ÷ 2
2. 5.4 ÷ 9
3. 3.5 ÷ 5
4. 9.6 ÷ 8
5. 6.6 ÷ 6
6. 12.1 ÷ 11
7. 10.8 ÷ 12

Use short division to work out:

8. 29.1 ÷ 3
9. 41.5 ÷ 5
10. 71.4 ÷ 7
11. 15.6 ÷ 4
12. 98.1 ÷ 9
13. 2.58 ÷ 6
14. 9.96 ÷ 12

A gardener has 14.4 kg of compost. How much does she put in each pot if she shares it equally between:

15. 12 pots?
16. 8 pots?
17. 9 pots?
18. The perimeter of a regular hexagon is 52.2 cm. What is the length of each side?

Set B

Work out:

1. 4.9 ÷ 7
2. 7.2 ÷ 3
3. 9.6 ÷ 6
4. 0.81 ÷ 9
5. 0.48 ÷ 4
6. 0.85 ÷ 5
7. 0.84 ÷ 3

Use written division to help you work out:

8. 5.85 ÷ 9
9. 9.87 ÷ 3
10. 9.3 ÷ 6
11. 14.6 ÷ 4
12. 22.86 ÷ 9
13. 46.5 ÷ 15

14. A garden path is 8.82 m long and is made from 9 identical slabs. How long is each slab?
15. Six identical wheels of cheese weigh 53.28 kg. How much does each wheel of cheese weigh?
16. Raj buys 12 lightbulbs for £17.52. How much was each lightbulb?

Set C

Work out:

1. 0.96 ÷ 4
2. 4.98 ÷ 3
3. 42.84 ÷ 6
4. 16.44 ÷ 12
5. 7.4 ÷ 4
6. 9.6 ÷ 5
7. 42.8 ÷ 8

Use long division to help you work out:

8. 38.52 ÷ 18
9. 50.08 ÷ 16
10. 60.72 ÷ 24
11. 46.9 ÷ 14
12. 94.8 ÷ 15
13. 83.5 ÷ 25

14. Four adult tickets to a theme park cost £98.24. How much does each ticket cost?
15. A baker shares 19.6 g of yeast equally between 8 bread mixes. How much is in each bread mix?
16. Brad runs 16 laps of a track. His total distance is 37.6 km. How long is each lap?

I can divide decimals by whole numbers.

Writing Fractions as Decimals

To write a fraction as a decimal, find an equivalent fraction with a denominator of 10, 100 or 1000.
You can also use short division — just divide the numerator by the denominator.

Examples

Write $\frac{18}{200}$ as a decimal.

Find an equivalent fraction:

$$\frac{18}{200} \overset{\div 2}{=} \frac{9}{100} = \mathbf{0.09}$$

Write $\frac{1}{8}$ as a decimal.

Find an equivalent fraction:

$$\frac{1}{8} \overset{\times 125}{=} \frac{125}{1000} = \mathbf{0.125}$$

You could also do 1 ÷ 8 using short division:

$$8\overline{)1\,.\,{}^{1}0\,{}^{2}0\,{}^{4}0} = \mathbf{0\,.\,1\,2\,5}$$

Write $\frac{1}{6}$ as a decimal, rounded to 3 decimal places.

Use short division:

$$6\overline{)1\,.\,{}^{1}0\,{}^{4}0\,{}^{4}0\,{}^{4}0} = \mathbf{0\,.\,1\,6\,6\,6}$$

0.1666 rounded to 3 decimal places is **0.167**

Set A

Find the missing number in the fraction, then write as a decimal:

1. $\frac{4}{5} = \frac{\square}{10} = \square$
2. $\frac{6}{50} = \frac{\square}{100} = \square$
3. $\frac{3}{20} = \frac{\square}{100} = \square$
4. $\frac{15}{25} = \frac{\square}{100} = \square$

Write as a decimal:

5. $\frac{1}{5}$
6. $\frac{8}{20}$
7. $\frac{14}{50}$
8. $1\frac{1}{2}$
9. $5\frac{1}{4}$

10. An eel is sixteen twentieths of a metre long.
    Write the length of the eel as a decimal.
11. Write $\frac{1}{3}$ as a decimal.
    Round your answer to 3 decimal places.

Set B

Find the missing number in the fraction, then write as a decimal:

1. $\frac{12}{20} = \frac{\square}{10} = \square$
2. $\frac{18}{50} = \frac{\square}{100} = \square$
3. $\frac{13}{25} = \frac{\square}{100} = \square$
4. $\frac{120}{500} = \frac{\square}{1000} = \square$

Write as a decimal:

5. $\frac{17}{20}$
6. $\frac{49}{50}$
7. $2\frac{32}{50}$
8. $1\frac{3}{200}$
9. $\frac{3}{8}$

10. A room is two and eight twenty-fifths metres wide.
    Write the width of the room as a decimal.
11. Write $\frac{2}{3}$ as a decimal.
    Round your answer to 3 decimal places.

Set C

Find the missing number in the fraction, then write as a decimal:

1. $\frac{72}{90} = \frac{\square}{10} = \square$
2. $\frac{17}{25} = \frac{\square}{100} = \square$
3. $\frac{64}{400} = \frac{\square}{100} = \square$
4. $\frac{12}{125} = \frac{\square}{1000} = \square$

Write as a decimal:

5. $\frac{58}{200}$
6. $\frac{379}{500}$
7. $\frac{960}{2000}$
8. $3\frac{19}{20}$
9. $1\frac{7}{8}$

10. Write $\frac{1}{9}$ as a decimal, to 3 decimal places.
11. Now write $\frac{4}{9}$ as a decimal. to 3 decimal places.
12. Rhonda's string is 1 m long. Tim's string is nineteen fortieths the length of Rhonda's. Write the length of Tim's string as a decimal.

I can write fractions as decimals.

Solving Problems with Decimals

You need to be able to add, subtract, multiply and divide with decimals. Once you've done the calculation you might have to round your answer. You can also use rounding to check that your answer is sensible.

Examples

A 476 cm piece of rope is cut into five equal pieces. What is the length of each piece? Give your answer to the nearest cm.

```
   9 5 . 2
5 |4 ⁴7 ²6 . ¹0
```

So each piece is **95 cm** to the nearest cm.

Jenny is sending two parcels. The first parcel weighs 2.58 kg and the second parcel weighs half as much. What is the total weight of the parcels?

You can do this using short division.

The second parcel weighs 2.58 ÷ 2 = 1.29 kg

So in total the parcels weigh 2.58 + 1.29 = **3.87 kg**

A dairy cow produces 6.38 litres of milk each day. How much milk will the cow produce in a week? Use estimation to check your answer is sensible.

1 week = 7 days

```
    6 3 8
  ×     7
  -------
  4 4 6 6
    2 5
```

So 6.38 × 7 = **44.66** litres.

Round the decimal to a whole number to check. → Check: 6 × 7 = 42, so the answer is sensible.

Set A

1. Harry has 73.2 ml of cordial and uses half of it to make some squash. How many ml are left in the bottle? Give your answer to the nearest ml.
2. An octagon has a perimeter of 84 cm. What is the length of each side to the nearest cm?
3. A bag of cement weighs 8.7 kg. How much do 9 bags of cement weigh?
   What calculation could you use to check your answer is sensible?
4. A construction crew can lay 983 m of road in 5 days. How much road can they lay each day?
5. Karen drives 9 laps around a motor racing track. She travels 23.4 miles in total. How many miles is one lap?
6. Mrs Jenkins spends £4.40 on lunch every day. How much does she spend in 4 days? Give your answer to the nearest £1.
7. A pipe leaks 3.7 litres of water in a day. How many litres of water does it leak in 8 days?
   What calculation could you use to check your answer is sensible?
8. Elek buys a 3.25 kg bale of hay. He uses 0.3 kg in his rabbit hutch each week. How much hay is left after 5 weeks?
9. Beth is thinking of a number. She multiplies it by 4, adds 4.7 and then divides by 7. She gets 4.1. What number did Beth start with?
10. Gia gets paid £9.40 an hour and Jay gets paid £9.20 an hour. How much do they get in total for working 5 hours?

Set B

1 Petra has 8 kg of rice. She stores 4.4 kg in a cupboard and splits the rest equally between 3 cooking pots. How much rice is in each pot?

2 Eight tickets for a water park cost £166. How much is each ticket to the nearest 10 pence?

3 A cyclist travels 0.39 km in a minute. How far does he travel in seven minutes? Round your answer to one decimal place.

4 A group of campers took 78.3 litres of water on a camping trip. They used a ninth of the water on the first night. How much did they have left?

5 A square of chocolate weighs 9.74 g. There are six squares of chocolate in a bar. How much does a bar of chocolate weigh?

What calculation could you use to check your answer is sensible?

6 Tom had £17.64 in his wallet. He spent £4.80 on some shopping. He then spent a quarter of the money he had left on a milkshake. How much was the milkshake?

The table shows the heights of some statues.

Statue A	1.78 m
Statue B	2.89 m
Statue C	5.75 m

7 A building is seven times as tall as statue A. How tall is the building?

What calculation could you use to check your answer is sensible?

8 The height of Statue D is exactly halfway between the heights of Statues B and C. How tall is statue D?

9 6 balls have the same mass as 4 bean bags. One ball weighs 92.4 g. How much does one bean bag weigh? Give your answer to the nearest gram.

Set C

1 15 pieces of wood flooring weigh 27 kg in total. What is the weight of each piece of wood flooring?

2 Mika gets paid £8.54 an hour to work at a car wash. She works for 6 hours and spends £5.25 on lunch. How much does she have left?

What calculation could you use to check your answer is sensible?

3 A sugar cube weighs 3.8 g and a sugar bowl weighs 420 g. What is the total mass of a sugar bowl containing 28 sugar cubes? Give your answer to the nearest gram.

4 There is 79.88 ml of olive oil in a bottle. A chef made 7 salads and used 8.59 ml of olive oil on each one. How much olive oil is left in the bottle? Give your answer to the nearest ml.

What calculation could you use to check your answer is sensible?

5 A water pipe is 10.84 m long. It is made from four equal length black pipes and one white pipe that is 2.2 m long. How long is each piece of black pipe?

6 A game show prize of £8754 is split equally between 4 contestants. One of the contestants spends half his money on a new bike. How much does he have left?

7 A fisherman has 350 m of fishing line. He puts an equal amount onto 6 fishing reels and has 45.8 m of line left. How much did he put on each reel?

8 12 tubes of tennis balls cost the same as 3 rackets. One racket costs £15.84. What is the cost of one tube of tennis balls?

9 Mala's car weighs 1912 kg. The car is 32 times heavier than Mala. How much does Mala weigh to the nearest kg?

10 A water trough can hold 87 litres of water. In the morning it was one quarter full, then 4.932 litres leaked out. Bob then poured away half of what was remaining. How much water was left in the trough? Round your answer to two decimal places.

I can solve problems involving decimals.     

Fraction, Decimal and Percentage Problems

You need to be able to convert between fractions, decimals and percentages to tackle these questions. Have a look at these examples first to get into the swing of things.

Examples

What proportion of this grid is shaded? Give your answer as a percentage and as a fraction in its simplest form.

15 out of 100 squares are shaded. So **15%** of the grid is shaded.

$15\% = \frac{15}{100} = \mathbf{\frac{3}{20}}$

32% of a movie cast are men, $\frac{2}{5}$ are women and the rest are children. What percentage of the movie cast are children?

$\frac{2}{5} = \frac{40}{100}$ = 40% are women

So 100% – 32% – 40% = **28%** are children

Abbey swam 0.57 km and Toby swam $\frac{13}{25}$ km. How much further did Abbey swim than Toby?

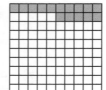

$\frac{13}{25} = \frac{52}{100}$ = 0.52 km

So Abbey swam 0.57 – 0.52 = **0.05 km** further.

Set A

What percentage of these shapes is shaded?

1 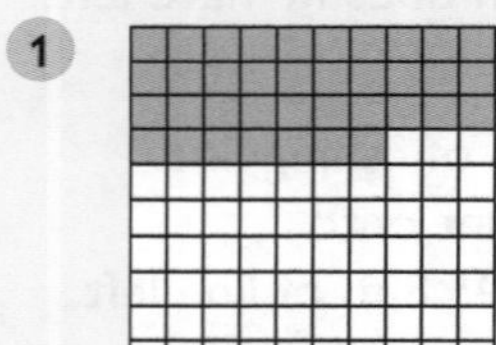

2

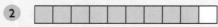

3

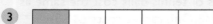

4 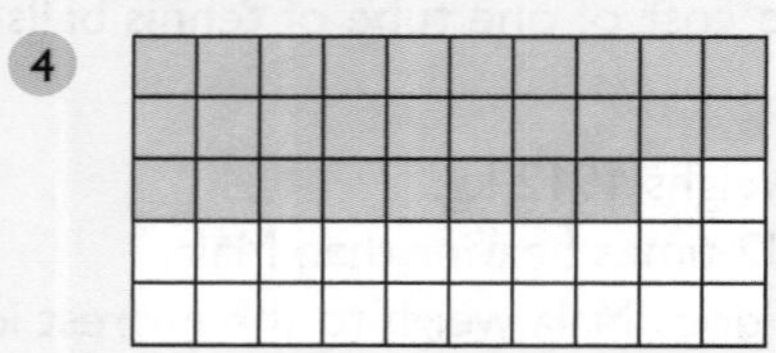

5 Copy and complete this table to show equivalent fractions, decimals and percentages. Give the fractions in their simplest form.

Fraction	Decimal	Percentage
$\frac{19}{50}$		
		80%
	0.26	

Which of these is bigger?

6 0.85 or 90%?

7 $\frac{3}{5}$ or 0.65?

8 $\frac{12}{50}$ or 25%?

9 Izzy has completed $\frac{36}{50}$ of a cycling race. What percentage of the race has she completed?

10 Sarah has a 1 kg bag of flour. She uses $\frac{3}{5}$ of the bag to make some bread. How much is left in the bag? Give your answer as a decimal.

11 Kim and Jin share a bag of popcorn. Kim eats 58% and Jin eats the rest. What fraction of the bag did Jin eat? Give your answer in its simplest form.

12 Kyle has a 1 litre bottle of milk. He uses 24% of the bottle to make some porridge. How much milk is left in the bottle? Give your answer as a decimal.

Set B

What percentage of these shapes is shaded?

1 

2

3 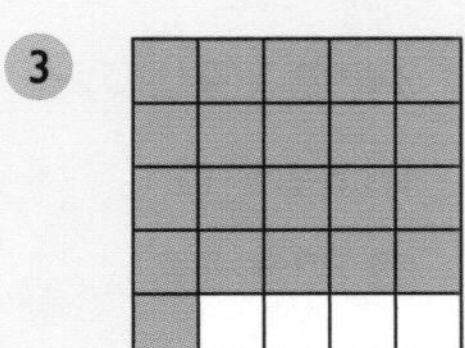

Which of these is smaller?

4 0.634 or 62%?

5 $\frac{1}{3}$ or 35%?

6 $\frac{7}{20}$ or 0.4?

Put these amounts in order. Start with the largest.

7 | 28% | $\frac{1}{5}$ | 0.25 |

8 | 0.8 | $\frac{17}{20}$ | 83% |

9 In a long jump competition, Olivia jumped $2\frac{2}{5}$ m and Gavin jumped 2.3 metres. Who jumped further? Explain your answer.

10 The label on a bottle of ketchup says it contains 68% tomatoes. What fraction of the ketchup is not tomatoes? Give your answer in its simplest form.

11 A butcher weighs two pieces of meat. The first piece weighs 0.87 kg and the second piece weighs $\frac{19}{20}$ kg. What is the total weight? Give your answer as a decimal.

Set C

1 Copy and complete this table to show equivalent fractions, decimals and percentages. Give the fractions in their simplest form.

Fraction	Decimal	Percentage
$\frac{3}{20}$		
		24%
	0.45	
$\frac{14}{40}$		

Put these amounts in order. Start with the smallest.

2 | $\frac{11}{25}$ | 47% | 0.434 |

3 | 0.64 | $\frac{2}{3}$ | 65% |

4 | 1.57 | $1\frac{3}{5}$ | 1.509 | $1\frac{27}{50}$ |

5 | $2\frac{11}{20}$ | 2.54 | $2\frac{14}{25}$ | 2.558 |

At a cafe 34% of customers order tea, $\frac{7}{25}$ order coffee and the rest order water.

6 What fraction of customers ordered tea or coffee? Give your answer in its simplest form.

7 What percentage of customers ordered water?

8 Ryan has a 1 litre bottle of lemonade. He poured 21% into a glass and spilt another $\frac{3}{20}$. What fraction of the lemonade is left in the bottle? Give your answer in its simplest form.

9 The temperature in Mary's kitchen is 22.8 °C. The temperature in her garage is $5\frac{27}{30}$ °C colder than in the kitchen. What is the temperature in her garage? Give your answer as a decimal.

10 Quinn reads $\frac{12}{40}$ of the pages in her book on Monday, 28% on Tuesday and $\frac{7}{50}$ on Wednesday. What percentage of the pages does she have left to read?

I can solve fraction, decimal and percentage problems.     

Fractions and Decimals — Review 3

Work out:

1. 0.3 × 3
2. 0.5 × 7
3. 0.02 × 9
4. 1.2 × 4
5. 3.1 × 6
6. 5.4 × 3
7. 8.9 × 8
8. 5.11 × 6
9. 6.08 × 9
10. 7.93 × 5
11. 3.62 × 7
12. 8.76 × 4

Use long multiplication to work out:

13. 7.8 × 12
14. 1.24 × 14
15. 2.47 × 22
16. 7.84 × 35

A bag of carrots weighs 0.9 kg.
How much will:

17. 5 bags of carrots weigh?
18. 11 bags of carrots weigh?

A pack of stamps costs £6.72.
What will be the total cost of:

19. 7 packs?
20. 14 packs?

Work out:

21. $5\overline{)7\ 8}$
22. $4\overline{)9\ 4}$
23. $8\overline{)6\ 8}$
24. $5\overline{)1\ 8\ 2}$
25. $4\overline{)3\ 8\ 5}$
26. $5\overline{)7\ 8\ 2\ 4}$
27. $12\overline{)2\ 7\ 2\ 7}$
28. $15\overline{)5\ 2\ 4\ 7}$

Work out:

29. 703 ÷ 5
30. 586 ÷ 4
31. 690 ÷ 8
32. 1473 ÷ 5
33. 3477 ÷ 12
34. 7024 ÷ 25

35. There are 8432 kg of concrete in a mixer. It is shared equally between 5 building sites. How much concrete is given to each building site?

Work out:

36. 1.8 ÷ 2
37. 10.8 ÷ 9
38. 9.5 ÷ 5
39. 0.49 ÷ 7
40. 0.99 ÷ 3
41. 0.84 ÷ 4

Work out:

42. 25.5 ÷ 5
43. 3.56 ÷ 4
44. 7.86 ÷ 3
45. 34.92 ÷ 9
46. 15.84 ÷ 12
47. 62.88 ÷ 24

Write as a decimal:

48. $\frac{3}{5}$
49. $\frac{34}{50}$
50. $\frac{7}{25}$
51. $2\frac{48}{50}$
52. $3\frac{112}{200}$
53. $\frac{7}{8}$

54. Francis has a 1 litre bottle of lemonade. He pours one third of the lemonade into a glass. How many litres are in the glass? Give your answer as a decimal to 3 decimal places.

55. A large bag of sugar weighs 2.6 kg. A small bag of sugar weighs 0.5 kg. Lois buys 3 large bags and 1 small bag. How much sugar does she buy in total?

56. A car travels 89.54 m in 11 seconds, at a constant speed. How far did the car travel each second? Round your answer to one decimal place.

57. Copy and complete this table to show equivalent fractions, decimals and percentages. Give the fractions in their simplest form.

Fraction	Decimal	Percentage
		60%
$\frac{42}{50}$		
	0.16	

On a school trip, 48% of the people were schoolgirls, $\frac{9}{20}$ were schoolboys and the rest were teachers.

58. What fraction of people were children?
59. What percentage of people were teachers?

You smashed through all those decimal questions — well done!

Fractions and Decimals — Challenges

Clara is moving three files on her computer.

Artist: Dessi Mall
Song Title: Places
Size: 3.55 MB

Film Title: Fraction Man
Length: 1 hr 55 mins
Size: 1770 MB

Document Title: Clara's Homework
Word Count: 2100
Size: 20 055 kB

What is the size of the:

a) song file, in kilobytes (kB)?

b) film file, in gigabytes (GB)?

c) document file, in megabytes (MB)?

Use these conversions to answer the questions:

1 megabyte (1 MB) = **1000 kilobytes** (1000 kB)

1000 megabytes (1000 MB) = **1 gigabyte** (1 GB)

One third of a shape is shown on the right.
The rest of the shape is also made up of blue and white squares of the same size.

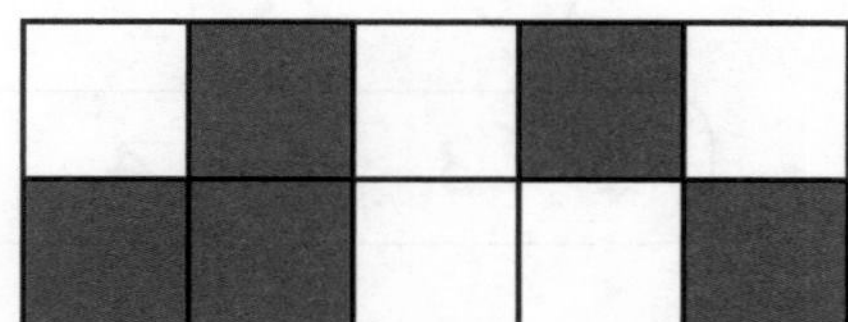

Miro says, "One fifth of the whole shape is blue."

Is it possible that Miro is correct?
Explain your answer.

A delivery company uses a conveyor belt to move boxes.
Each box has its mass, in kg, printed on the side.

Warning!
When more than 3 kg is on the conveyor belt, it will stop moving.

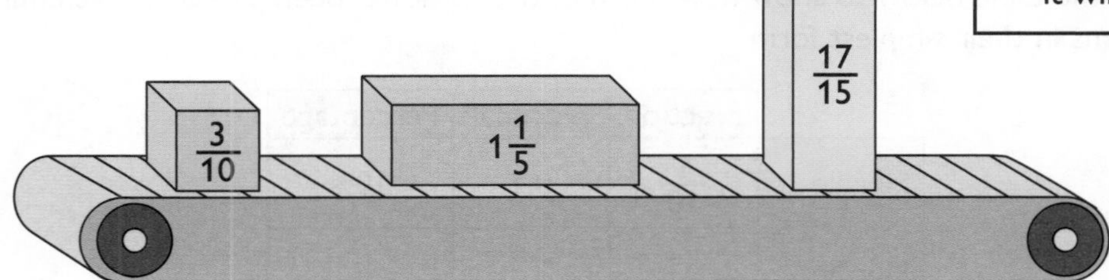

Is the conveyor belt moving?
Explain your answer.

Damien and Tara are talking about simplifying fractions:

You can always simplify a fraction which has a denominator that is twice as big as its numerator.
You can always simplify a fraction which has an even numerator and denominator.
Damien
Tara

Discuss with a partner whether you think Damien and Tara's statements are true. Explain your reasons. If you think a statement is false, write down an example to show it is false.

Complete the missing number problems below using the digits in the boxes. Use each digit only once. There is more than one possible answer for each.

a) Multiply two proper fractions:

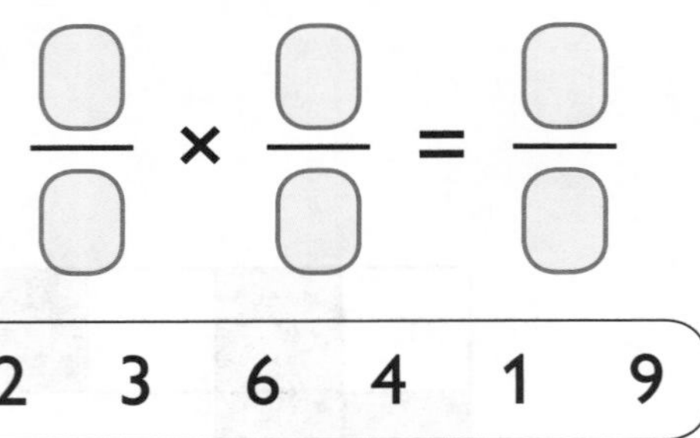

2 3 6 4 1 9

b) Divide a proper fraction by a whole number:

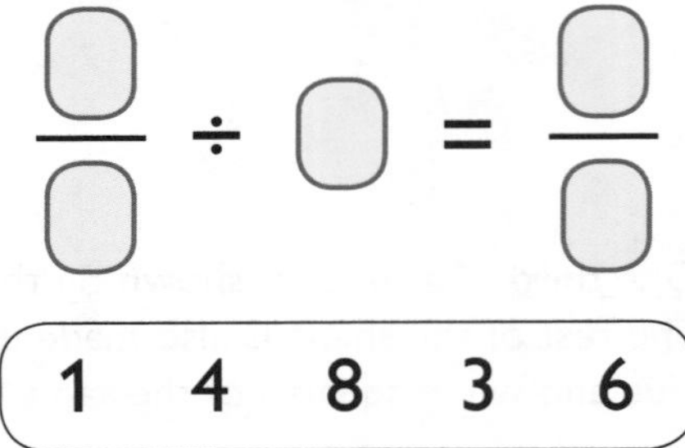

1 4 8 3 6

An athlete is practising for a 100 m hurdle race. The track is divided into 10 equal sections.

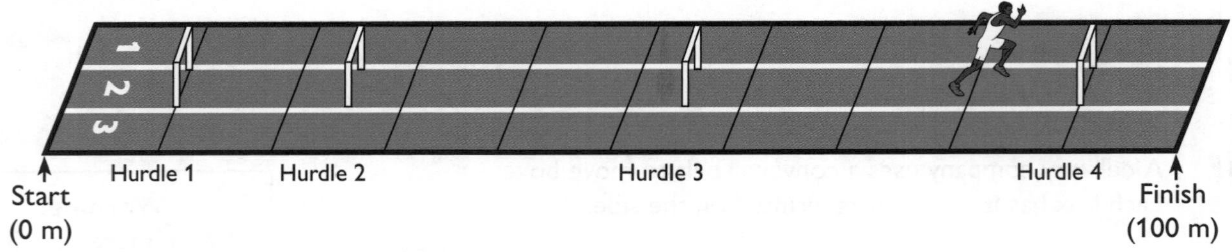

Copy and fill in the table below to show how much of the track has been passed at each hurdle. Give the fractions in their simplest form.

	Fraction	Decimal	Percentage
Hurdle 1	$\frac{1}{10}$	0.1	10%
Hurdle 2			
Hurdle 3			
Hurdle 4			

7 Ancient Egyptians wrote their fractions as a sum of unit fractions.

A unit fraction is a fraction with a numerator of 1.

Cleo wrote the following instructions to turn a fraction into an Egyptian fraction:

1. If the fraction is bigger than $\frac{1}{2}$, subtract $\frac{1}{2}$.
2. If the fraction is smaller than $\frac{1}{2}$ but bigger than $\frac{1}{3}$, subtract $\frac{1}{3}$.
3. If the fraction is smaller than $\frac{1}{3}$ but bigger than $\frac{1}{4}$, subtract $\frac{1}{4}$.
4. ... and so on. Keep going until you're left with a unit fraction — then you're done!

Cleo uses the method above to write $\frac{9}{10}$ as an Egyptian fraction:

- $\frac{9}{10}$ is bigger than $\frac{1}{2}$, so she does $\frac{9}{10} - \frac{1}{2} = \frac{2}{5}$. So $\frac{9}{10} = \frac{1}{2} + \frac{2}{5}$.
- $\frac{2}{5}$ is smaller than $\frac{1}{2}$, but bigger than $\frac{1}{3}$, so she does $\frac{2}{5} - \frac{1}{3} = \frac{1}{15}$. So $\frac{2}{5} = \frac{1}{3} + \frac{1}{15}$.
- $\frac{1}{15}$ is a unit fraction, so $\frac{9}{10} = \frac{1}{2} + \frac{1}{3} + \frac{1}{15}$.

Help Cleo write these as Egyptian fractions:

a) $\frac{11}{12}$

b) $\frac{3}{10}$

8 A party shop sells pumpkin baskets in small boxes of three or large boxes of five.

Small Box
3 baskets for £6.45

Large Box
5 baskets for £10.50

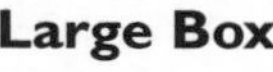

a) Which box is better value per pumpkin basket? Explain your answer.

Hugo has invited 17 guests to his Halloween party. He wants to give each guest a pumpkin basket.

He knows he can't buy exactly 17 pumpkin baskets, so he works out whether it is cheaper to buy 6 small boxes or 4 large boxes.

b) Which does Hugo find cheaper: 6 small boxes or 4 large boxes?

c) Can you find a cheaper way for Hugo to buy his pumpkin baskets? Explain your answer.

You're a fraction superhero in the making — great work!

Scaling

To scale a quantity up you multiply and to scale a quantity down you divide.

Example

Flo earns £4 each week delivering newspapers. After three weeks she has £12.

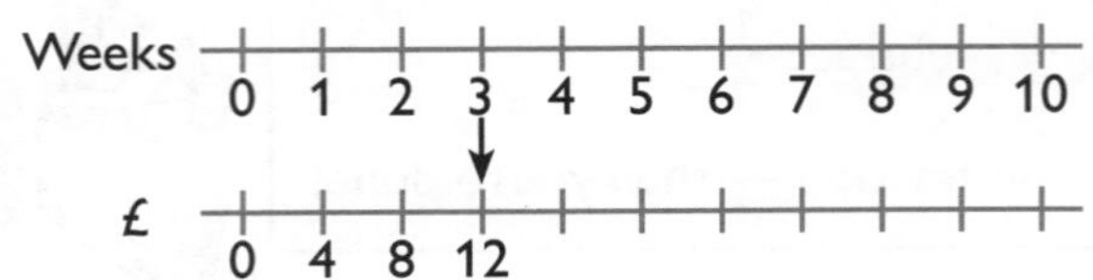

How much money will Flo have after 8 weeks?

Count in 4s to complete the second number line.

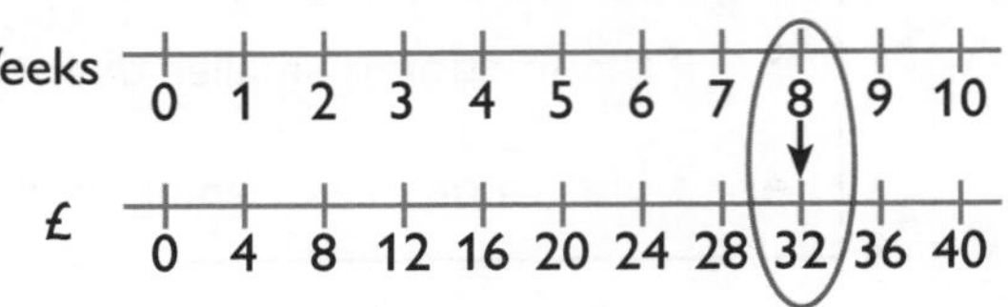

So after 8 weeks Flo will have **£32**.

Set A

Draw number lines to answer the questions below.

1. Marcellus eats 3 plums a week. How many plums has he eaten after 5 weeks?
2. Cara swims 5 times a month. How many months will it take her to go swimming 45 times?

It costs £400 for 4 tyres. Complete the sentences:

3. 1 tyre will cost £400 ÷ ☐ = £ ☐
4. 5 tyres will cost £ ☐ × 5 = £ ☐
5. 10 tyres will cost £ ☐ × 10 = £ ☐

One deluxe muffin weighs 150 g. How much will:

6. 4 deluxe muffins weigh?
7. 10 deluxe muffins weigh?
8. Matt drinks the same amount of water each day. He drinks 14 litres in 7 days. How much water did he drink each day?

Set B

A pencil costs 30p. How much will:

1. 10 pencils cost?
2. 25 pencils cost?

£100 can buy 80 litres of petrol. How many litres can you buy:

3. with £10?
4. with £60?

Kaya finds the recipe below.

Sponge Cake
3 small eggs
250 g butter
200 g flour

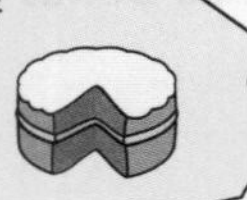

How much:

5. flour is needed for 6 sponge cakes?
6. butter is needed to make half a sponge cake?

One 400 g bucket can carry 1500 ml. Maisy has 8 empty buckets.

7. How much do her buckets weigh in total?
8. How many buckets does she need to fill to carry 4500 ml?

Maisy collected 12 000 ml of water from a well using 2 buckets at a time.

9. How many trips did she make?

Set C

1. 52 m² of fabric are used to make shirts for 13 people. How much fabric is used to make a single shirt?

10 school uniforms cost £250. A school has 4 classes of 30. How much will it cost to buy one uniform each for:

2. one class?
3. half of the school?

Look at the map below.

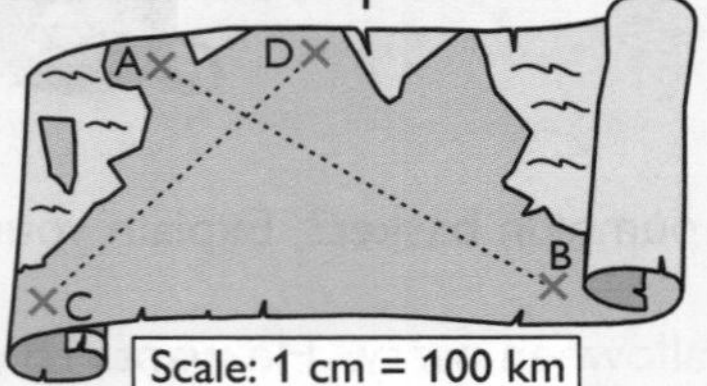

Use a ruler to find out how many km there are between:

4. A and B.
5. C and D.

A chocolate milkshake is made with 40 g cocoa powder, 600 ml milk and 30 ml chocolate syrup.

6. Kyla makes a milkshake using 10 g cocoa powder. How much milk should she use?

180 ml of chocolate syrup is used to make some milkshakes.

7. How much of the other ingredients are needed?

I can scale values up or down.

Proportion

Proportions compare a part to the whole thing. This makes them similar to fractions, except they are given in words like '1 in every 5' (instead of $\frac{1}{5}$).

Example

3 in every 5 children say they have two best friends.
30 children were asked.
How many said they have two best friends?

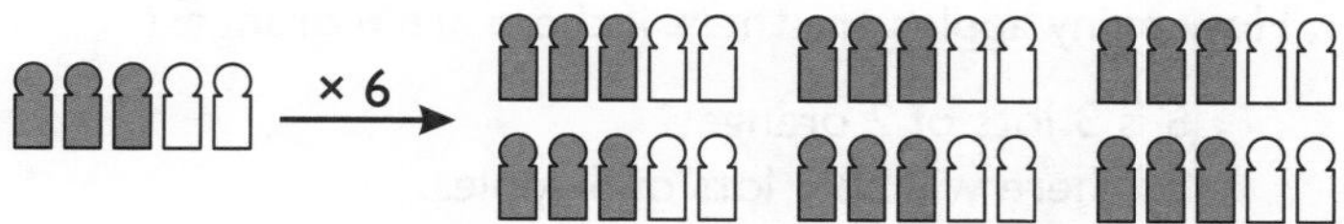

30 is 6 lots of 5.
6 × 3 = **18 children**.

Set A

1 in every 6 magicians has a wand.
How many wands are there for:

1. 12 magicians?
2. 30 magicians?

2 in every 3 magic tricks use cards.
How many tricks use cards in:

3. 9 magic tricks?
4. 15 magic tricks?

There are 50 pupils in Year 6.

Hair	No. of pupils
Blond	15
Brown	30
Red	5

How many Year 6 pupils:

5. in every 50 have blond hair?
6. in every 25 have brown hair?

7. 3 in every 7 clowns wear hats. A circus has 21 clowns. How many wear hats?

Bob saw 20 vans drive past school.
7 in every 10 vans were red.

8. How many vans were red?

He also saw 50 cars drive past.
3 in every 5 cars were red.

9. How many cars were not red?

Set B

1. 1 in every 5 hares is brown.
4 in every 5 hares are grey.

Copy and complete the table:

Brown	Grey	Total
1	4	5
		20
		50
	80	

3 in every 25 sales staff earn a bonus. How many will earn a bonus if the company has:

2. 100 sales staff?
3. 150 sales staff?
4. 200 in every 1000 bikes are BMXs. 8000 bikes are sold.
How many were BMXs?

Medhi has 300 balls. One third of them are white, seventy are black, eighty are blue, and fifty are red.

Find the missing numbers below:

5. 1 in every ☐ balls are white.
6. 7 in every ☐ balls are black.
7. ☐ in every 30 balls are blue.
8. ☐ in every 12 balls are red.

Set C

A recipe for 2 buns uses 150 g flour and 20 ml milk.
Clara uses 750 g flour.

1. How many buns is Clara making in total?
2. What volume of milk does Clara need to use?

2 in every 9 people don't like buns.
Clara gives buns to 90 people.

3. How many people like them?

There are 450 shapes in a box:

- 150 are squares.
- 180 are triangles.
- the rest are stars.

Find the missing numbers below:

4. 18 in every ☐ shapes is a triangle.
5. 10 in every ☐ shapes is a square.
6. ☐ in every 15 shapes is a star.

Keith uses 6 tubes of glue for every 200 models he builds.
He buys 30 tubes of glue.

7. How many models can Keith build?

Keith paints 5 in every 10 models.
He sells 2 in every 5 painted models.
How many models are sold if:

8. Keith builds 20 models?
9. Keith builds 50 models?

I understand and can use proportions.

Ratio

Ratios compare the amounts of two things. The two amounts are written with a colon (:) between them, e.g. 1:3. This means that for every 1 part of something, there are 3 parts of something else (totalling 4 parts overall).

Example

In a shop, the ratio of apples to oranges is 5:2.
How many apples are there if there are 6 oranges?

6 is 3 lots of 2 oranges.
So there will be 3 lots of 5 apples.
3 × 5 = **15 apples**

Set A

Look at the grid below.

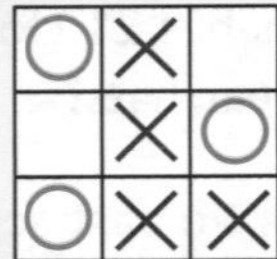

1. Write the ratio of noughts to crosses.
2. How many crosses would there be if there were 3 grids identical to the one above?

There is 1 frog for every 2 goldfish in a pond.

3. Write the ratio of frogs to goldfish.
4. How many frogs would there be if there were 8 goldfish in the pond?
5. How many goldfish would there be if there were 8 frogs in the pond?

The ratio of boys to girls in an archery class is 3:1.

6. Give the ratio of girls to boys.
7. There are 6 girls, how many boys are there?
8. The ratio of cats to dogs at a shelter is 3:4. How many cats are there if there are 8 dogs?

Set B

An ice cream van sells 2 strawberry ice creams for every 5 vanilla ice creams they sell.

1. Write the ratio of strawberry to vanilla ice creams sold.

The ice cream van sells 25 vanilla ice creams.

2. How many strawberry ice creams did the van sell?

There are 10 ants for every 3 ladybirds in a field.

3. Write the ratio of ants to ladybirds.
4. How many ants would there be if there were 24 ladybirds in the field?
5. How many ladybirds would there be if there were 150 ants in the field?

Kai and Lewis share a bag of sweets in the ratio 6:9. Lewis gets the bigger share. How many sweets does Kai get:

6. if Lewis gets 18 sweets?
7. if Lewis gets 45 sweets?
8. Complete the sentence: For every 3 sweets that Lewis gets, Kai gets ☐.

Set C

In Kate's CD collection there are 15 rock CDs for every 30 pop CDs. How many of her CDs are:

1. rock if she has 90 pop CDs?
2. pop if she has 60 rock CDs?

Kate says "You can write the ratio of rock CDs to pop CDs in my collection as 1:2."

3. Do you agree? Explain your answer.

Jo and Nick share their pocket money equally.

4. In what ratio is this?

Ian and Paula share their pocket money in the ratio of letters in their name.

5. In what ratio is this?
6. If Ian gets £2.40 pocket money how much does Paula get?

7. The ratio of red to blue pens in a box is 5:4. There are 20 blue pens in one box. How many red pens are in 3 boxes?
8. The ratio of hot to cold water in a bath was 7:3. 24 litres of cold water were used. How many litres of water were used in total?

I understand and can use ratios.

Sharing Problems

These pages will help prepare you to deal with any pesky sharing problems you might come across. Remember to work out the total number of shares first to make dividing up the total much simpler.

Examples

Nico and Karen read books in the ratio of 5:1. If they read 42 books in total, how many does Nico read?

There are 5 + 1 = 6 shares in total.
1 share = 42 ÷ 6 = 7 books
Nico reads 5 shares, so he reads 5 × 7 = **35 books.**

For every 2 paintings that Michelle finishes, Deirdre finishes 3.
They finish 75 paintings in total. How many paintings does each artist finish?

    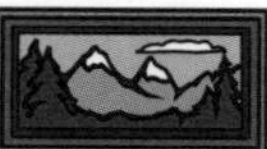

For every 2 paintings Michelle finishes... Deirdre finishes 3.

There are 2 + 3 = 5 shares in total.
1 share = 75 ÷ 5 = 15 paintings.
Michelle has 2 shares, so does 2 × 15 = **30 paintings.**
Deirdre has 3 shares, so does 3 × 15 = **45 paintings.**

Check your answer by making sure it adds to the total: 30 + 45 = 75 paintings.

Set A

A pack of chewy sweets has 3 bubblegum chews for every cola chew. In a pack of 20 chewy sweets:

1. how many are cola chews?
2. how many are bubblegum chews?

A garage has 2 cars for every motorbike.

3. How many cars are there if there are 12 vehicles in the garage?
4. How many motorbikes are there if there are 30 vehicles in the garage?

The ratio of peacocks to parrots in the bird enclosure at a zoo is 1:4. There are 20 peacocks and parrots altogether in the enclosure.

5. How many peacocks are there?
6. How many parrots are there?

In the zoo's kangaroo enclosure there are 3 females for every male.

7. How many males are in the enclosure if there are 40 kangaroos?

For every one card Tom collects, Luke collects six. How many cards does each boy collect if they collect a total of:

8. 21 cards?
9. 70 cards?

A chef served 1 vegetarian main course for every 3 non-vegetarian main courses.

10. The chef served 32 main courses. How many were vegetarian?

The chef also served 3 starters for every 2 desserts.

11. He served 50 starters and desserts in total. How many desserts did the chef serve?

The ratio of white loaves to brown loaves made at a bakery is 7:2.

12. On Monday they make 36 loaves. How many of them are white?
13. On Tuesday they make 54 loaves. How many of them are brown?

Set B

A carpenter is making a table.
He uses one screw for every five nails.
He uses 60 screws and nails in total.

1. How many screws did he use?
2. How many nails did he use?

In a cafe, for every 2 cups of coffee that George makes, Harris makes 3. How many cups does:

3. George make if 35 cups are made in total?
4. Harris make if 60 cups are made in total?

5. A farmer's field contains some cows and sheep. For every 3 cows there are 7 sheep. There are 150 animals in the field in total.

   How many cows are there in the field?

Tara and Ewan pay for a video game in the ratio 3:4. The game costs £42.

6. How much does Tara pay?
7. How much does Ewan pay?

Sheds are made out of oak and pine logs.
5 oak logs are used for every 7 pine logs.

8. How many oak logs are used to build a shed that uses 48 logs?
9. How many pine logs are used to build a shed that uses 144 logs?

10. After winning at bingo, Miriam and Bert share £200. For every £30 Miriam gets, Bert gets £20.
    How much money does Bert get?

11. Diaz ran 51 km over a weekend. The ratio of the distance he ran on Saturday to the distance he ran on Sunday is 12:5.

    How far did he run on Sunday?

12. Ozzy and Tay share 10 lollies and 8 biscuits. Ozzy gets 3 lollies for every 2 that Tay gets. Ozzy gets 1 biscuit for every 3 that Tay gets.

    How many treats does Ozzy get in total?

Set C

For every 5 cakes Spencer bakes, Julie bakes 4 cakes.
On Friday they baked 54 cakes in total.

1. How many cakes did Spencer bake?

Dean bakes 3 tarts for every 6 cakes Spencer bakes.

2. How many tarts did Dean bake on Friday?

3. For every 8 bags of gravel a garden centre sells, they sell 3 bags of sand. 110 bags are sold in total.

   How many of the bags sold contained sand?

For every 14 peanuts in a bowl there are 6 cashew nuts. How many:

4. peanuts are in a bowl of 80 nuts?
5. cashew nuts are in a bowl of 200 nuts?

Dev and Eric share their water in the ratio 3:8.
How much water does:

6. Eric have if they have 990 ml in total?
7. Dev have if have 2200 ml in total?

8. In a forest, there are 9 deer for every 6 foxes and there are 3 mice for every deer. There are 90 deer and foxes altogether.
   How many mice are there?

9. Sandra and Wilt buy 63 g of popping candy. They share it in the ratio 4:3. How much more does Sandra get than Wilt?

10. In a volleyball season, the Spikers won 7 games for every 5 games the Bluechips won. The two teams won 48 games in total.
    How many fewer games did the Bluechips win than the Spikers?

For every 7 backflips Magda does, Titus does 8.
On Tuesday, they do 150 backflips in total.

11. How many backflips did Magda do on Tuesday?

On Monday Titus did 5 more backflips than Magda.

12. How many backflips did they do in total on Monday?

I can solve problems involving unequal sharing.

Ratio and Proportion — Review 1

Draw number lines to answer the questions below.

1. Alice eats 5 yoghurts a week. How many yoghurts will she have eaten after 6 weeks?
2. Bruno jogs 8 miles every month. How many miles will he have jogged after 4 months?
3. Davina reads for 30 minutes every day. How many days will it take her to do 120 minutes of reading?

It costs £6 for one portion of fish and chips.

4. How much will 5 portions cost?
5. How much will 15 portions cost?
6. How much will 25 portions cost?

Thirty spinning tops cost £60.

7. How much will ten spinning tops cost?
8. How much will sixty spinning tops cost?

Look at the instructions on the right:

9. How many medium cubes are there in 5 robots?
10. How many small cubes are there in 30 robots?
11. How many small spheres are there in 400 robots?

Robot Kit:

To make one robot, this kit contains:

6 rectangular blocks
8 small cubes
1 large cube
3 medium cubes
2 bendy rods
2 straight short rods
4 small spheres

Faizel makes cheese wheels.
3 in every 5 cheese wheels he makes are soft cheese.
2 in every 10 cheese wheels he makes are blue cheese.
How many wheels of soft cheese and blue cheese are there if he makes:

12. 50 cheese wheels?
13. 700 cheese wheels?

14. Maggie keeps 2 in every 5 scarves she knits and sells the rest for £5 each. Maggie knits 100 scarves. How much money does she earn?

There are 200 buttons in a jar. 70 are red, 50 are blue and the rest are white.
Find the missing numbers below:

15. ☐ in every 100 buttons are red.
16. 10 in every ☐ buttons are blue.
17. 2 in every ☐ buttons are a white.

Look at the pattern on the right.

18. Write the ratio of moons to stars.
19. How many stars would there be in 5 patterns identical to the one on the right?

The pieces in a breakfast cereal are in the shape of circles, hearts and arrows. There are 7 circles for every heart. There are 35 circles in each box of cereal.

20. Write the ratio of circles to hearts.
21. How many hearts are there in each a box?

The cereal also has 2 arrows for every circle.

22. How many arrows are there in a box?

The ratio of cars to bikes in a village is 5:2.
There are 350 cars in the village.

23. How many bikes are there?

A larger village has 200 bikes.
The ratio of cars to bikes in this village is 9:4.

24. How many cars are there in this village?

The ratio of rollerbladers to skateboarders in a skate park is 3:5. There are 40 people in the skate park.

25. How many rollerbladers are there?
26. How many more skateboarders than rollerbladers are there?

Stacey and Liam have 90 marbles in total.

27. How many marbles would they each have if they split them in the ratio 5:4, with Stacey getting the bigger share?
28. How many more marbles would Stacey have than Liam if they split them in the ratio 4:1?

For every 5 raisins that Dougan ate, Kerry ate 15.
300 raisins were eaten in total.

29. How many raisins did they each eat?

The raisins cost £3.00. They split the cost in the same proportion to how many raisins that they ate.

30. How much did Kerry pay?

Excellent job doing these questions — your brainpower must be off the scale!

Scale Factors

When a shape is enlarged, every side is multiplied by a scale factor.
You can also divide by scale factors to work out the original size of shapes... useful stuff!

Examples

Look at the shape on the grid below.
Enlarge it by a scale factor of 2.

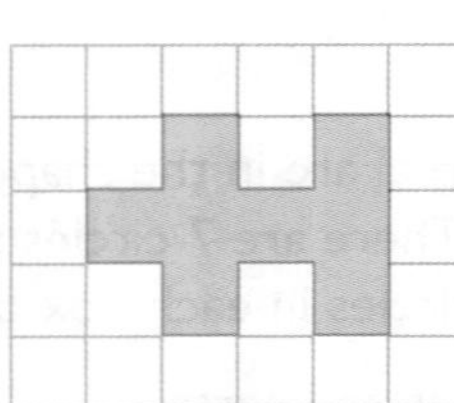

Multiply every length by the scale factor.
So all the sides 1 square long become:
1 × 2 = **2 squares long.**
And the side that is 3 squares long becomes:
3 × 2 = **6 squares long.**

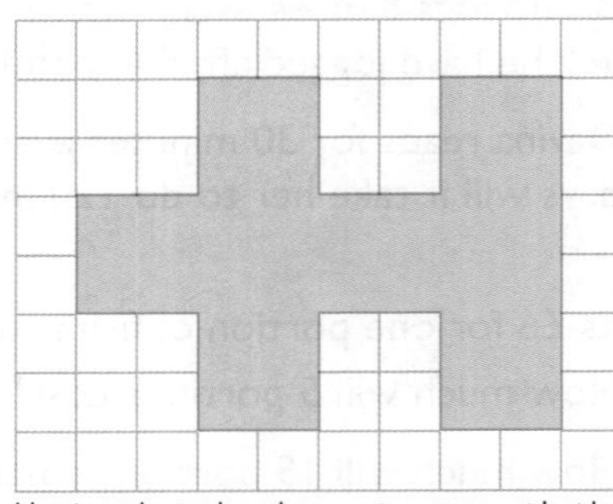

Notice that the shape stays exactly the same — it just becomes twice as big!

Look at the shapes on the right.
Shape A is enlarged by a scale factor of 9 to give shape B.
Find the length of side 'x'.

To work out the original length,
divide the enlarged length by the scale factor:
63 ÷ 9 = 7.
So 'x' = **7 cm**.

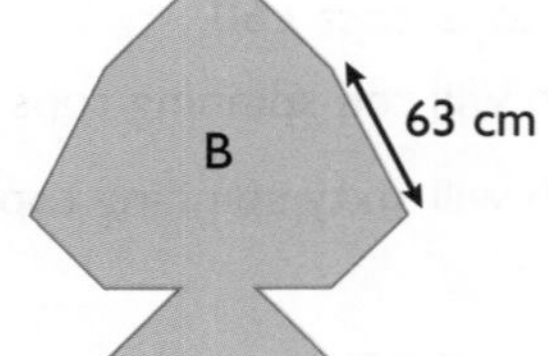

Set A

On squared paper, enlarge each of the shapes below using the scale factors given.

1. Enlarge by a scale factor of 2.

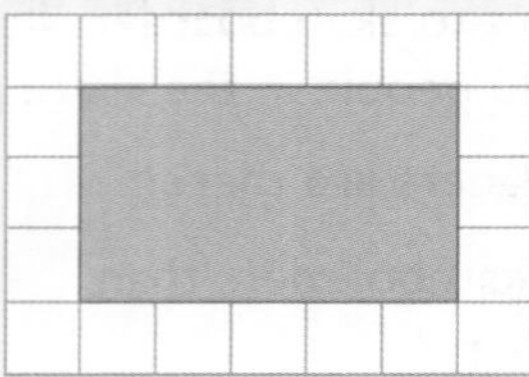

2. Enlarge by a scale factor of 3.

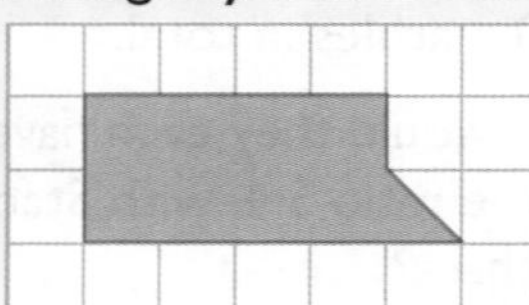

3. Enlarge by a scale factor of 5.

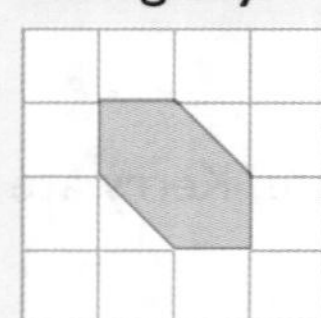

What scale factor would be used to enlarge a square's sides:

4. from 2 cm to 14 cm?
5. from 5 cm to 50 cm?

Shape A is enlarged to make shape B in each question below.
Work out the length of each side 'x'.

6. Scale factor = 2

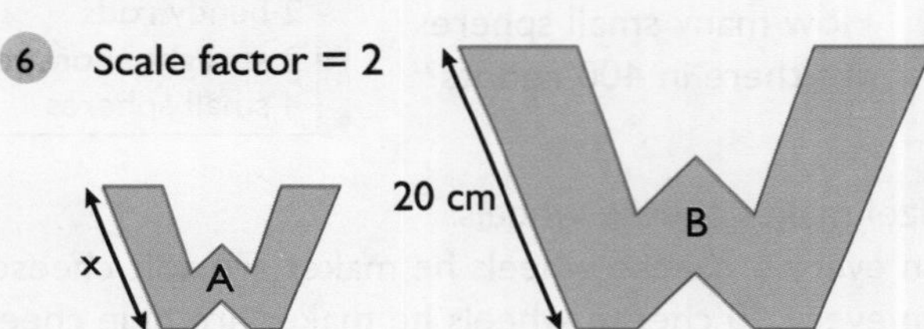

7. Scale factor = 7

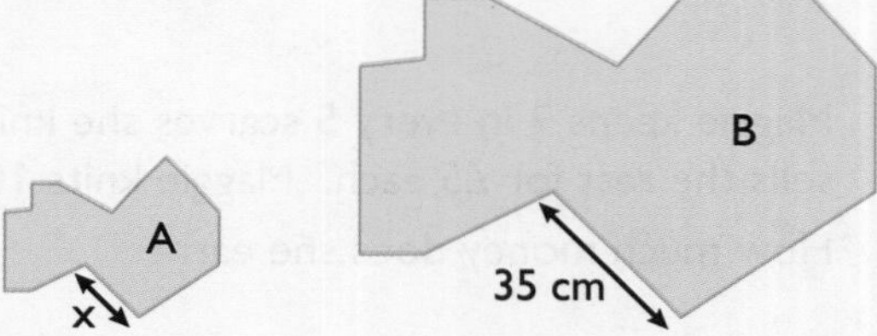

8. Scale factor = 20

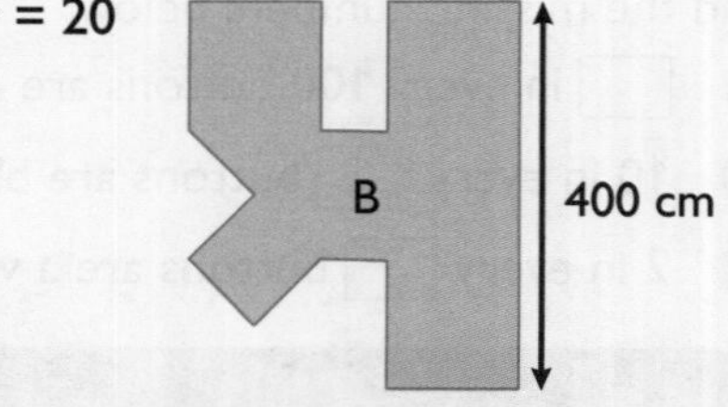

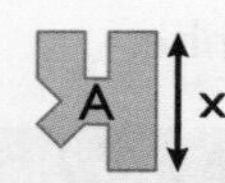

Set B

On squared paper, enlarge each of the shapes below using the scale factors given.

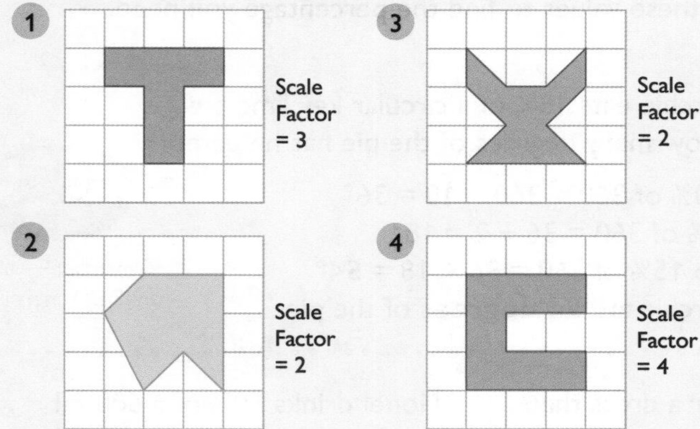

Work out the original length of a side that is now:

5 40 cm after being enlarged by a scale factor of 4.

6 77 cm after being enlarged by a scale factor of 7.

Work out the new length of a side if it was:

7 5 cm before being enlarged by a scale factor of 8.

8 4 cm before being enlarged by a scale factor of 20.

Work out the scale factor of enlargement from shape A to shape B.

9
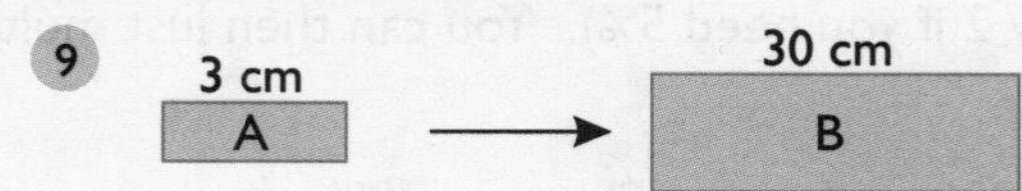

10
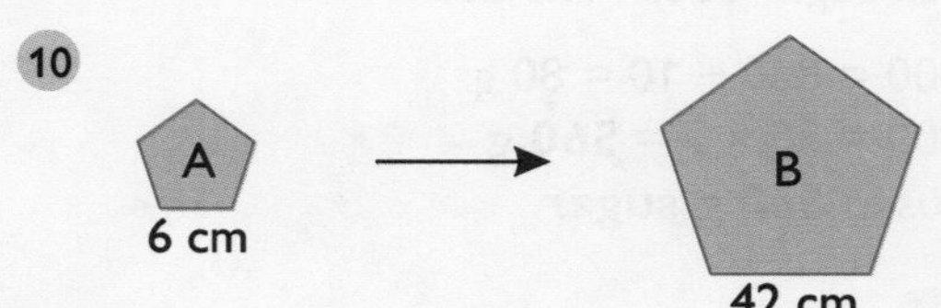

11
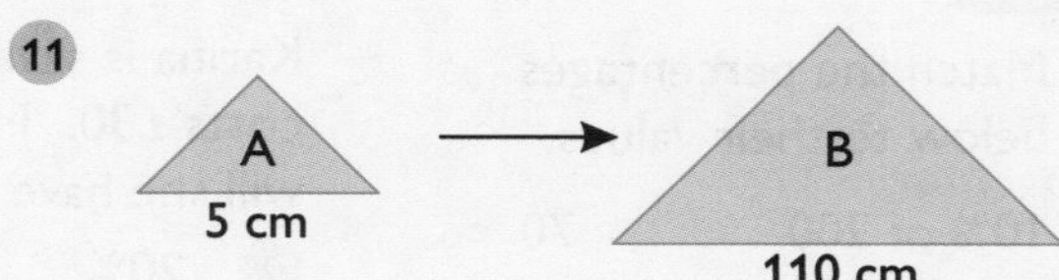

12
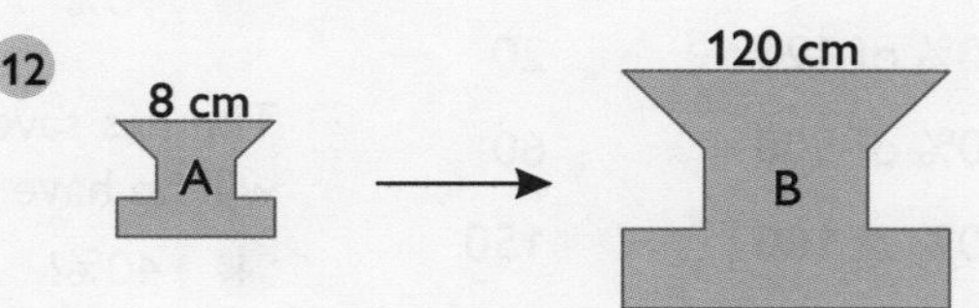

Set C

Work out the scale factor of enlargement from shape A to shape B.

1
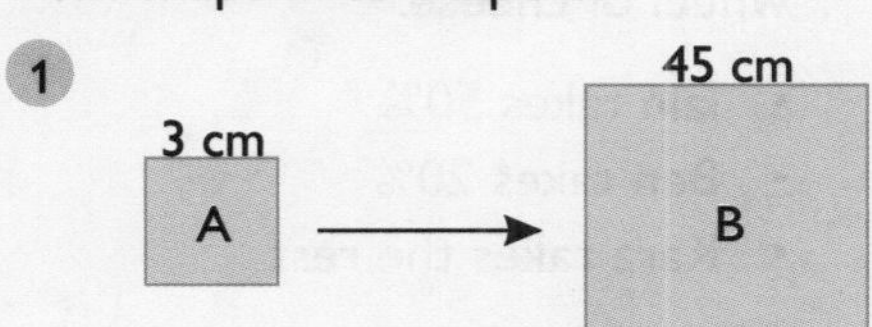

2
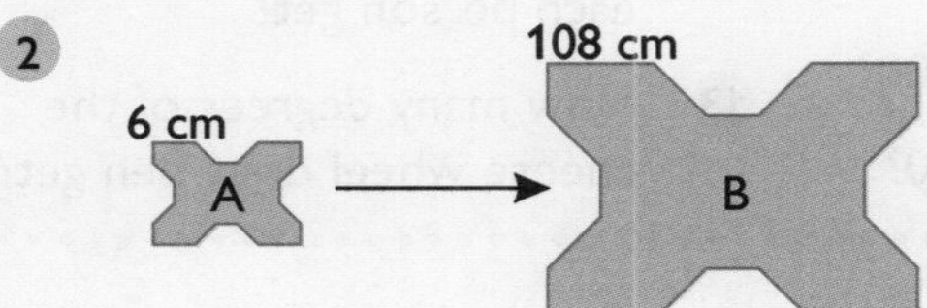

3
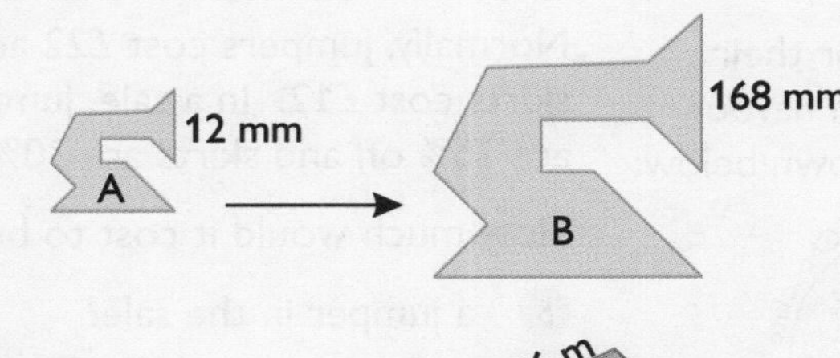

4
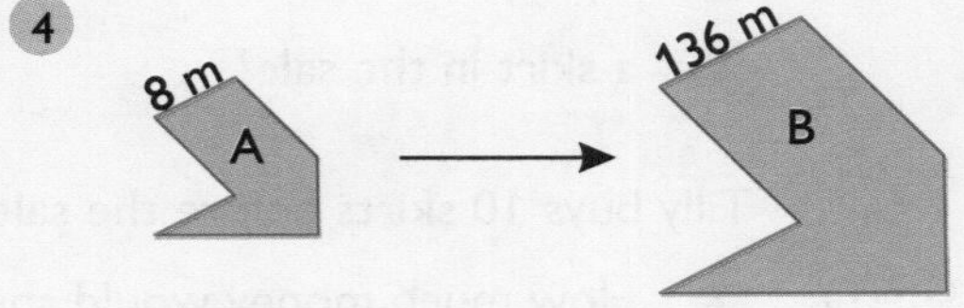

Enlarge each shape labelled 'A' below by a scale factor of 3 and label your enlarged shape 'B'. Then enlarge each 'B' by a scale factor of 2 and label your enlarged shape 'C'.

5
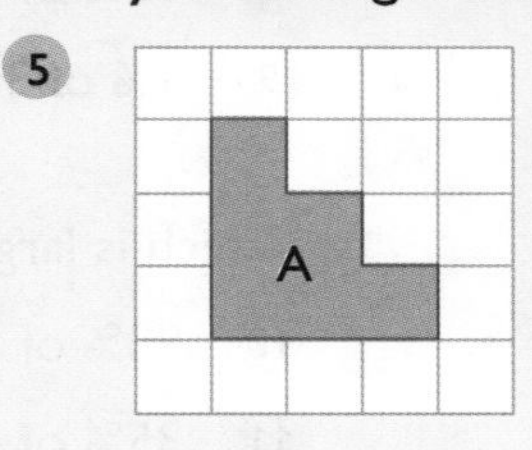

7
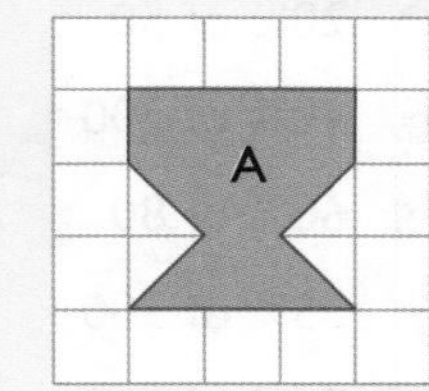

6
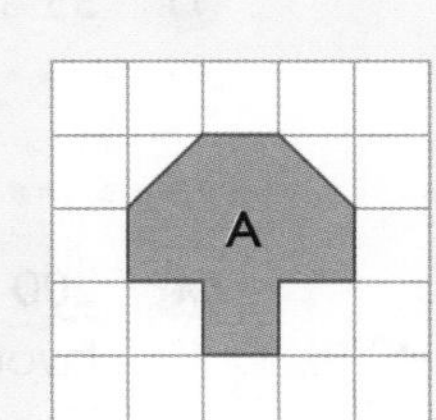

8
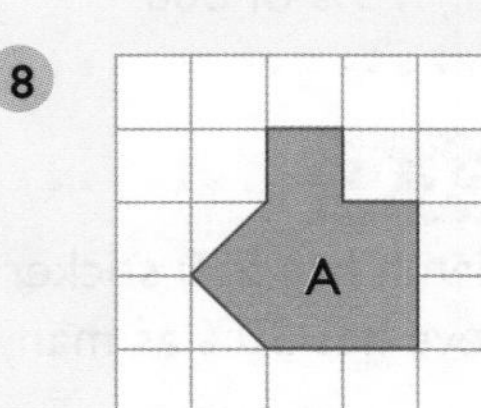

9 A hexagon has a perimeter of 36 cm. It is enlarged by a scale factor of 2. Arun says: "The perimeter of the enlarged hexagon is twice the perimeter of the original hexagon."

Is he correct?
Explain your answer.

I can use scale factors on 2D shapes.

Percentages of Amounts

Finding percentages is mostly straightforward — the whole amount is 100%. Divide by 10 to find 10% (and then by 2 if you need 5%). You can then just multiply these values to find the percentage you need.

Examples

Nina has 800 g of sugar. She uses 70%.
How much sugar does Nina use?

10% of 800 = 800 ÷ 10 = 80 g
70% of 800 = 80 × 7 = **560 g**
So Nina used **560 g sugar**.

Archie eats 15% of a circular key lime pie.
How many degrees of the pie has he eaten?

10% of 360 = 360 ÷ 10 = 36°
5% of 360 = 36 ÷ 2 = 18°
So 15% of 360 = 36 + 18 = **54°**
Archie ate **54 degrees** of the pie.

Remember — there are 360° in a circle.

Set A

1 Match the percentages below to their values.

10% of 200	70
20% of 150	180
50% of 120	20
30% of 500	60
70% of 100	150
90% of 200	30

Karina is saving for a dress that costs £30. How much money will she have after she has saved:

2 20%?

3 90%?

Tim has saved £70. How much will he have if he spends:

4 40%?

5 70%?

Lionel drinks 50% of a 600 ml bottle of cola. Rick drinks 65% of a 800 ml bottle.

6 Who drank the most?

7 How much did they drink in total?

Sarah drank everything that was left over by Lionel and Rick.

8 In ml, how much was left over for Sarah to drink?

Set B

Work out each of the percentages below.

1 10% of 400

2 20% of 50

3 40% of 200

4 60% of 80

5 55% of 300

6 75% of 800

Which is smaller:

7 25% of 200 or 20% of 150?

8 60% of 600 or 50% of 700?

9 1% of 300 or 4% of 100?

Which is larger:

10 90% of 700 or 60% of 1000?

11 35% of 400 or 25% of 700?

Three friends share a 2 kg wheel of cheese:

- Iain takes 50%
- Ben takes 20%
- Kara takes the rest

12 In g, how much cheese does each person get?

13 How many degrees of the cheese wheel does Ben get?

Set C

Niamh has 550 stickers.
Steve has 30% as many as Niamh.

1 How many stickers do they have in total?

Niamh loses 40% of her stickers.

2 How many stickers does she have now?

3 What percentage of Niamh's total stickers does Steve have now?

4 200 people vote for their favourite ice-cream flavour. The results are shown below:

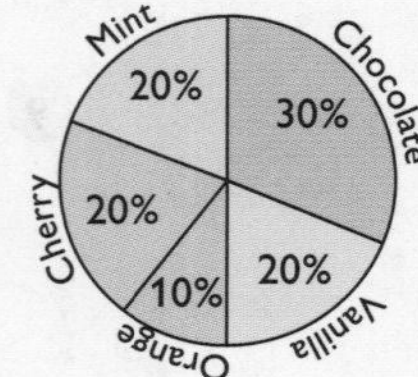

How many people said cherry or mint was their favourite?

Normally, jumpers cost £22 and skirts cost £12. In a sale, jumpers are 25% off and skirts are 30% off.

How much would it cost to buy:

5 a jumper in the sale?

6 a skirt in the sale?

Tilly buys 10 skirts before the sale.

7 How much money would she have saved in the sale?

I can find a percentage of an amount.

Comparing Percentages

Now, it's fantastic that you can find percentages — but you've got to compare them as well.

Example

There is a sale at a clothes shop.
A top that normally costs £25 has £10 off.
A dress that normally costs £50 has £15 off.

Which item has the larger percentage discount?

Put the money off as the numerator. Put the total price as the denominator.

top: $\frac{10}{25} = \frac{40}{100} = \mathbf{40\%}$ (×4)

dress: $\frac{15}{50} = \frac{30}{100} = 30\%$ (×2)

Find an equivalent fraction with a denominator of 100.

So the **top** has the larger percentage discount with **40% off**.

Set A

A games console costs £300.
Nolan has saved £120.

1. What percentage has Nolan saved?
2. What percentage of the cost is £90?
3. A bag has 10 red marbles and 15 blue marbles.

   What percentage of the marbles are red?

4. There are 50 chocolates in a box. 15 chocolates are eaten.

   What percentage of chocolates are left in the box?

5. A butcher makes 400 sausages and 200 burgers. He sells 240 sausages and 140 burgers.

   Which food did he sell the larger percentage of?

6. A fruit farmer grows 50 plums, 80 pears and 70 apples.

   What percentage of the fruits are pears?

7. Look at the table below.

Item	Original	Sale
Hat	£50	£20 off
Bag	£100	£30 off

Which item has the bigger percentage discount?

Set B

A kennel has 5 dogs, 20 cats and 25 rabbits.

1. What percentage of the pets are dogs?

15 of the cats are adopted.
9 of the rabbits are adopted.

What percentage:

2. of cats are adopted?
3. of rabbits are not adopted?
4. There is a sale at a music shop. A guitar that originally cost £50 has £7 off. A bongo that originally cost £20 has £3 off.

   Which instrument has the bigger percentage discount?

5. Which bag gives greater percentage of free potatoes?
   Bag A: 1.5 kg + 0.5 kg free
   Bag B: 0.7 kg + 0.3 kg free

Look at the table below.

Watch	Original	Sale
A	£200	£50 off
B	£300	£105 off
C	£400	£160 off

6. Which watch has the biggest percentage discount?
7. Which watch has the smallest percentage discount?

Set C

Which is the bigger percentage discount:

1. £5 off £50 or £3 off £20?
2. £132 off £300 or £168 off £400
3. £670 off £1000 or £350 off £500?
4. £1350 off £1500 or £1700 off £2000?
5. Marcus has 600 ml of water and drinks 240 ml of it. Renee has 800 ml of water and drinks 360 ml of it.

   Who drank the higher percentage of their water?

6. A belt costs £25. It is reduced by £3.50.

   What percentage discount has it been given?

People get into teams for a hide-and-seek competition:

- 16 people join team A
- 12 people join team B
- 22 people join team C

7. What percentage of people are not on team C?
8. 150 more people join team C. What percentage of people are now on team B?

I can use percentages to compare amounts.      

Ratio and Proportion — Review 2

Enlarge each of the shapes below on a grid using the scale factors given.

1 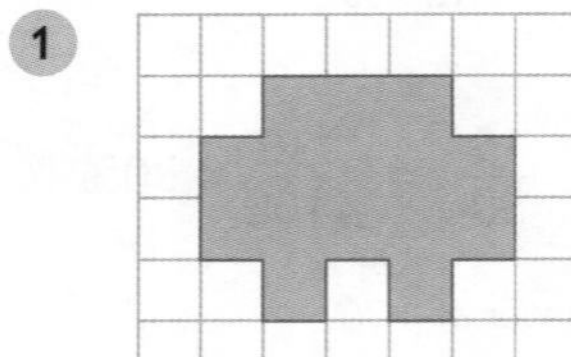

Scale Factor = 2

2 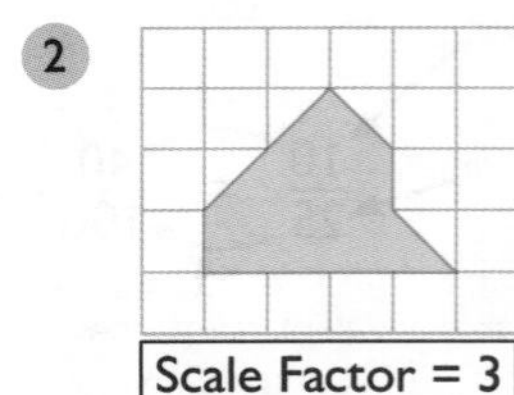

Scale Factor = 3

Shape A is enlarged to make shape B below. Use the scale factors given to work out the length of each side labelled 'x'.

3 Scale Factor = 5

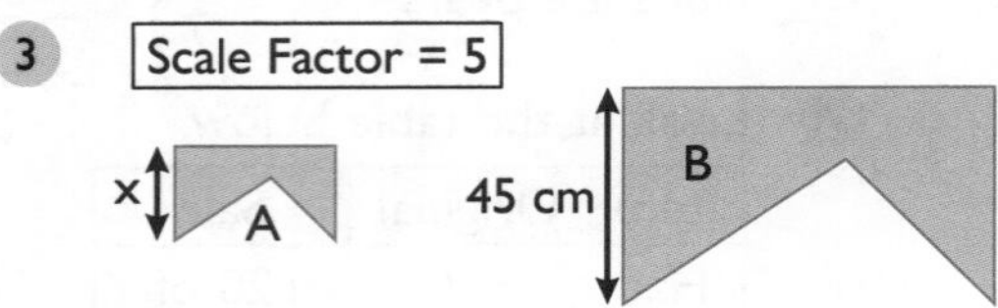

4 Scale Factor = 7

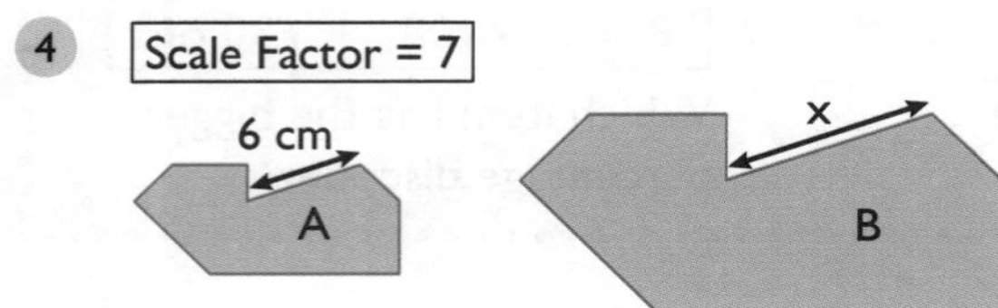

5 What scale factor would enlarge a square's sides from 6 cm to 72 cm?

6 An octagon has 4 sides of 1 cm and 4 sides of 2 cm. The octagon is enlarged by a scale factor of 9. What is the octagon's new perimeter?

Max is saving for a £60 computer game. How much money will he have after:

7 saving 30%?

8 saving 50%?

9 saving 45%?

10 Four friends share 500 ml of juice:

- Izzy drinks 20%
- Sanjay drinks 30%
- Ola drinks 10%
- Linda drinks 40%

How much juice does each person drink?

200 people were asked what type of pet they had. 50% had a cat, 25% had a dog, 20% had fish, and 5% had no pet.

11 How many people have a pet?

12 How many more people have a cat than a fish?

13 Order the amounts below from smallest to largest.

A 20% of £400

B 5% of £1200

C 80% of £200

D 55% of £300

E 90% of £100

F 15% of £700

In a sale, capes are 75% off and masks are 60% off. Capes normally cost £50 and masks cost £25. How much would it cost to buy:

14 a cape in the sale?

15 a mask in the sale?

A school gym has 40 footballs, 20 basketballs, 30 rugby balls, 50 tennis balls and 60 cricket balls.

16 What percentage of the balls are footballs?

17 What percentage of the balls are not cricket balls?

18 Look at the table below.

Item	Original	Sale
Car	£6000	£900 off
Piano	£1200	£300 off

Which item has the greater percentage discount?

A triathlete swims 2 km, cycles 40 km and runs 8 km.

19 What percentage of the total distance does she run?

20 How much greater a percentage of the total distance is cycled than swam?

180 people entered the triathlon. 15% gave up after the swim and a further 13 people gave up later in the race.

21 How many people finished the event?

22 Sean has 200 m of wood and uses 80 m. Ellie has 300 m of wood and uses 135 m. Who used the higher percentage of their wood?

You must be at least 80% genius now that you've tackled all these questions!

Ratio and Proportion — Challenges

1 On holiday Ben saw a castle that he liked so much he decided to do a scale drawing of it.

He bought a blueprint with the diagram below. It came with a scale.

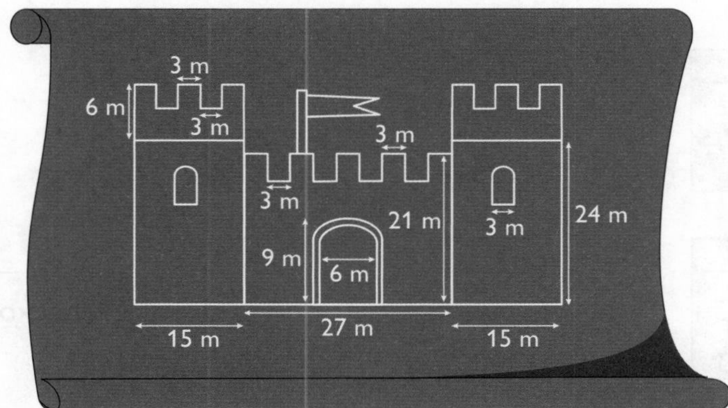

Scale: 1 cm = 3 m

a) Use Ben's blueprint and the scale above to draw your own castle on centimetre square paper. Create your own flag for the castle.

b) Can you add a moat and a bridge to your diagram?

2 Tom has a bag of 9 marbles, which are either blue or red.

He pulls out 3 marbles:

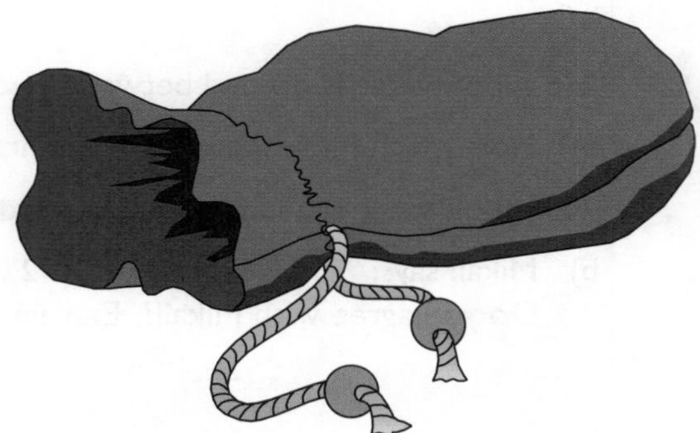

He says, "1 in 3 marbles left in the bag are red."

Can he be correct? Explain your answer.

3 A band called Dizzy Ballerina have 400 000 tickets for their tour.
The band give away 5% of the tickets for free to fans and to charities.

a) How many tickets will be given away for free?

25% of the free tickets are given to a charity. The charity sells every ticket for £10.

b) How many of the free tickets are not given to the charity?

c) How much money does the charity raise from selling their tickets?

Clarissa needs one of each of the four coloured items below.

You will need to guide Clarissa from the start to the checkout by buying one item in each column.

Clarissa follows the rules below, in order:

- She will not buy an item with a percentage discount of less than 35%.
- She will always choose the cheapest item.

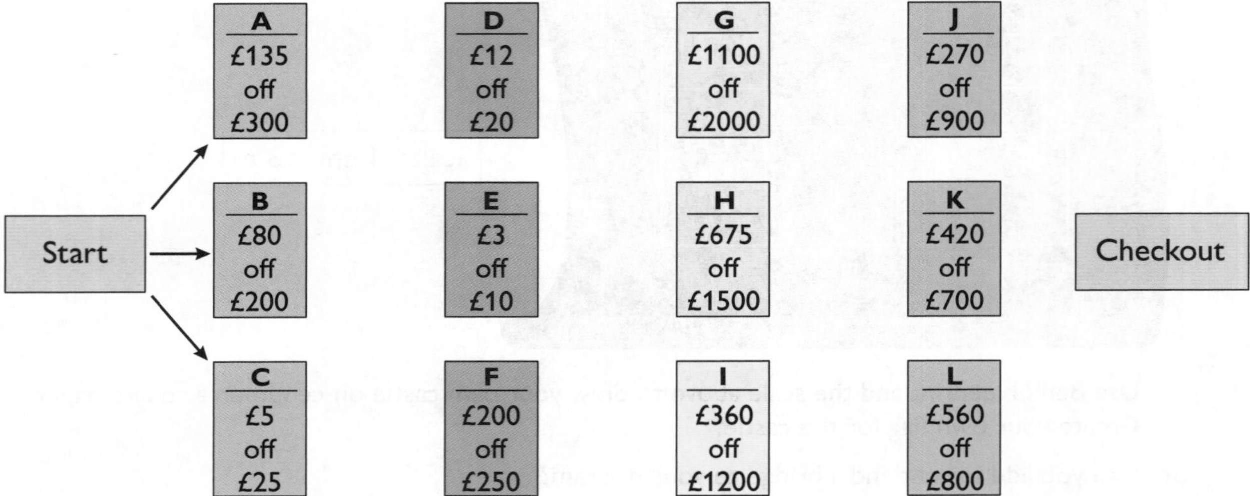

275 ml of water is divided between two flasks in the ratio 7:4.

a) How much more water is in the first flask than the second?

200 ml of water is added to the second flask.

b) Mikail says: "The new ratio is 7:12".
Do you agree with Mikail? Explain your answer.

There are three treasure caves on an island. Six identical treasure chests are split across the caves:

Cave 1

Cave 2

Cave 3

Four pirates go to the island one at a time and choose a cave.
If more than one pirate choose the same cave they must share the treasure equally between them.
Each pirate chooses the cave that will give them the most treasure after sharing.
The treasure isn't actually shared out until all of the pirates have chosen a cave.

Explain why the fourth pirate will get the same amount whichever cave he chooses.

These challenges were no walk in the park — give yourself a massive pat on the back!

Formulas — 1

Formulas are just maths rules that help you work out a quantity using other quantities that are connected to it.

Examples

This formula connects the number of bananas and pineapples needed to make a smoothie:

number of bananas = 3 × number of pineapples

If you use 2 pineapples, how many bananas do you need?

number of bananas = 3 × 2 = **6**

If you use 15 bananas, how many pineapples do you need?

15 = 3 × number of pineapples
So number of pineapples = 15 ÷ 3 = **5**

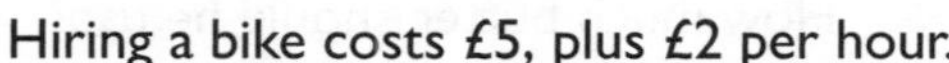

Hiring a bike costs £5, plus £2 per hour.

Write a formula that connects the total cost of hiring a bike with the number of hours.

Cost of hiring a bike = 5 + (2 × number of hours)

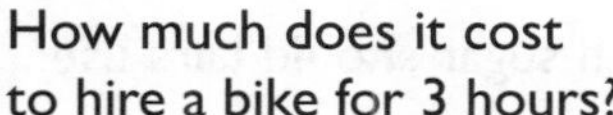

How much does it cost to hire a bike for 3 hours?

Cost of hiring a bike = 5 + (2 × 3)
= 5 + 6 = **£11**

Mina paid £9 to hire a bike. How many hours did she hire it for?

9 = 5 + (2 × number of hours)

2 × number of hours = 9 – 5 = 4

number of hours = 4 ÷ 2 = **2 hours**

Set A

1. The total number of stickers is given by the formula:

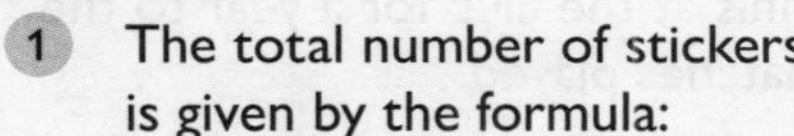

number of stickers = 6 × number of packs

How many stickers are there in 3 packs?

The total number of wheels on the cars in a car park is given by the formula:

number of wheels = 4 × number of cars

2. How many wheels are there in the car park when 9 cars are there?
3. There are 44 wheels in the car park. How many cars are there?

A biscuit recipe uses 5 cherries for each biscuit.

4. Complete the formula:
number of biscuits = number of cherries ÷ ☐

Use your formula to work out:

5. how many biscuits you could make if you had 40 cherries.
6. how many cherries are needed for 6 biscuits.

The amount of pocket money Pam gets depends on the number of times she walks the dog each week:

pocket money (£) = (2 × number of walks) + 1

7. How much pocket money will she get if she walks the dog twice in one week?
8. One week Pam got £9 pocket money. How many times did she walk the dog that week?
9. Hiring a hall for a party costs £20, plus £3 for each guest. Complete the formula:

cost of hall = ☐ + (number of guests × ☐)

A pet shop uses this formula to work out how many grams of food to put into a fish tank:

Amount of food (g) = (3 × number of fish) + 10

10. How much food should they put in a tank with 5 fish?
11. Hannah puts 40 g of food in a tank. How many fish are there in the tank?

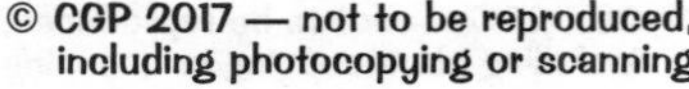

Set B

This formula connects the number of tomatoes and peppers needed to make a sauce.

number of tomatoes = 5 × number of peppers

1. How many tomatoes do you need if you use 7 peppers?
2. How many peppers do you need if you use 45 tomatoes?

The number of carrots needed for the sauce is twice the number of peppers.

3. Write a formula that connects the number of carrots with the number of peppers.

A hotel owner uses this formula to decide how many slices of toast to make for breakfast each day.

number of slices = (2 × number of guests) + 12

4. How many slices should he make if there are 15 guests staying at the hotel?
5. One day he makes 56 slices of toast. How many guests are there?

Alice works in a TV shop. She earns £45 a day, plus £5 for every TV she sells.

6. Write a formula that connects the amount Alice earns each day to the number of TVs she sells.
7. How much does Alice earn if she sells 5 TVs?
8. Alice earned £90 one day. How many TVs did she sell that day?

A cake recipe has this formula connecting the amounts of flour and butter, in grams.

$$\text{amount of butter} = \frac{3 \times \text{amount of flour}}{5}$$

9. Lars makes a cake with 100 g of flour. How much butter should he use?

To find the amount of sugar, you double the amount of butter, and then divide by three.

10. Write a formula for working out the amount of sugar from the amount of butter.
11. How much sugar should Lars use?

Set C

1. A chef uses this formula to work out how many eggs she uses, based on how many poached eggs and omelettes she makes:

   eggs used = poached eggs + (3 × omelettes)

   How many eggs does she use if she makes 8 poached eggs and 4 omelettes?

2. This formula is for how long it takes to cook a piece of beef, in minutes.

   time = (30 × weight in kg) + 20

   How long should a piece of beef weighing 2.5 kg be cooked for?

A taxi driver uses this formula to work out the cost of a journey.

cost = (£1.50 × number of miles) + £3.75

3. Emma travels 6 miles in the taxi. What is the cost, in £?
4. Dev's journey costs £8.25. How many miles did he travel?

It costs £25 to join a tennis club for a year, plus £1.50 for each match you play.

5. Write a formula that connects the total cost of playing tennis at the club for a year to the number of matches played.
6. Andy played 9 matches in a year. What was Andy's total cost over the year?
7. Jamie paid a total of £55 over a year. How many matches did Jamie play?

These formulas tell you how much red, blue and white paint are needed to make purple paint.

$$\text{amount of blue paint} = \frac{2}{3} \times \text{amount of red paint}$$

$$\text{amount of white paint} = \frac{1}{2} \times \text{amount of blue paint}$$

8. If Clare has 150 ml of red paint, how much blue paint should she use?
9. Write a formula that connects the amount of white paint to red paint.
10. Use your formula to work out how much red paint Clare needs if she has 75 ml of white paint.

I can use formulas written in words.     

Formulas — 2

Sometimes formulas use letters instead of words. Don't be put off — it's just a shorter way of writing formulas.

Examples

Daffodils have 6 petals. Write a formula for the number of petals p on d daffodils.

p = 6d ⟵ This means 6 × d.

You can check your formula works. You'd expect two daffodils to have 12 petals — put d = 2 into the formula to check: p = 6 × 2 = 12.

This formula gives the area A of a triangle. b is the length of the base and h is the height.

$$A = \frac{bh}{2}$$ ⟵ This means b × h.

What is the area when b = 2 cm and h = 3 cm?

$$A = \frac{2 \times 3}{2} = \frac{6}{2} = \mathbf{3\ cm^2}$$

Set A

Look at the formula below:

k = 8m

What is the value of k when:

1. m = 6?
2. m = 10?
3. A shirt has 10 buttons. Write a formula for the number of buttons b on s shirts.

Look at the formula below:

R = d × e

What is the value of R when:

4. d = 7 and e = 4?
5. d = 10 and e = 2?
6. e = 9 and d = 6?
7. Write a formula for the number of legs L on D dogs.

8. The perimeter p of a triangle with side lengths f, g and h is given by the formula:

   p = f + g + h

   What is the value of p when f = 3 m, g = 7 m and h = 5 m?
9. Write a formula for the perimeter p of a square with side length s.

Set B

1. Look at the formula below:

   $$T = \frac{xy}{2}$$

   Find the value of T when x = 5 and y = 6.
2. A book has 50 pages. Write a formula for the number of pages p, in c copies of the book.
3. Write a formula for the perimeter p of a rectangle with width w and height h.
4. The area A of a rhombus with width w and height h is:

   A = wh

   Work out the width of a rhombus with an area of 28 cm^2 and height of 4 cm.

The cost c, in £, of going to the village fair if you play g games is:

c = 1 + 2g

What is the cost if you play:

5. 5 games?
6. 20 games?
7. Tariq spent a total of £15 at the fair. How many games did he play?

Set C

The amount of money m, in £, that Sarah sponsors her friends for running d km is given by:

m = 10 + 3d

1. How much money will Sarah sponsor Harvey for running 4 km?
2. Sarah gives Latika £25 in sponsorship. How far did Latika run?
3. Look at this formula:

   V = LWH

   Work out the value of H when V = 24, L = 3 and W = 2.

Write a formula for:

4. the perimeter p of a regular octagon with side length a.
5. the perimeter q of a regular polygon with n sides of length b.
6. The size x of an angle inside a regular polygon with s sides is:

   $$x = 180 - \frac{360}{s}$$

   What is the size of an angle inside a regular hexagon?
7. Hiring a boat costs £5, plus £3 per person. Write a formula for the cost c of hiring a boat for p people.

I can use formulas written using letters.      

Sequences — 1

Sequences are patterns of numbers connected by a rule — you might have to figure the rule out for yourself.

Examples

The first term in a sequence is 7.
The rule for the sequence is "add 8".

Find the first five terms in the sequence.

7, 15, 23, 31, 39

Look at this sequence: 51, 42, 33, 24

Write down the rule for the sequence and find the next 3 terms.

The rule is **subtract 9**.
The next three terms are **15, 6, –3**.

Set A

Use the rules for these sequences to find the next three terms.

1. Add 7:
   3 10 ☐ ☐ ☐
2. Subtract 11:
   67 56 ☐ ☐ ☐
3. Add 5:
   –12 –7 ☐ ☐ ☐

Find the first 4 terms in each sequence.

4. first term: 12
   rule: add 6
5. first term: 24
   rule: subtract 3
6. first term: 5
   rule: subtract 2
7. first term: –9
   rule: add 4

Write down the rule for the sequence, and find the next 3 terms.

8. 7, 11, 15, 19
9. 35, 29, 23, 17
10. –5, –2, 1, 4

Find the missing numbers in each of these sequences:

11. 21 24 27 ☐ ☐
12. ☐ 55 50 45 ☐

Set B

Find the first 5 terms in each sequence.

1. first term: 28
   rule: add 13
2. first term: 22
   rule: subtract 11
3. first term: 4.5
   rule: subtract 0.2
4. first term: 1
   rule: add $\frac{1}{3}$

For each sequence below, write down the rule, and the next 3 terms.

5. 9, 17, 25, 33
6. 54, 61, 68, 75
7. 81, 75, 69, 63
8. 4, –5, –14, –23
9. $\frac{5}{7}$, $1\frac{1}{7}$, $1\frac{4}{7}$, 2
10. 1.4, 1.9, 2.4, 2.9

Find the missing numbers in these sequences:

11. 86 ☐ ☐ 65 58
12. 150 ☐ 450 600 ☐
13. ☐ $\frac{4}{5}$ $1\frac{1}{5}$ $1\frac{3}{5}$ ☐

14. The rule for a sequence is add 3. The first term is 10. What is the 11th term?

Set C

Find the first 5 terms in each sequence.

1. first term: 99
   rule: subtract 19
2. first term: –30
   rule: add 12
3. first term: $3\frac{1}{4}$
   rule: subtract $\frac{1}{2}$
4. first term: 7.7
   rule: subtract 0.3

Write down the rule for each sequence, and the next 3 terms.

5. 46, 57, 68, 79
6. 165, 150, 135, 120
7. –3.6, –3.2, –2.8, –2.4

Find the missing numbers:

8. 64 78 ☐ ☐ 120
9. ☐ –18 –11 –4 ☐
10. $3\frac{1}{3}$ ☐ $3\frac{2}{3}$ ☐ 4

Find the first term in each sequence:

11. rule: subtract 8
    third term: 6
12. rule: add 9
    fifth term: 60
13. rule: subtract 11
    fourth term: 18
14. The rule for a sequence is add 4. The first term is 3. What is the 101st term?

I can generate and describe number sequences.

Sequences — 2

You can use rules to generate sequences. They're just like formulas — you replace the letters with numbers.

Examples

The rule for a sequence is 2n + 5.
Find the first 3 terms of the sequence.

First put n = 1 into the formula: $2 \times 1 + 5 = 7$
Next put in n = 2: $2 \times 2 + 5 = 9$
Then put in n = 3: $2 \times 3 + 5 = 11$

So the first three terms are **7**, **9**, **11**.

Set A

The rule for a sequence is 2n + 3. Find the value when:

1. n = 1
2. n = 2
3. n = 3
4. n = 4
5. n = 5
6. n = 10
7. n = 50

Look at the sequences below.

A: 3, 6, 9, 12
B: 4, 5, 6, 7
C: 4, 7, 10, 13
D: 2, 5, 8, 11

Which sequence can be generated using the rule:

8. 3n + 1?
9. 3n – 1?

Find the first 3 terms in the sequences generated by these rules:

10. n + 4
11. n – 1
12. 2n + 2
13. 3n + 5
14. 2n – 3
15. 4n + 5

Set B

Look at the sequences below.

A: 4, 8, 12, 16, 20
B: 1, 5, 9, 13, 17
C: 7, 11, 15, 19, 23
D: 6, 11, 16, 21, 26

Which sequence can be generated using the rule:

1. 4n – 3?
2. 5n + 1?

Find the first 4 terms in the sequences generated by these rules:

3. 2n + 4
4. 3n – 3
5. n – 6
6. 6n + 2
7. 10 – 2n
8. 50 + 10n

The rule for a sequence is 5n – 2.

9. Find the first 4 terms of the sequence.
10. Which of the rules below describes how to get from one term to the next?
    A: Subtract 5 B: Add 3
    C: Subtract 10 D: Add 5
11. What is the 10th term in the sequence?

Set C

Find the first 5 terms in the sequences generated by these rules:

1. 3n + 2
2. 7n – 4
3. 2n – 5
4. 4 – 3n
5. 6 – 4n
6. 8 + 7n

Look at this sequence:

2, 5, 8, 11, 14

7. Which of the rules below generates this sequence?
   A: n + 1 B: 4n – 2
   C: 3n – 1 D: 2n
8. Which of the numbers below is not in the sequence?
   17, 23, 32, 42

Three rules for sequences are shown below:

2n + 9 5n + 3 9n – 1

9. For each sequence, find the first 4 terms, and describe how to get from one term to the next.
10. What pattern can you see between the rules given and your answers to Q9?

I can generate sequences using formulas.

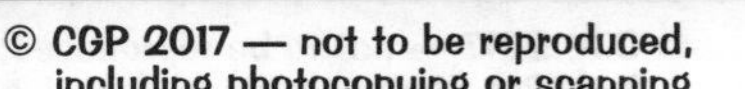

Algebra — Review 1

The total number of tentacles in an octopus tank is given by the formula:

number of tentacles = 8 × number of octopuses

1. How many tentacles are there in a tank of 7 octopuses?
2. Janine counts 32 tentacles in a tank. How many octopuses are there?

A cake recipe requires 50 g of sugar for each layer of the cake, and an extra 20 g for decoration.

3. Complete the formula: sugar needed = (☐ × number of layers) + ☐

Use your formula to work out:

4. the amount of sugar needed for a cake with 3 layers.
5. how many layers you could make if you had 370 g of sugar.

A school budget has rules for the amount of art supplies each class can have:

number of brushes = 3 × number of pupils

number of paint pots = 5 × number of brushes

There are 20 pupils in class 6R.

6. How many brushes can class 6R have?
7. Write a formula that connects the number of paint pots to the number of pupils.
8. How many paint pots can class 6R have?

Look at the formula below:

$t = 50 - 3w$

9. What is the value of t when w = 7?
10. What is the value of w when t = 20?

Terrence collects stamps — he already has 150 stamps. Each year he adds 45 stamps to his collection.

11. Write a formula for the number of stamps, s, Terrence will have after y years.
12. Use your formula to work out how many stamps he will have after 4 years.

Find the first 4 terms in each sequence.

13. first term: 9
rule: add 10
14. first term: 220
rule: subtract 6
15. first term: –1
rule: subtract 7
16. first term: –6
rule: add 0.5

Write down the rule for each of these sequences:

17. 4, 10, 16, 22
18. 150, 180, 210, 240
19. 45, 34, 23, 12
20. 0.6, 1.1, 1.6, 2.1
21. –3, 5, 13, 21
22. $\frac{1}{5}$, $\frac{3}{10}$, $\frac{2}{5}$, $\frac{1}{2}$

Find the missing numbers in these sequences:

23. 95 ☐ ☐ 65 55
24. ☐ $1\frac{1}{2}$ $2\frac{1}{4}$ 3 ☐
25. 5.6 6.4 ☐ 8 ☐
26. –11 ☐ –1 ☐ 9

Look at the sequences below:

A:	13, 19, 25, 31
B:	4, 9, 14, 19
C:	13, 10, 7, 4
D:	11, 9, 7, 5
E:	7, 11, 15, 19

Which can be generated using the rule:

27. $5n - 1$?
28. $6n + 7$?
29. $13 - 2n$?

Find the first 4 terms in the sequences generated by these rules:

30. $n + 10$
31. $2n + 8$
32. $4n - 2$
33. $17 - 3n$
34. $15 + 25n$
35. $4 - 5n$

36. The terms in a sequence are generated by the rule $7n - 5$. Describe, in words, how to get from one term to the next.

Well done on getting through this work — now you'll be spotting sequences everywhere you go!

Missing Number Problems

Algebra might seem a bit scary — but it can make problems with missing numbers easier to deal with.

Examples

What is the value of ● in this equation?

● + 5 = 11

Method 1:

Think... what number equals 11 when you add 5 to it?
That's **6**.

Method 2 — use algebra:

● + 5 = 11

● = 11 – 5 = **6**

Subtract 5 from both sides to get ● on its own.

What is the value of p in this equation?

$3p = 12$

Method 1:

Think... what number do you multiply 3 by to get 12?

$3 \times 4 = 12$, so $p = \mathbf{4}$.

Method 2 — use algebra:

$3p = 12$

$p = 12 \div 3 = \mathbf{4}$

Divide both sides by 3 to get p on its own.

Jimmy thinks of a number, ▲.
He multiplies by 2 and then subtracts 6 to get 4.

Write an equation involving ▲.

2▲ – 6 = 4

Use your equation to find the value of ▲.

2▲ = 4 + 6 = 10 *Add 6 to both sides to get 2▲ on its own.*

▲ = 10 ÷ 2 = **5** *Divide both sides by 2 to find ▲.*

Set A

Use the equation to find the value of each shape:

1. ● + 3 = 9, so ● = 9 – 3 = ☐
2. 2⬢ = 8, so ⬢ = 8 ÷ 2 = ☐
3. ⯃ ÷ 3 = 7, so ⯃ = 7 × 3 = ☐
4. 10 – ⬟ = 1, so ⬟ = ☐
5. 5◆ = 30, so ◆ = ☐

Find the value of the letter in each equation:

6. $u + 6 = 18$
7. $v - 2 = 12$
8. $7 + w = 15$
9. $3x = 15$
10. $60 = 3y$
11. $\frac{z}{4} = 9$

Tilly thinks of a number, ▲.
She subtracts 7 from it to get 9.

12. Write an equation involving ▲.
13. What is the value of ▲?

Hassan thinks of a different number, ●.
He multiplies it by 4 to get 20.

14. Write an equation involving ●.
15. What is the value of ●?

16. Here are some numbers:

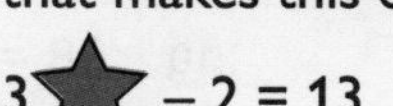

Which number is the value of ★ that makes this equation true?

3★ – 2 = 13

The perimeter of this square is 24 cm.

s cm

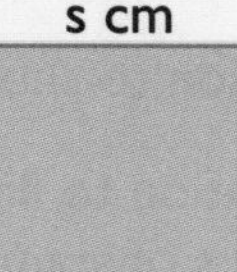

17. Write an equation involving s.
18. What is the value of s?

Set B

Find the value of the shape in each equation.

1. △ + 15 = 20
2. ◇ ÷ 3 = 3
3. 30 – ⬡ = 18
4. 108 = 9 × ●

Find the value of the letters in each equation.

5. 2m = 24
6. $\frac{28}{n} = 7$
7. 35 – p = 16

Use the numbers in the box below to answer the following questions.

6	3	7	2	10

8. Which number is the value of d in the equation d + 6 = 10 – d?
9. Which two numbers are the values of e and f in this equation 2e – f = 0?

Find the value of the letter in each equation.

10. 2a + 1 = 5
11. 3b – 2 = 1
12. 3 + 2c = 7
13. 2d + 1 = 9
14. 3e + 1 = 10
15. 4f – 3 = 5

Sarah thinks of a number, ■.

She multiplies it by 3, then subtracts 2 to get 16.

16. Write an equation involving ■.
17. What is the value of ■?

The perimeter of this rectangle is 40 cm.

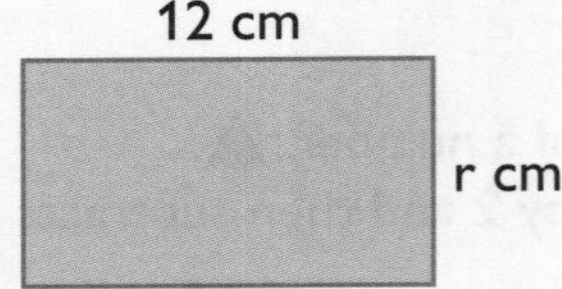

18. Write an equation involving r.
19. What is the value of r?

Set C

Find the value of the shape in each equation.

1. 37 + ■ = 63
2. 12 ★ = 72
3. ◇ – 19 = 58
4. 75 ÷ ⬡ = 25

Find the value of the letter in each equation.

5. 6a = 42
6. 4 + 4b = 12
7. 13 = 5c – 7
8. $\frac{d}{3} - 5 = 4$
9. 6e – 9 = 9
10. 38 = 20 + 2f

A post office sells stamps in books of 6. One day they start with 90 stamps, and sell b books of stamps. They're left with 48 stamps.

11. Write an equation to show this.
12. Solve your equation to find the number of books of stamps sold.

13. Look at this equation:

3q + 4 = 2q + 6

What is the value of q?

The angles below make a right angle.

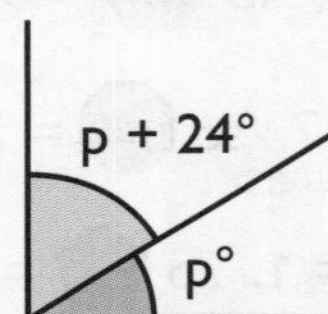

14. Write an equation involving p.
15. What is the value of p?

Look at the bar diagram below.
The two rows add up to the same amount.

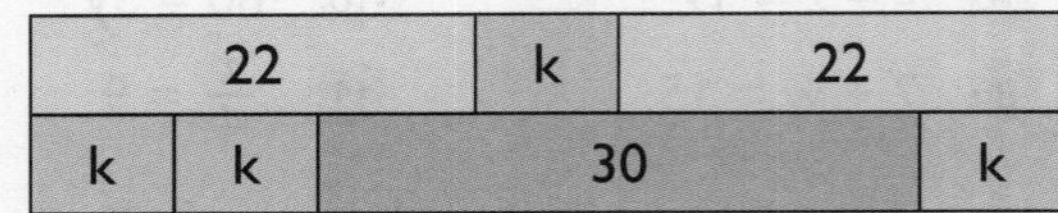

16. Write an equation involving k.
17. What is the value of k?

I can solve missing number problems.

Two Missing Numbers

Some problems have two missing numbers — there's often more than one possible answer, so be careful.

Examples

In the equation below, ▲ and ■ are whole numbers that are bigger than zero.

▲ × ■ = 12

Write down all the possible pairs of values for ▲ and ■.

▲ = 1, ■ = 12   **▲ = 4, ■ = 3**

▲ = 2, ■ = 6   **▲ = 6, ■ = 2**

▲ = 3, ■ = 4   **▲ = 12, ■ = 1**

Find all the pairs of numbers that multiply together to give 12. Be careful not to miss any out — for example you need to write down both ▲ = 1, ■ = 12 and ▲ = 12, ■ = 1.

A dictionary is 3 cm thick and an atlas is 1 cm thick. Jonathan puts D dictionaries and A atlases in a pile, with at least one of each in his pile. The pile is 10 cm high.

Write an equation that gives this information.   (3 × D) + (1 × A) = 10, so **3D + A = 10**

Write down all the possible pairs of values for D and A.

D = 1, A = 7   **D = 2, A = 4**   **D = 3, A = 1**

Put values for D into the equation, starting at D = 1. (3 × 1) + A = 10, so A = 10 – 3 = 7.

Check your answers make sense — if D is bigger than 3 then A is negative, and you can't have –2 atlases...

Set A

1 Look at this equation: ● + ▲ = 11
Write down all the options below that would make this equation true.

A: ● = 2 ▲ = 9

B: ● = 5 ▲ = 7

C: ● = 7 ▲ = 4

D: ● = 8 ▲ = 4

Look at this equation: ⬟ × ■ = 24

2 If ⬟ = 4, what is the value of ■ ?

3 If ■ = 2, what is the value of ⬟ ?

4 Look at this equation: ★ – ▲ = 6
Write down three different pairs of values for ★ and ▲, where both values are between 0 and 10, that would make this true.

Pessy has p books and Harry has h books. They have 10 books in total.

5 Write an equation that gives this information.

6 Write down two possible pairs of values for p and h.

For each of the equations below, find all possible solutions for x and y, where both x and y are whole numbers bigger than zero:

7 $x + y = 8$

8 $9 - x = y$

9 $xy = 16$

10 $20 \div x = y$

11 $x + 2y = 7$

12 $4x + y = 18$

13 Tom has t goldfish. Ellie has e goldfish. Tom has twice as many goldfish as Ellie. Which equation shows this information?

A: $t = e + 2$ C: $e = 2t$

B: $t = 2e$ D: $t = e - 2$

Binita has b tomatoes. Ryan has r tomatoes — he has half as many tomatoes as Binita.

14 Write an equation that gives this information.

15 They both have less than 10 tomatoes. Write down all possible pairs of values for b and r.

Set B

1 In the equation below, and are whole numbers that are bigger than zero.

× = 18

Write down all the possible pairs of values for and .

2 In the equation below, and are whole numbers that are bigger than zero.

+ 3 = 10

Write down all the possible pairs of values for and .

In the equation below, c and d are whole numbers that are bigger than zero.

$2c + d = 8$

3 If c = 1, what is the value of d?

4 Write down all the other possible pairs of values for c and d.

For each of the equations below, find all possible solutions for x and y, where both x and y are whole numbers bigger than zero:

5 $x = 7 - y$

6 $y = \frac{30}{x}$

7 $2x + y = 11$

8 $12 - 2x = y$

9 $5 - \frac{x}{2} = y$

10 $4x + 2y = 14$

11 In the equation below, f and g are whole numbers that are bigger than zero.

$$10 = f - 3g$$

Find the three possible pairs of values of f and g with the smallest values of f.

A cherry weighs 4 grams. A raisin weighs 1 gram. Sunita has c cherries and r raisins. They weigh 23 grams in total.

12 Which equation shows this information?

A: $4c - r = 23$ C: $4c = 23 + r$

B: $4c + r = 23$ D: $4r + c = 23$

13 Write down all the possible pairs of values for c and r.

Set C

In the equations below, and are whole numbers that are bigger than zero. Write down all the possible pairs of values for and .

1 2 + = 9

2 3 × × = 18

3 5 + = 21

In the equation below, c and d are whole numbers that are bigger than zero.

$$2c + 4d = 16$$

4 Why is there no solution where c = 1?

5 Write down all the possible pairs of values for c and d.

6 Look at this equation: $m - n = 19$

m and n are greater than 0 and m is a factor of 100. Write down all possible pairs of values for m and n.

For each of the equations below, find all possible solutions for x and y, where both x and y are whole numbers bigger than zero:

7 $6x = 25 - y$

8 $\frac{32}{y} = x$

9 $3x + 4y = 17$

10 $5xy = 100$

In the equation below, j and k are whole numbers that are bigger than zero.

$$4j + 3k = 35$$

11 Write down the solution for where j = k.

12 Write down all other solutions.

A cake costs £3. A pie costs £2. Paul buys c cakes and p pies for a party. He spends £21.

13 Write an equation to show this information.

14 Paul buys twice as many pies as cakes. How many of each does he buy?

I can solve problems with two missing numbers.

Algebra — Review 2

Use the equation to find the value of each shape.

1. 26 + ★ = 40, so ★ = ☐
2. ● × 6 = 24, so ● = ☐
3. 9 = 26 – ⬢, so ⬢ = ☐
4. ▲ ÷ 2 = 21, so ▲ = ☐
5. 64 = 40 + 2■, so ■ = ☐

Find the value of the letters in each equation.

6	$3a = 15$	11	$2f + 8 = 20$
7	$12 - b = 4$	12	$5 = 20 - 5g$
8	$c + 98 = 101$	13	$7h - 9 = 61$
9	$14 \div d = 2$	14	$121 - 12j = 1$
10	$\frac{e}{10} = 6$	15	$\frac{16}{k} - 2 = 2$

Use the numbers in the box below to answer the following questions.

11	9	8	2	4	6

16. Which number is the value of w in the equation $9 + w = 17 - w$?
17. Which number is the value of x in this equation $2x = 24 - x$?

Two angles are shown on a straight line below.

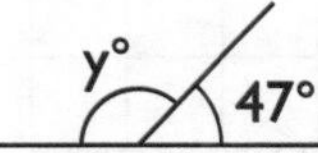

18. Write an equation involving y.
19. What is the value of y?

The large rectangle below is made from 6 smaller rectangles. All the green rectangles are the same size.

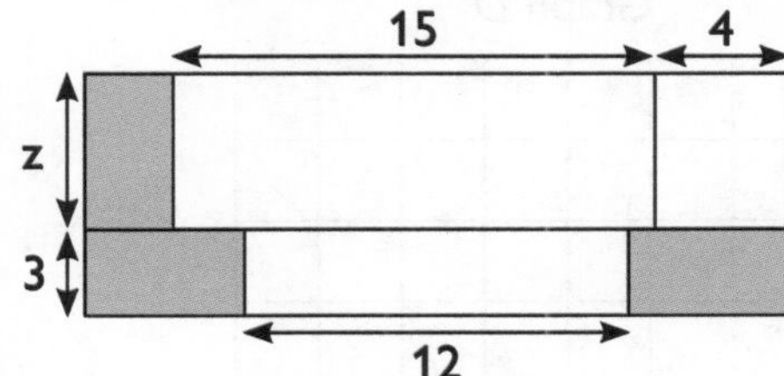

20. Write an equation involving z for the perimeter of the large rectangle.
21. What is the value of z?

In the equations below, ⬟ and ● are whole numbers that are bigger than zero. Write down <u>all</u> the possible pairs of values for ⬟ and ●.

22. ⬟ = 5 – ●
23. ⬟ × ● = 21
24. 25 = 5⬟ + ●

25. Harriet has h lemons. Ian has i lemons — which is one more than double the number Harriet has. Which equation shows this information?

A: $h = 2i + 1$	C: $i = 2 + h$
B: $h = 2i - 1$	D: $i = 2h + 1$

26. Look at the equation below.

   $a + b = 30$

   a and b are both whole numbers bigger than zero, and a is a multiple of 8. Write down <u>all</u> possible pairs of values for a and b.

27. Look at the equation below.

   $4c = 25 - d$

   c and d are both whole numbers bigger than zero, and c is a prime number. Write down <u>all</u> possible pairs of values for c and d.

For each of the equations below, find all possible solutions for x and y, where both x and y are whole numbers bigger than zero:

28	$5 - x = y$	32	$2x + 6y = 28$
29	$x \times y = 26$	33	$5x = 28 - 3y$
30	$\frac{15}{x} = y$	34	$5xy = 70$
31	$x + 2y = 9$	35	$\frac{18}{x} = 9 - y$

A taxi can carry 4 passengers, and a minibus can carry 7 passengers. There are 50 people going to a party — they completely fill t taxis and m minibuses.

36. Write an equation to show this information.
37. Write down all the possible pairs of values for t and m.

If you managed to find all of those missing numbers then give yourself a pat on the back!

Algebra — Challenges

1 Each box below contains numbers that belong to a sequence, but the numbers have been mixed up.

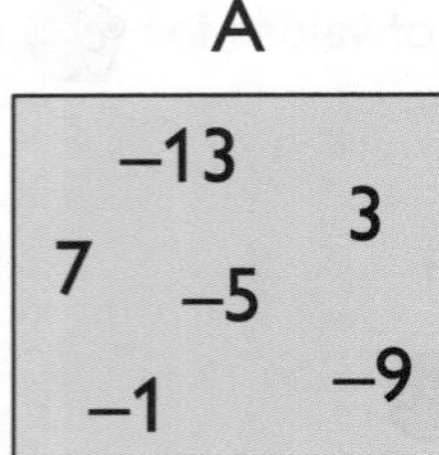

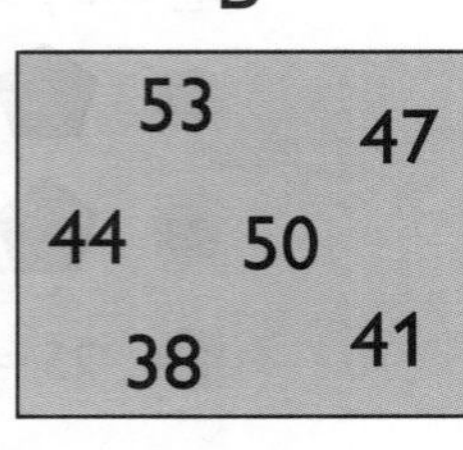

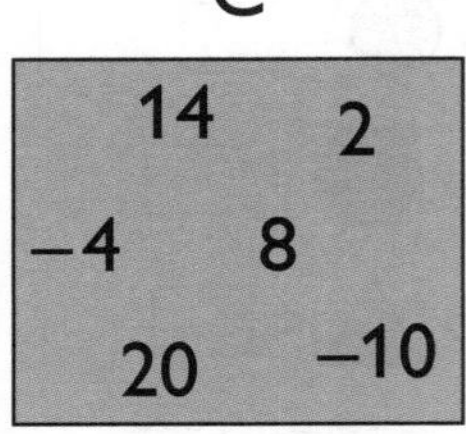

One of the rules below belongs to each sequence:

Add 6 **Subtract 4** **Subtract 3**

a) Use this information to work out what each sequence looked like before it was mixed up.

b) Write down the next 3 terms in each sequence.

2 For each equation below, Rhodri finds all the pairs of numbers that make the equation true. x and y are whole numbers that are bigger than zero.

$x + y = 8$ $x \times y = 4$ $x = 5 - y$ $x \times y = 8$

He plots the pairs of numbers on a graph. For example, if x = 1, y = 2 made an equation true, he would plot the coordinates (1, 2). He plots a separate graph for each equation.

Which of the equations above matches each graph?

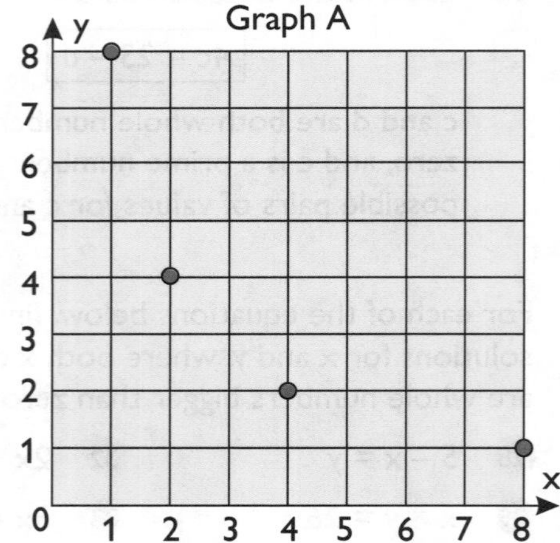

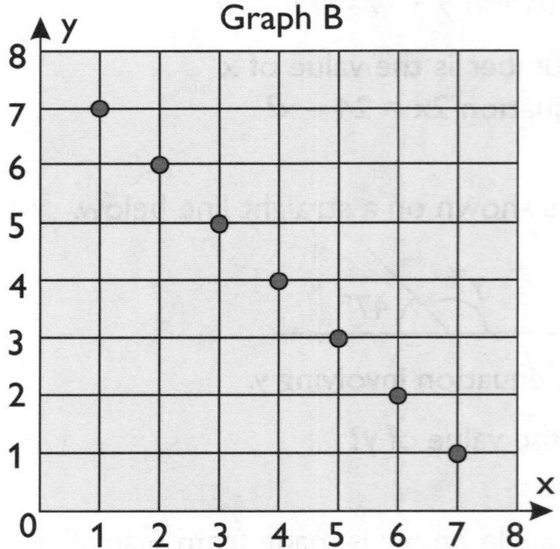

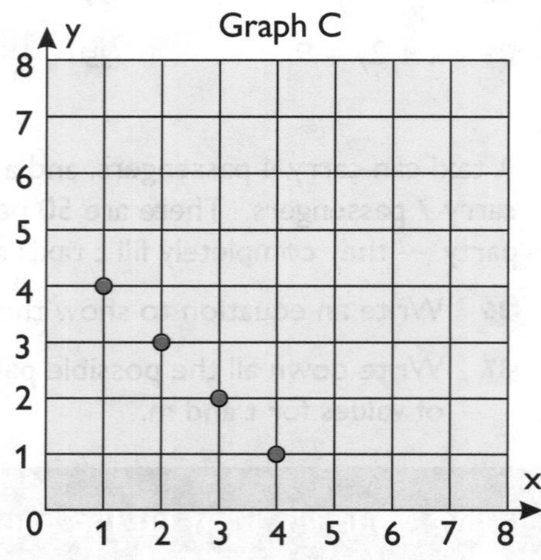

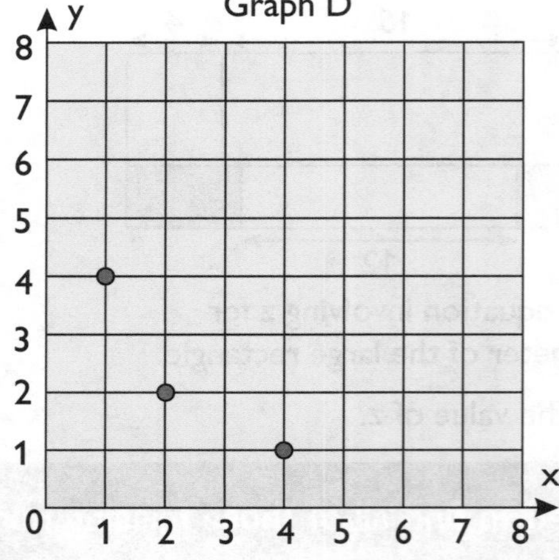

3 Abigail and Danny are playing a game where they send each other words in code.

In the code, each letter is represented by a number, as shown in the table below.

1	2	3	4	5	6	7	8	9	10	11	12	13	14	15	16	17	18	19	20	21	22	23	24	25	26
D	Q	Z	K	G	T	F	Y	A	P	J	N	W	C	S	M	V	L	R	X	B	I	O	U	E	H

Abigail and Danny make their code even harder to crack by sending the numbers as equations.

Here is an example: if Abigail sends the equation 3● = 9, Danny has to find the value of ● — that's 9 ÷ 3 = 3. Then he needs to look at the table — 3 corresponds to Z.

a) Danny sends Abigail five equations. The value of each shape in each equation should spell out a maths word, but Danny made a mistake. What word was he trying to spell out?

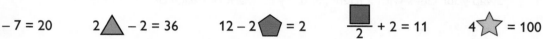

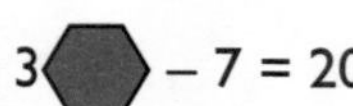 3⬢ − 7 = 20   2▲ − 2 = 36   12 − 2⬟ = 2   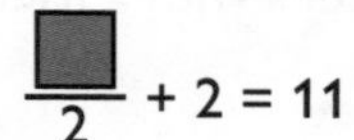 $\frac{■}{2}$ + 2 = 11    4☆ = 100

b) Suggest an equation that he could have used instead of the wrong one.

c) Try writing your own code like Danny's (but without mistakes!). Give your code to a classmate and see if they can crack it.

4 Some formulas are shown on the grid below:

	1	2	3	4
A	F + H = 2	W + B = 2	P = 3T	A = W × W
B	P = T + 3	A = 2W	H = 5 + F	B = 2W
C	W = A × A	T = 3P	W = B + 2	F = 5H
D	W = 2B	H = 5F	T = P × P × P	A = 4W

Write down the grid references for the following formulas (for example A1 for row A, column 1).

a) The formula for the number of wings W on B birds.

b) The formula for perimeter P of an equilateral triangle with side length T.

c) The formula for the number of fingers F on H hands.

d) The formula for the area A of a square with side length W.

Now try coming up with a word formula that would match the formulas in:

e) B3

f) D3

5 Anna has written these clues to help you guess the number she is thinking of.

- Take the second term in the sequence generated by $3n - 1$.
- Add the fourth term in the sequence generated by $2n + 3$.
- Then divide by the third term in the sequence generated by $5n - 7$.

a) What is Anna's number?

b) Write your own clues for finding a number, using terms from these three sequences:

$3n + 5$ $\quad$ $4n - 2$ $\quad$ $6n - 3$

Swap your clues with a friend, and try to work out each other's numbers.

6 Kamal has bought some packets of peppers, potatoes and apples.
These formulas connect the number of items with the number of packets.

number of peppers = 3 × number of packets

number of potatoes = 12 × number of packets

number of apples = 6 × number of packets

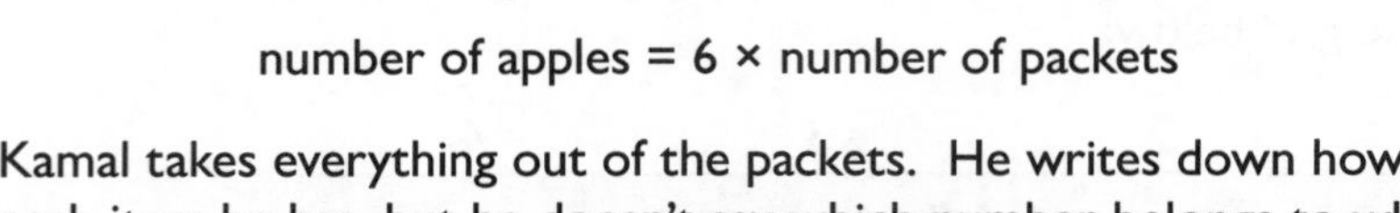

a) Kamal takes everything out of the packets. He writes down how many of each item he has, but he doesn't say which number belongs to which item...

36	18	21

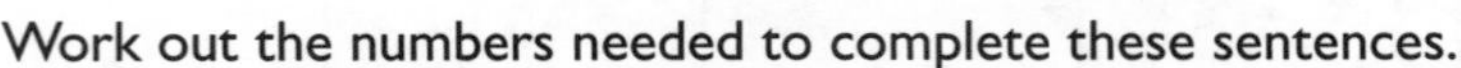

Work out the numbers needed to complete these sentences.

Kamal bought ☐ packets of peppers.

Kamal bought ☐ packets of potatoes.

Kamal bought ☐ packets of apples.

Simona also buys packets of peppers, potatoes and apples. She buys 48 items in total.

b) How many of each thing could she have bought?
Copy and complete the table below to work out all possible solutions.

Potatoes	36								
Apples	6								
Peppers	6								

c) Simona bought exactly 10 packets in total. How many of each thing did she buy?

Well done, you've made it — that's the end of algebra!

Length — 1

You'll often see length measured in metric units like millimetres, centimetres, metres and kilometres. On this page, you'll practise using multiplication and division to convert between these units.

Examples

Convert 1.35 m to cm.

1 m = 100 cm, so multiply by 100:

1.35 × 100 = **135 cm**

If you're converting from a bigger unit to a smaller unit, then multiply.

Convert 11.56 mm to cm.

1 cm = 10 mm, so divide by 10:

11.56 ÷ 10 = **1.156 cm**

If you're converting from a smaller unit to a bigger unit, then divide.

Convert 9.568 km to m.

1 km = 1000 m, so multiply by 1000:

9.568 × 1000 = **9568 m**

Set A

Complete the conversions below.

1. 5.1 cm = ☐ mm
2. 7.2 m = ☐ cm
3. 4.6 km = ☐ m
4. 2.55 m = ☐ cm
5. 1.35 cm = ☐ mm
6. 9.05 km = ☐ m

Complete the conversions below.

7. 219 cm = ☐ m
8. 13.8 mm = ☐ cm
9. 914 cm = ☐ m
10. 1925 m = ☐ km
11. 16.93 mm = ☐ cm
12. 2275 m = ☐ km

Look at the lengths in the box below.

3.25 m	32.5 m
325 m	3250 m

Which length is equal to:

13. 325 cm?
14. 3.25 km?
15. 0.325 km?

Set B

Complete the conversions below.

1. 1.67 m = ☐ cm
2. 2459 m = ☐ km
3. 1.191 km = ☐ m
4. 3.052 cm = ☐ mm
5. 525.8 cm = ☐ m
6. 25.81 mm = ☐ cm

Convert the following:

7. 1328 m to km
8. 0.753 m to cm
9. 0.391 cm to mm
10. 10.68 mm to cm
11. 5.859 cm to mm
12. 0.004 km to m
13. 150.1 cm to m

Which symbol (<, > or =) should go in each box?

14. 35 m ☐ 0.035 km
15. 3 mm ☐ 0.03 cm
16. 2005 cm ☐ 20.5 m

Convert 132 mm to:

17. centimetres
18. metres

Set C

Convert the following:

1. 3594 m to km
2. 0.729 cm to mm
3. 15.14 mm to cm
4. 3.196 cm to mm
5. 4.521 km to m
6. 9.702 m to cm
7. 183.9 cm to m

Tim says, "You can convert millimetres to metres by dividing by 1000."

8. Convert 500 mm to cm, then into m.
9. Try converting 500 mm to m with Tim's method. Do you get the same answer as you did in Q8? Explain why.

Convert 0.079 km to:

10. metres
11. centimetres

Convert the following:

12. 0.05 m to mm
13. 600 cm to km
14. 95 mm to m

I can convert between metric units of length.      

Length — 2

Length can be measured in miles. '5 miles ≈ 8 km'. You can multiply or divide by 1.6 to roughly convert between miles and kilometres. Or, you can follow the methods in the examples below.

Examples

Approximately how many miles is 16 km?

To convert km to miles, first divide by 8: 16 ÷ 8 = 2

Then multiply by 5: 2 × 5 = **10 miles**

Approximately how many km is 15 miles?

To convert miles to km, first divide by 5: 15 ÷ 5 = 3

Then multiply by 8: 3 × 8 = **24 km**

These are only approximate conversions because 8 km isn't exactly 5 miles.

Set A

Find the missing numbers:

1. 24 ÷ 8 = 3
   3 × 5 = 15
   So 24 km ≈ ☐ miles
2. 10 ÷ 5 = 2
   2 × 8 = ☐
   So 10 miles ≈ ☐ km
3. 64 ÷ 8 = 8
   8 × 5 = ☐
   So 64 km ≈ ☐ miles

Divide by 8 and then multiply by 5 to convert these to miles:

4. 40 km ≈ ☐ miles
5. 88 km ≈ ☐ miles
6. 800 km ≈ ☐ miles

Divide by 5 and then multiply by 8 to convert these to km:

7. 100 miles ≈ ☐ km
8. 200 miles ≈ ☐ km

Complete the conversions below.

9. 32 km ≈ ☐ miles
10. 48 km ≈ ☐ miles
11. 35 miles ≈ ☐ km
12. 50 miles ≈ ☐ km
13. 72 km ≈ ☐ miles
14. 60 miles ≈ ☐ km
15. 500 miles ≈ ☐ km

Set B

Complete the conversions below.

1. 32 km ≈ ☐ miles
2. 56 km ≈ ☐ miles
3. 640 km ≈ ☐ miles
4. 25 miles ≈ ☐ km
5. 450 miles ≈ ☐ km
6. 1000 miles ≈ ☐ km

Which is further:

7. 72 km or 55 miles?
8. 400 miles or 650 km?

Ben travels 104 km by coach, and then 600 miles by plane. Approximately how long was:

9. his coach journey in miles.
10. his plane journey in km.

Do the approximate conversions below.

11. 1.6 km to miles
12. 1.5 miles to km
13. 2.5 miles to km
14. Jess lives 4.8 km away from the park. Approximately how many miles is this?

Set C

Complete the conversions below.

1. 40 km ≈ ☐ miles
2. 65 miles ≈ ☐ km
3. 320 km ≈ ☐ miles
4. 300 miles ≈ ☐ km
5. 896 km ≈ ☐ miles
6. 340 miles ≈ ☐ km

Do the approximate conversions below.

7. 4.8 km to miles
8. 3.5 miles to km
9. 6.4 km to miles
10. 4.5 miles to km
11. 8.64 km to miles
12. 5.75 miles to km

13. Abid swims 2 miles per day for ten days. Approximately how many km is this in total?
14. Liz cycles 30 km four times a week. Approximately how many miles is this in total?
15. Fay runs 5.5 miles each day. Approximately how many km will she run in 5 days?

I can convert between miles and kilometres.      

Mass and Capacity

You can measure mass in kilograms or grams. Capacity (or 'volume') can be measured in litres or millilitres. To convert between kg and g or litres and ml, just multiply or divide by 1000.

Examples

Convert 1847 ml to litres.

1 litre = 1000 ml, so divide by 1000:

1847 ÷ 1000 = **1.847 litres**

If you're converting from a smaller unit to a bigger unit, then divide.

A puppy weighs 2.958 kg.
How much does it weigh in grams?

1 kg = 1000 g, so multiply by 1000:

2.958 × 1000 = **2958 g**

If you're converting from a bigger unit to a smaller unit, then multiply.

Set A

Complete the conversions below.

1. 1.3 litres = ☐ ml
2. 4.7 litres = ☐ ml
3. 5.15 kg = ☐ g
4. 6.75 kg = ☐ g
5. 3.54 litres = ☐ ml
6. 7.25 kg = ☐ g

Complete the conversions below.

7. 1200 ml = ☐ litres
8. 1800 ml = ☐ litres
9. 5270 g = ☐ kg
10. 8990 g = ☐ kg
11. 3580 ml = ☐ litres
12. 6840 g = ☐ kg

Which value from the box is equal to:

13. 3.298 litres?

3298 ml	32.98 ml
32890 ml	329.8 ml

14. 6185 g?

61.85 kg	618.5 kg
0.6185 kg	6.185 kg

Set B

Complete the conversions below.

1. 3.68 litres = ☐ ml
2. 4540 g = ☐ kg
3. 2.05 kg = ☐ g
4. 3.54 litres = ☐ ml
5. 5870 ml = ☐ litres
6. 6680 g = ☐ kg

Convert the following:

7. 0.28 kg to g
8. 960 ml to litres
9. 0.002 litres to ml
10. 0.058 kg to g
11. 3525 g to kg
12. 625 g to kg
13. 95 ml to litres

Which is greater:

14. 2.273 litres or 2275 ml?
15. 90 g or 0.009 kg?
16. 0.08 litres or 800 ml?
17. 0.65 kg or 640 g?
18. A pencil weighs 0.045 kg. How much does it weigh in grams?

Set C

Convert the following:

1. 2369 g to kg
2. 1.285 kg to g
3. 0.161 litres to ml
4. 35 ml to litres
5. 6 g to kg
6. 9 ml to litres
7. 8.605 kg to g

Which is greatest:

8. 83 ml, 0.09 litres or 50 ml?
9. 0.13 kg, 1350 g or 1.3 kg?
10. 0.05 litres, 5 ml or 500 ml?
11. 1.938 litres, 1928 ml or 1958 ml?
12. 5.007 kg, 5070 g or 5.7 kg?
13. 0.004 litres, 40 ml or 0.4 litres?
14. 4259 g, 4.254 kg or 4.252 kg?

Complete these calculations.

15. 1550 ml + 43 ml = ☐ litres
16. 7.05 kg + 8.57 kg = ☐ g
17. 8 ml + 0.003 litres = ☐ litres
18. 559 g + 10.52 kg = ☐ g
19. 3657 g + 3.5 kg = ☐ kg

I can convert between metric units of mass and capacity.

Time

Time can be measured with all sorts of units, including seconds, minutes, hours, days, weeks and years. On this page, you'll practise converting between these different units.

Examples

Patrick's guitar lesson was $2\frac{1}{3}$ hours long.
How long was his lesson in minutes?

2 hours = 2 × 60 = 120 minutes

$\frac{1}{3}$ of an hour = 60 ÷ 3 = 20 minutes

So Patrick's guitar lesson was 120 + 20 = **140 minutes** long.

How many hours are in 2 weeks?

2 weeks is 2 × 7 = 14 days

14 days is: → 24 × 14 = 96 + 240 = **336 hours**

So there are **336 hours** in 2 weeks.

Set A

Complete these conversions:

1. 5 weeks 3 days = ☐ days
2. 2 hrs 23 mins = ☐ mins
3. 4 mins 39 secs = ☐ secs
4. 10 hrs 16 mins = ☐ mins
5. 3 days 7 hrs = ☐ hrs
6. 2 normal years 40 days = ☐ days

Convert the following:

7. $2\frac{1}{2}$ hrs = ☐ mins
8. $1\frac{1}{2}$ days = ☐ hrs
9. $3\frac{1}{4}$ mins = ☐ secs
10. $2\frac{1}{3}$ mins = ☐ secs
11. $4\frac{3}{4}$ hrs = ☐ mins

Use the numbers in the box below to complete the questions.

1440	60	120
3600	24	7200

12. 1 hr = ☐ mins = ☐ secs
13. 2 hrs = ☐ mins = ☐ secs
14. 1 day = ☐ hrs = ☐ mins

Set B

Complete these conversions:

1. $3\frac{1}{3}$ hrs = ☐ mins
2. $2\frac{1}{6}$ mins = ☐ secs
3. $3\frac{5}{7}$ weeks = ☐ days
4. $\frac{5}{6}$ leap year = ☐ days
5. $2\frac{5}{8}$ days = ☐ hrs

Convert the following:

6. 420 secs = ☐ mins
7. 180 mins = ☐ hrs
8. 120 hrs = ☐ days
9. 56 days = ☐ weeks
10. 60 hours = ☐ days ☐ hrs
11. 330 secs = ☐ mins ☐ secs

Multiply by 60 twice to convert:

12. 1 hr to secs
13. 5 hrs to secs
14. 10 hrs to secs

Multiply by 24, then 60 to convert:

15. 1 day to mins
16. 5 days to mins

Set C

Complete these conversions:

1. $3\frac{1}{6}$ hrs = ☐ mins
2. $9\frac{4}{7}$ weeks = ☐ days
3. $5\frac{7}{12}$ days = ☐ hrs
4. $5\frac{4}{5}$ hrs = ☐ mins
5. $4\frac{3}{8}$ days = ☐ hrs

Convert the following:

6. 68 days to weeks and days
7. 285 mins to hrs and mins
8. 435 secs to mins and secs
9. 134 hrs to days and hrs
10. 978 hrs to days and hrs
11. 1425 secs to mins and secs

Convert the following:

12. 4 weeks = ☐ days = ☐ hrs
13. 3 hrs = ☐ mins = ☐ secs
14. 2 days = ☐ hrs = ☐ mins
15. 10 weeks = ☐ hrs
16. 20 hrs = ☐ secs
17. 2 normal years = ☐ hrs

I can convert between different units of time.

Solving Problems with Measure

To solve the problems on these pages, you'll need to convert between units of length, mass, capacity and time. You might also have to do some adding, subtracting, multiplying and dividing.

Examples

A jug contains 1.436 litres of orange juice. Pam pours 512 ml into a glass.

How much orange juice is left in the jug? Give your answer in ml.

Convert the amount that was in the jug into ml: 1.436 × 1000 = 1436 ml

Subtract the amount that was poured into the glass:

$$\begin{array}{r} \overset{}{\cancel{1}}\overset{14}{\cancel{4}}36 \\ -\ 512 \\ \hline \mathbf{924} \end{array}$$

So there is **924 ml** of orange juice left in the jug.

Anna is going on holiday. Her journey to the airport takes 2 hours.

Her flight is $1\frac{1}{4}$ hours longer than her journey to the airport.

How long is her flight in minutes?

Her flight is $2 + 1\frac{1}{4} = 3\frac{1}{4}$ hours long.

3 hours = 3 × 60 = 180 minutes

$\frac{1}{4}$ of an hour = 60 ÷ 4 = 15 minutes

So her flight is 180 + 15 = **195 minutes** long.

Set A

1. Harry's backpack weighs 2.3 kg.
   How many grams does it weigh?

It takes Elena 4 hours to paint a picture.

2. How many minutes does it take her?
3. It takes Roger $1\frac{1}{2}$ hours longer to paint his picture than Elena. How many minutes does Roger spend painting?

A bag of sugar weighs 1.8 kg.

4. How many grams does the bag of sugar weigh?
5. Kayla uses 643 g of the sugar.
   How much sugar is left?
   Give your answer in grams.

A vase contains 0.75 litres of water.

6. How many ml of water does it contain?
7. Jonny adds 95 ml of water to the vase.
   How much water is in the vase now?
   Give your answer in litres.

Lora's hair is 35.2 cm long.

8. How many mm long is Lora's hair?
9. Lora cuts her hair so that it is 190 mm shorter.
   How many cm long is her hair now?

The table shows the length of three different routes around a lake.

Route A	Route B	Route C
5.5 km	7500 m	6.75 km

10. How much longer is route B than route A?
    Give your answer in km.
11. How much shorter is route A than route C?
    Give your answer in m.
12. What is the total length of all three routes?
    Give your answer in km.
13. Sophia drives 40 km a day.
    8 km is approximately 5 miles.

    Approximately how many miles does she drive in 2 days?

Set B

Nabil's fish tank can hold 7.8 litres of water.

1 How many ml of water can it hold?

2 Ciara's fish tank can hold 2500 ml more water than Nabil's fish tank. How much water can Ciara's tank hold? Give your answer in litres.

Nawra has decided to run 25 miles for charity. 5 miles is approximately 8 km.

3 Approximately how many km is Nawra going to run?

4 Rose runs 16 km further than Nawra. How many miles does Rose run?

Jordan's piano lesson usually lasts 165 minutes.

5 How long is his lesson in hours and minutes?

6 On Thursday, his lesson is 20 minutes shorter than usual. How many seconds shorter is it?

7 Hannah's lessons last for 1 hour 20 minutes. How many minutes shorter are Hannah's lessons than Jordan's?

In one second, Speedy the snail moves 1.383 cm. Sammy the snail moves 13.48 mm.

8 Which snail travels further?

9 What is the difference between how far the two snails travel? Give your answer in mm.

10 How far do the snails travel in total? Give your answer in cm.

Yassir and Joe recorded how far they walked in one day. In total they walked 9.482 km.

11 Joe walked 4.371 km. How far did Yassir walk? Give your answer in m.

12 How much further did Yassir walk than Joe? Give your answer in m.

13 Maggie walked 255 m further than Joe. How far did she walk in km?

14 Gareth has 7.96 kg of luggage in his bag. He removes an 850 g pair of boots and a 480 g pair of jeans. How many kg of luggage does he have in his bag now?

Set C

The table shows how much food three pigs eat a day.

Betsy	Percy	Barny
2.67 kg	2450 g	2.3 kg

1 How many kg of food do the 3 pigs eat in total each day?

2 How much more food does Betsy eat than Percy? Give your answer in grams.

3 How many kg of food does Percy eat in 3 days?

4 How many more grams of food does Barny need to eat each day to eat as much as Betsy?

Camilla drives 360 km from her home in Coventry to Carlisle. 8 km is approximately 5 miles.

5 Approximately how many miles does Camilla travel?

6 She visits a friend on the way back home and drives an extra 240 miles. Approximately how far does she travel on the way home? Give your answer in km.

The apple tree in Hamid's garden is 475 cm tall. The pear tree is 1793 mm tall.

7 How many metres tall is the apple tree?

8 How much smaller than the apple tree is the pear tree? Give your answer in cm.

A large sink can hold 11.873 litres of water.

9 How many ml of water is this?

10 A sports bottle can hold 655 ml of water. How many litres less than the sink can the sports bottle hold?

11 Ryan has 1.023 litres of orange squash. 93 ml of squash is needed per serving. How many servings can he make?

It takes Rachel 2 days and 5 hours to travel from England to New Zealand.

12 How long does it take her in minutes?

13 Rachel spends 960 minutes of the journey asleep. How many hours of the journey is she awake for?

I can solve problems involving measurement.

Measurement — Review 1

Complete the conversions below:

1. 4.8 cm = □ mm
2. 2.7 km = □ m
3. 17.25 cm = □ mm
4. 8.75 m = □ cm
5. 4.38 km = □ m
6. 1.525 km = □ m
7. 1.295 m = □ cm
8. 0.645 cm = □ mm

Convert the following:

9. 453 cm to m
10. 3550 m to km
11. 9230 cm to m
12. 20.52 mm to cm
13. 75.6 cm to m
14. 7541 m to km
15. 62 m to km
16. 167.2 cm to m

Which symbol (< , > or =) should go in each box?

17. 3 cm □ 0.03 m
18. 71 km □ 7100 m
19. 45 mm □ 4.5 cm
20. 0.24 m □ 240 km
21. 1.7 cm □ 170 mm
22. 850 m □ 85 cm

8 km is approximately 5 miles.
Complete the conversions below:

23. 16 km ≈ □ miles
24. 24 km ≈ □ miles
25. 56 km ≈ □ miles
26. 400 km ≈ □ miles
27. 480 km ≈ □ miles
28. 880 km ≈ □ miles

Complete the conversions below.

29. 20 miles ≈ □ km
30. 40 miles ≈ □ km
31. 60 miles ≈ □ km
32. 150 miles ≈ □ km
33. 200 miles ≈ □ km
34. 500 miles ≈ □ km

Do the approximate conversions below:

35. 3.2 km to miles
36. 3.5 miles to km
37. 9.6 km to miles
38. 6.25 miles to km
39. 8.95 miles to km
40. 10.56 km to miles

Complete the conversions below:

41. 6.4 litres = □ ml
42. 8.25 kg = □ g
43. 2.36 litres = □ ml
44. 3.755 kg = □ g

Convert the following:

45. 1900 g to kg
46. 1340 ml to litres
47. 7234 g to kg
48. 29 ml to litres

Which is greater:

49. 3.456 litres or 345.6 ml?
50. 0.04 kg or 4 g?
51. 23.73 litres or 2373 ml?
52. 3.225 kg, 3.255 kg or 3252 g?

Convert the following:

53. $4\frac{1}{4}$ hours = □ minutes
54. $5\frac{1}{3}$ minutes = □ seconds
55. $2\frac{3}{4}$ days = □ hours
56. $7\frac{3}{7}$ weeks = □ days

Complete these conversions:

57. 4 minutes 41 seconds = □ seconds
58. 8 days 3 hours = □ hours
59. 6 weeks 4 days = □ days
60. 90 days = □ weeks □ days
61. 173 hours = □ days □ hours
62. 4 hours = □ minutes = □ seconds
63. 2 days = □ minutes

64. Samir has a 1.85 m long piece of ribbon.
He cuts a 125 cm piece off the ribbon.
How many cm of ribbon does he have left?

65. Polly watches two films.
The first film is 1 hour 50 minutes long.
The second film is 105 minutes longer.
How long is the second film
in hours and minutes?

66. One serving of cereal weighs 27 g.
Freddie has 0.972 kg of cereal.
How many servings does he have?

Great work recapping all of those measurement topics!

Area of a Triangle

To work out the area of a triangle you need to know the height of the triangle and the length of its base. You can then use a formula to work out the area. Let's take a look at what you need to do...

Examples

Work out the area of the triangles below.

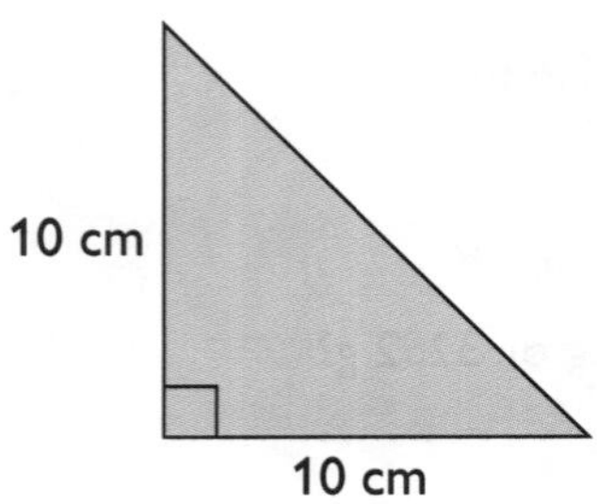

$\text{Area} = \frac{1}{2} \times 10 \times 10 = \mathbf{50\ cm^2}$.

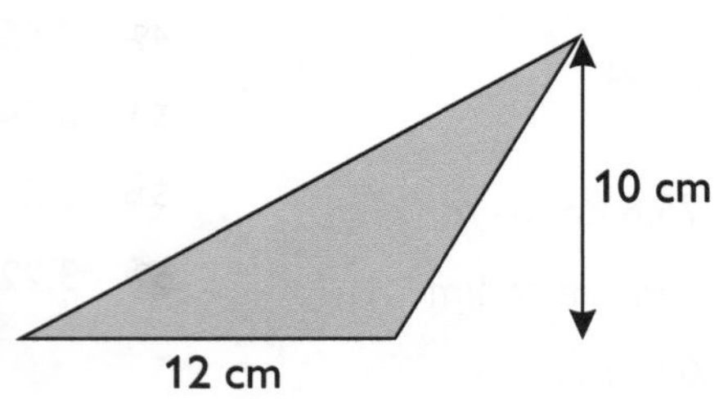

$\text{Area} = \frac{1}{2} \times 12 \times 10 = \mathbf{60\ cm^2}$.

To work out the area of a triangle, just use the formula:

$\text{Area of triangle} = \frac{1}{2} \times \text{base} \times \text{height}$.

The area of this triangle is 30 cm². Find the height of the triangle.

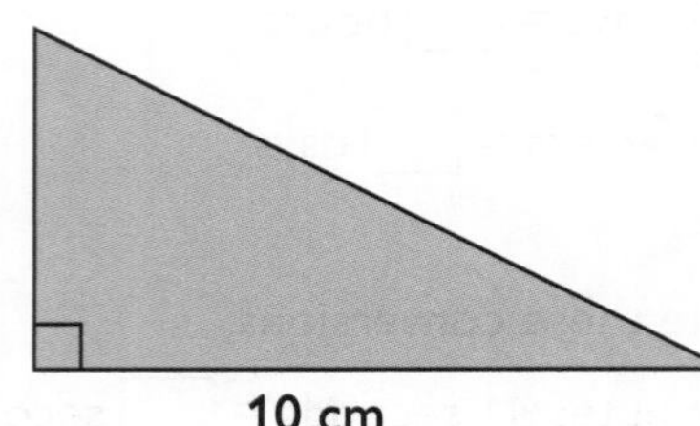

Put the values you know into the area formula:

$30 = \frac{1}{2} \times 10 \times \text{height}$

$30 = 5 \times \text{height}$

So height $= 30 \div 5 = \mathbf{6\ cm}$

Set A

Use the calculations to find the area of these triangles:

1

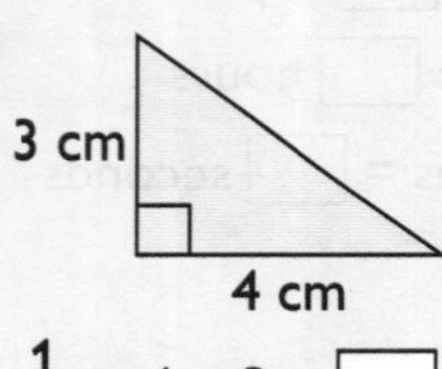

$\frac{1}{2} \times 4 \times 3 = \square$

2

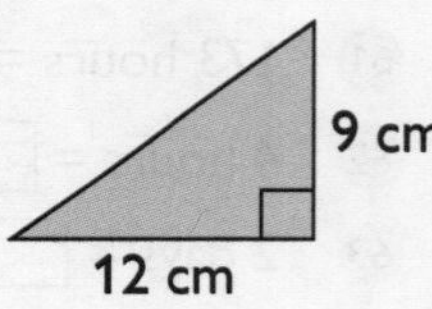

$\frac{1}{2} \times 12 \times 9 = \square$

3

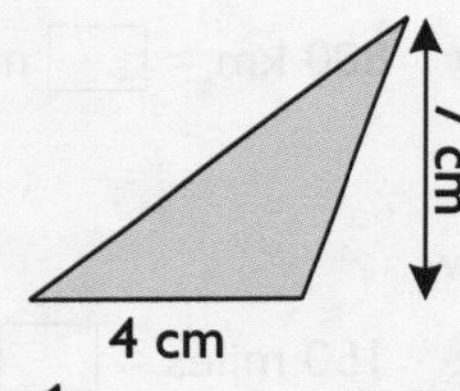

$\frac{1}{2} \times 4 \times 7 = \square$

4

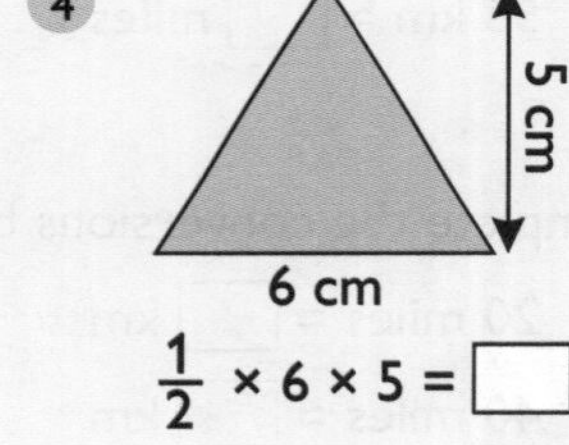

$\frac{1}{2} \times 6 \times 5 = \square$

Work out the area of these triangles:

5

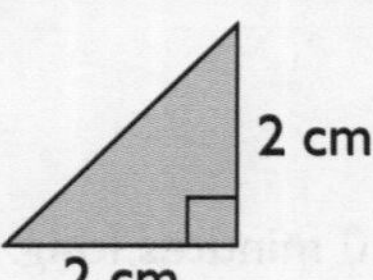

6

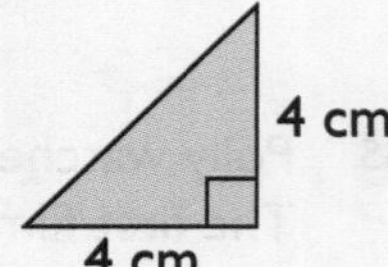

7

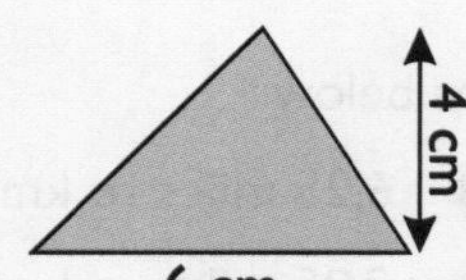

8

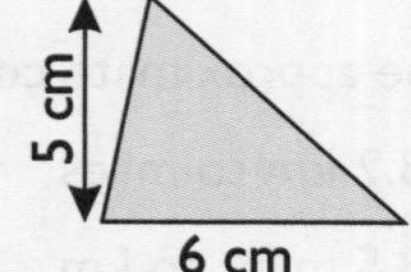

9 Find all of the triangles with an area of 6 cm².

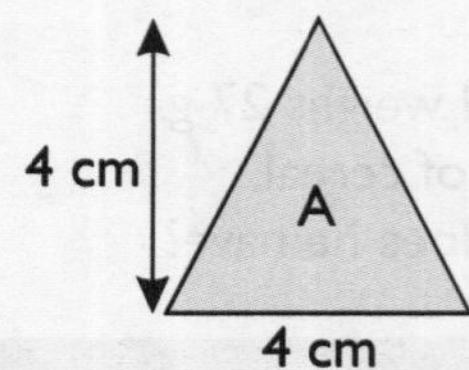

3 cm B 4 cm

2 cm C 6 cm

D 3 cm 3 cm

Set B

Find the area of these triangles:

1
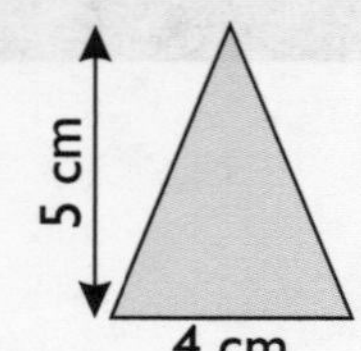

2
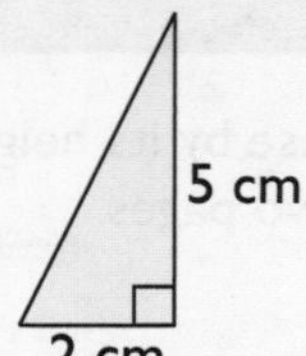

3
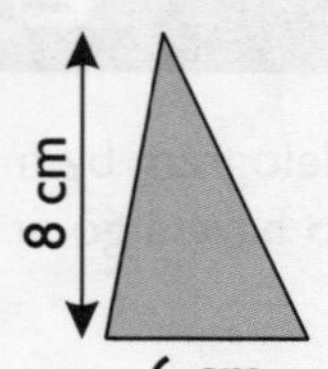

4
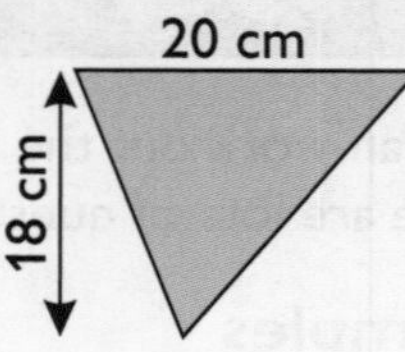

5
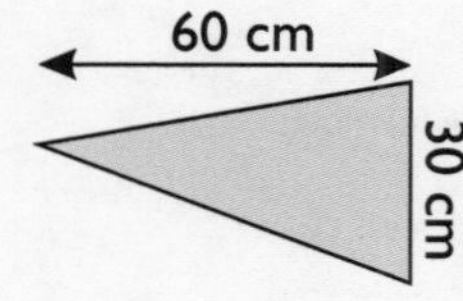

6
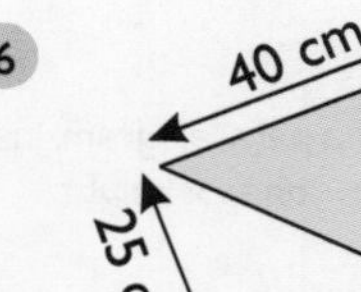

7
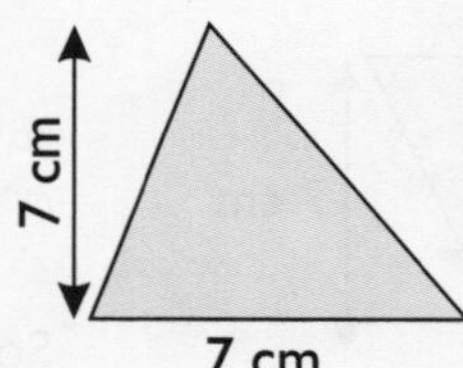

8
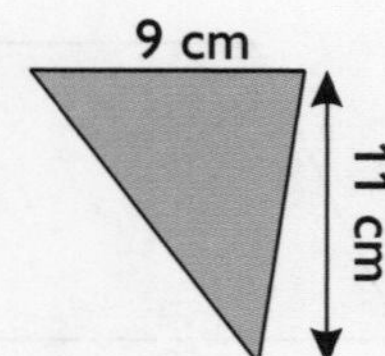

Find the area of a triangle with:

9 a height of 7 cm and a base of 8 cm.

10 a height of 20 cm and a base of 15 cm.

11 a height of 11 cm and a base of 11 cm.

12 The area of the triangle below is 16 cm^2. Find the length of the base.

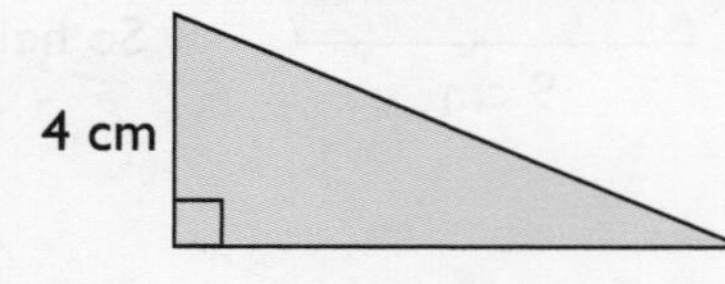

13 Find the area of each triangle in the rectangle below.

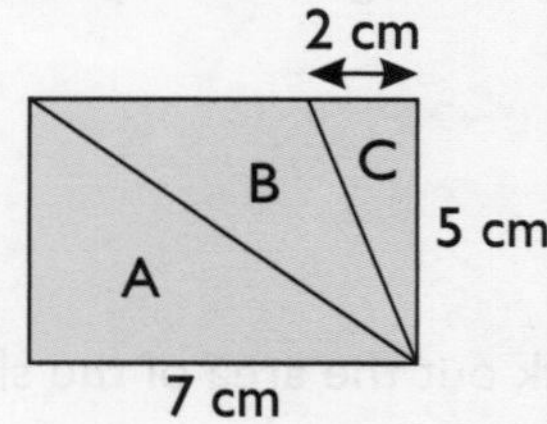

Set C

Find the area of these triangles:

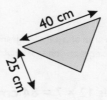

1
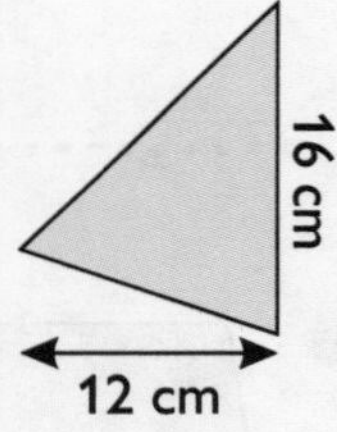

2
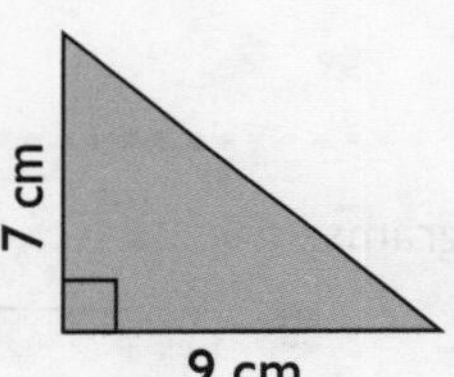

3
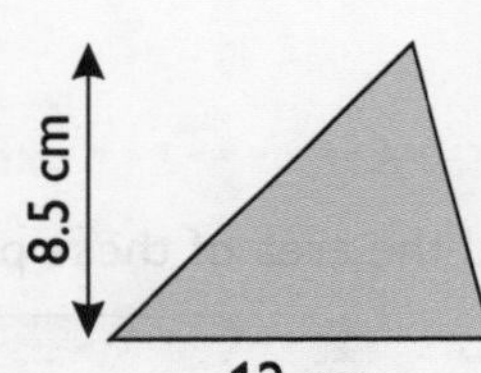

4
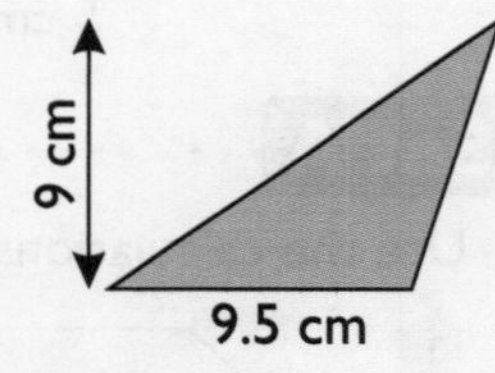

5 The rectangles below are each made up from three triangles. Find the area of each triangle.

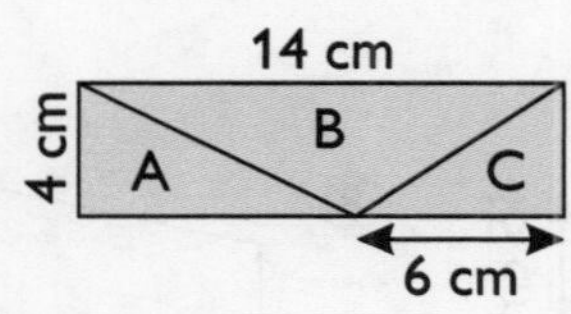

6 Copy and complete the table below to show the height, base and area of different triangles:

Height	Base	Area
7 cm	12 cm	
	9 cm	36 cm^2
6 cm		12 cm^2

Find the area of the shaded part of these shapes:

7
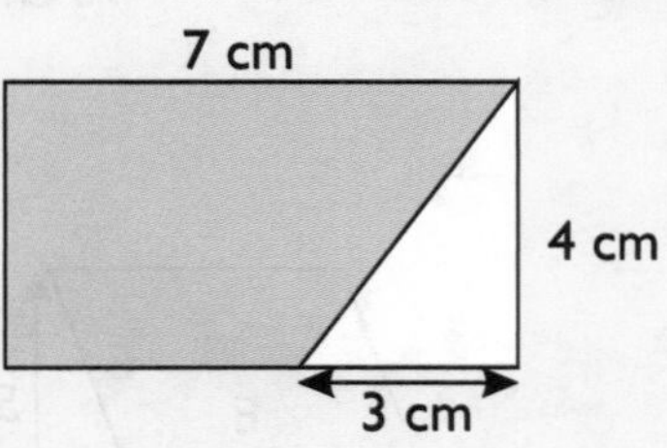

8
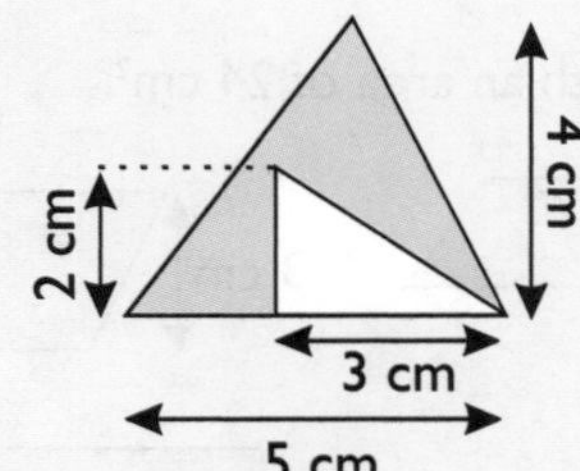

9
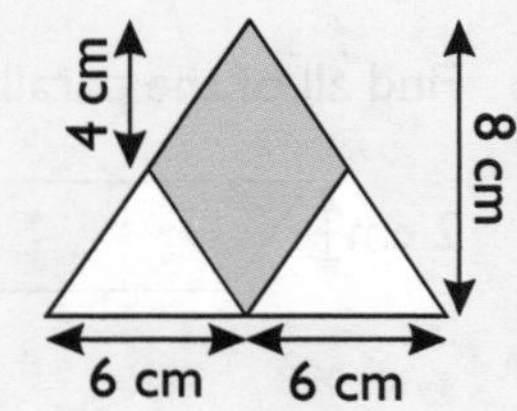

I can find the area of a triangle.

Area of a Parallelogram

You can work out the area of a parallelogram by multiplying its base by its height.
There are lots of questions for you to have a go at on the next two pages.

Examples

Work out the area of this parallelogram.

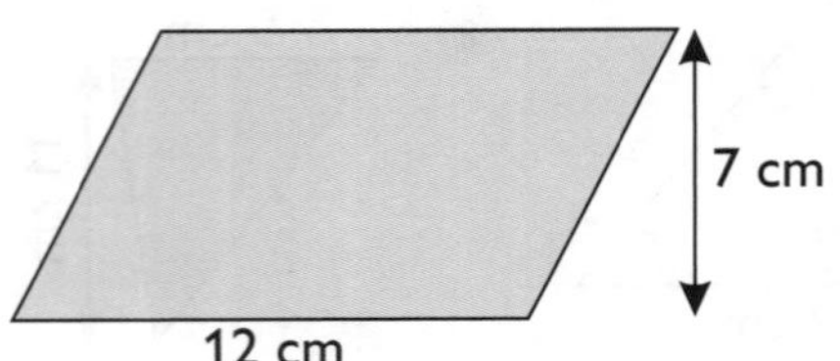

To work out the area of a parallelogram, just use the formula:
Area of a parallelogram = base × height.

So the area is 12 × 7 = **84 cm²**

The area of this parallelogram is 72 cm².
Find the height of the parallelogram.

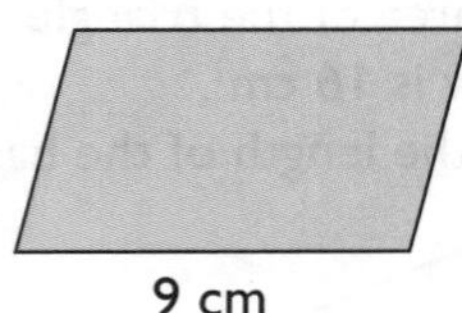

Put the values you know into the area formula:

72 = 9 × height

So height = 72 ÷ 9 = **8 cm**

Work out the area of the shaded part of this shape:

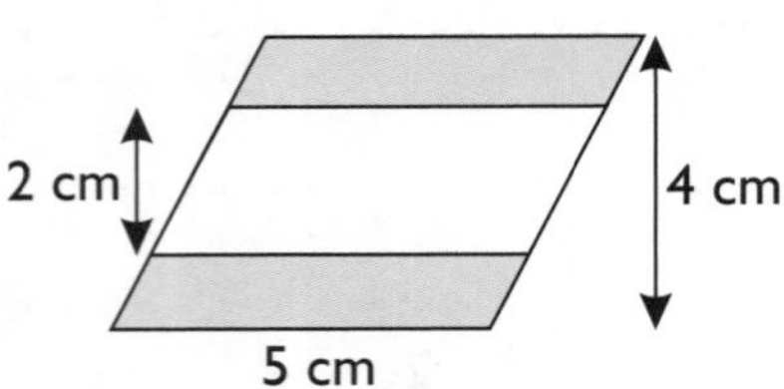

The area of the whole parallelogram is 5 × 4 = 20 cm².

The area of the white part is 5 × 2 = 10 cm².

So the area of the shaded part is 20 cm² – 10 cm² = **10 cm²**.

Set A

Use the calculations to find the area of these parallelograms:

1
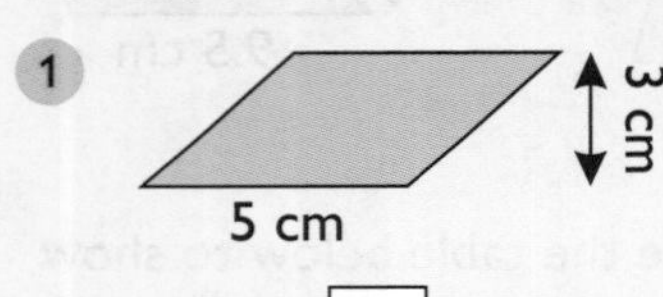

5 × 3 = ☐

2
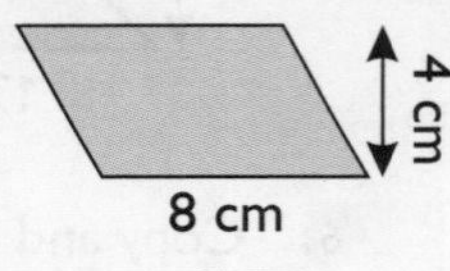

8 × 4 = ☐

3
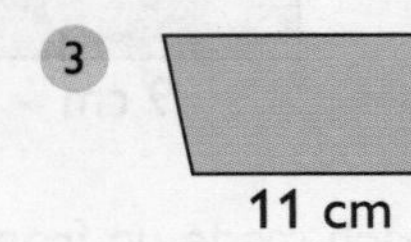

11 × 7 = ☐

4
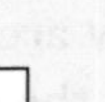

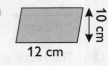

10 cm
12 cm

12 × 10 = ☐

Find the area of these parallelograms:

5
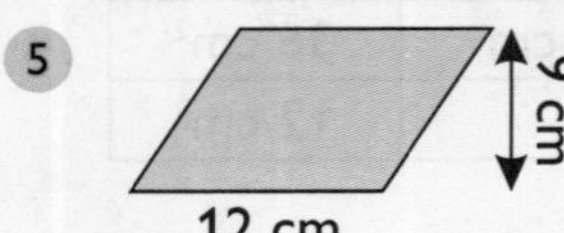

6
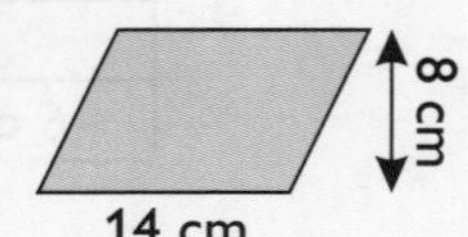

7
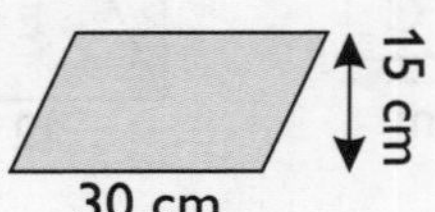

8
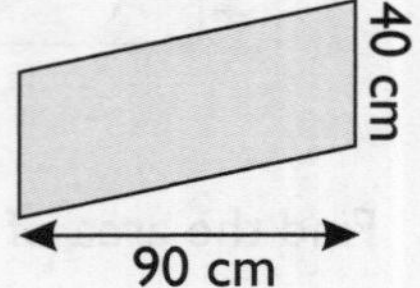

9 Find all of the parallelograms with an area of 24 cm².

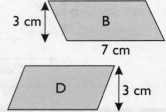

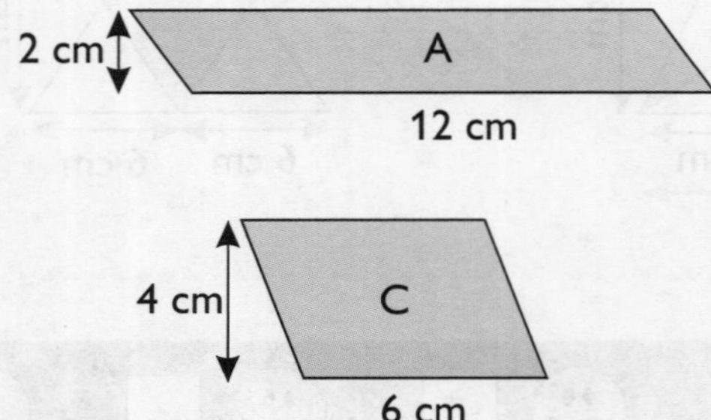

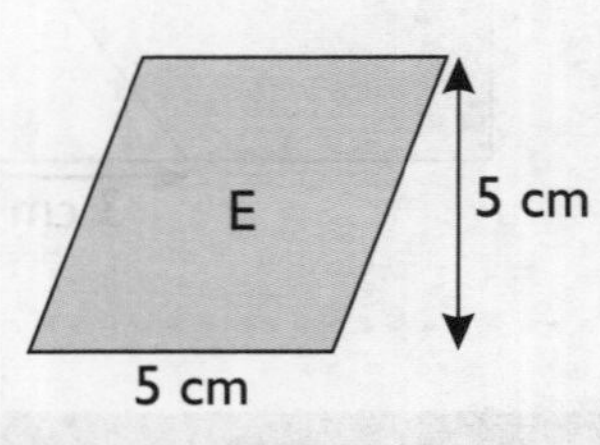

Set B

Find the area of these parallelograms:

1 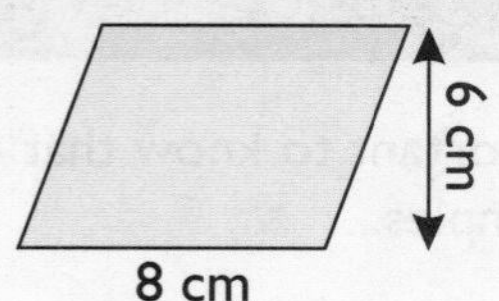

2 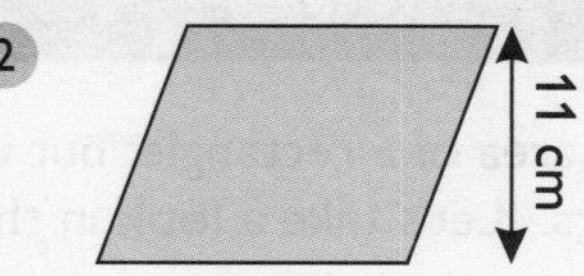

3 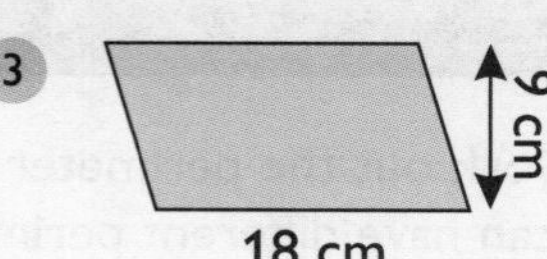

4 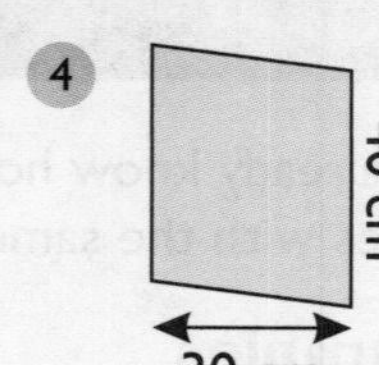

5 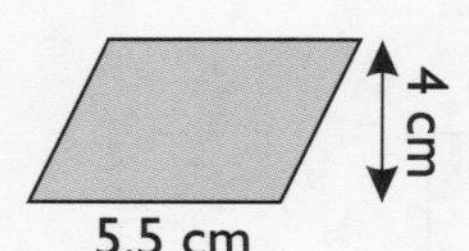

6 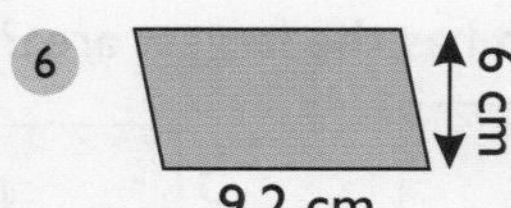

7 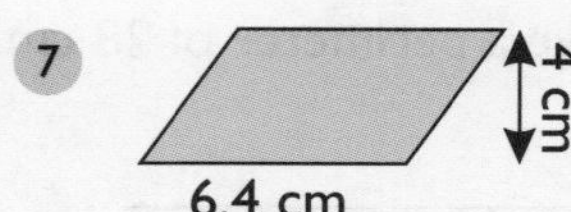

8

9 The table on the right shows the heights and base lengths of three parallelograms.

Copy and complete the table to show the area of the different parallelograms.

Height	Base	Area
4 cm	7 cm	
5 cm	13 cm	
4.5 cm	8 cm	

10 The parallelograms on the right both have an area of 18 cm².

Find the height of each parallelogram.

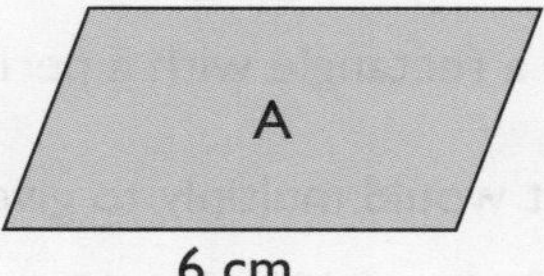

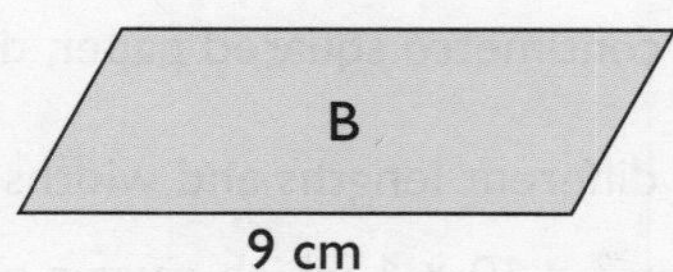

Set C

Find the area of these parallelograms in cm²:

1 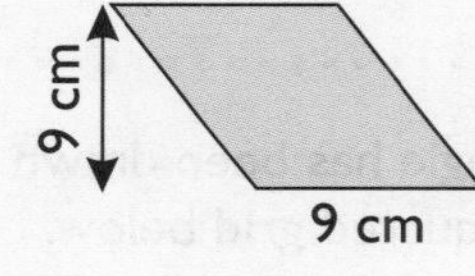

2 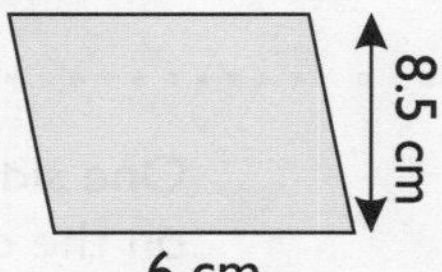

3 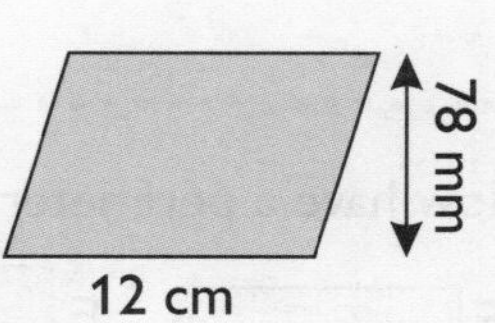

4 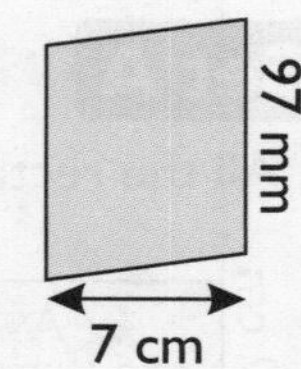

Work out the total area of these shapes:

5 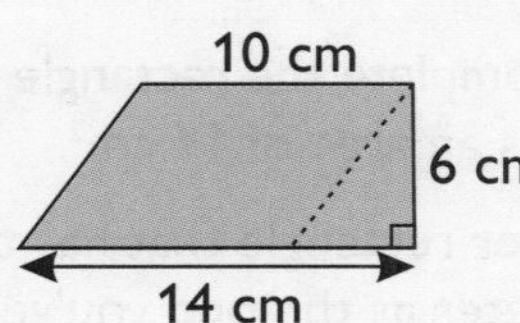

6 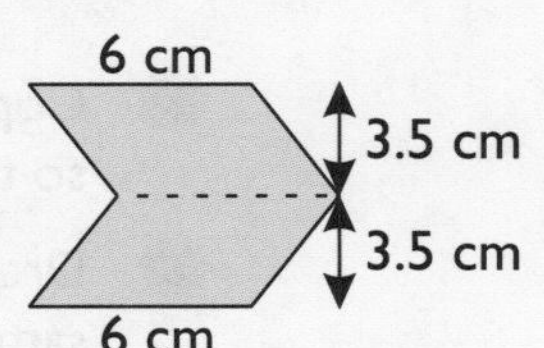

7 Copy and complete the table below to show the height, base and area of these parallelograms:

Height	Base	Area
6 cm	8 cm	
	7 cm	42 cm²
9 cm		27 cm²

Find the area of the shaded part of these shapes:

8 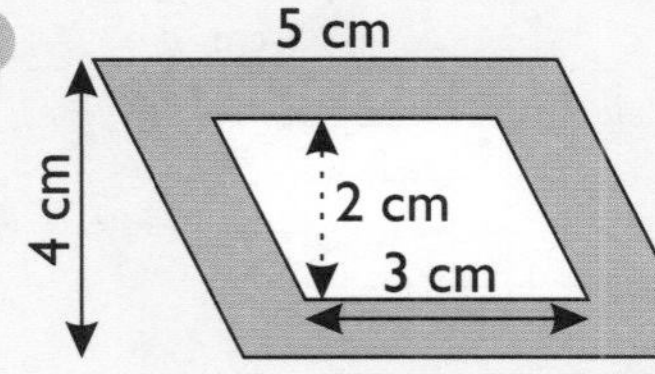

9 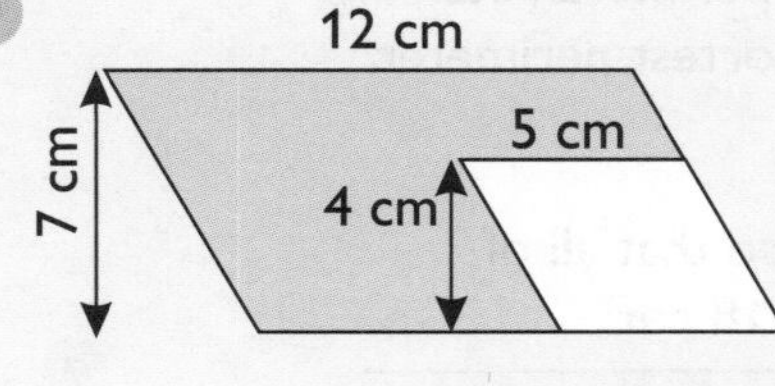

10 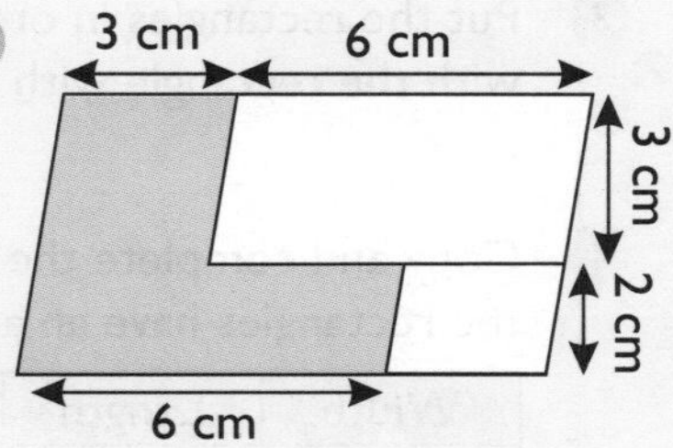

I can find the area of a parallelogram.

Perimeter and Area

You already know how to work out the perimeter and area of a rectangle, but it's important to know that shapes with the same area can have different perimeters. Let's take a look in the examples...

Examples

All of these rectangles have a perimeter of 28 cm. Which has the largest area?

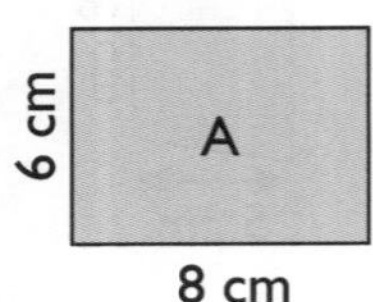

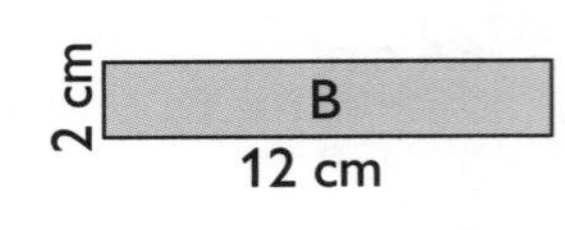

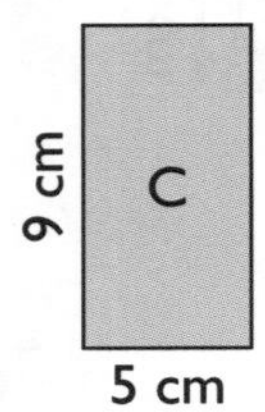

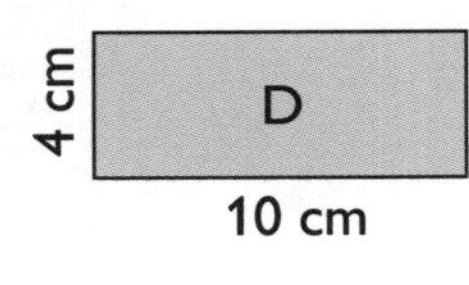

Area of A = $6 \times 8 = 48$ cm^2

Area of B = $2 \times 12 = 24$ cm^2

Area of C = $9 \times 5 = 45$ cm^2

Area of D = $4 \times 10 = 40$ cm^2

So **rectangle A** has the largest area.

On centimetre squared paper, draw a rectangle with a perimeter of 14 cm and an area of 10 cm^2.

Try different lengths and widths that would multiply to give an area of 10 cm^2:

10 cm^2 = 10×1 which gives a perimeter of $10 + 1 + 10 + 1 = 22$ cm

10 cm^2 = 5×2 which gives a perimeter of $5 + 2 + 5 + 2 = 14$ cm

So a rectangle with length 5 cm and width 2 cm has a perimeter of 14 cm and an area of 10 cm^2.

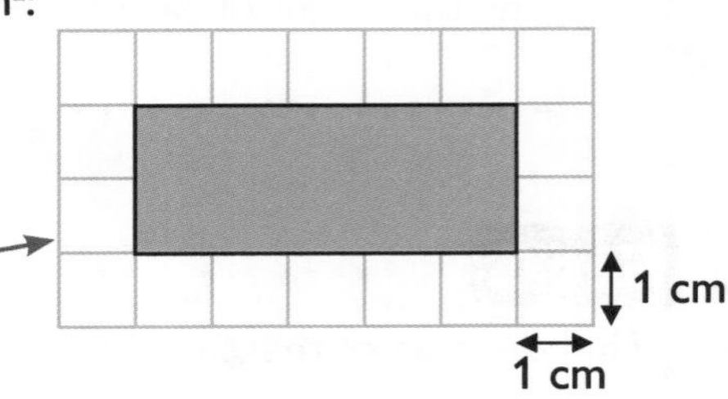

Set A

All the rectangles below have a perimeter of 20 cm.

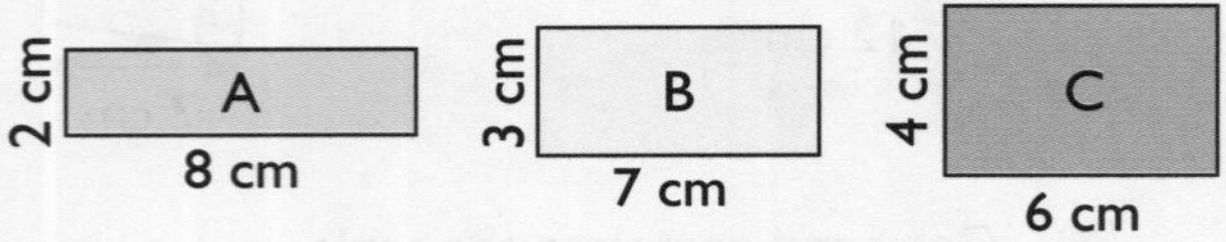

1. Which rectangle has the largest area?
2. Which rectangle has the smallest area?

All the rectangles below have an area of 24 cm^2.

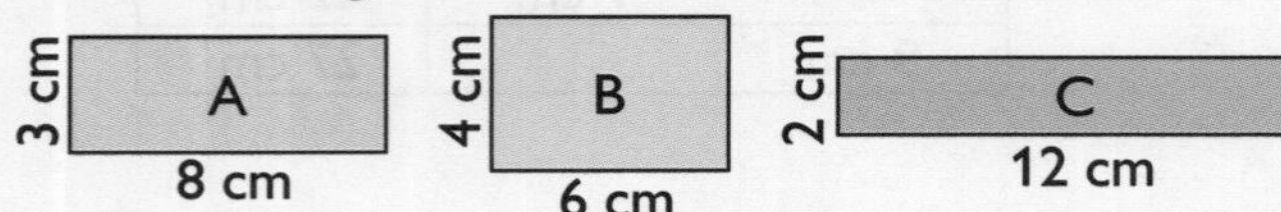

3. Put the rectangles in order of perimeter, starting with the rectangle with the shortest perimeter.

4. Copy and complete the table so that all of the rectangles have an area of 18 cm^2.

Width	Length	Perimeter	Area
1 cm			18 cm^2
2 cm			18 cm^2
	6 cm		18 cm^2

One side of a rectangle has been drawn on the centimetre squared grid below.

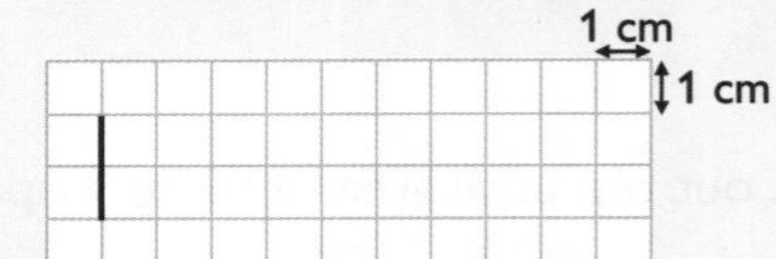

5. Copy and complete the rectangle so that it has an area of 14 cm^2.
6. Draw another rectangle that has the same perimeter as the one you've just drawn. What is its area?

The side of another rectangle has been drawn on the centimetre squared grid below.

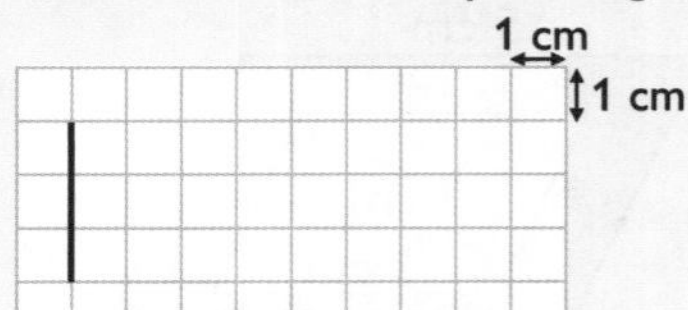

7. Copy and complete the rectangle so that it has a perimeter of 12 cm.
8. Draw another rectangle that has the same area as the one you've just drawn. What is its perimeter?

Set B

All of the shapes below have the same perimeter.

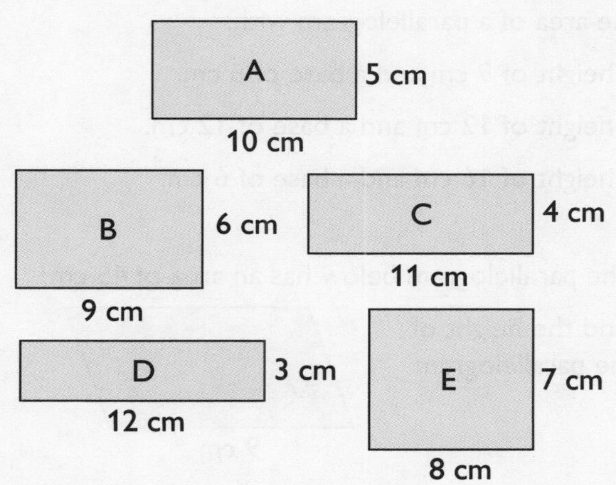

1. What is the perimeter of each shape?
2. Which shape has the biggest area?
3. Which shape has the smallest area?
4. Which shape has an area of 54 cm^2?
5. Which shape has an area 14 cm^2 bigger than shape D?

6. On centimetre squared paper, draw three different rectangles with areas of 16 cm^2. Calculate the perimeter of each rectangle you have drawn.

On centimetre squared paper, draw a rectangle with:

7. a perimeter of 12 cm and an area of 8 cm^2.
8. a perimeter of 20 cm and an area of 24 cm^2.

9. Copy and complete the table so that all of the rectangles have perimeters of 22 cm.

Width	Length	Area
2 cm		
4 cm		
	6 cm	
	8 cm	

Set C

1. A rectangle has an area of 12 cm^2 and a perimeter of 14 cm. What is the length and width of the rectangle?

The incomplete table below shows the measurements of rectangles with a perimeter of 24 cm. The lengths are always longer than the widths.

Width	Length	Area
1 cm		
2 cm		
	9 cm	
		35 cm^2
		32 cm^2

2. Copy and complete the table.
3. Complete this statement:
   "The rectangle with the longest possible length gives the rectangle with the ☐ possible area."

4. Rectangle A has an area of 28 cm^2 and a perimeter of 32 cm. Rectangle B has the same area but a larger perimeter. The side lengths of both rectangles are given in cm and are whole numbers. What is the perimeter of Rectangle B?

On a centimetre squared grid, draw a rectangle made up of whole grid squares with:

5. a perimeter of 30 cm and the largest area possible.
6. a perimeter of 30 cm and the smallest area possible.
7. an area of 10 cm^2 and the largest perimeter possible.
8. an area of 36 cm^2 and the smallest perimeter possible.

9. Three sides of a shape have been drawn on the centimetre squared grid below.

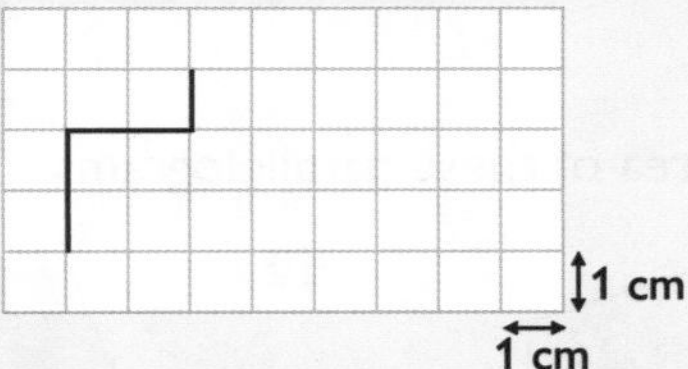

Draw three more lines to make a shape with a perimeter of 18 cm and an area of 16 cm^2.

I know that shapes with the same area can have different perimeters and vice versa.

Measurement — Review 2

Find the area of these triangles.

1 3

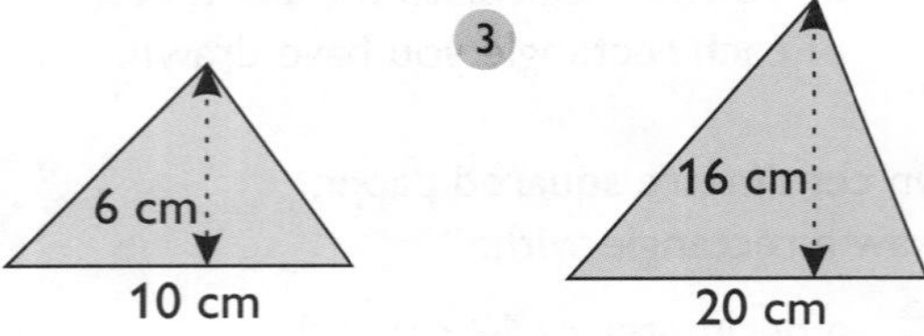

2 4

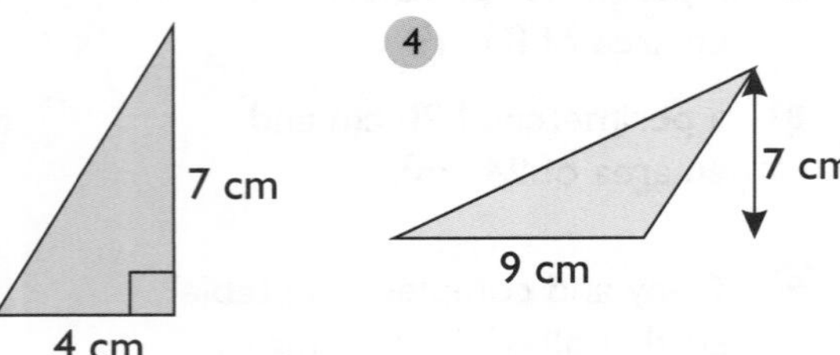

5 Which of the triangles below has an area of 15 cm^2?

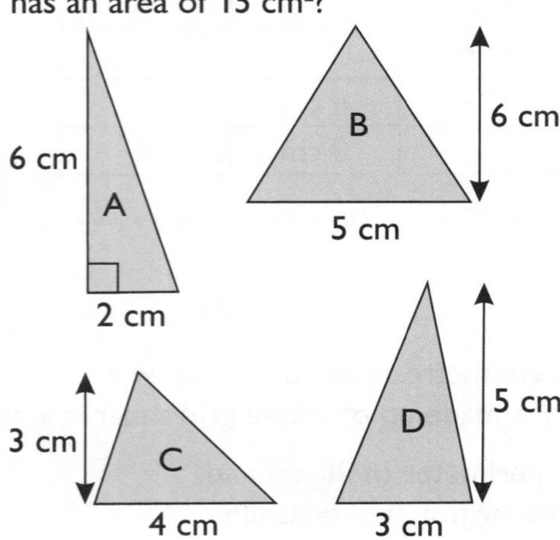

Find the area of a triangle with:

6 a height of 4 cm and a base of 9 cm.

7 a height of 12 cm and a base of 7 cm.

8 The rectangle on the right is made from three triangles.

Find the area of each triangle.

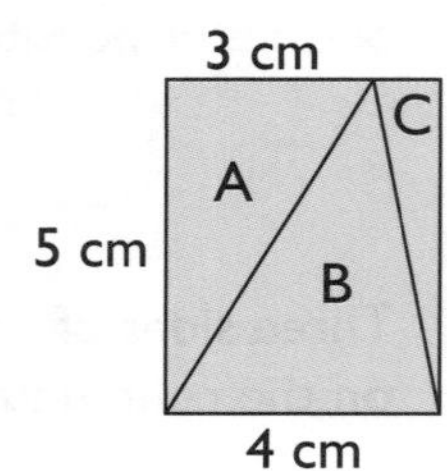

Find the area of these parallelograms:

9

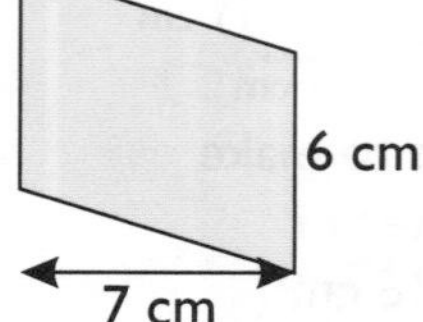

10

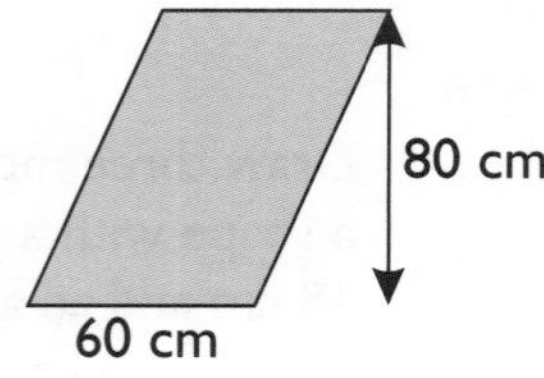

Find the area of a parallelogram with:

11 a height of 9 cm and a base of 6 cm.

12 a height of 12 cm and a base of 12 cm.

13 a height of 16 cm and a base of 6 cm.

14 The parallelogram below has an area of 45 cm^2.

Find the height of the parallelogram.

15 Find the total area of this shape:

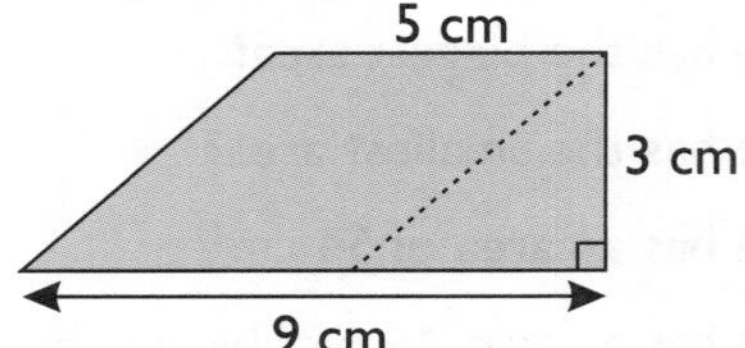

All the rectangles below have a perimeter of 26 cm.

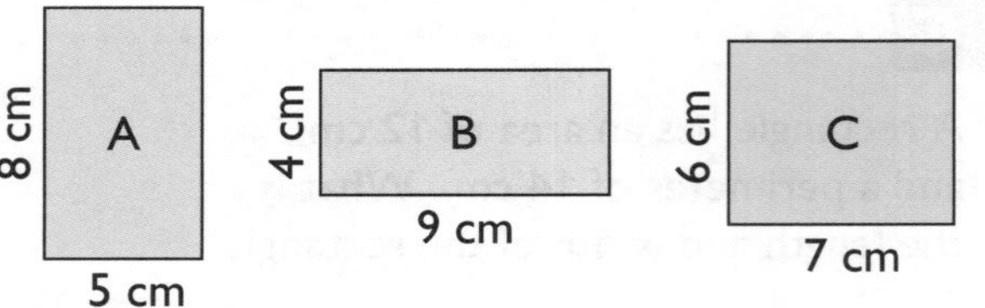

16 Which rectangle has the largest area?

17 Which rectangle has the smallest area?

All the rectangles below have an area of 48 cm^2.

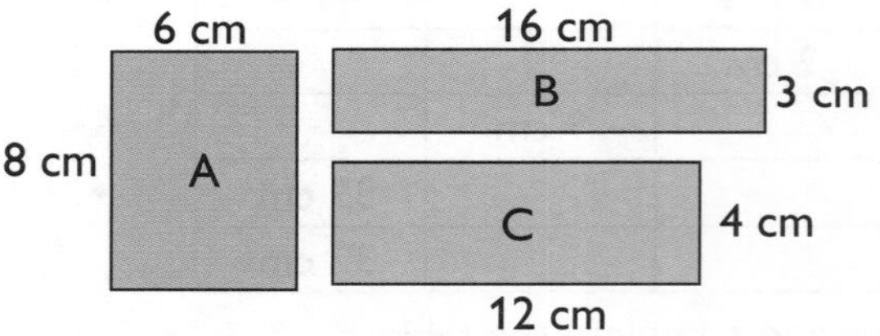

18 Put the rectangles in order of perimeter, starting with the rectangle with the longest perimeter.

On centimetre squared paper, draw a rectangle with:

19 a perimeter of 16 cm and an area of 7 cm^2.

20 a perimeter of 18 cm and an area of 20 cm^2.

21 a perimeter of 26 cm and the largest area possible.

Wow, you really are an area and perimeter expert!

Calculating Volume

Volume is the amount of space that something takes up.
You can work out the volume of a cube or cuboid by multiplying the length, width and height together.

Examples

Work out the volume of the cuboid below.

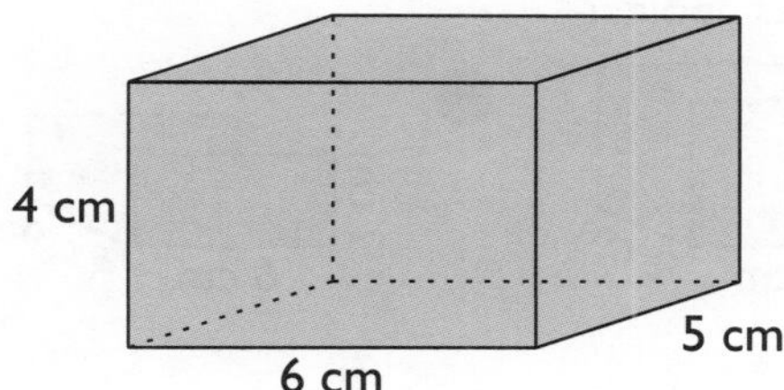

Use the formula: Volume = Length × Width × Height

Length = 5 cm

Width = 6 cm

Height = 4 cm So volume = 5 × 6 × 4 = **120 cm³**

The cuboid below has a volume of 96 cm³.
Work out the height of the cuboid.

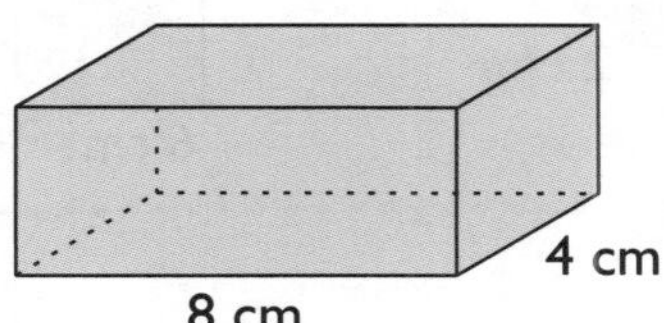

Put the values you know into the volume formula:

96 = 4 × 8 × height

24 = 8 × height

So height = 24 ÷ 8 = **3 cm**

Set A

Find the volume of the following cubes and cuboids.

They are made out of 1 cm³ cubes.

1 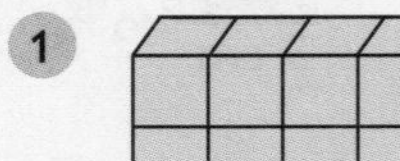

2 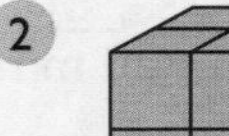

3 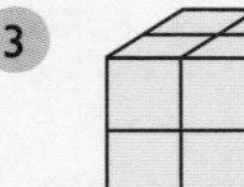

4 

Find the missing numbers in the formula to find the volume of the cuboids below.

5 2 cm, 2 cm, 3 cm

3 × 2 × ☐ = ☐

6 2 cm, 4 cm, 3 cm

3 × 4 × ☐ = ☐

7 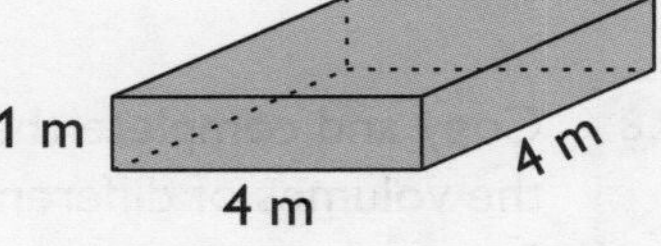

4 × ☐ × 1 = ☐

Work out the volume of these cubes and cuboids:

8 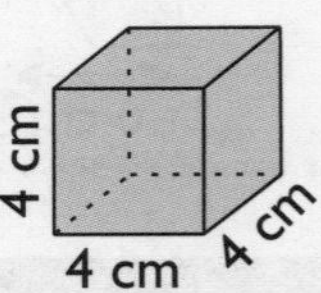

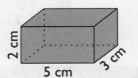

9 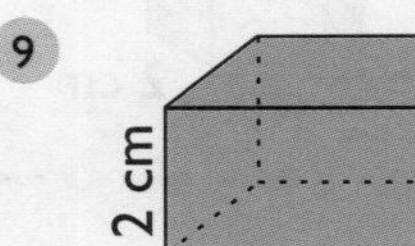

10  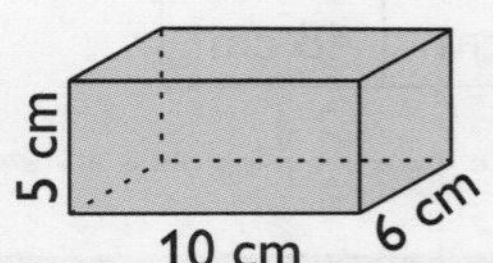

11  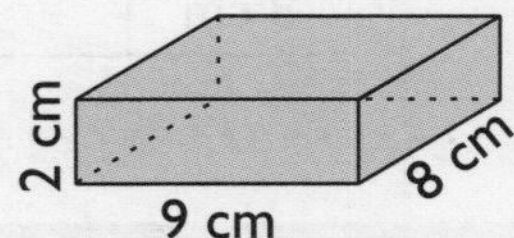

Set B

Work out the volume of the cubes and cuboids below.

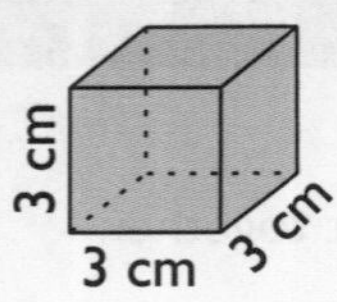

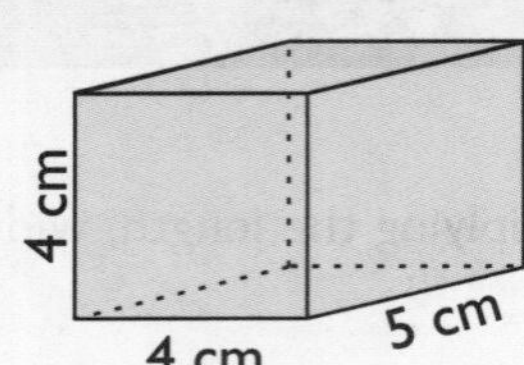

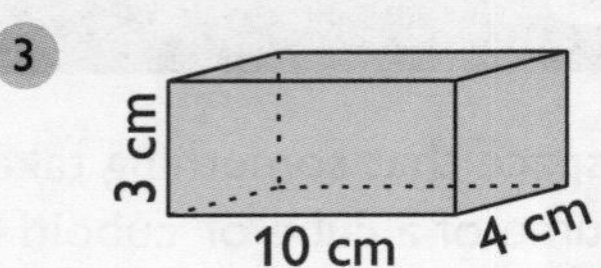

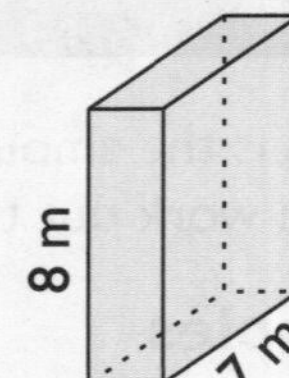

Find the volume of the cuboids below. They are made out of 2 cm³ cubes.

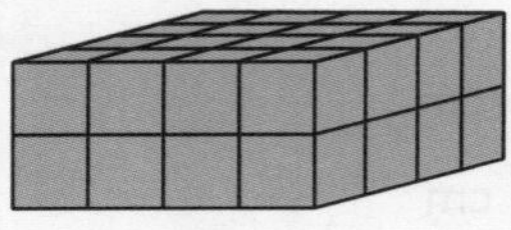

How many 1 cm cubes would fit into these cuboids?

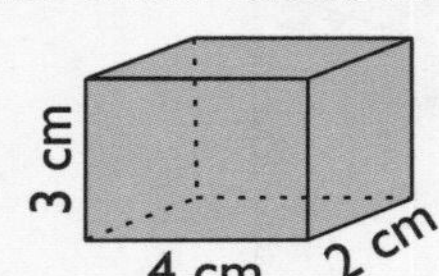

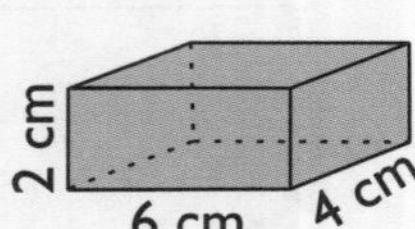

9 This cuboid has a volume of 144 cm³. What is the length of side x?

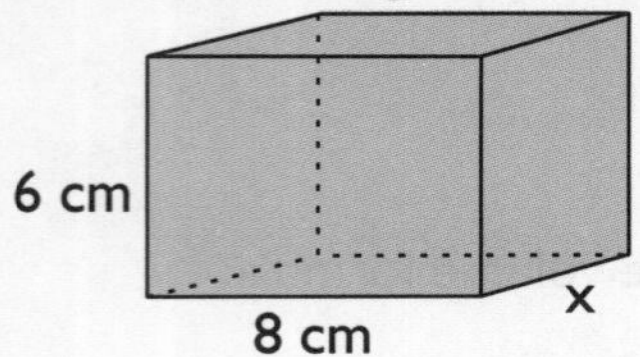

Find the total volume of each shape:

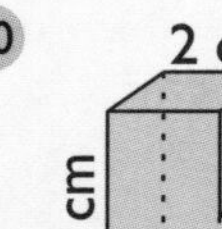

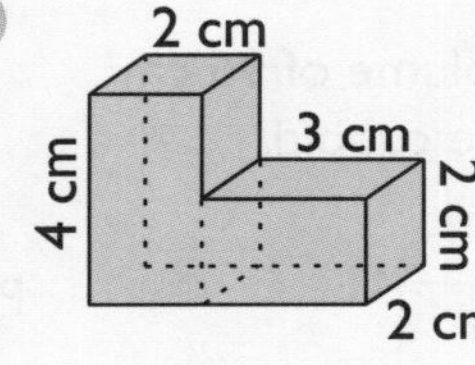

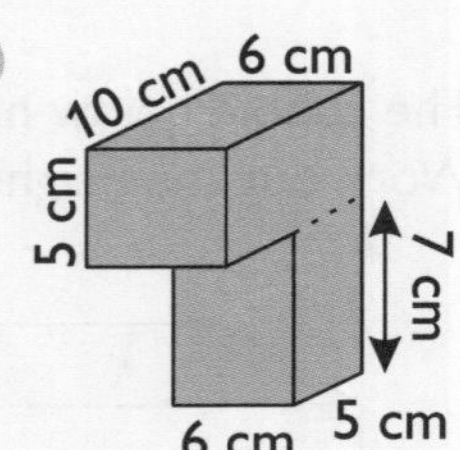

Set C

Find the volume of these cuboids in cm³:

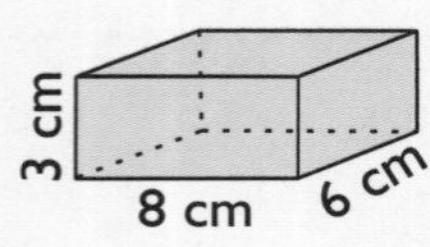

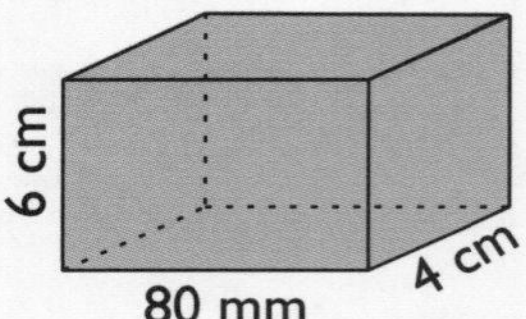

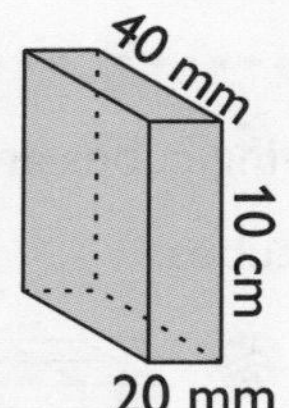

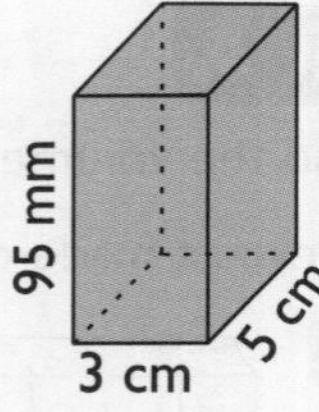

Find the volume of the cuboids below. They are made out of 5 cm³ cubes.

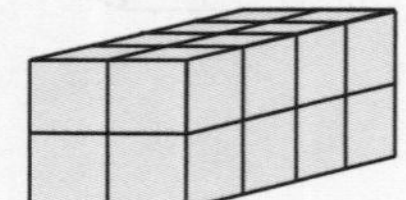

7 This cuboid has a volume of 60 cm³. What is the length of side x in cm?

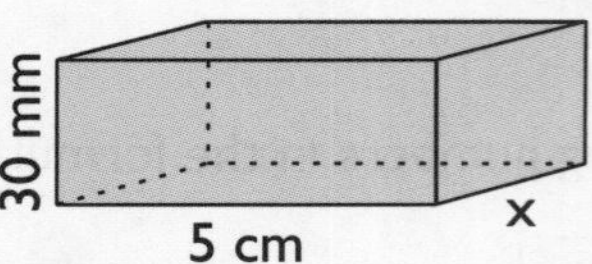

8 Copy and complete the table to show the volumes of different cuboids.

Length	Width	Height	Volume
5 m	4 m	3 m	
3 mm	2 mm		6 mm³
	6 cm	7 cm	84 cm³
8 cm		2 cm	48 cm³

Find the total volume of each shape:

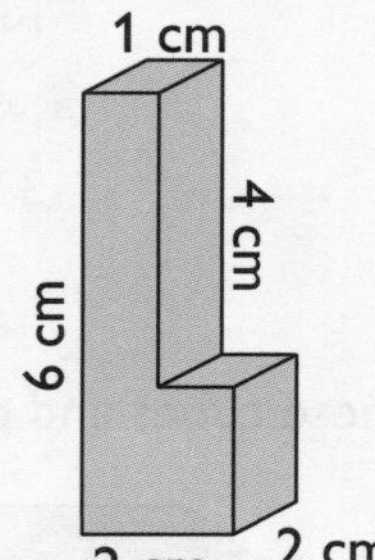

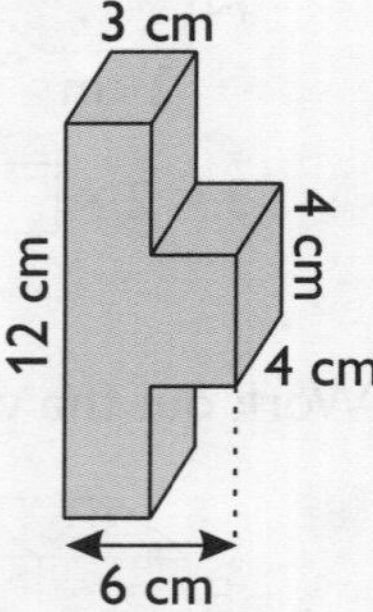

I can calculate the volume of cubes and cuboids.

Comparing Volume

Now it's time to put your knowledge of calculating volume to the test — let's take a look...

Examples

The cuboids below are made from cubes with a volume of 1 cm³.
What is the difference in volume between the two cuboids?

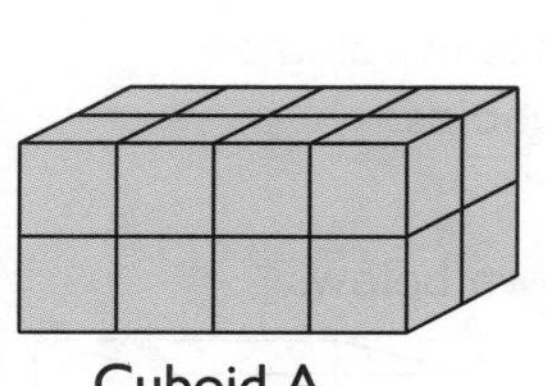
Cuboid A

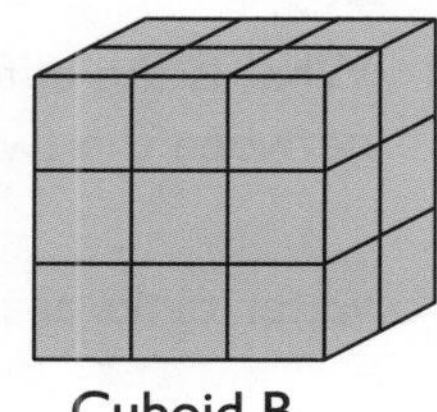
Cuboid B

Cuboid A is made of 2 × 4 × 2 = 16 cubes.
So cuboid A has a total volume of 16 cm³.

Cuboid B is made of 2 × 3 × 3 = 18 cubes.
So cuboid B has a total volume of 18 cm³.

So the difference in volume is 18 – 16 = **2 cm³**

Look at the two cuboids below.

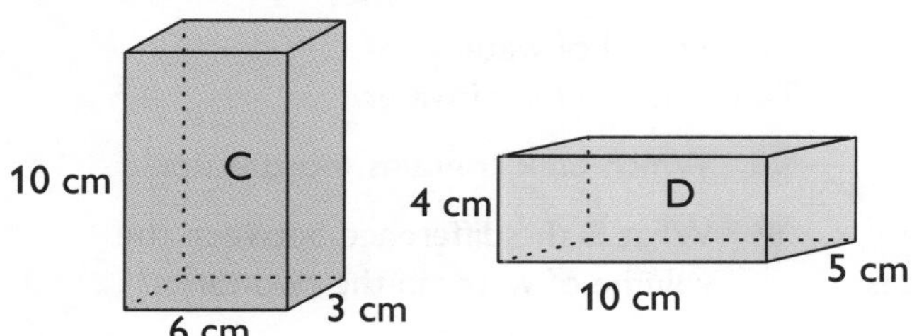

Which cuboid has the bigger volume?

Cuboid C = 3 × 6 × 10 = 180 cm³

Cuboid D = 5 × 10 × 4 = 200 cm³

So **cuboid D** has the bigger volume.

Set A

The cuboids below are made from cubes with a volume of 1 cm³.

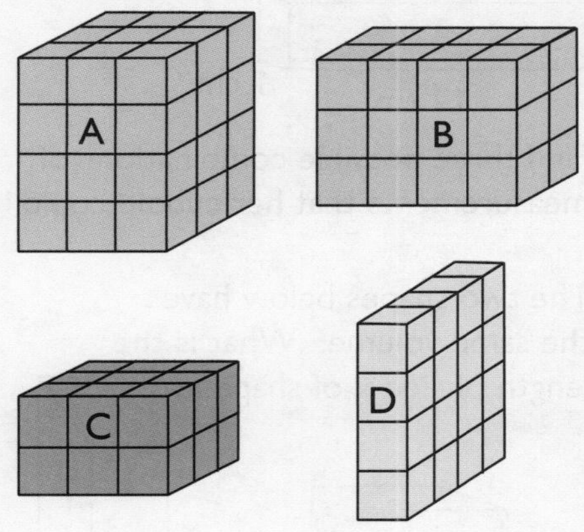

1. Which has the biggest volume — cuboid A or cuboid B?
2. Which has the smallest volume — cuboid C or cuboid D?
3. What is the difference in volume between cuboid A and cuboid C?
4. What is the difference in volume between cuboid B and cuboid D?
5. The volume of cuboid K is half the volume of cuboid B. What is the volume of cuboid K?

Look at the cuboids below.

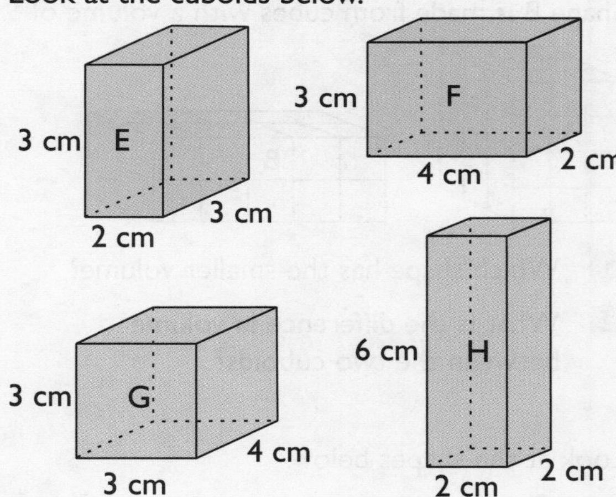

6. Which cuboids have the same volume?
7. Which cuboid has the biggest volume?
8. Which cuboid has the smallest volume?

Look at the cuboids below.

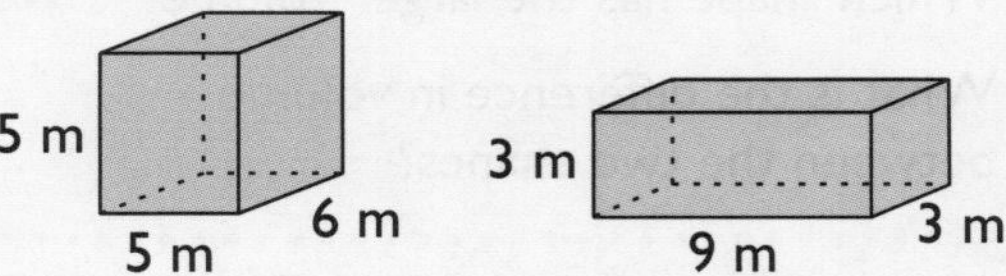

9. What is the difference in volume between the two cuboids?

Set B

Look at the cubes and cuboids below.

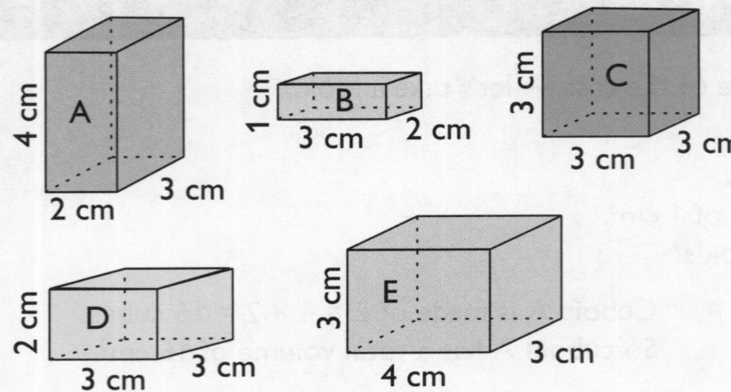

Which of the shapes above has:

1. the smallest volume?
2. the biggest volume?
3. a volume bigger than shape A but smaller than shape E?

Shapes F and G are made of 2 cm³ cubes.

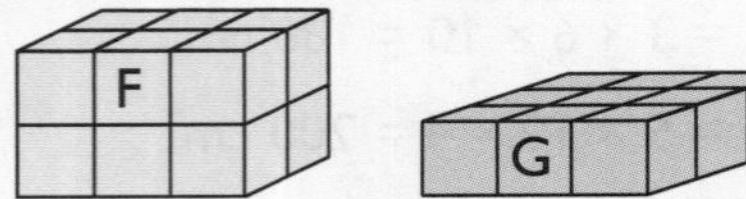

4. What is the difference in volume between the shapes?

Look at the cuboids below.

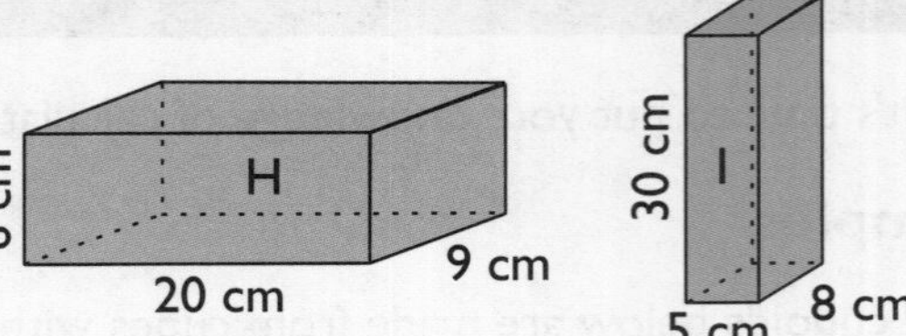

5. Which shape has the smaller volume?
6. What is the difference in volume between the two cuboids?

Two water tanks are shown below.

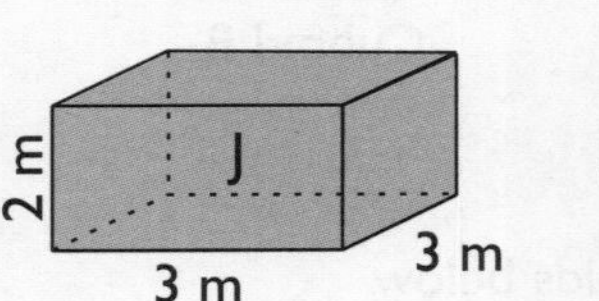

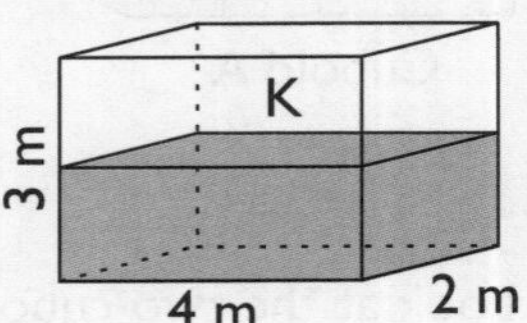

Tank J is full of water.
Tank K is half full of water.

7. Which tank contains more water?
8. What is the difference between the volume of water in the two tanks?

Set C

Shape A is made from cubes with a volume of 3 cm³.
Shape B is made from cubes with a volume of 5 cm³.

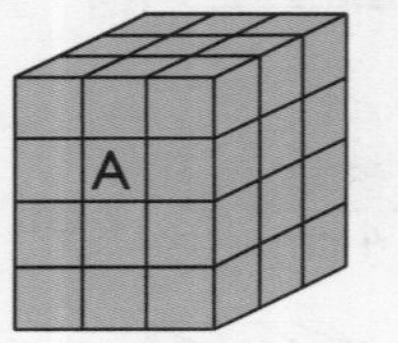

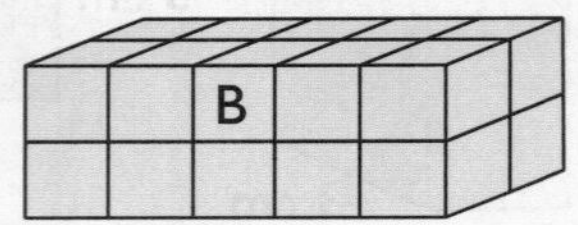

1. Which shape has the smaller volume?
2. What is the difference in volume between the two cuboids?

Look at the shapes below.

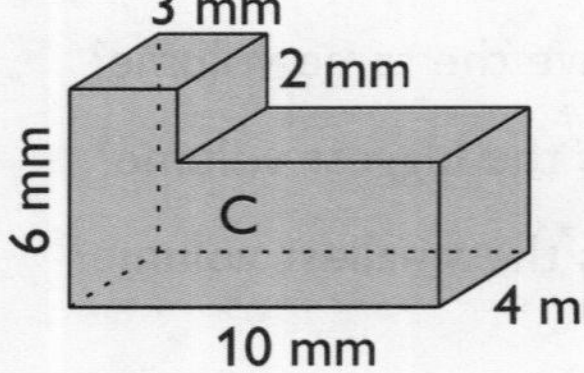

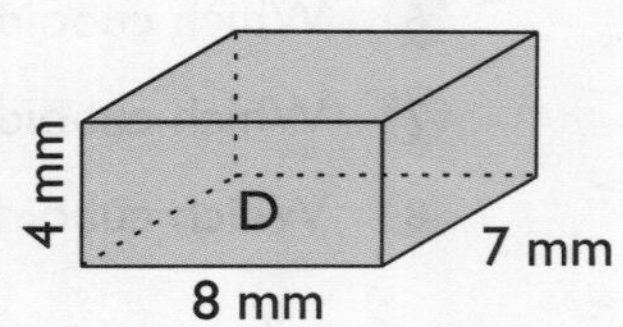

3. Which shape has the larger volume?
4. What is the difference in volume between the two shapes?

Laura wants to draw another cuboid with the same volume as the cuboid below.

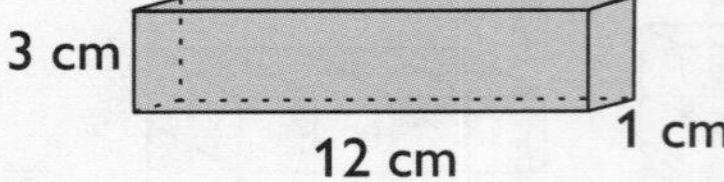

5. Find three possible combinations of measurements that her cuboid could have.
6. The two shapes below have the same volume. What is the length of side x of shape F?

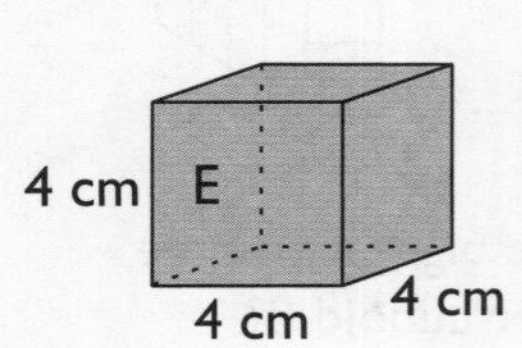

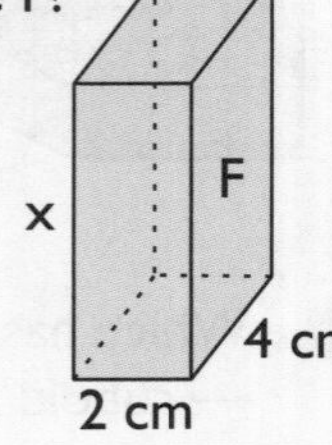

7. Monib has two cuboids, G and H. Cuboid G is half the volume of cuboid H. Cuboid G has side lengths of 8 cm, 10 cm and 5 cm. Cuboid H is 4 cm tall and 4 cm wide — how long is it?

I can compare the volume of different shapes.

Measurement — Review 3

Find the volumes of the cuboids below.

1 This cuboid is made from 1 cm^3 cubes.

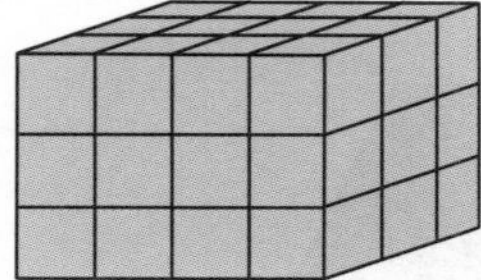

2 This cuboid is made from 2 cm^3 cubes.

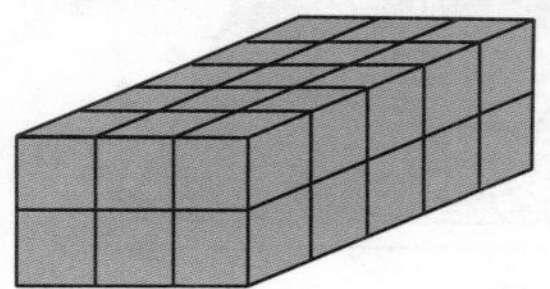

3 This cuboid is made from 4 cm^3 cubes.

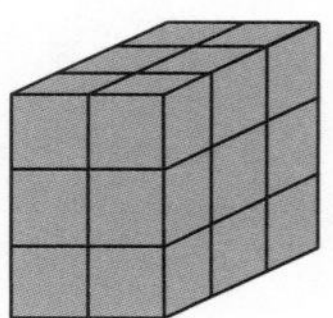

Find the volume of the cuboids below.

4

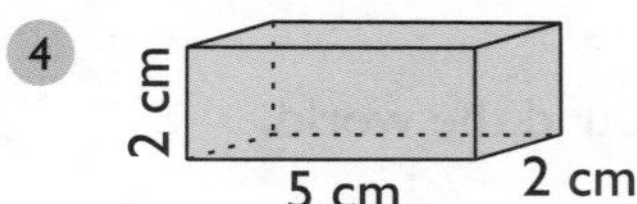

5

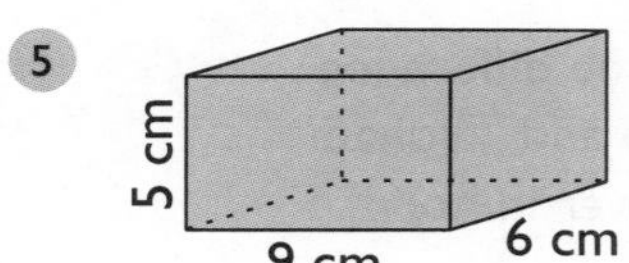

6

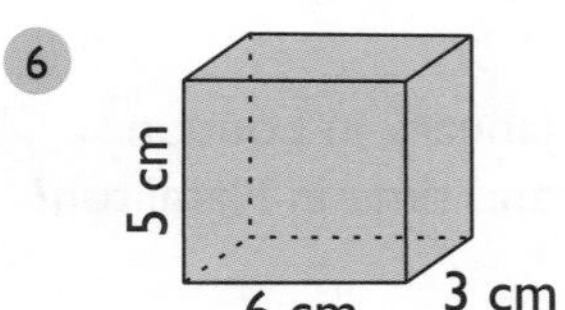

7 This cuboid has a volume of 120 cm^3.

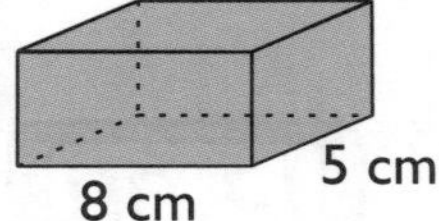

What is the height of the cuboid?

8 This cuboid has a volume of 80 cm^3.

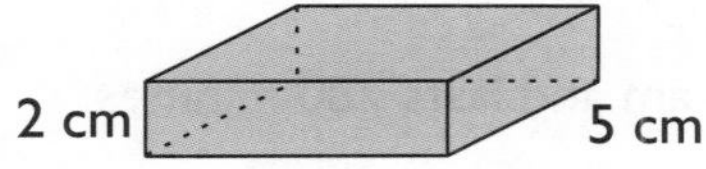

What is the width of the cuboid?

Work out the volume of the shapes below.

9 10

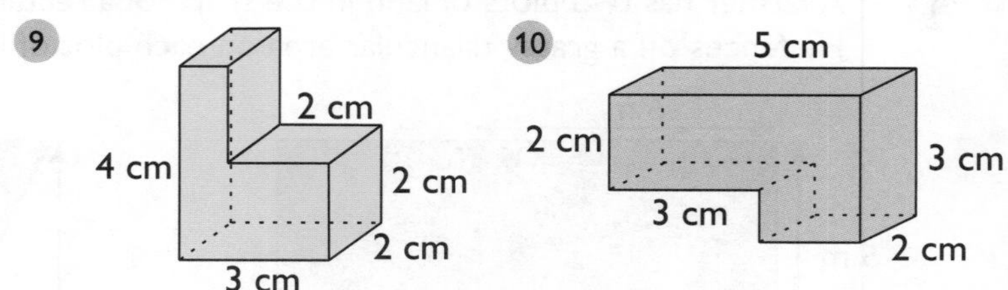

Look at shapes A to D below:

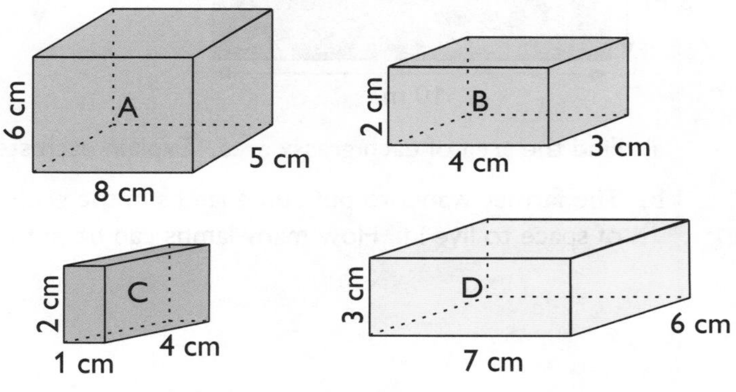

11 Which shape has the smallest volume?

12 Which shape has the biggest volume?

13 Which shapes have a volume bigger than 100 cm^3?

14 Copy and complete the sentence:
The volume of shape B is ☐ times bigger than the volume of shape C.

Look at the pair of shapes below.

Shape G is made from 3 cm^3 cubes.

Shape H is made from 4 cm^3 cubes.

G H

15 Which shape has the bigger volume?

16 What is the difference in volume between the two cuboids?

17 The two shapes below have the same volume. What is the length of side x of shape Z?

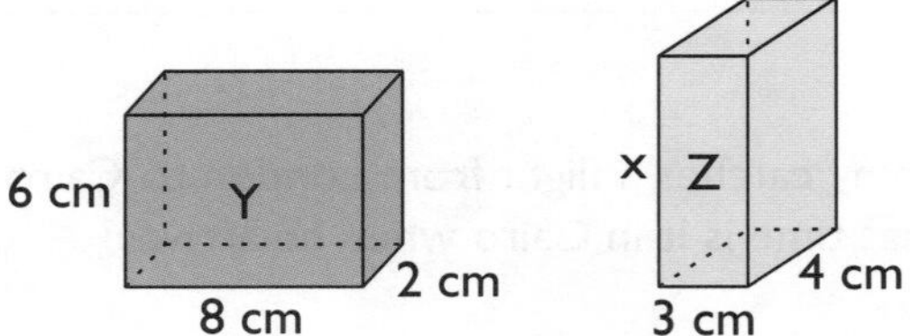

Wow, there were some tricky questions there — well done for getting to the end!

Measurement — Challenges

A farmer has two plots of land in the shape of a rectangle and a parallelogram.
He fences off a grassy triangular area on each plot of land, as shown below.

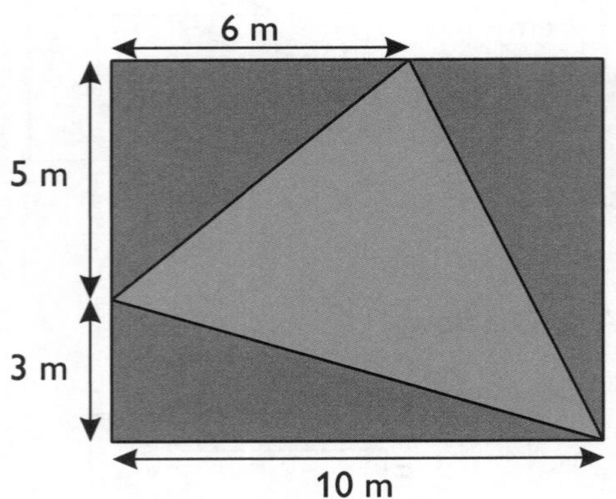

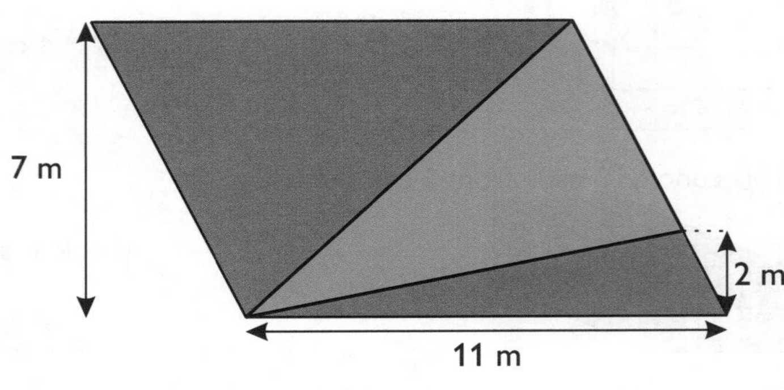

a) Find the area of each grassy area. Explain each step in your method.

b) The farmer wants to put some lambs in the grassy areas. Each lamb needs 2 m^2 of space to live in. How many lambs can he put in the grassy areas in total?

The table shows the time difference between London, UK and different places around the world.

Place	Time difference
Taiohae, Marquesas Islands	– 570 minutes
Calgary, Canada	– 7 hours
Hamilton, Bermuda	– 14 400 seconds
Buenos Aires, Argentina	– 180 minutes
Cairo, Egypt	+ 7200 seconds
Mumbai, India	+ 5 hours 30 minutes
Sydney, Australia	+ 36 000 seconds
Wellington, New Zealand	+ 12 hours

a) What is the time difference between Cairo and Taiohae? Give your answer in hours.

b) It is 3 am on 3rd January in London. What is the date and time in Hamilton?

c) It is 11.35 am in Buenos Aires. What time is it in Sydney?

d) This 24-hour clock shows the time where Rana is.

It is 18:30 in Wellington. In which of the places in the table is Rana?

e) Sammy catches a flight from London to Cairo. His flight leaves at 7:05 am and lasts 280 minutes. What time is it in Cairo when he arrives?

3 The map below shows some routes to different places on an island.

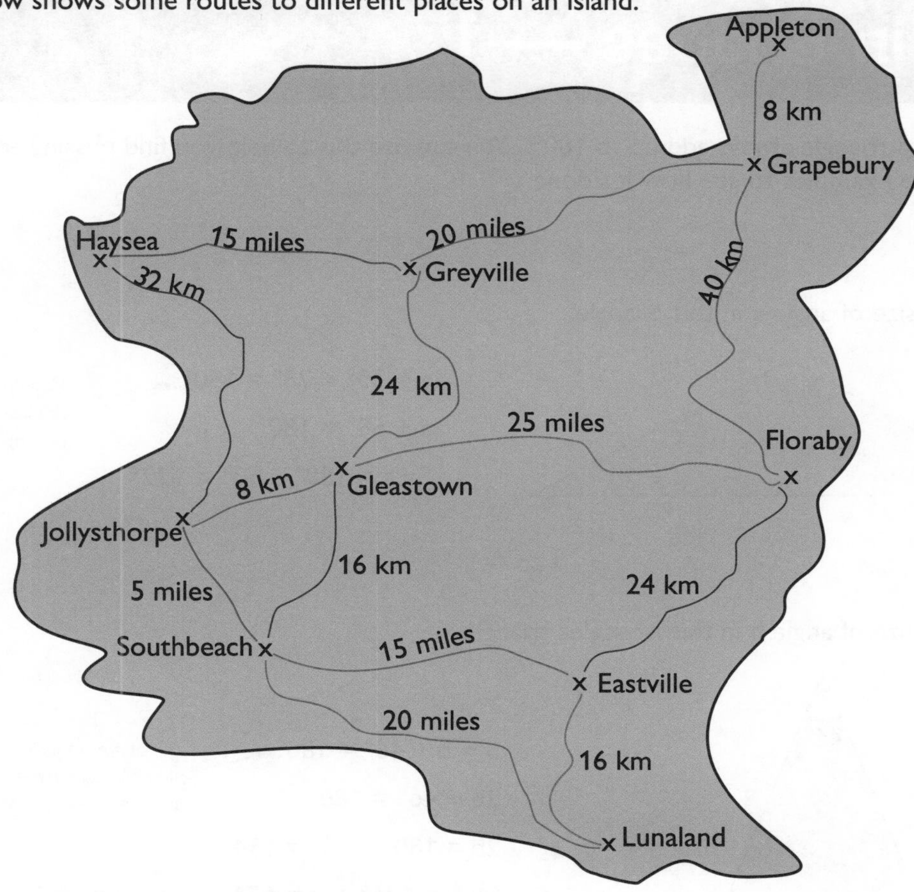

a) Mona lives in Gleastown and wants to take the shortest route to Grapebury. Should she travel through Greyville or Floraby?

b) Carrie travels 55 miles from Haysea to Floraby.
   (i) Which towns does she go through?
   (ii) Can you find a shorter route she could take?

c) Danny leaves Jollysthorpe and travels for 48 km. Which town could he be in? Can you find more than one possible answer?

d) Kev wants to drive clockwise around the outside of the island starting in Appleton. He uses 500 ml of petrol for every 10 miles he travels, and he has 4.5 litres of petrol. Which two towns will he be between when he runs out of petrol?

4 In a chewing gum factory, packs of chewing gum are put into small boxes of 24. Each small box measures 12 cm × 12 cm × 12 cm. Small boxes are then packed into larger boxes. The factory owners order some large boxes and are sent some measuring 0.35 m × 0.45 m × 0.45 m.

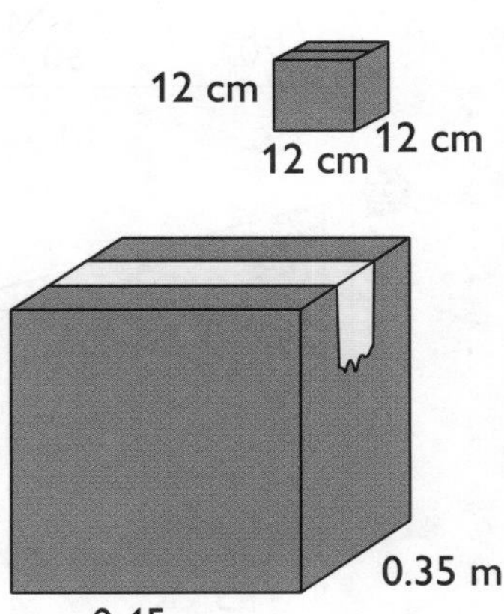

a) How many pieces of chewing gum in total can be packed into a large box?

The factory owners want to order some different large boxes so that when they are filled with small boxes, there is no empty space.

b) What are the smallest amounts they could increase the dimensions of the large boxes by? Give your answers in cm.

c) If they increased the dimensions of the large boxes by the amounts you said in b), how many pieces of chewing gum could fit inside a large box?

You've made it through the challenges — good job!

Angles in Shapes — 1

The angles inside a triangle always add up to 180°. You can use this to help you find missing angles. Have a look at the examples to see how it's done...

Examples

Work out the size of angle a in this triangle.

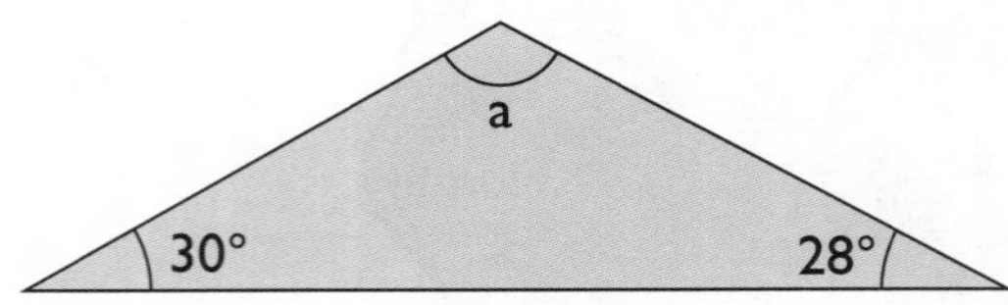

a + 30° + 28° = 180°

a + 58° = 180°

So a = 180° – 58° = **122°**

Remember all of the angles in a triangle add up to 180°.

Work out the size of angle b in this isosceles triangle.

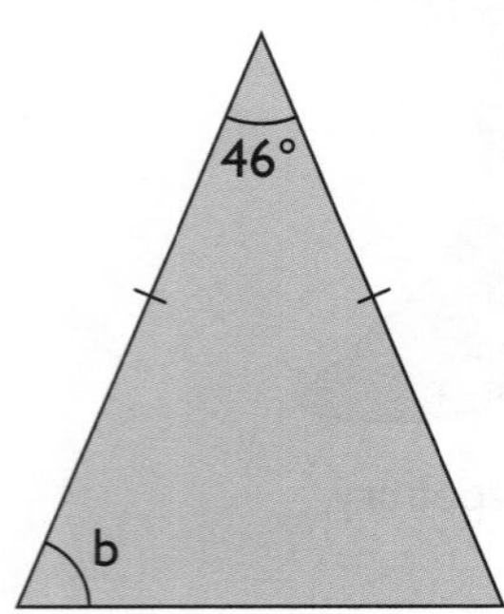

b + b + 46° = 180°

2b + 46° = 180°

2b = 180° – 46° = 134°

So b = 134° ÷ 2 = **67°**

The other angle is also b because it's an isosceles triangle.

Set A

Complete the calculations below to find the missing angle in each of these triangles:

1

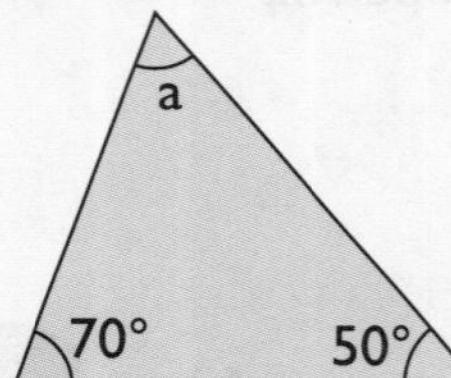

a + 70° + 50° = 180°

a + ☐ = 180°

a = 180° – ☐ = ☐

2

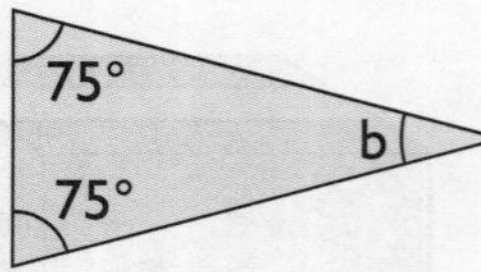

b + 75° + 75° = 180°

b + ☐ = 180°

b = 180° – ☐ = ☐

3

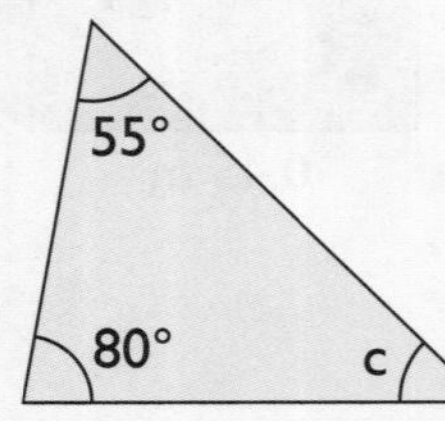

c + 55° + 80° = 180°

c + ☐ = 180°

c = 180° – ☐ = ☐

Find the missing angles in these triangles:

4

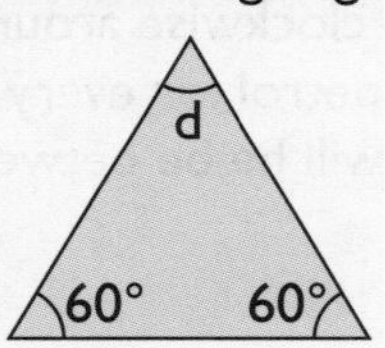

5

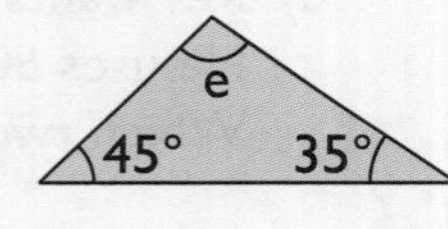

6

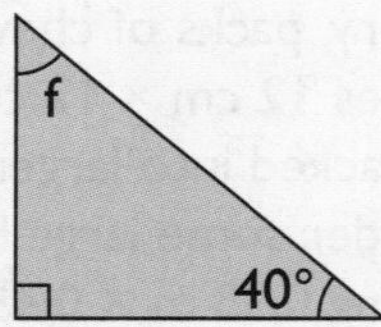

7

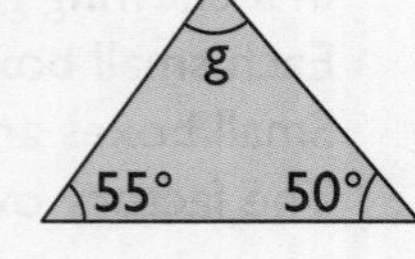

8 Complete the calculations below to find the missing angles in this isosceles triangle.

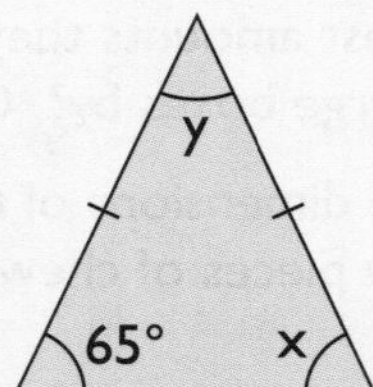

x = ☐

y + 65° + ☐ = 180°

y + ☐ = 180°

y = 180° – ☐ = ☐

Set B

Find the missing angles in these triangles:

1
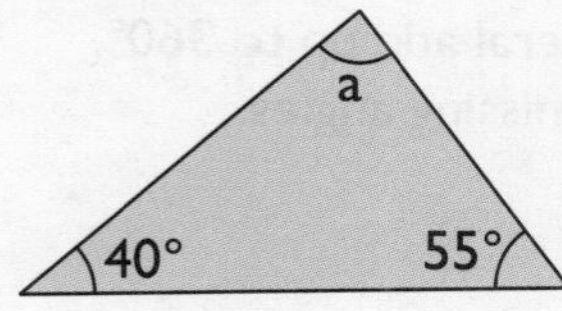

2
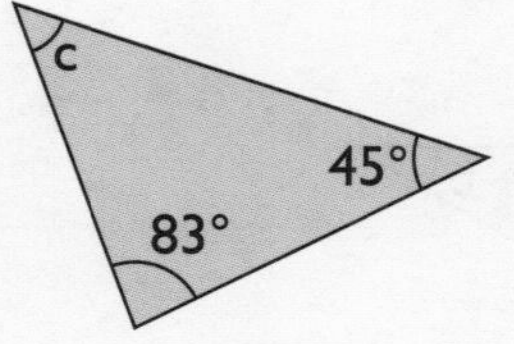

3
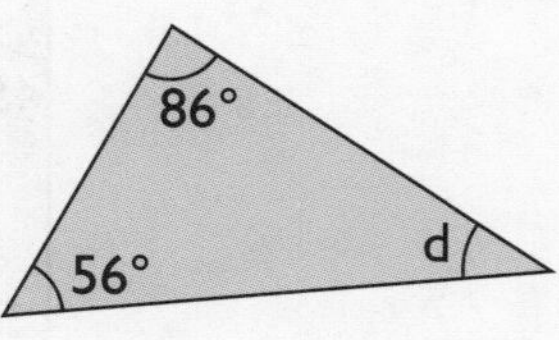

4
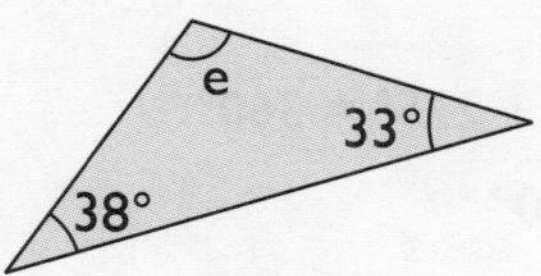

5
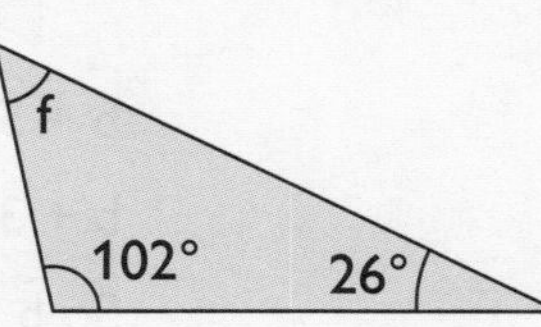

6
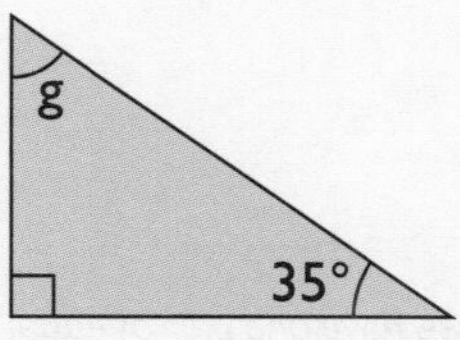

7
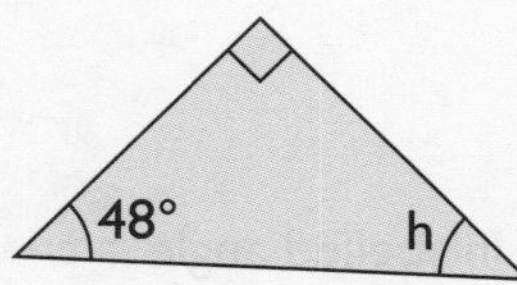

8

Find all of the missing angles in these isosceles triangles:

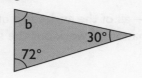

9
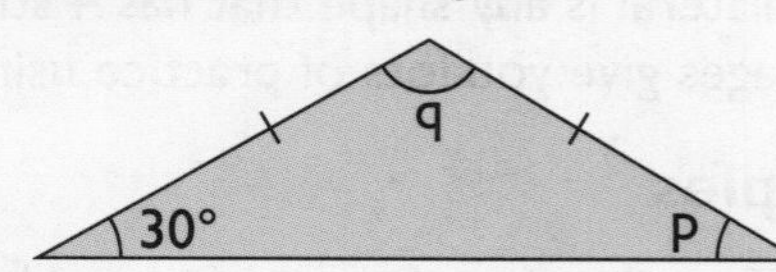

10
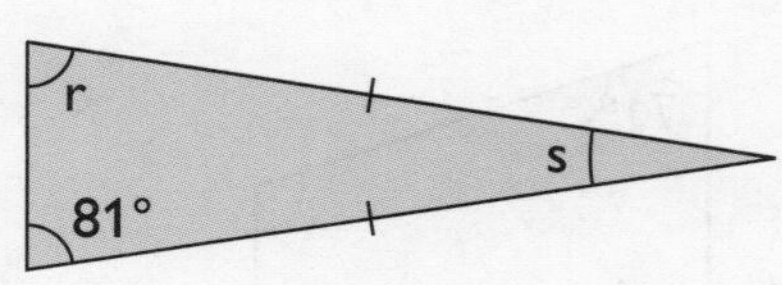

11
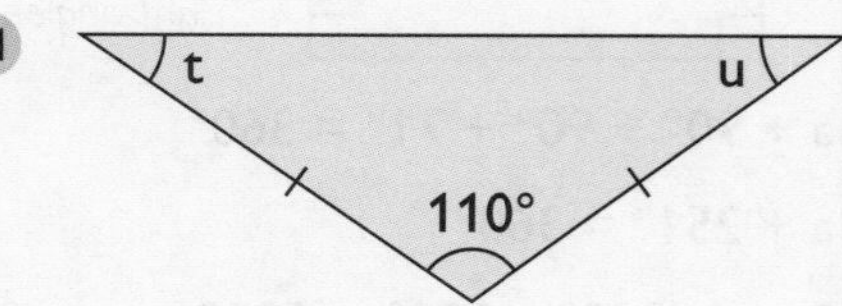

12
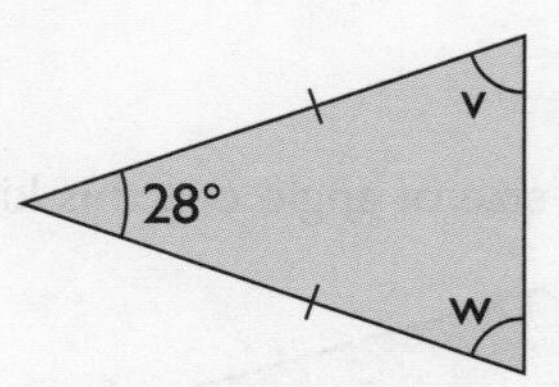

Set C

Find the missing angles in these triangles:

1
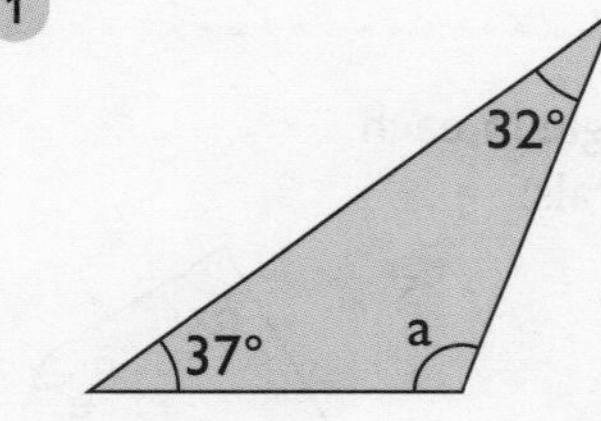

2
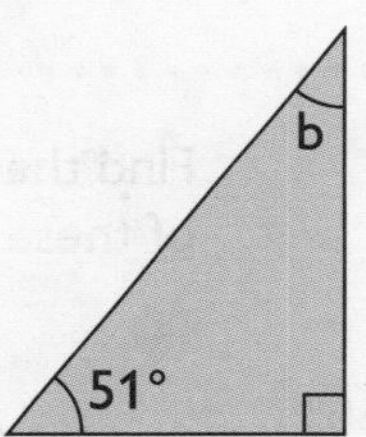

Find all the labelled angles in these isosceles triangles:

3
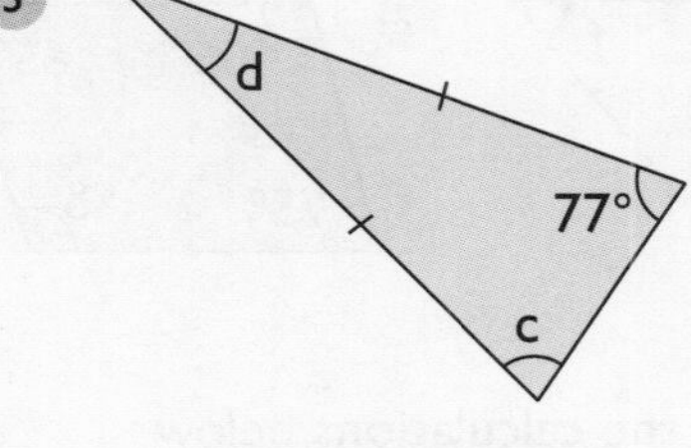

4
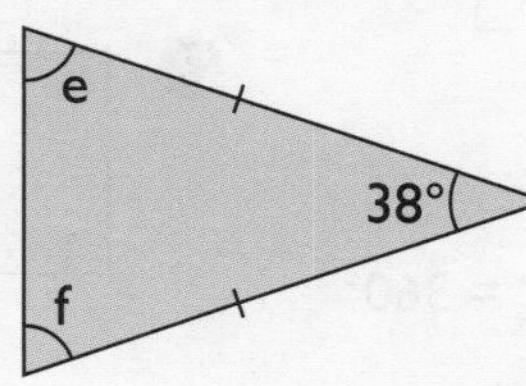

5
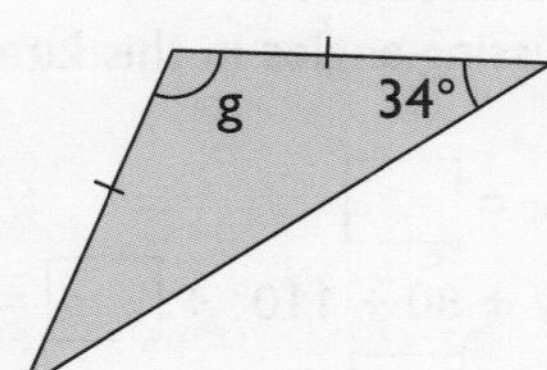

6
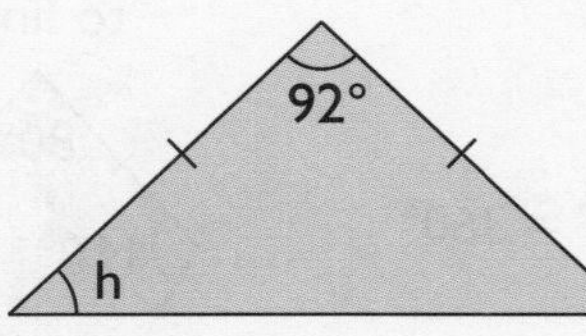

Two angles in a triangle are given below. Work out the size of the final angle and decide whether the triangle is equilateral, isosceles or scalene.

7 54° and 72°

8 30° and 65°

9 60° and 60°

10 102° and 39°

11 Identify the triangles whose angles must have been labelled incorrectly.

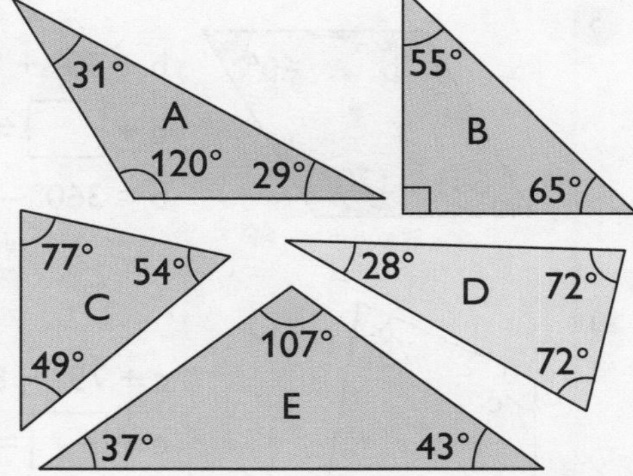

I can find missing angles in triangles.

Angles in Shapes — 2

A quadrilateral is any shape that has 4 straight sides — all of the angles in a quadrilateral add up to 360°. These pages give you lots of practice using this information to work out the size of missing angles.

Examples

Work out the size of the missing angles in these quadrilaterals.

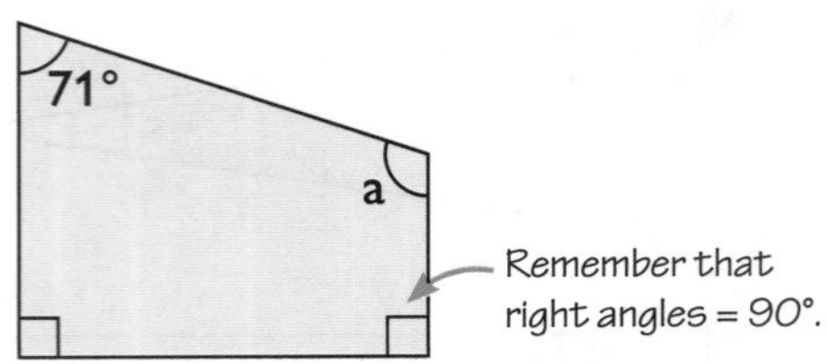

Remember that right angles = 90°.

$a + 90° + 90° + 71° = 360°$

$a + 251° = 360°$

So $a = 360° - 251° =$ **109°**

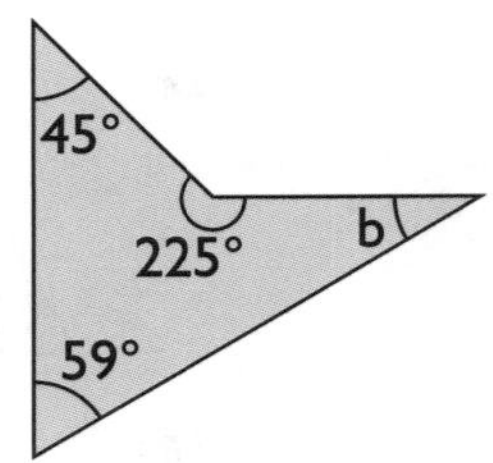

$b + 59° + 45° + 225° = 360°$

$b + 329° = 360°$

So $b = 360° - 329° =$ **31°**

Work out the size of angle c in this kite.

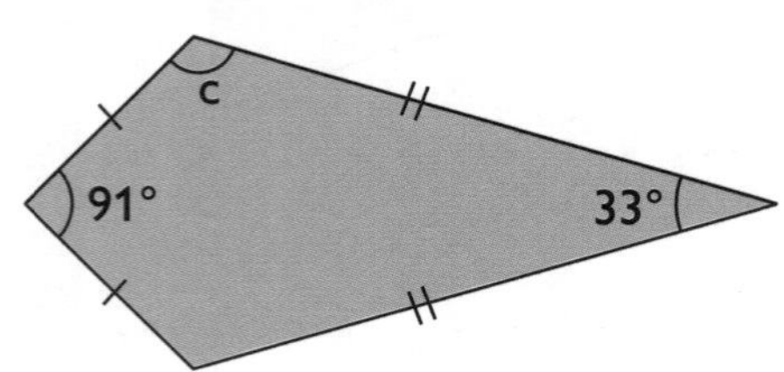

Unlabelled angle = c

Kites have one pair of equal angles opposite each other.

$c + 33° + c + 91° = 360°$

$2c + 124° = 360°$

$2c = 360° - 124° = 236°$

So $c = 236° \div 2 =$ **118°**

Set A

Complete the calculations below to find the missing angle in each of these quadrilaterals:

1

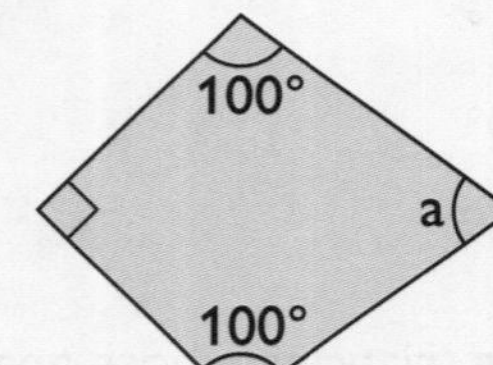

$a + 100° + 90° + 100° = 360°$

$a + \square = 360°$

$a = 360° - \square = \square$

2

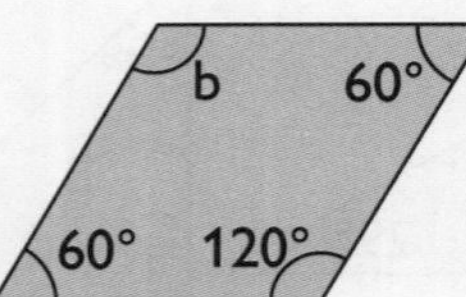

$b + 60° + 120° + 60° = 360°$

$b + \square = 360°$

$b = 360° - \square = \square$

3

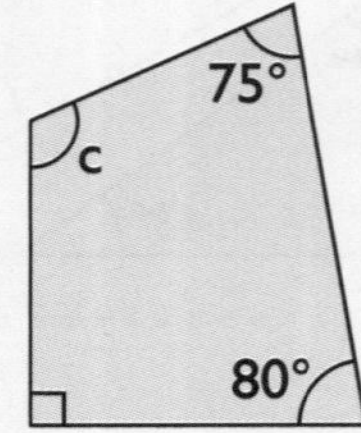

$c + 75° + 80° + 90° = 360°$

$c + \square = 360°$

$c = 360° - \square = \square$

Find the missing angle in each of these quadrilaterals:

4

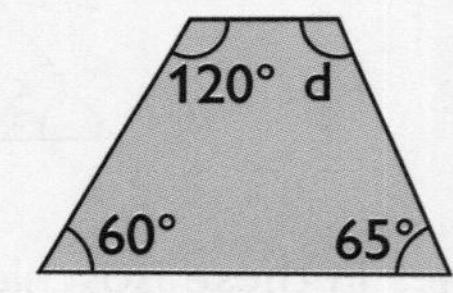

5

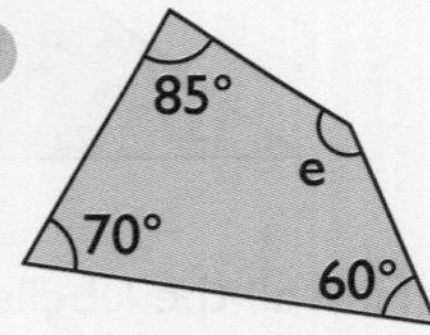

6

f

130°

7

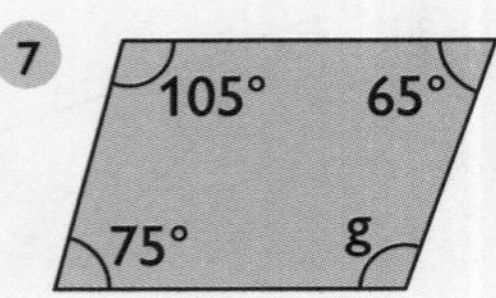

8 Complete the calculations below to find the missing angles in this kite.

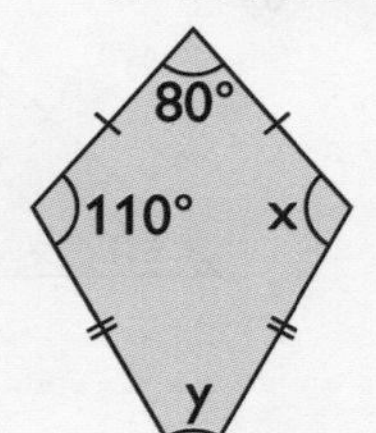

$x = \square$

$y + 80 + 110° + \square = 360°$

$y + \square = 360°$

$y = 360° - \square = \square$

Set B

Find the missing angle in each of these quadrilaterals:

1 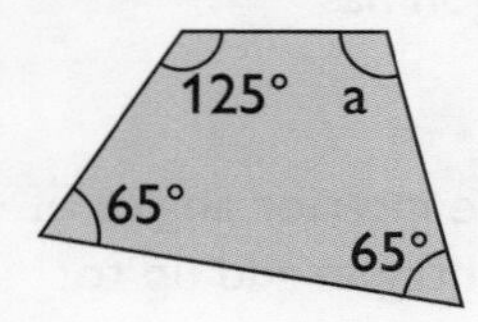

2 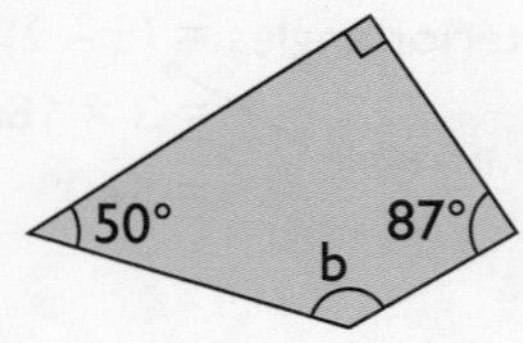

3 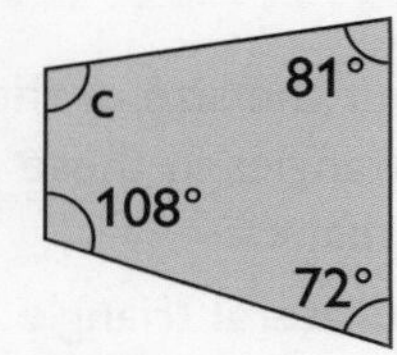

4 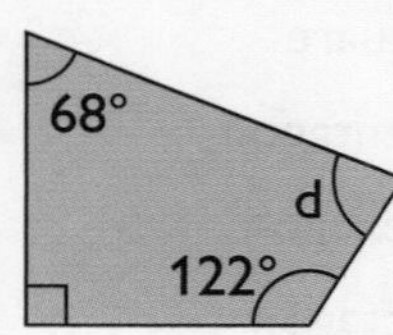

Find all the missing angles in these kites:

5 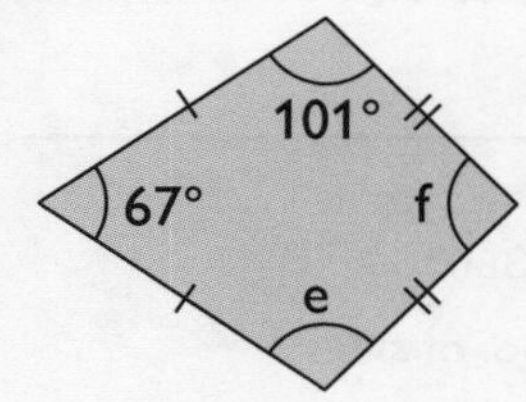

6 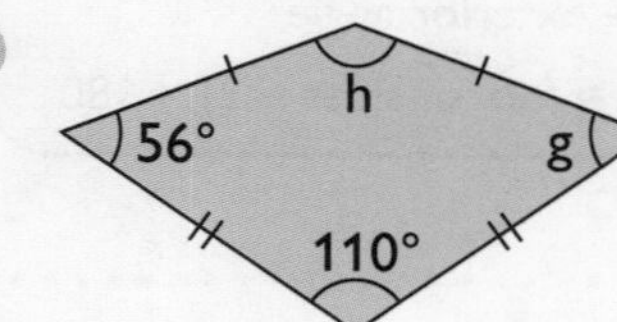

7 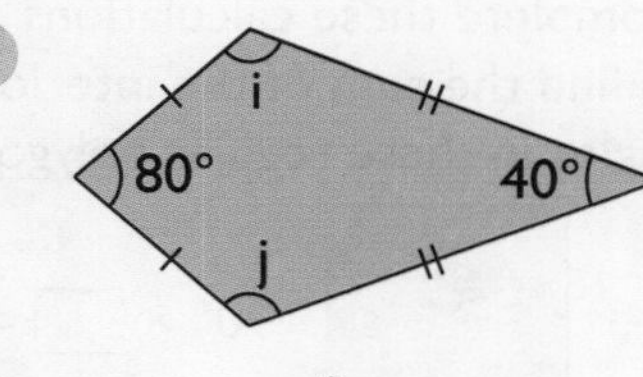

8 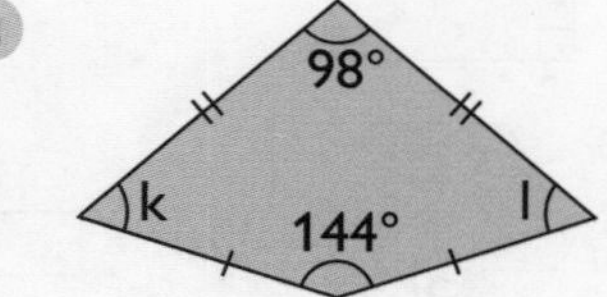

Find all the missing angles in these parallelograms:

9 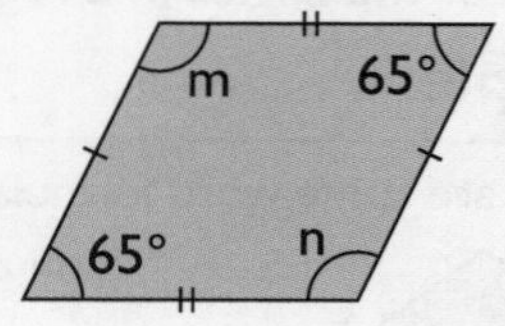

10 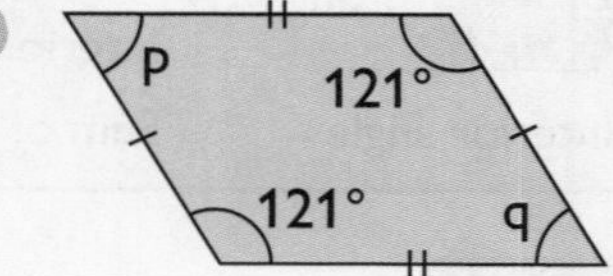

11 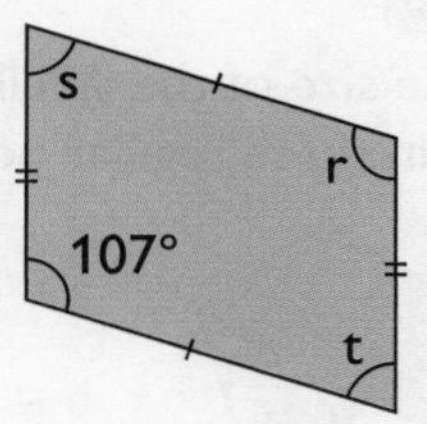

12 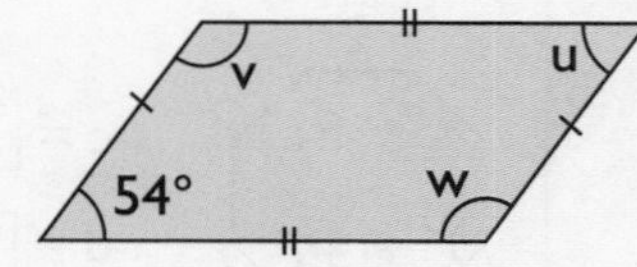

Set C

Find all the missing angles in each of these quadrilaterals:

1 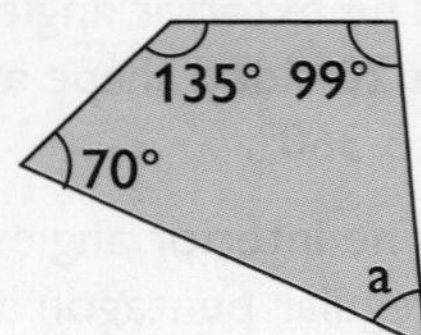

2 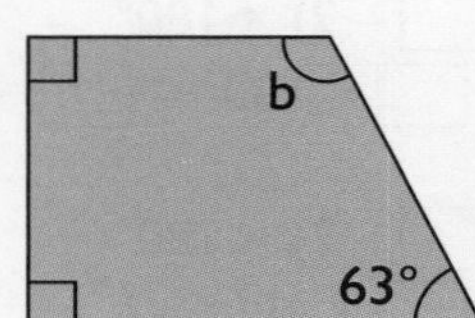

Use the properties of these quadrilaterals to help you find the labelled angles:

3 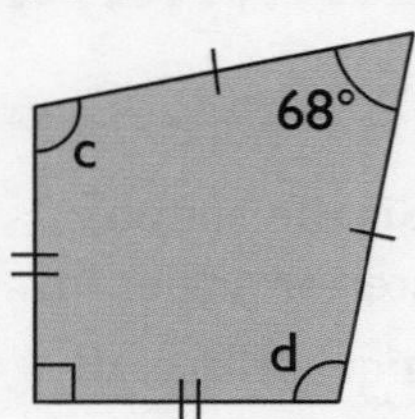

4 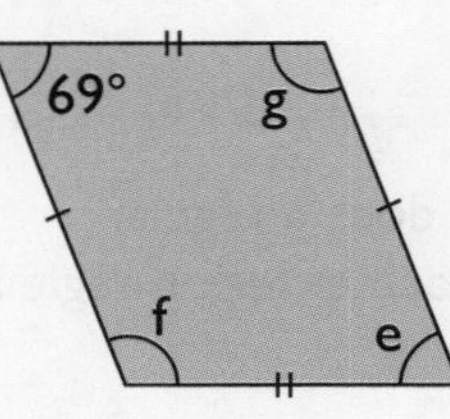

5 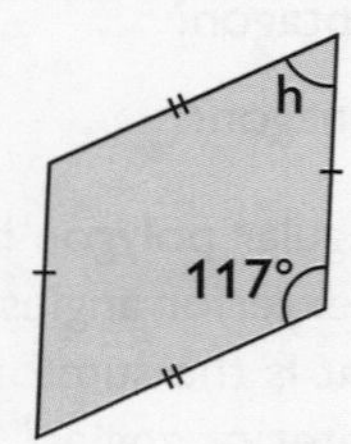

6 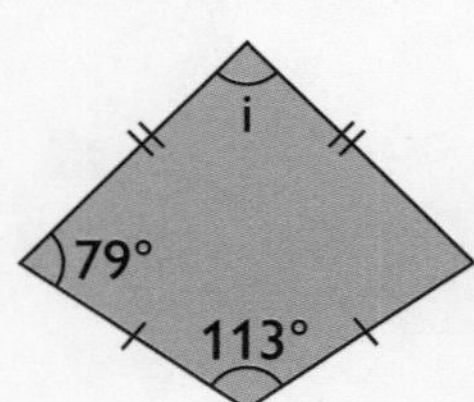

7 Match the name of each quadrilateral to the group of angles it could have:

Kite	64° 107° 116° 73°
Rhombus	90° 109° 109° 52°
Trapezium	65° 115° 115° 65°

8 Identify the quadrilaterals whose angles are labelled incorrectly.

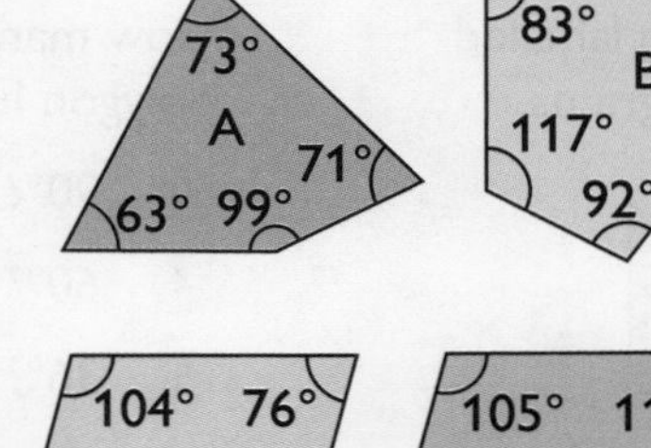

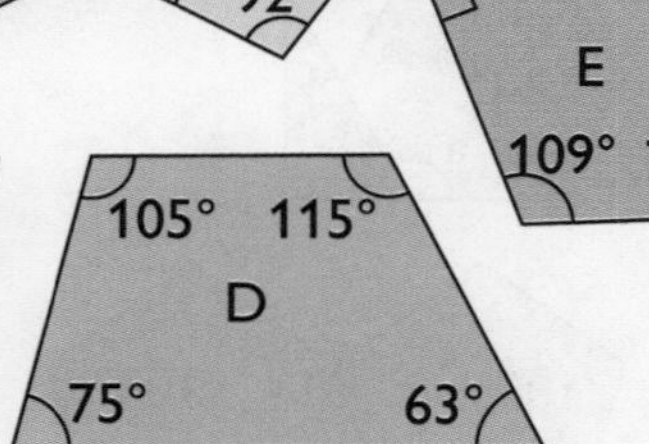

I can find missing angles in quadrilaterals.     

Angles in Shapes — 3

The size of the angles in a regular polygon depends on how many sides the regular polygon has.

Example

Here are some word formulas to use on this page:

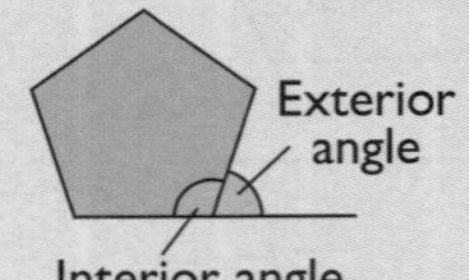

Sum of exterior angles = 360°

Exterior angle = 360° ÷ no. of sides

Interior angle = 180° – exterior angle

Sum of interior angles = (no. of sides – 2) × 180°

What do the interior angles of a regular pentagon add up to?

Sum of interior angles = (5 – 2) × 180°
= 3 × 180°
= **540°**

Pentagons have 5 sides.

Set A

Find the size of the labelled angles in these regular polygons.

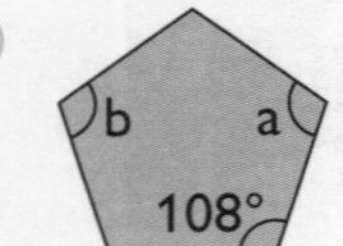

a = ☐
b = ☐

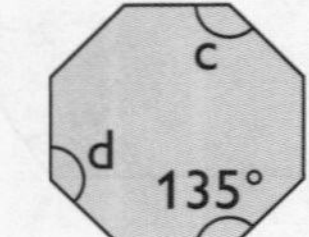

c = ☐
d = ☐

Complete these calculations to find the sum of the interior angles in these regular polygons:

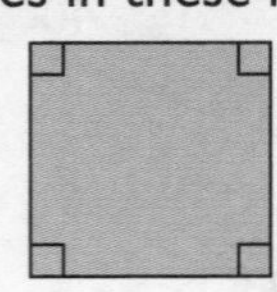

90° × ☐ = ☐

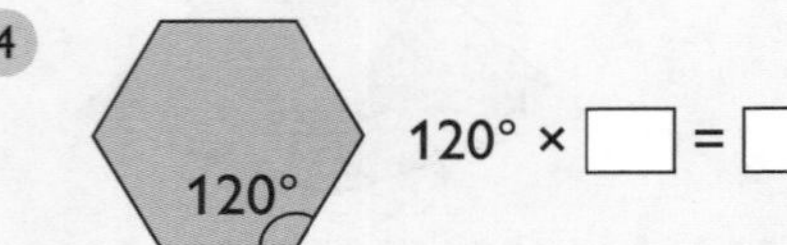

Work out the size of the exterior angles in these regular shapes:

5. equilateral triangle
6. square
7. pentagon
8. hexagon
9. octagon
10. decagon

Set B

Find the size of the labelled angles in these diagrams.

1. 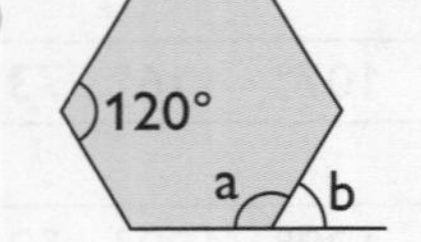

a = ☐
b = ☐

2. 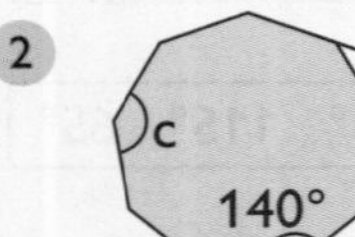

c = ☐
d = ☐

Find the sum of the interior angles in these regular polygons:

3. 
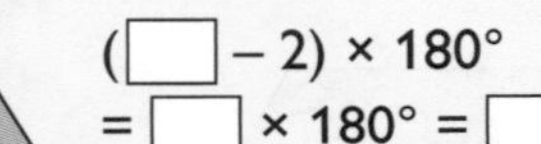

(☐ – 2) × 180°
= ☐ × 180° = ☐

4. 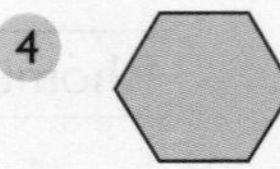
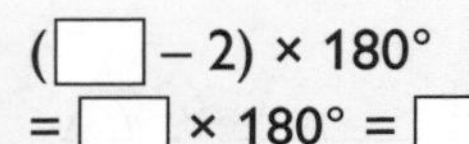

(☐ – 2) × 180°
= ☐ × 180° = ☐

5. 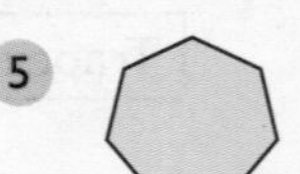

(☐ – 2) × 180°
= ☐ × 180° = ☐

True or false? Explain your answers.

6. The exterior angles in a 20-sided shape add up to 360°.
7. The interior angles of a regular pentagon add up to 900°.
8. Each exterior angle of a regular decagon is 36°.

Set C

Find the size of the labelled angles in these diagrams.

1. 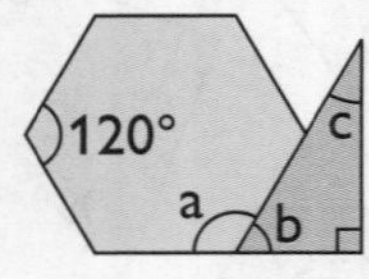

2. 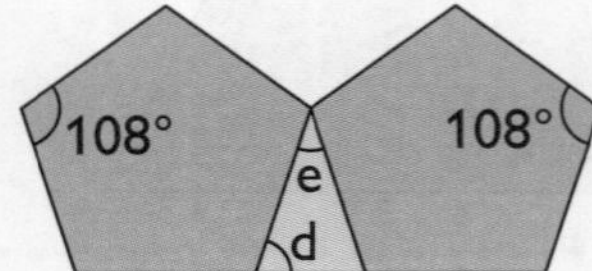

How many sides does a regular polygon have if each exterior angle is:

3. 90°?
4. 60°?
5. 36°?
6. 18°?
7. 12°?
8. 6°?

What is the sum of the interior angles in:

9. a quadrilateral?
10. a heptagon?
11. a nonagon?
12. A regular polygon has 30° exterior angles. What is the sum of its interior angles?

I can find missing angles in regular polygons.

Angle Rules

Knowing your angle rules can be really useful, especially if you have to work out the size of a missing angle. On these pages, you'll practise finding angles that are on a straight line, around a point and vertically opposite.

Examples

Work out the size of angle a:

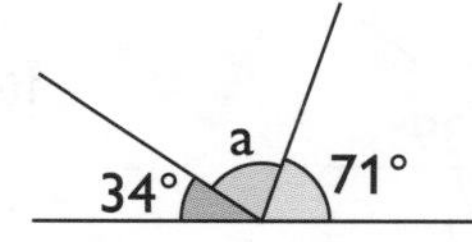

b + 34° + 71° = 180° ← *Angles on a straight line add up to 180°.*

b + 105° = 180°

So b = 180° – 105° = **75°**

Work out the size of angle b:

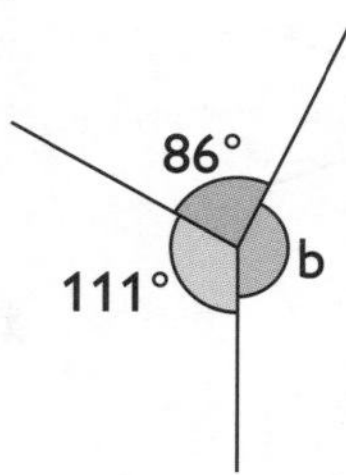

a + 111° + 86° = 360° ← *Angles around a point add up to 360°.*

a + 197° = 360°

So a = 360° – 197° = **163°**

Work out the size of angles c and d:

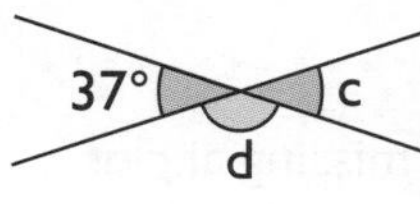

c = **37°** ← *When two lines cross you get two sets of opposite angles. The angles vertically opposite each other are equal.*

d + 37° = 180°

So d = 180° – 37° = **143°**

Set A

Work out the missing angles:

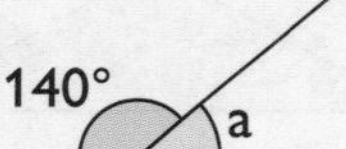

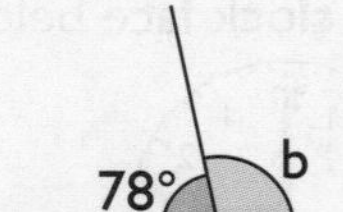

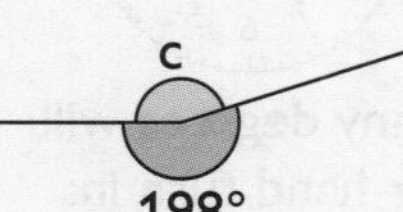

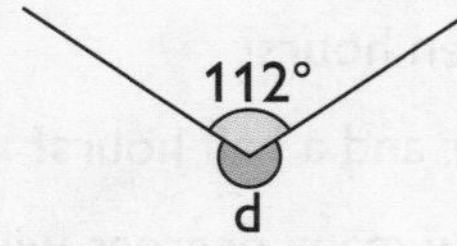

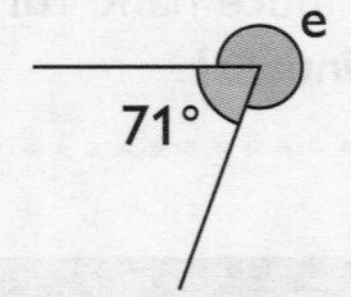

Work out the missing angles:

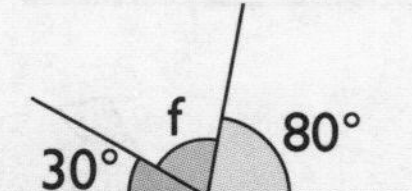

7

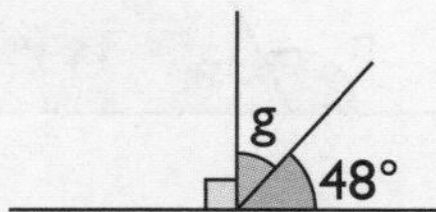

8

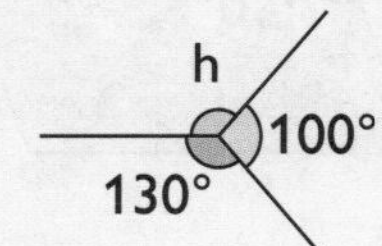

9

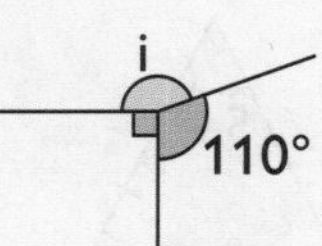

10

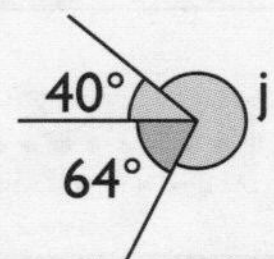

Find the labelled angles:

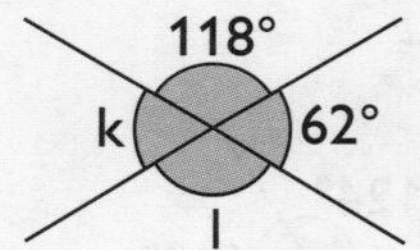

12

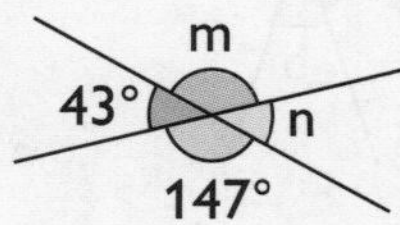

Complete the calculations below to work out the missing angles.

13

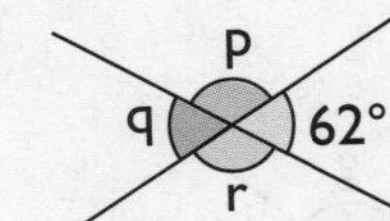

p + ☐ = 180°

So p = 180° – ☐ = ☐

q = ☐

r = ☐

Set B

Work out the missing angles:

1

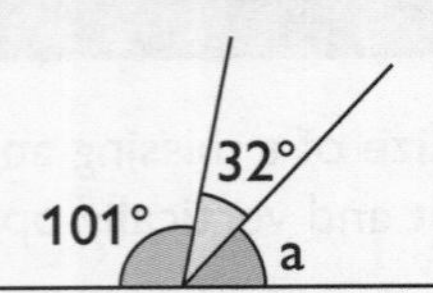

2

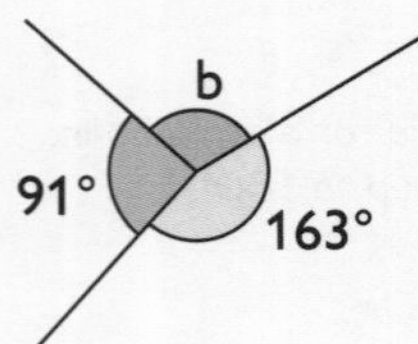

3

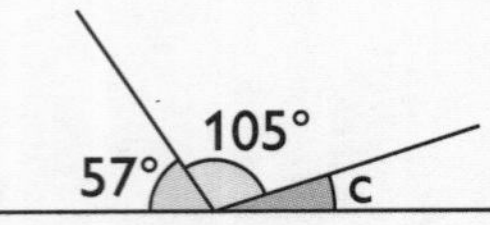

4

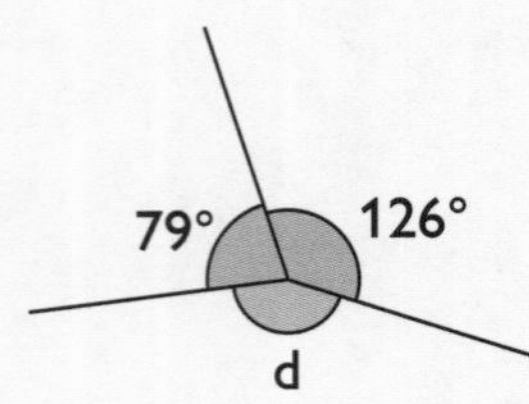

Find the labelled angles:

5

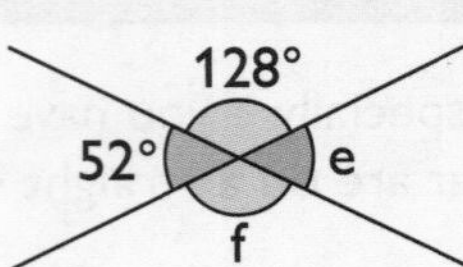

6

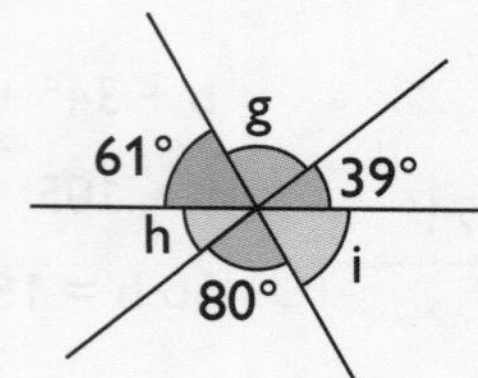

7

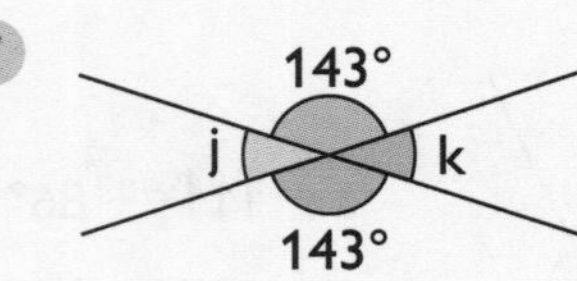

8

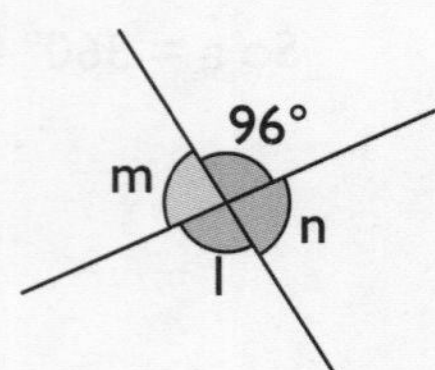

Work out the missing angles on these diagrams:

9

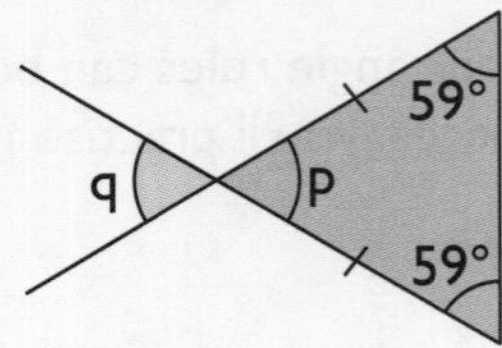

10

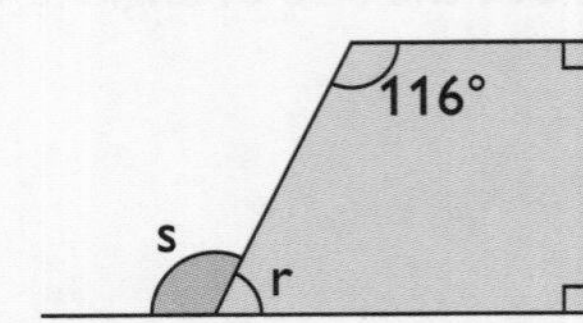

11

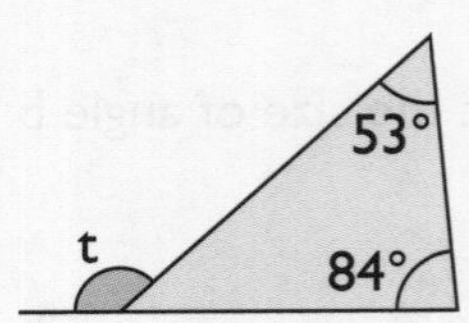

12

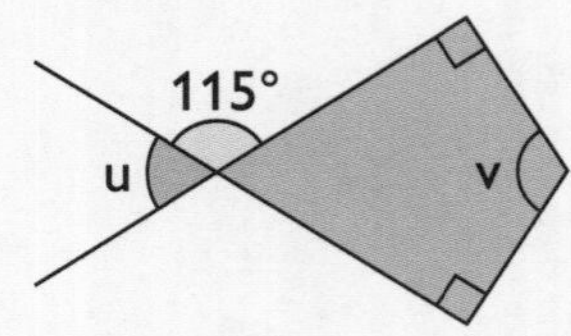

Set C

Work out the missing angles:

1

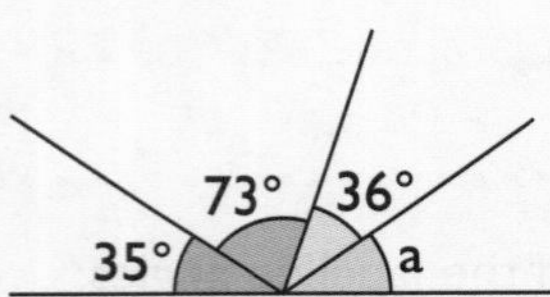

2

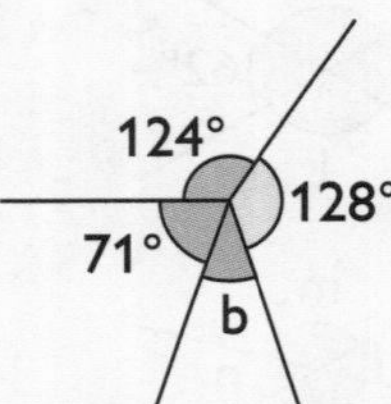

3

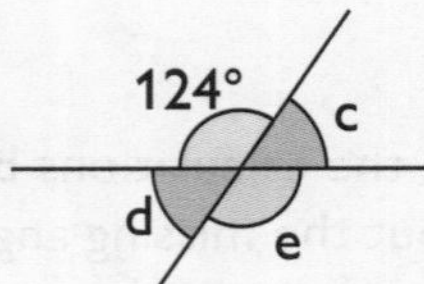

4

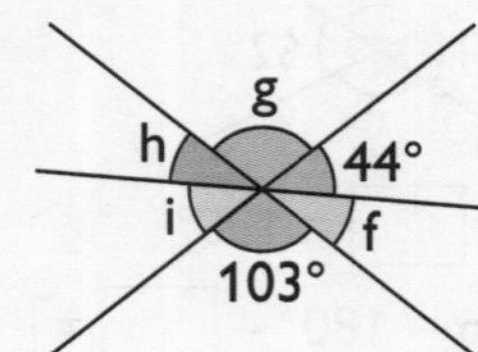

Work out the missing angles on these diagrams:

5

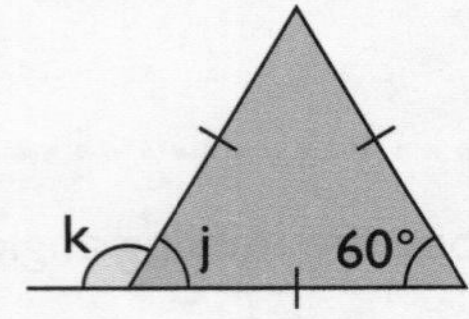

6

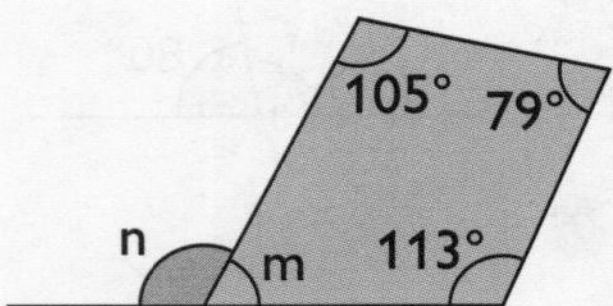

7

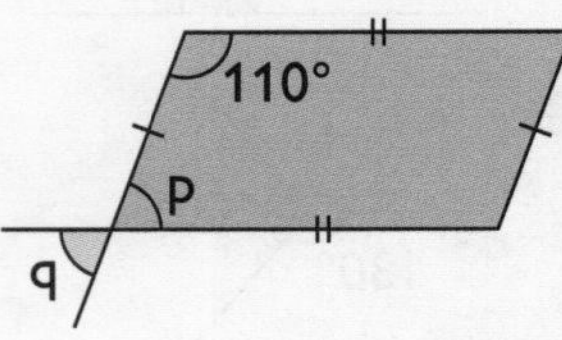

8

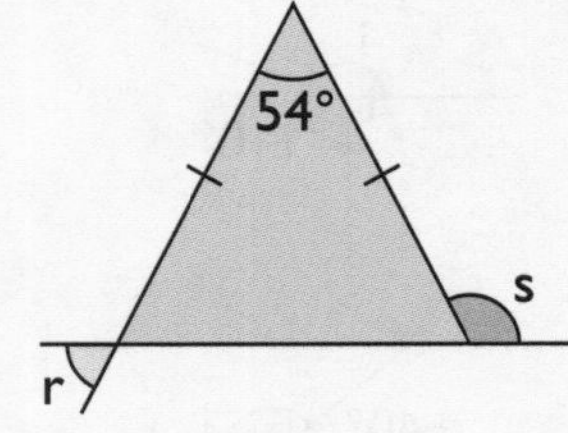

9 Ida has joined four isosceles triangles together to make a rectangle. Calculate the size of angles x and y.

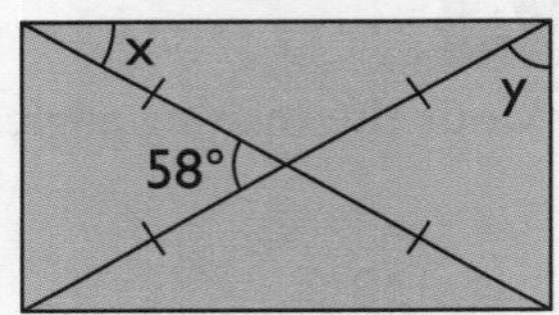

Look at the clock face below.

How many degrees will the hour hand turn in:

10 one hour?

11 seven hours?

12 four and a half hours?

13 How many degrees will the minute hand turn in 18 minutes?

I know and can use different angle rules.

Geometry — Review 1

Work out the missing angles:

1 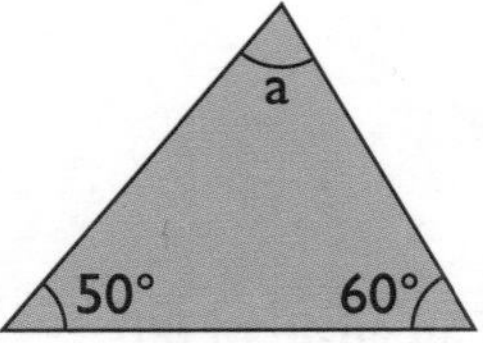

3 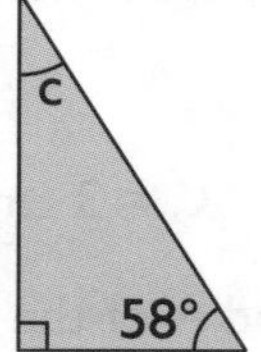

2 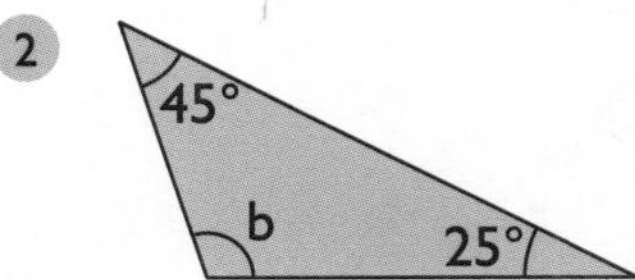

4 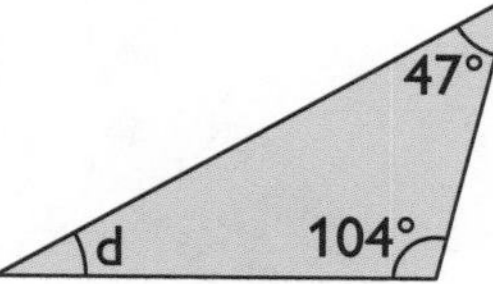

Work out the missing angles in these isosceles triangles:

5 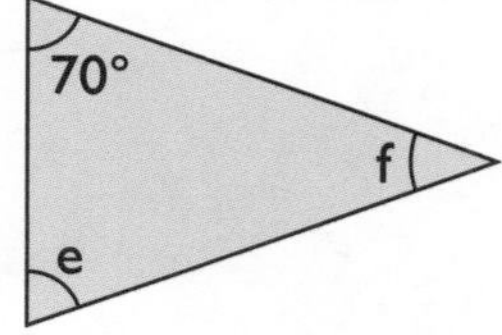

6 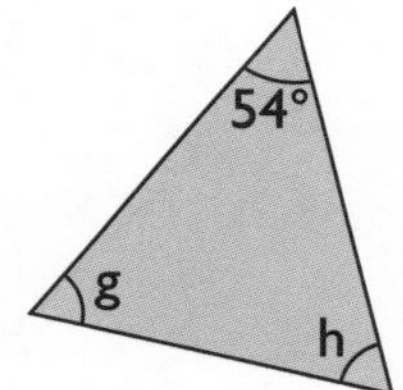

Work out the missing angles:

7 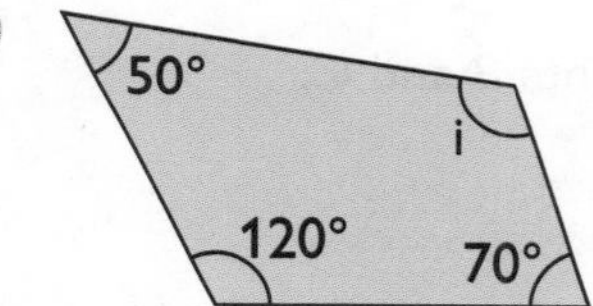

9 

8 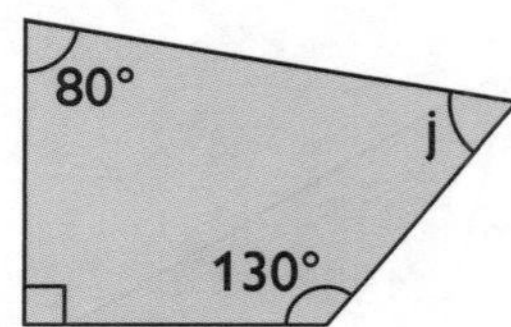

10 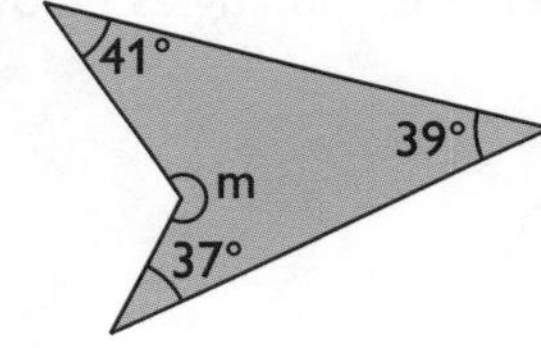

Use the properties of these quadrilaterals to help you find the labelled angles:

11 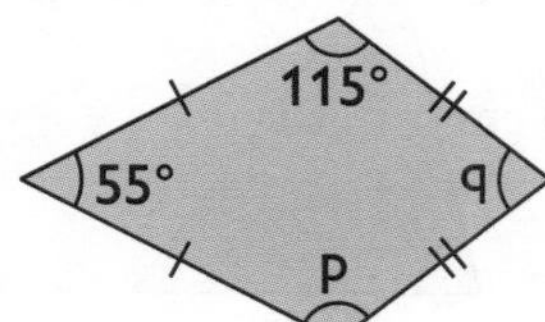

13 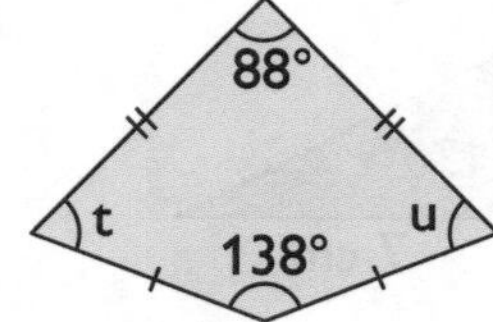

12 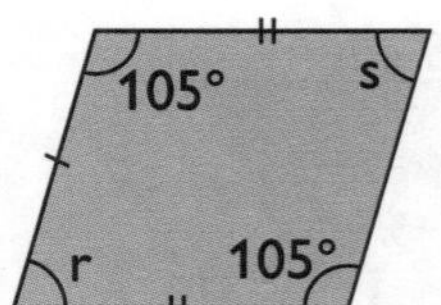

14 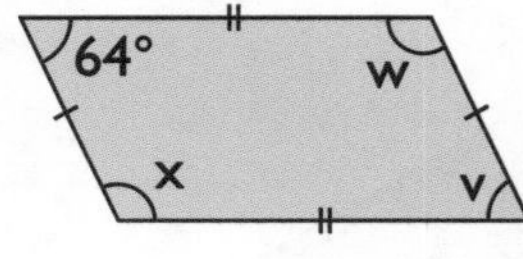

15 Copy and complete the table to show the size of each exterior angle and interior angle in these regular polygons:

Regular Shape	Exterior angle	Interior angle
Square		
Hexagon		
Nonagon		
Decagon		

Work out the sum of the interior angles of the following shapes:

16 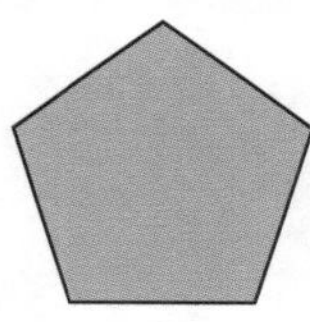

17 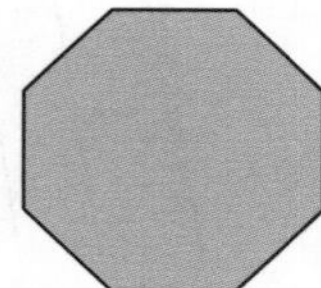

Work out the size of the missing angles:

18 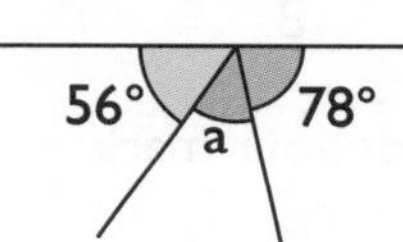

20 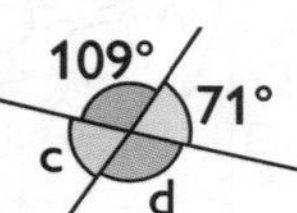

19 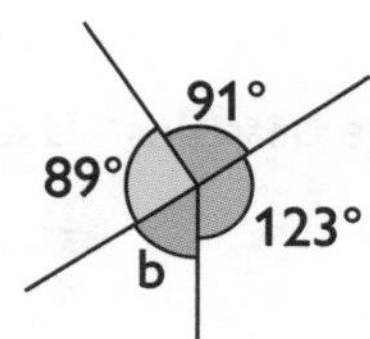

21 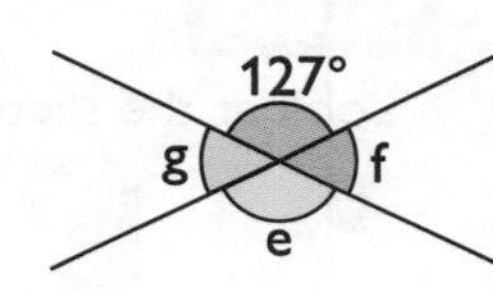

22 The diagram on the right is made from two isosceles triangles. Work out the size of angle x.

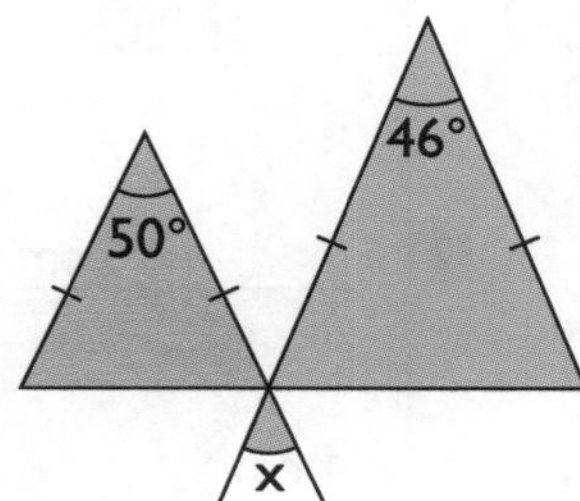

Look at the clock face on the right.

How many degrees will the hour hand turn between:

23 09:00 and 11:00?

24 04:00 and 10:30?

Great work taking on all those questions!

Drawing Triangles

You need to be able to draw triangles with certain side lengths and angles.
For this, you'll need a ruler and a protractor. Check out the example, then give it a go.

Example

Draw triangle ABC where line AB = 3.5 cm, angle A = 80° and line AC = 3 cm.

1. Draw the line AB with a ruler. Label the ends A and B.

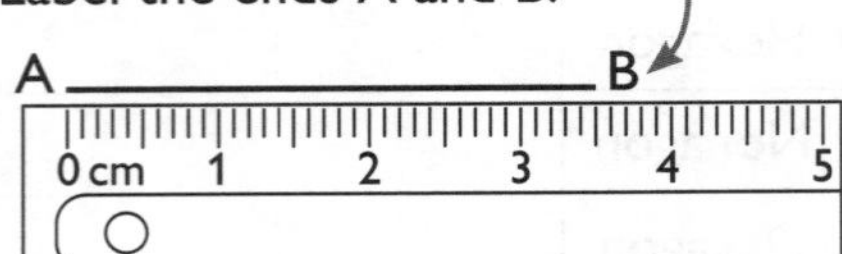

2. From end A of the line, mark an angle of 80°.

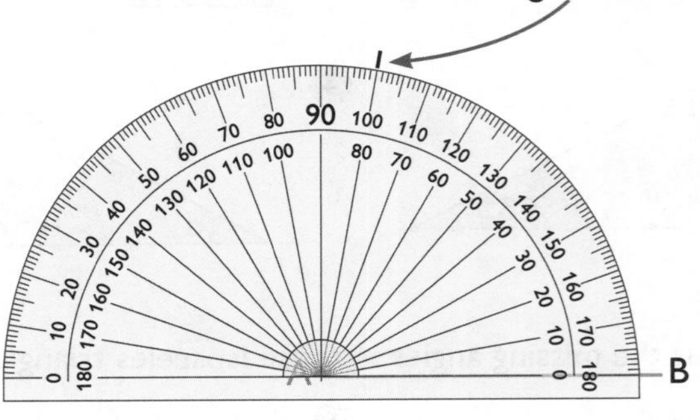

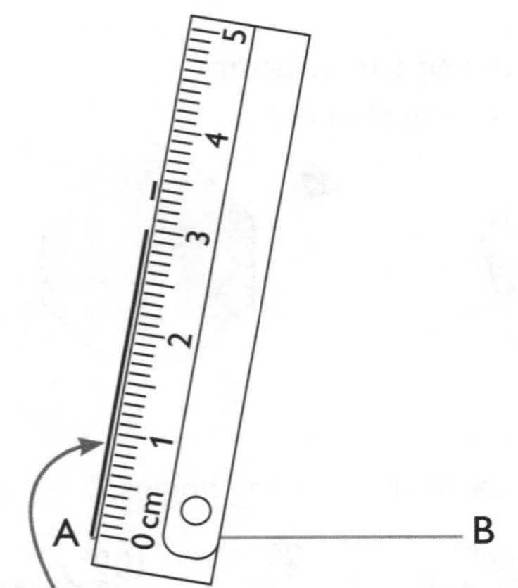

3. Draw line AC towards your mark — it should be 3 cm long.

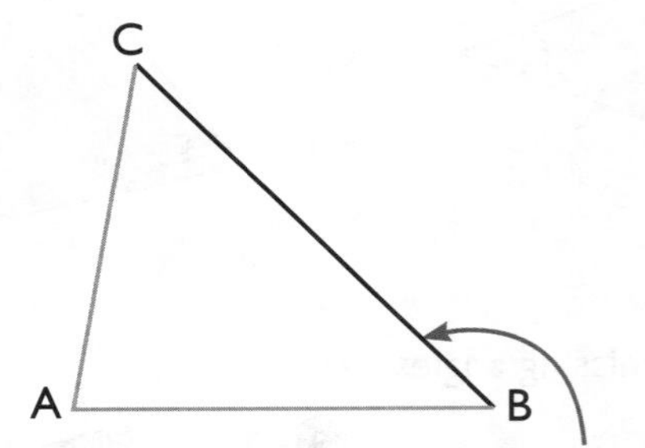

4. Draw a line to connect points B and C.

Set A

Look at the sketches of these triangles. Use the side lengths and angles below to draw them accurately:

1. 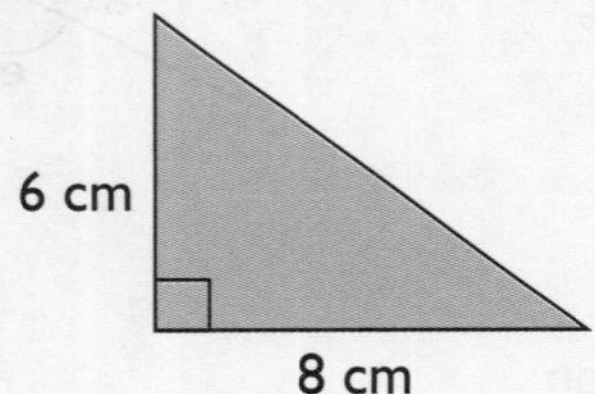

2. 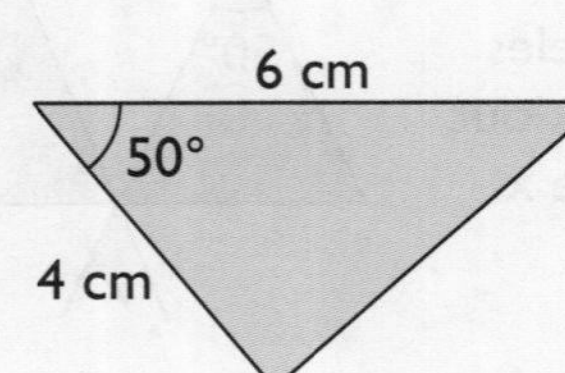

3. 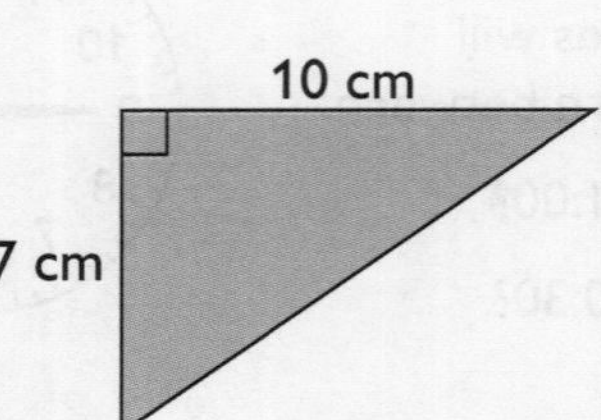

4. 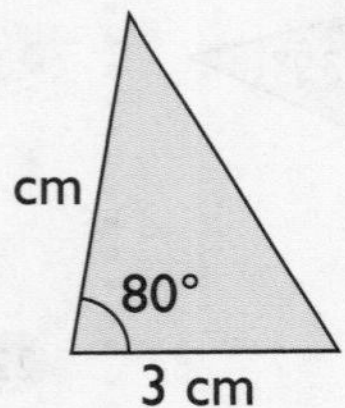

5. 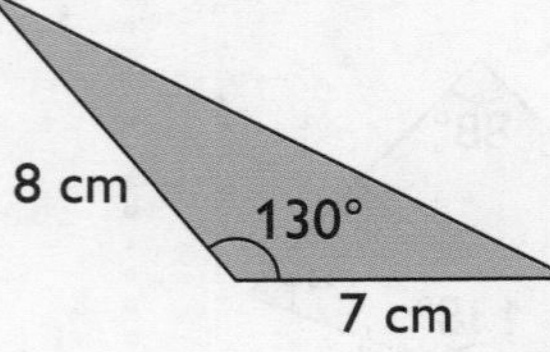

6. 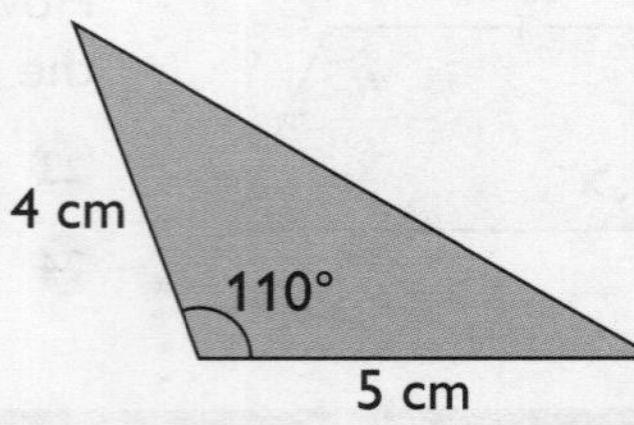

7. 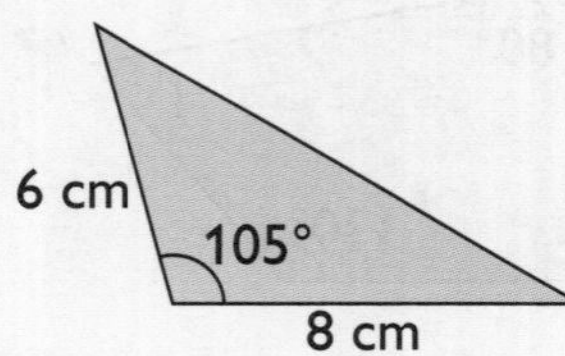

8. 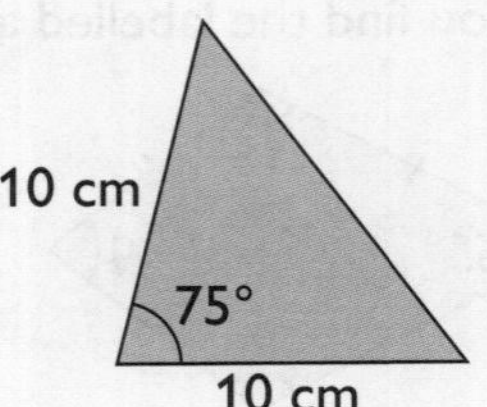

9. 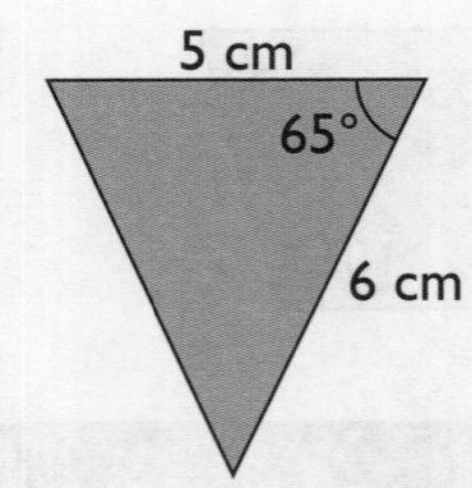

Set B

Accurately draw the sketched triangles below, then find the value of 'x' to the nearest mm or the nearest degree.

1
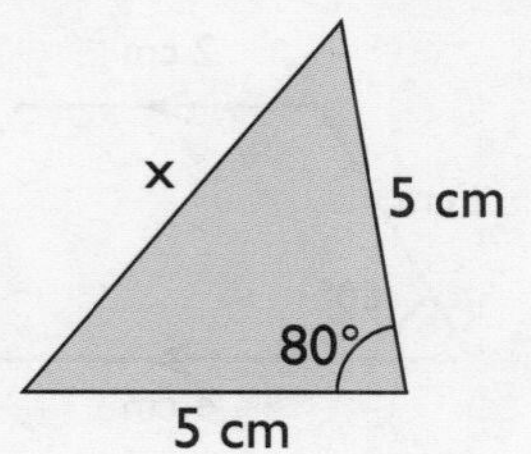

2
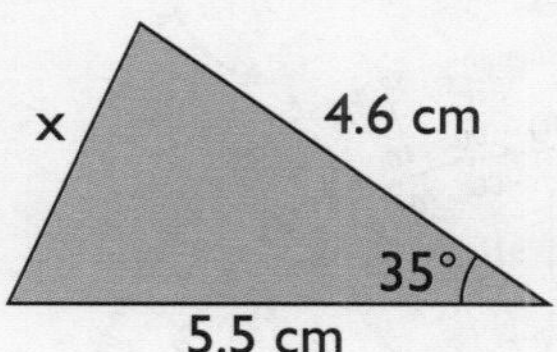

3
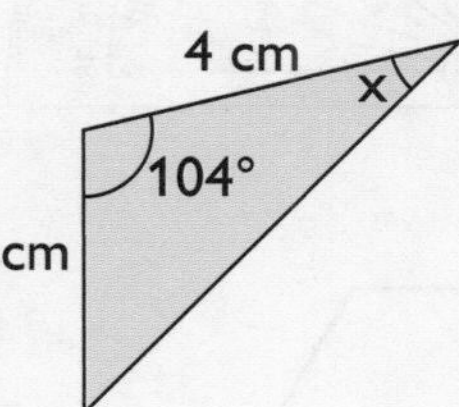

4
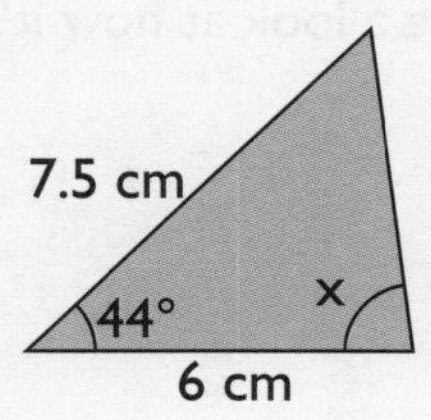

5
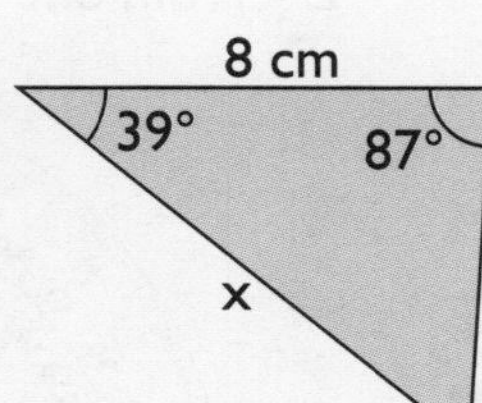

6
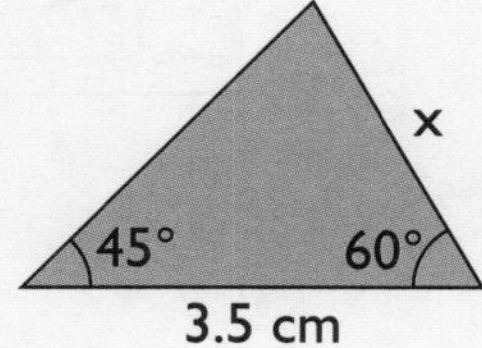

Draw the triangles using the measurements given below:

7 Triangle ABC where:
line AB = 7 cm
angle A = 75°
line AC = 5 cm

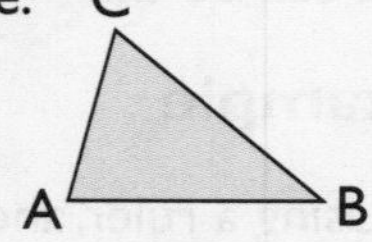

8 Triangle DEF where:
line DE = 4 cm
angle E = 50°
line EF = 6 cm

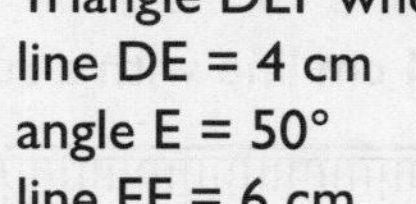

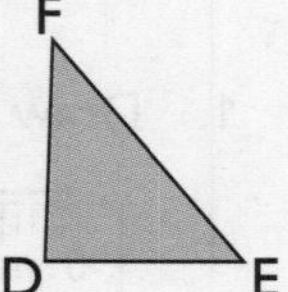

9 Triangle GHI where:
line HI = 3 cm
angle I = 90°
line IG = 5.5 cm

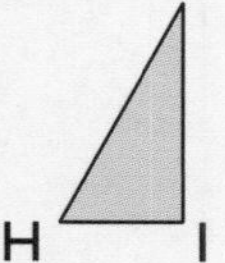

10 Triangle JKL where:
line JK = 7.5 cm
angle K = 35°
line KL = 4 cm

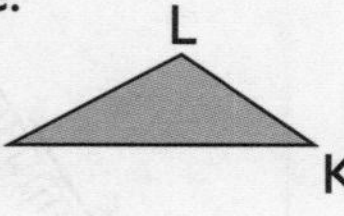

Set C

Accurately draw the sketched triangles, then find the value of 'x' to the nearest mm or degree.

1
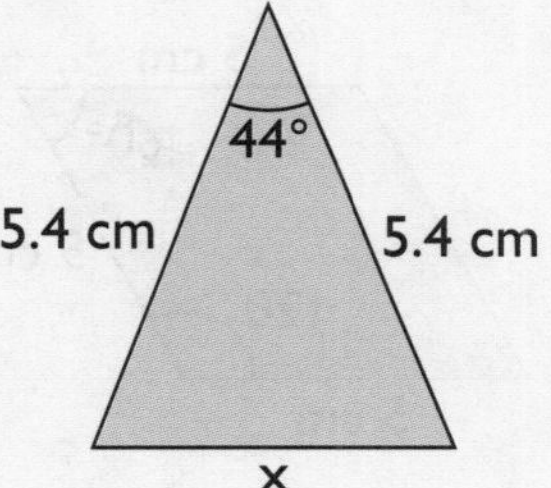

2

3
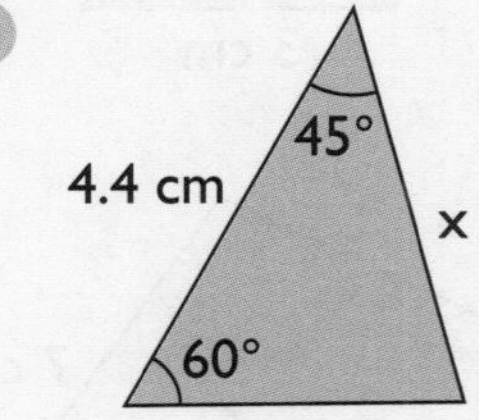

Draw the triangles using the measurements given below:

4 Triangle ABC where:
angle A = 72°
line AB = 8 cm
line CA = 5 cm

5 Triangle DEF where:
angle D = 45°
line DE = 6.4 cm
line FD = 5 cm

6 Triangle GHI where:
angle G = 54°
angle H = 30°
line GH = 4 cm

7 Triangle JKL where:
angle J = 34°
angle K = 112°
line JK = 7 cm

Measure and copy these triangles. Start by measuring angle A.

8
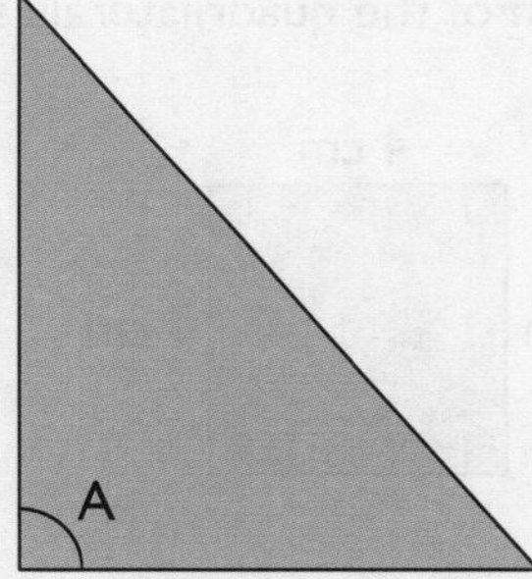

9
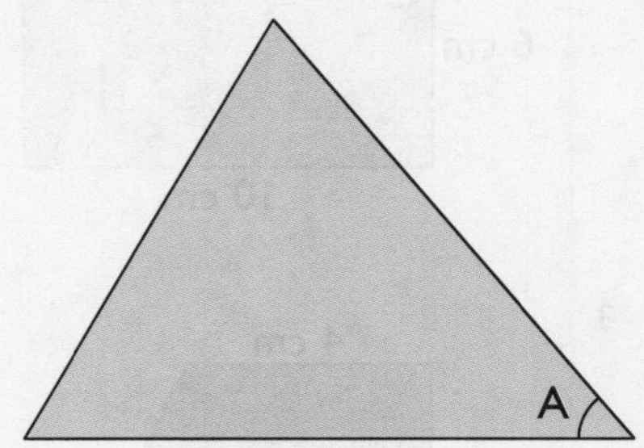

I can draw triangles accurately.

Drawing Quadrilaterals

It's important that you know how to draw quadrilaterals with exact angles and side lengths. You can do this with a ruler and protractor — let's take a look at how it's done.

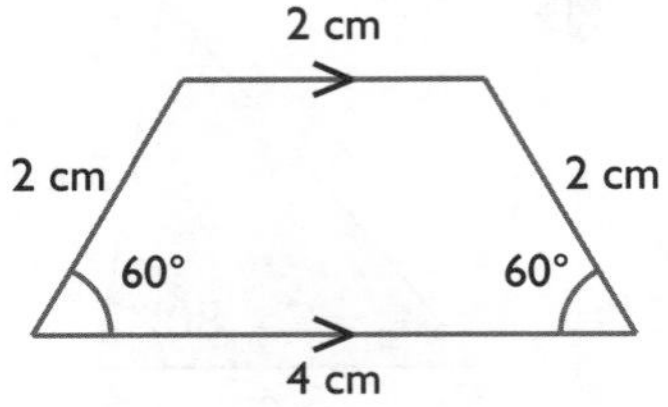

Example

Using a ruler and protractor, accurately draw the trapezium that has been sketched on the right.

1. Draw the 4 cm line with a ruler.

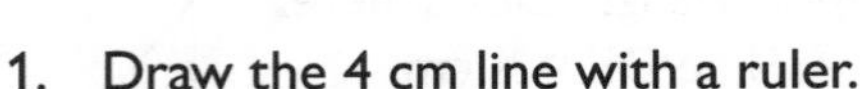
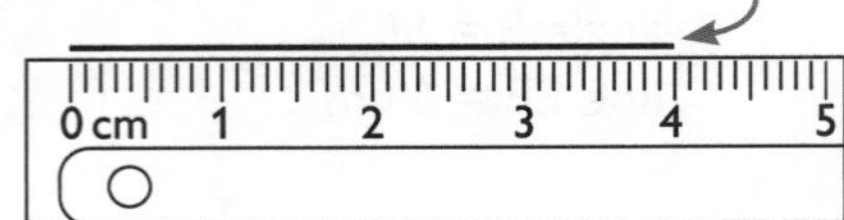

2. From one end of the 4 cm line, mark an angle of 60°.

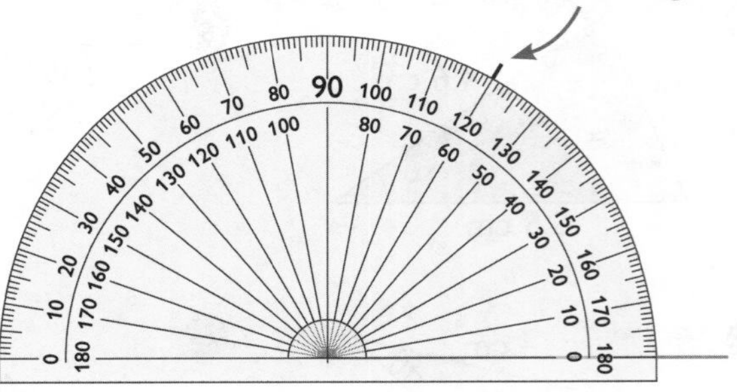

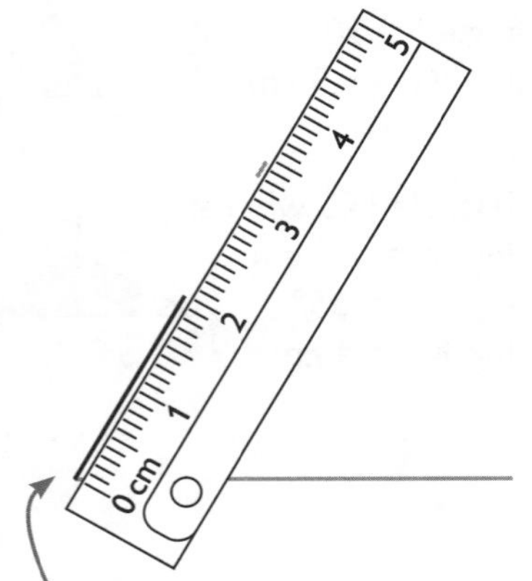

3. Draw a 2 cm line towards your mark.

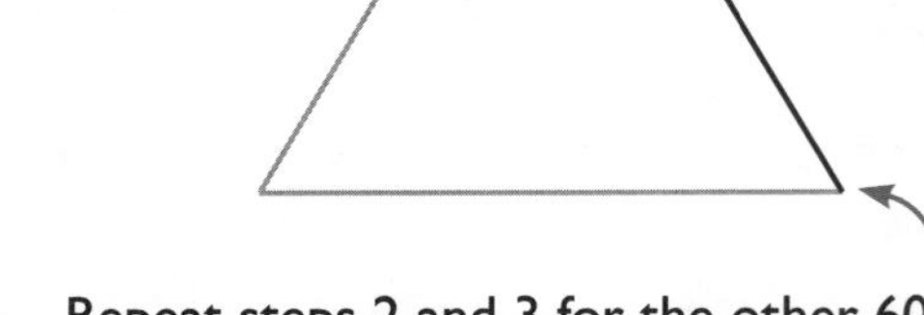

4. Repeat steps 2 and 3 for the other 60° angle. Join the lines to complete the trapezium.

Set A

Draw each of the quadrilaterals sketched below using the given side lengths and angles:

1
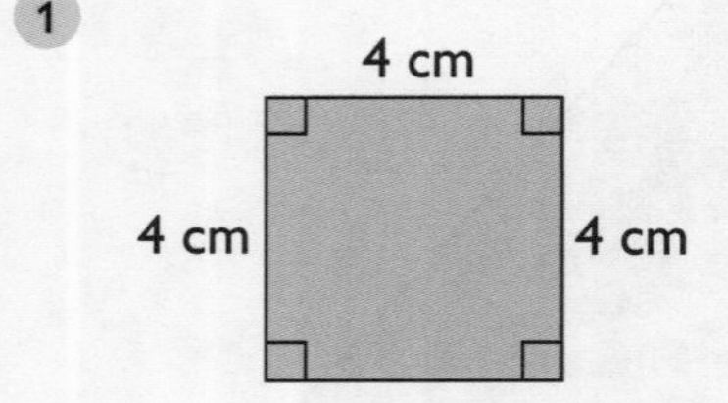

2
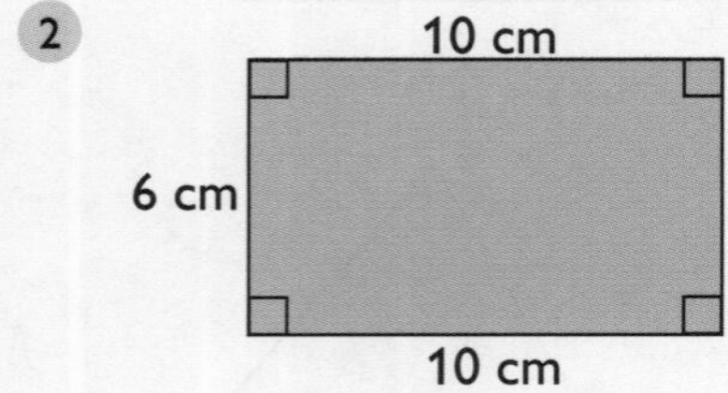

3
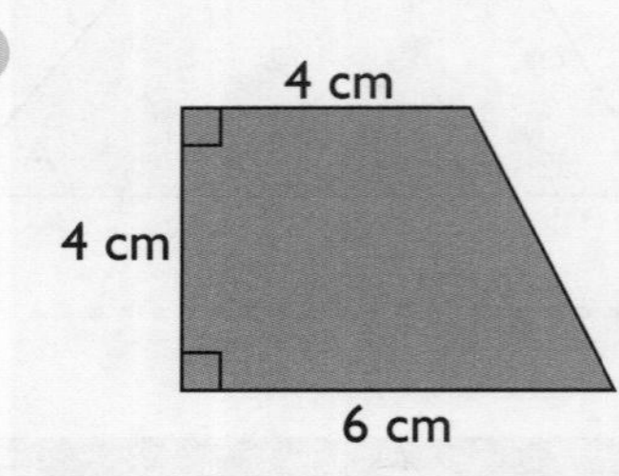

4
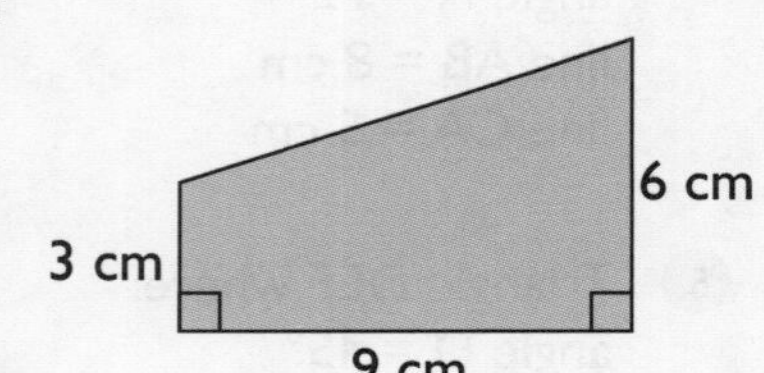

5
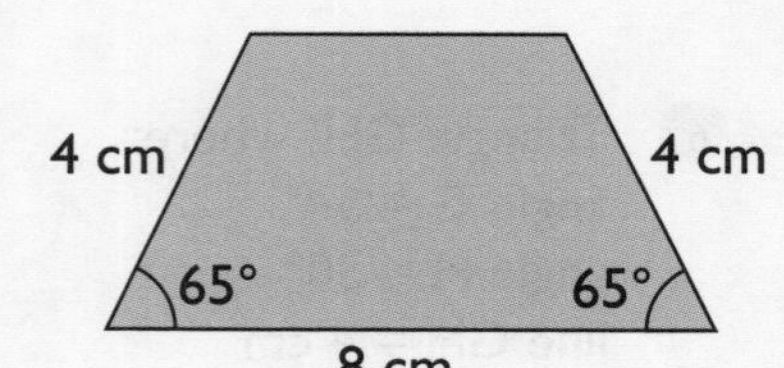

6
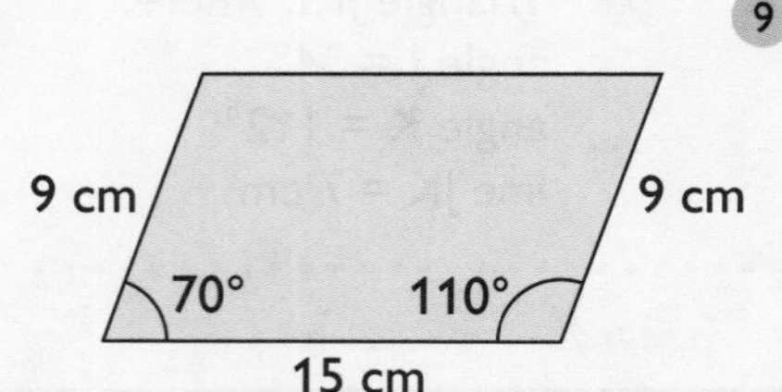

7
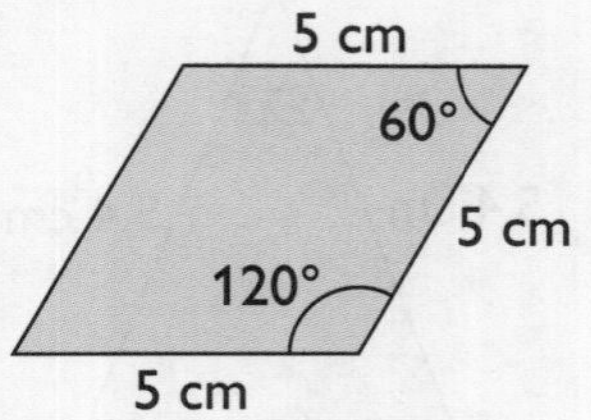

8
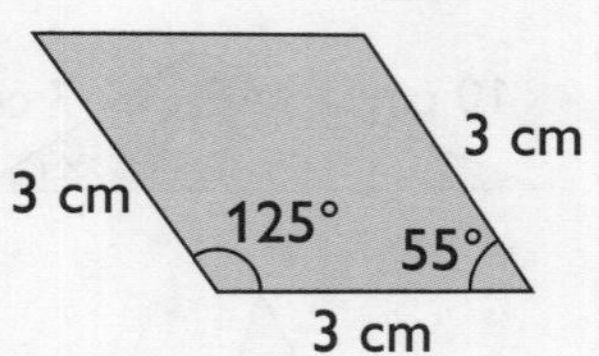

9
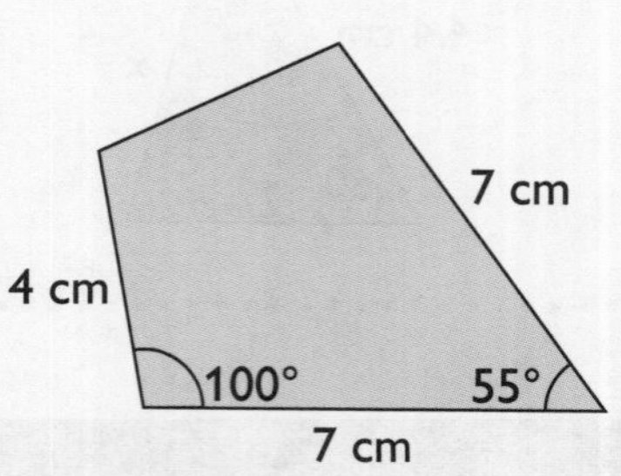

Set B

Draw and name each of the quadrilaterals that have been sketched below:

1
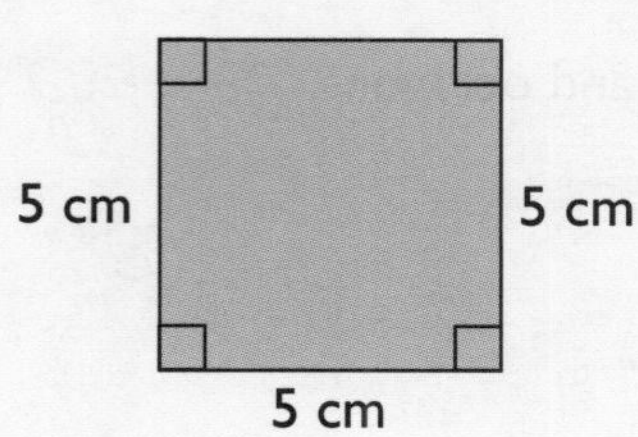

2

10 cm
8 cm
10 cm

3
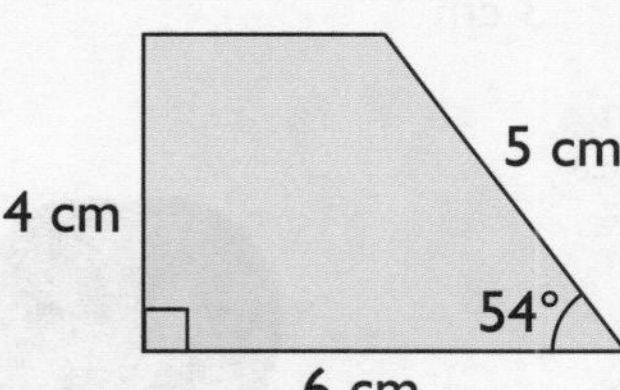

4
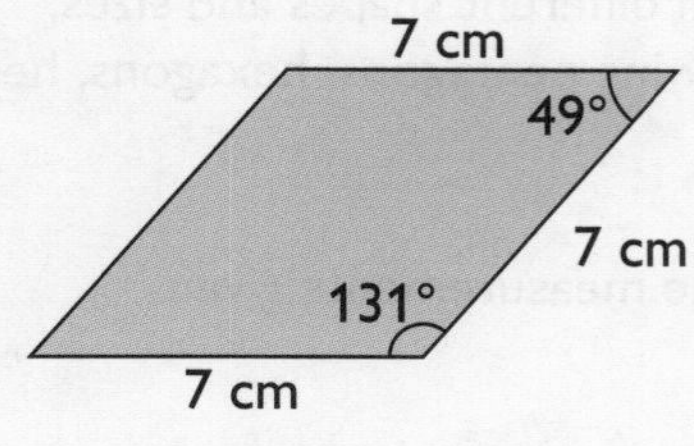

5

4 cm
3 cm
61°
108°
4 cm

6
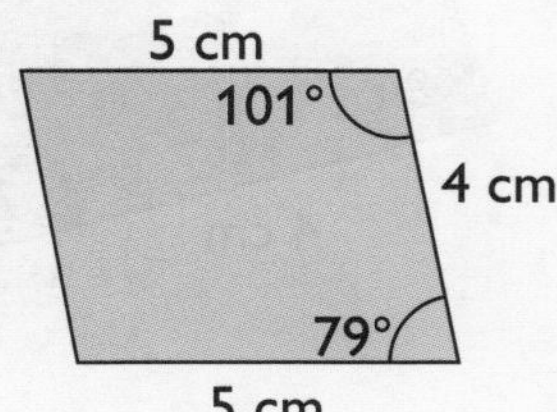

Draw the quadrilaterals sketched below and find the size of 'x' to the nearest mm or the nearest degree.

7
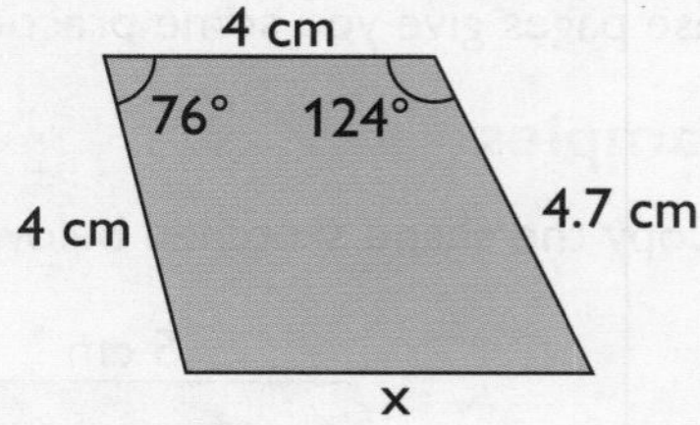

8
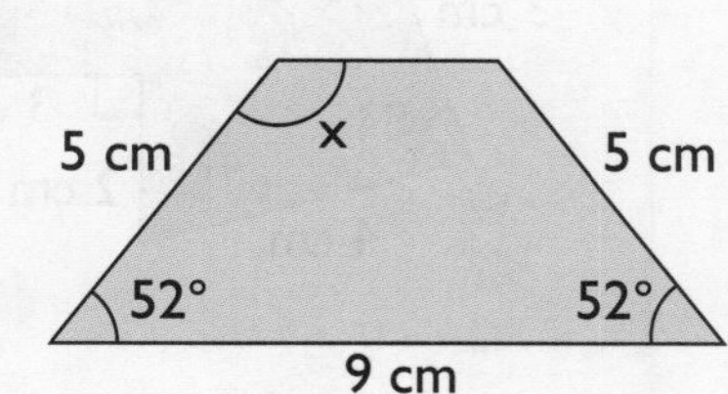

9
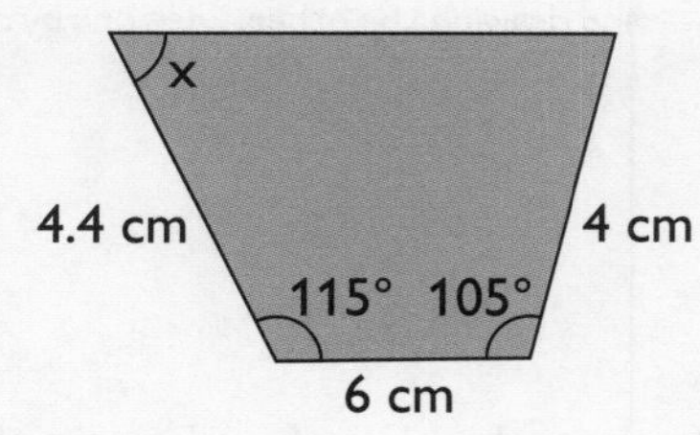

Set C

Draw the quadrilaterals that have been sketched below and find 'x' to the nearest mm or the nearest degree.

1
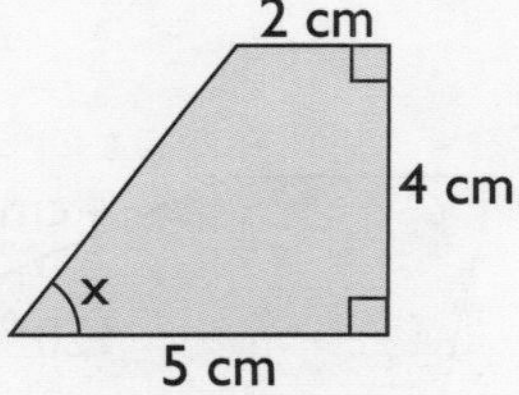

2
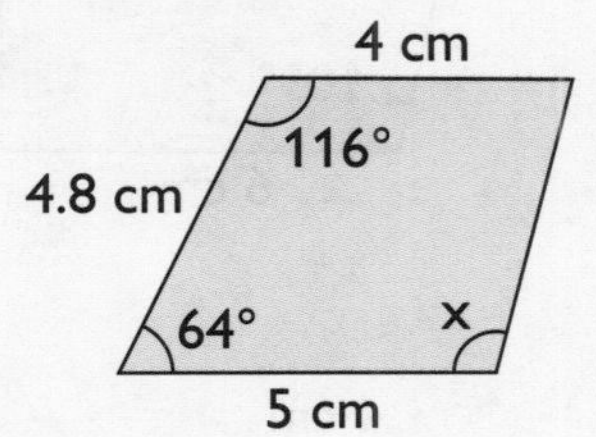

3
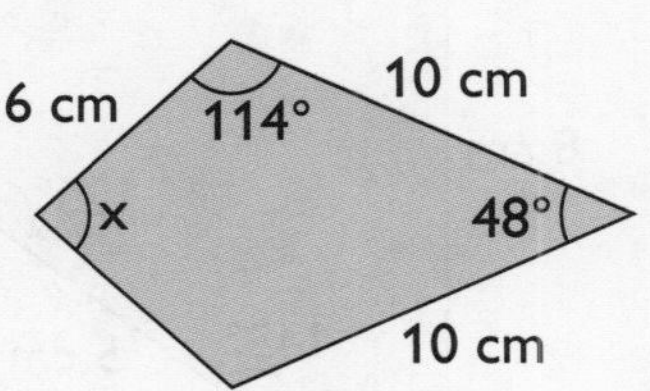

4
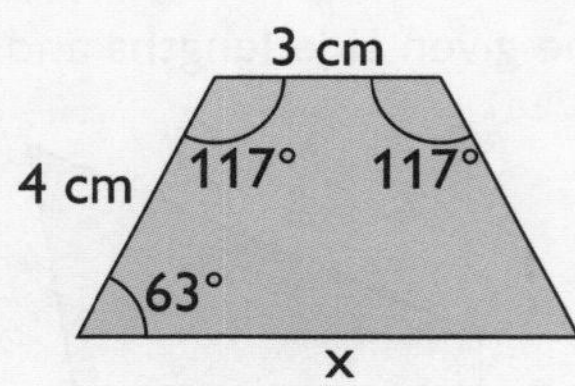

5
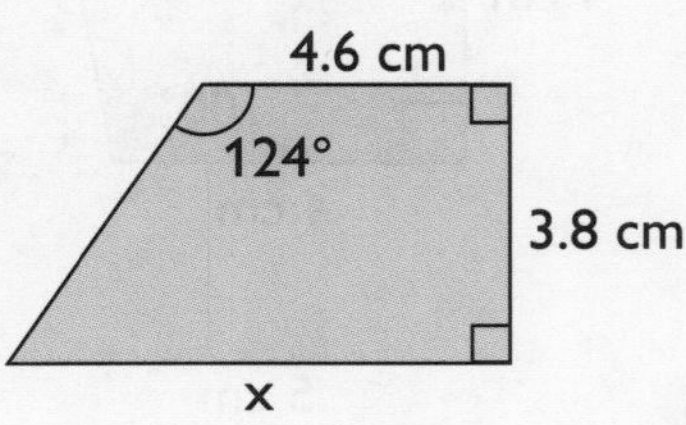

6
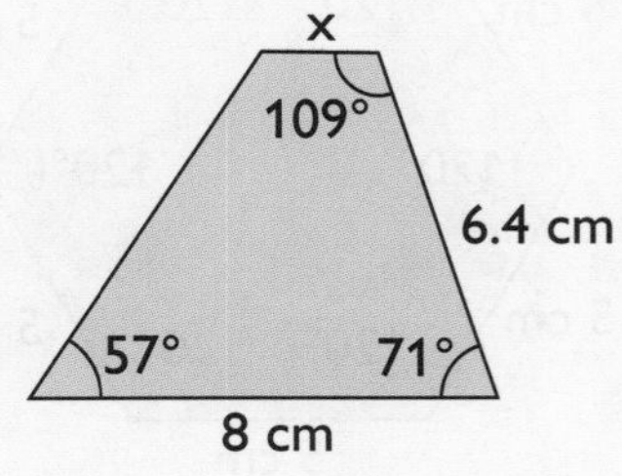

Draw the quadrilaterals described below:

7. A square with sides of 3.7 cm.

8. A trapezium with a horizontal side of length 4.2 cm and vertical sides of length 2.1 cm and 3.3 cm.

9. A rectangle with sides of 4.5 cm and 2.5 cm.

10. A rhombus with sides of 5 cm and angles of 65° and 115°.

11. A parallelogram with sides of 6.2 cm and 4.9 cm, and angles of 130° and 50°.

12. A kite with sides of 5 cm and 7 cm, 2 angles of 102° and 1 angle of 94°.

I can draw quadrilaterals accurately.    

Drawing Other Shapes

You need to be able to draw polygons of all different shapes and sizes.
These pages give you some practice at drawing pentagons, hexagons, heptagons and octagons.

Examples

Copy the shape sketched below using the measurements given.

5 cm
3 cm
111°
x
84°
3 cm
75°
2 cm
4 cm

Use a ruler and protractor to draw the shape accurately.

Start off by drawing one of the sides. Then go around the shape marking the angles and drawing the other sides one by one.

5 cm
111°
x
3 cm
3 cm
84°
2 cm
75°
4 cm

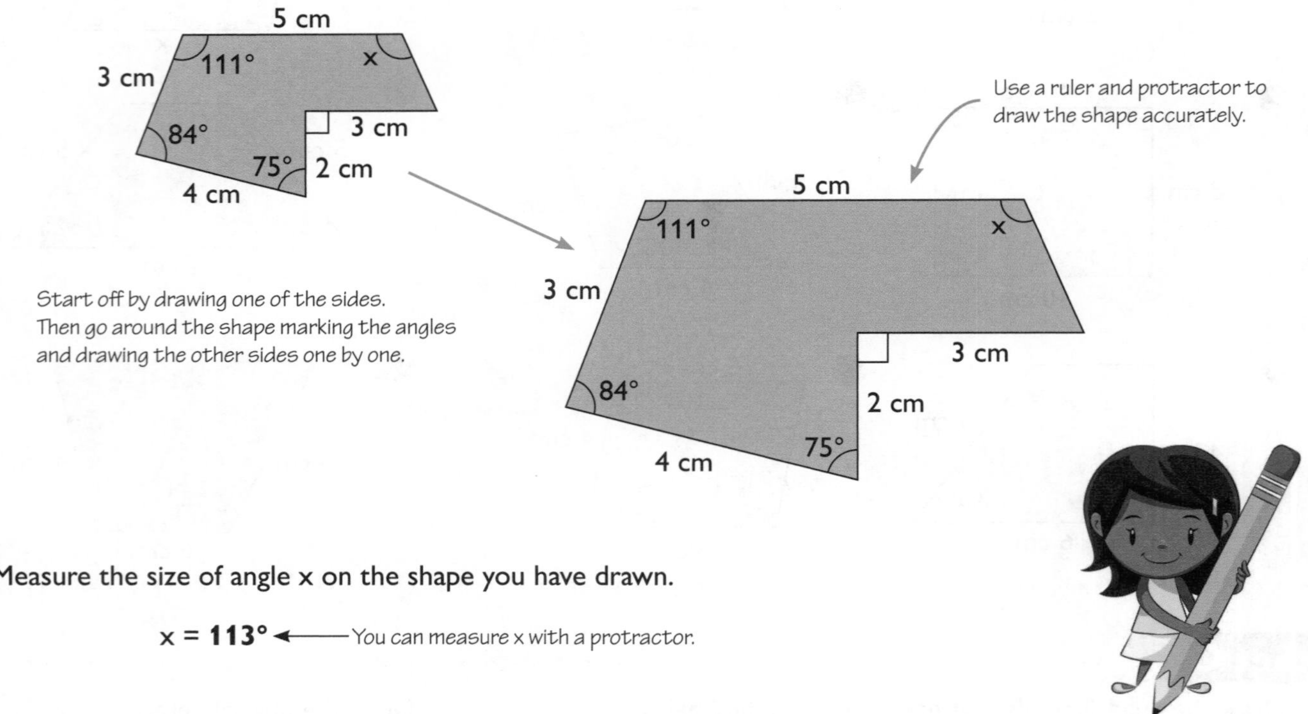

Measure the size of angle x on the shape you have drawn.

x = **113°** ← *You can measure x with a protractor.*

Set A

Draw the polygons sketched below using the given side lengths and angles:

1

5 cm
80°
5 cm
8 cm

2

4 cm
7 cm
100°
4 cm

3

4 cm
120°
9 cm
6 cm
105°
6 cm

4

3 cm
4 cm
95°
2 cm
80°
115°
3 cm

5

5 cm
5 cm
120°
120°
5 cm
120°
120°
5 cm
120°
120°
5 cm
5 cm

6

4 cm
8 cm
3 cm
125°
145°
5 cm
3 cm

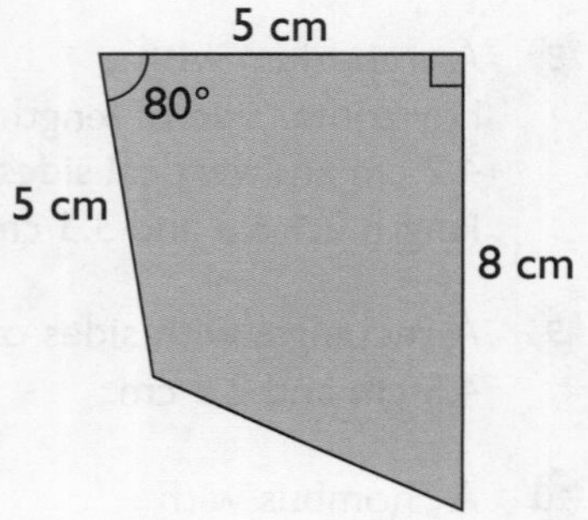

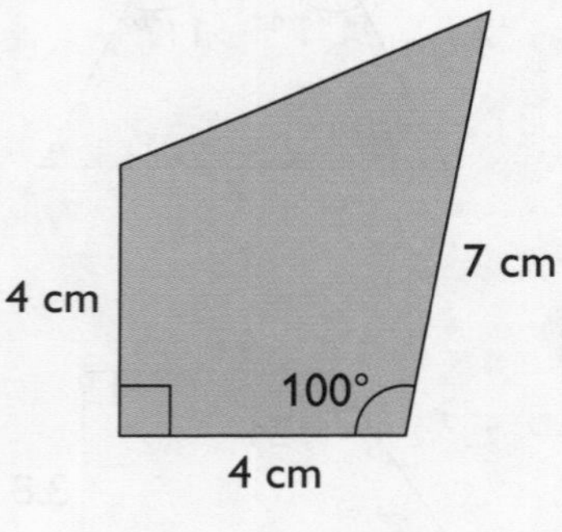

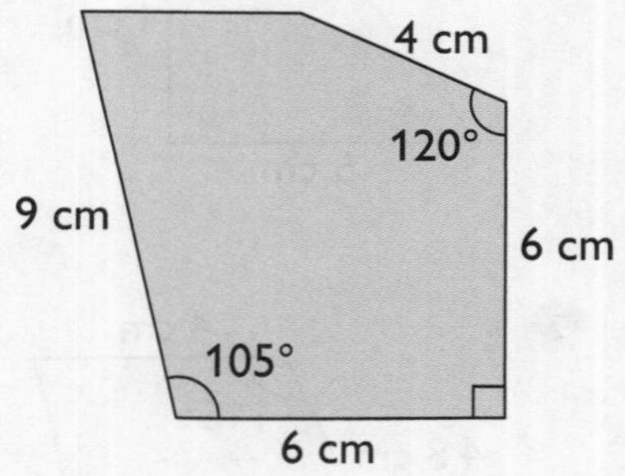

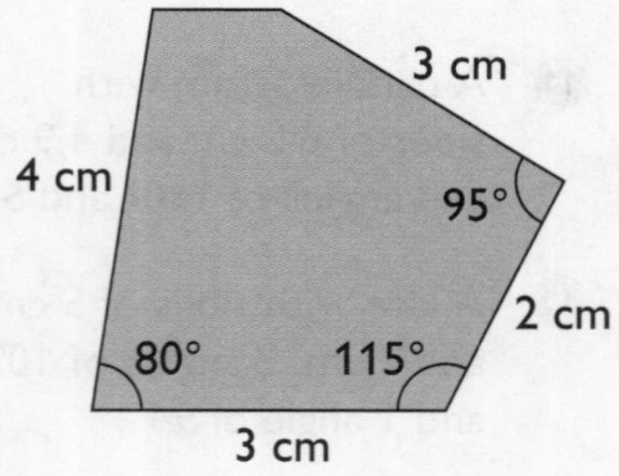

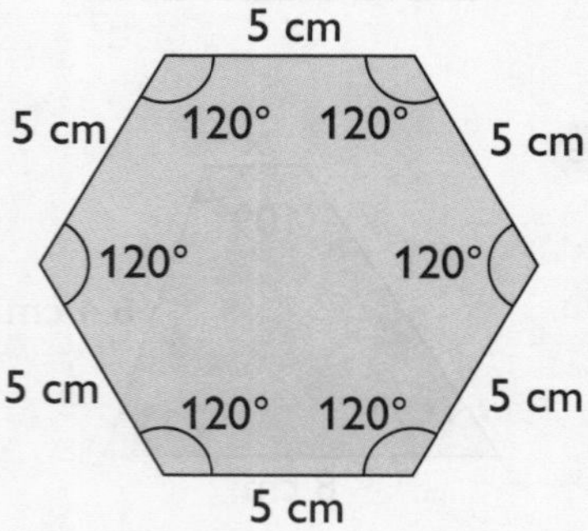

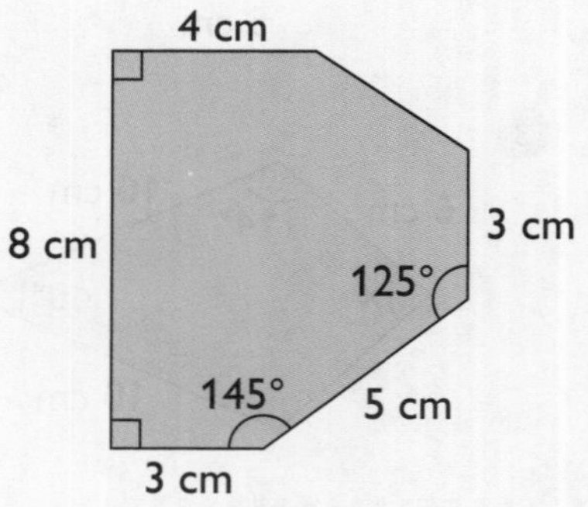

Set B

Draw and name each of the polygons that have been sketched below:

1
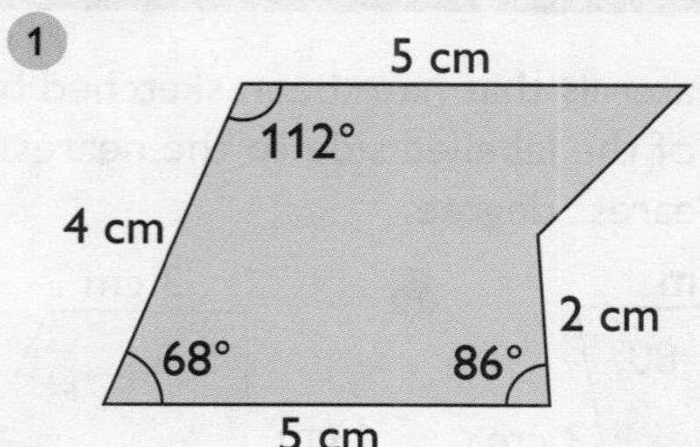

2
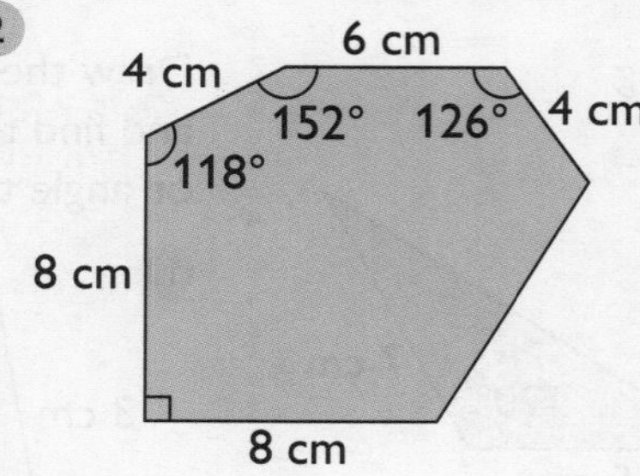

3
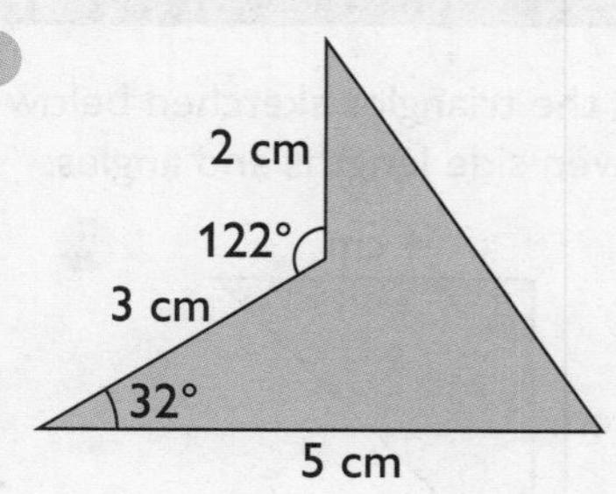

Draw the polygons sketched below and find the size of 'x' to the nearest mm or the nearest degree.

4
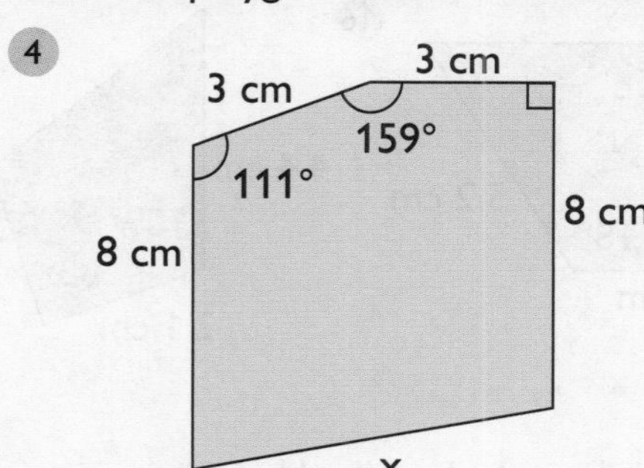

5
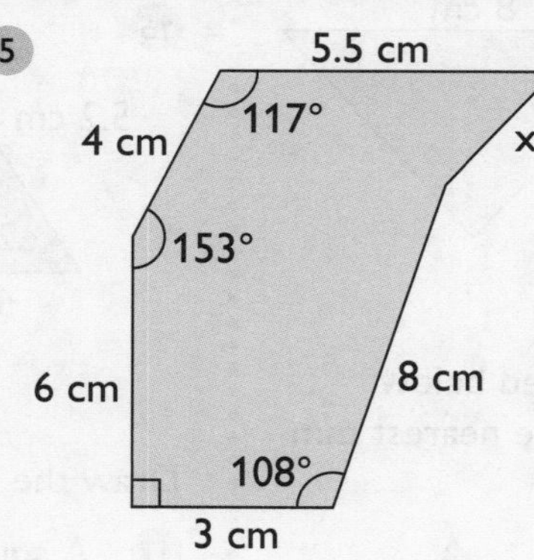

6
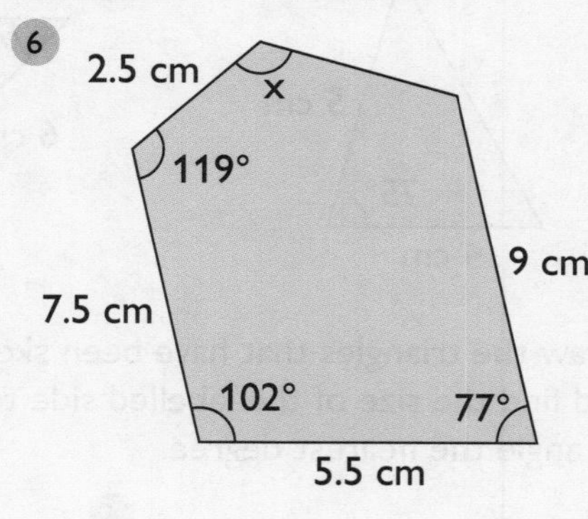

Set C

Draw the polygons that have been sketched below and find the size of the labelled side to the nearest mm or angle to the nearest degree.

1
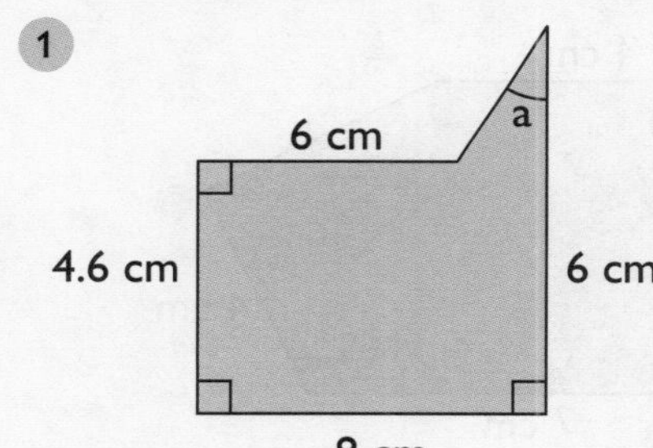

2
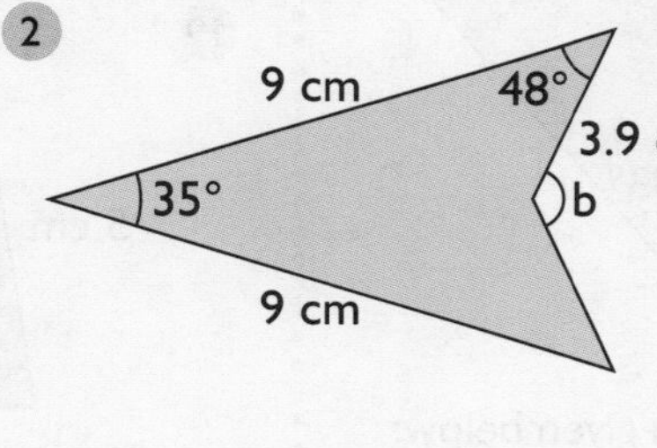

3
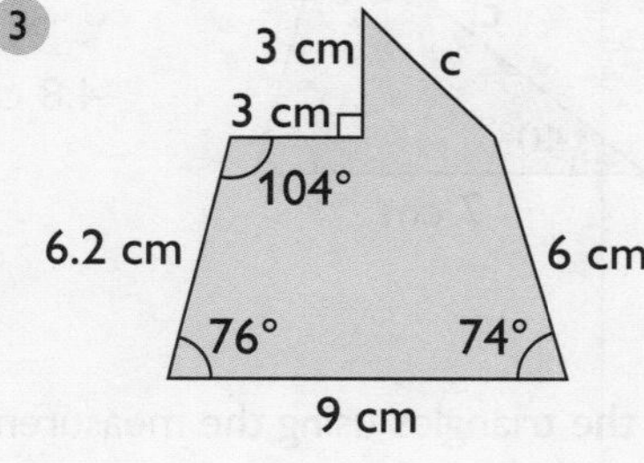

4
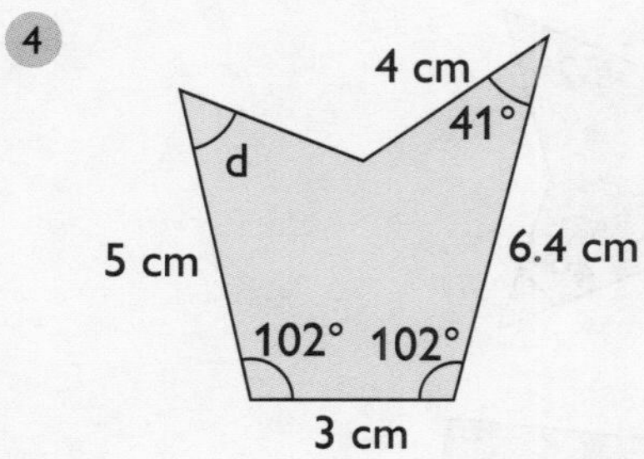

5
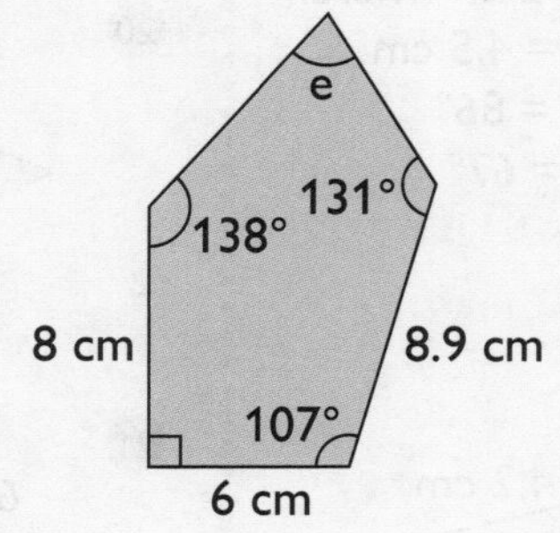

6
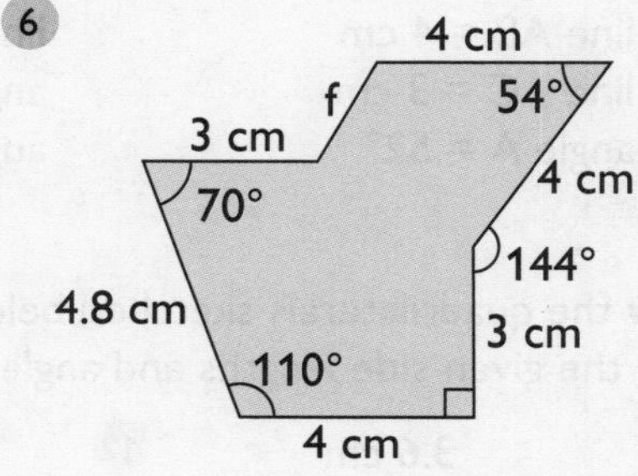

Draw the polygons using the measurements given below.

7 A regular pentagon with 4 cm sides and 108° angles.

8 A regular hexagon with 5.5 cm sides and 120° angles.

9 A regular octagon with 4.2 cm sides and 135° angles.

I can draw other 2D shapes accurately.

Geometry — Review 2

Draw the triangles sketched below using the given side lengths and angles:

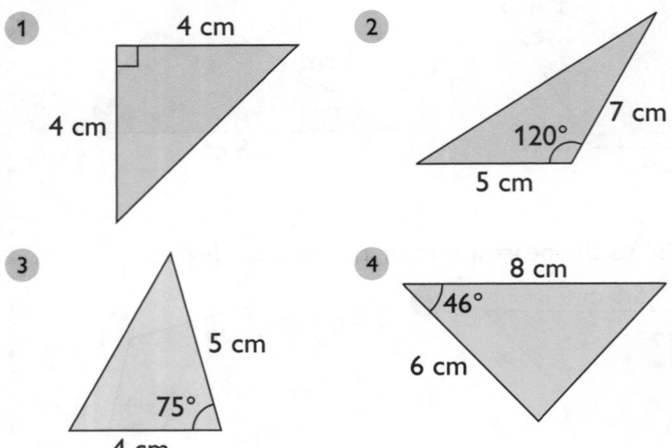

Draw the triangles that have been sketched below and find the size of the labelled side to the nearest mm or angle the nearest degree.

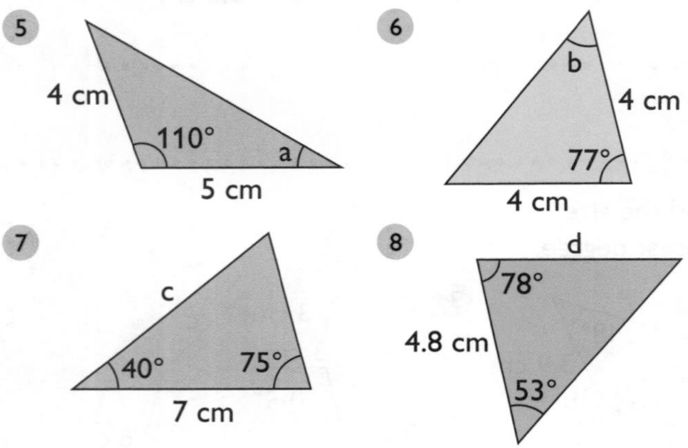

Draw the triangles using the measurements given below:

9 Triangle ABC where:
line AB = 4 cm
line AC = 3 cm
angle A = 52°

10 Triangle DEF where:
line DE = 4.5 cm
angle D = 86°
angle E = 67°

Draw the quadrilaterals sketched below using the given side lengths and angles:

11

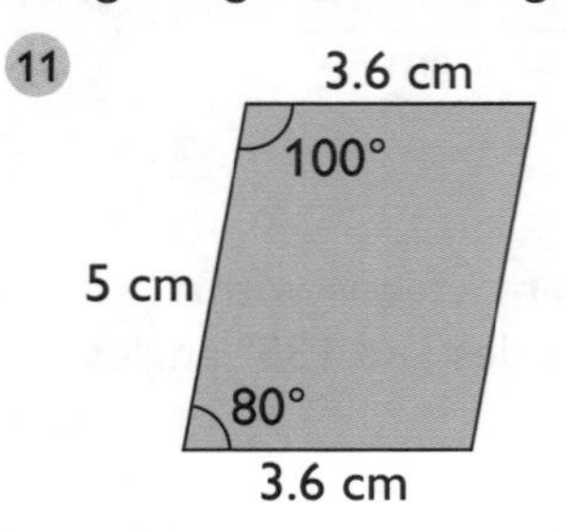

12

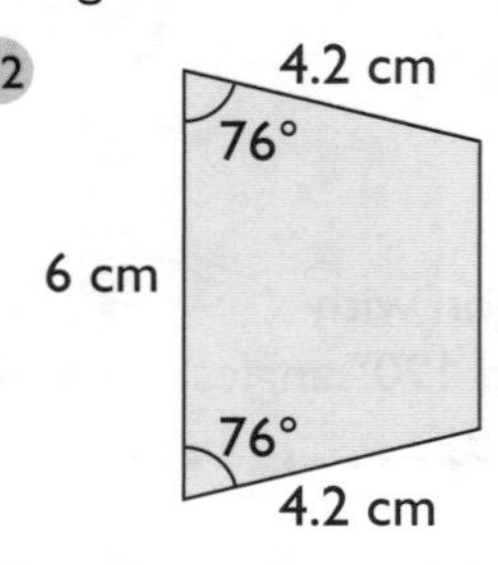

Draw the quadrilaterals that have been sketched below and find the size of the labelled side to the nearest mm or angle to the nearest degree.

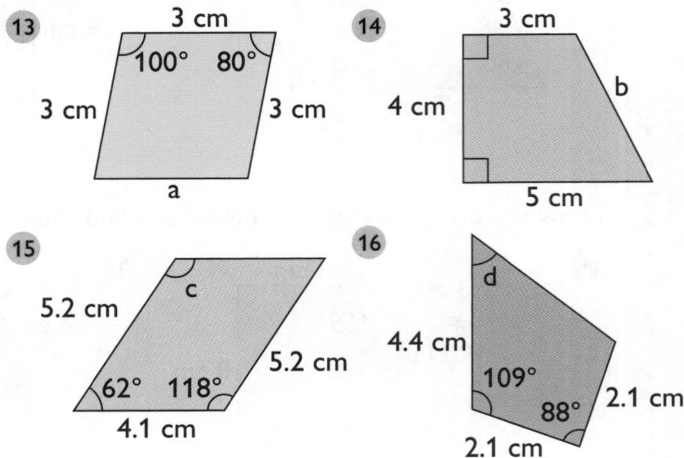

Draw the quadrilaterals described below:

17 A square with sides of 5.5 cm.

18 A rhombus with sides of 3.8 cm and angles of 125° and 55°.

Draw the polygons sketched below using the given side lengths and angles:

19

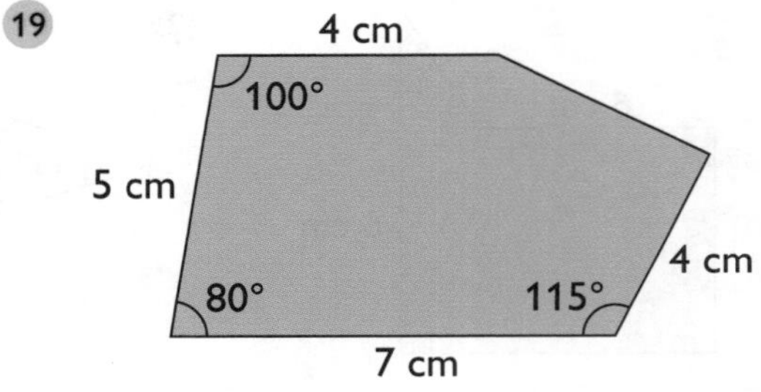

20

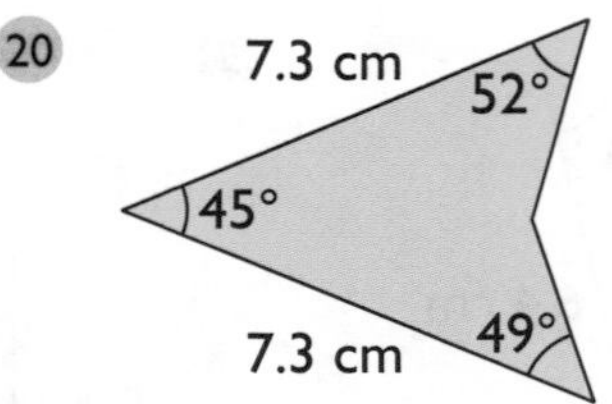

21

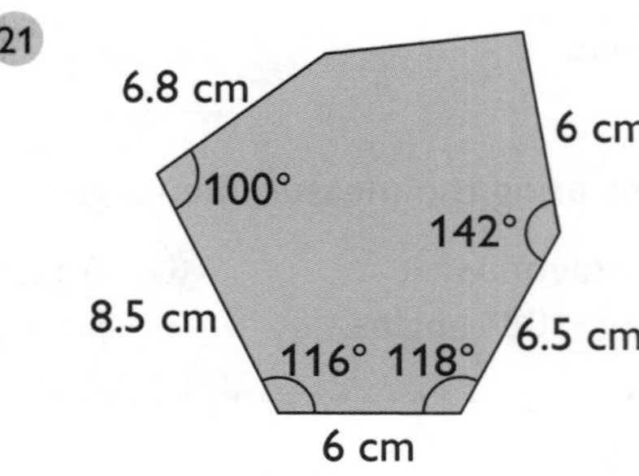

That was a lot of shapes to draw — well done for giving it a go!

2D Shapes

These pages will test your knowledge of 2D shapes and their properties.
Make sure you remember the names of all the different triangles, quadrilaterals and polygons with more sides.

Examples

Look at these shapes.

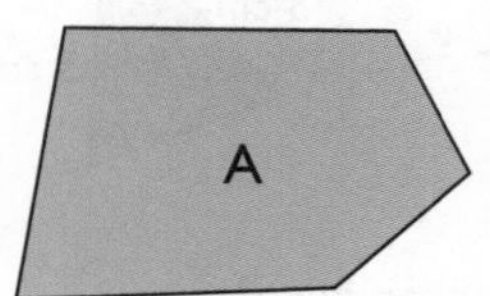

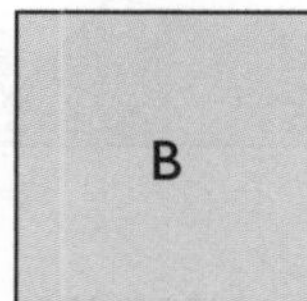

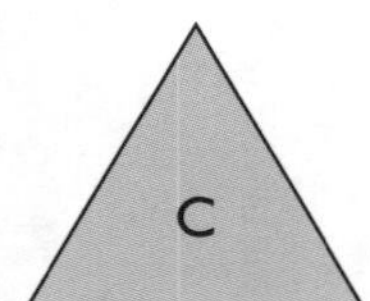

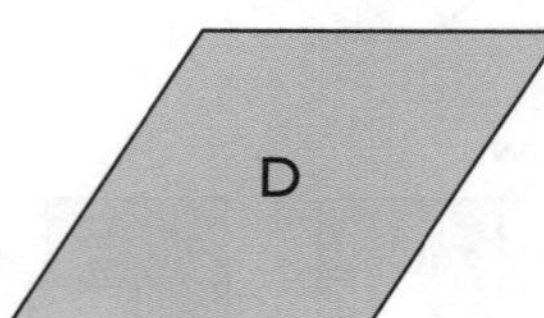

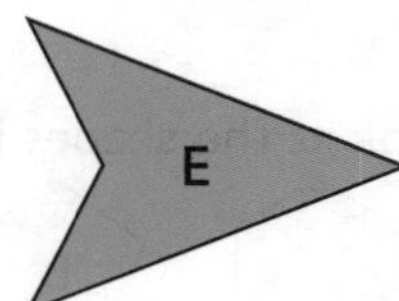

Identify the regular polygons.

The regular polygons are shapes **B** and **C**. ← *Regular polygons are shapes where all sides and angles are equal.*

Which shape has exactly two obtuse angles?

Shape **D** has exactly two obtuse angles. ← *Obtuse angles are angles greater than 90° but less than 180°.*

Which shapes have fewer than two lines of symmetry?

Shape A has 0 lines of symmetry.
Shape B has 4 lines of symmetry.
Shape C has 3 lines of symmetry.
Shape D has 2 lines of symmetry.
Shape E has 1 line of symmetry.

So shapes **A** and **E** have fewer than two lines of symmetry.

Set A

Copy and complete these sentences for each shape below:

The shape has ☐ sides.
It has ☐ lines of symmetry.
This shape has ☐ acute angles.

1 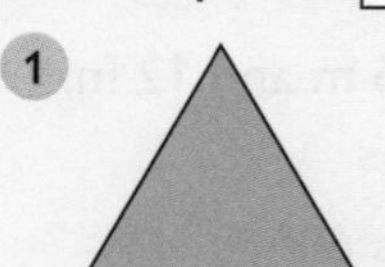

2 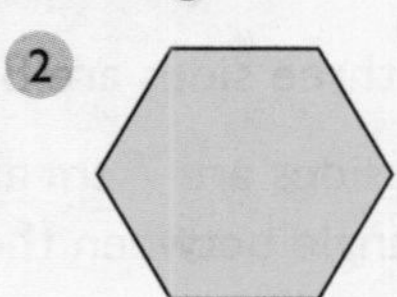

Look at the shapes below.

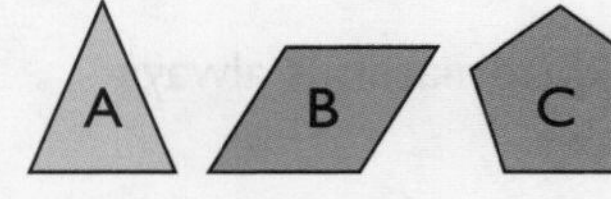

Which shape has each of the following properties?

3 5 lines of symmetry
4 Contains right angles
5 Two pairs of parallel sides
6 No obtuse angles

Look at the quadrilaterals below.

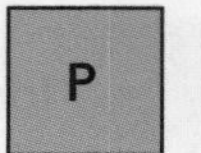

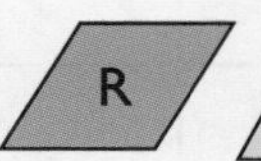

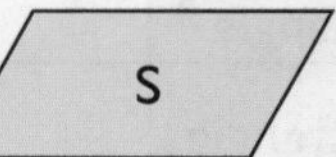

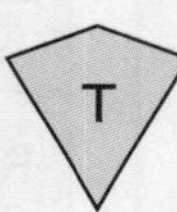

Write the letters of all the shapes that match these descriptions:

7 Is a regular polygon.
8 Has no acute angles.
9 Has no perpendicular sides.
10 Has diagonals that cross at right angles.
11 Has exactly two lines of symmetry.

Which number is greater:

12 The number of equal sides of a regular octagon or the number of equal angles in a regular hexagon?
13 The number of obtuse angles in a square or the number of lines of symmetry in an isosceles triangle?
14 The number of pairs of parallel sides in a decagon or the number of lines of symmetry in a regular hexagon?

Set B

Copy and complete these sentences for each shape below:

This polygon is a ☐. It has ☐ pairs of parallel sides and ☐ lines of symmetry.

1 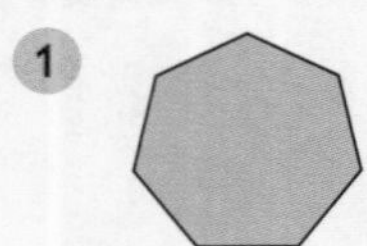

2 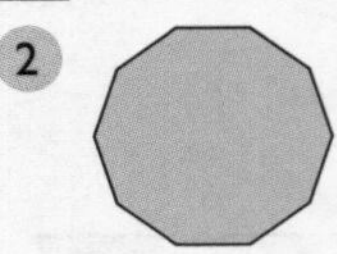

Look at the shapes below

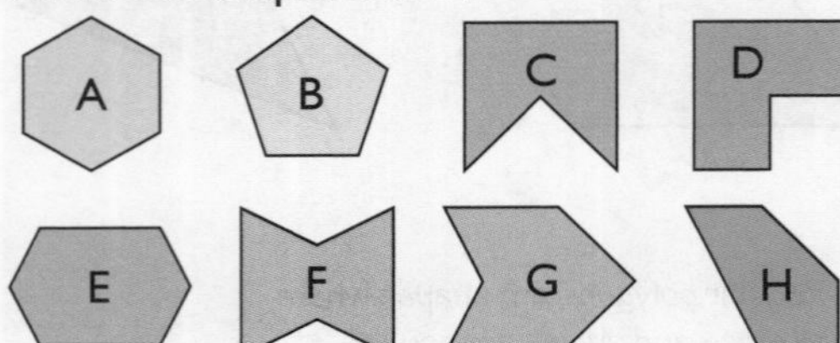

Write the letters of all the shapes that match these descriptions:

3 Is a regular polygon.

4 Has at least one pair of perpendicular sides.

5 Has exactly one pair of parallel sides.

6 Has exactly two lines of symmetry.

Identify whether these triangles are equilateral, isosceles or scalene. Explain your answer.

7 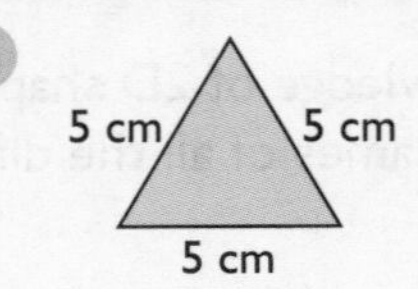

9 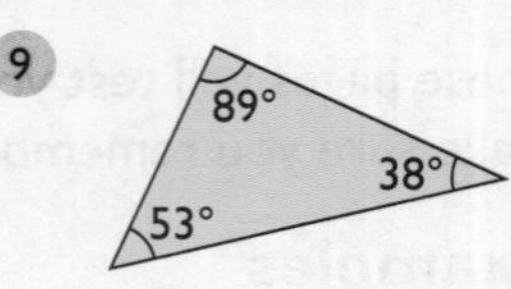

8 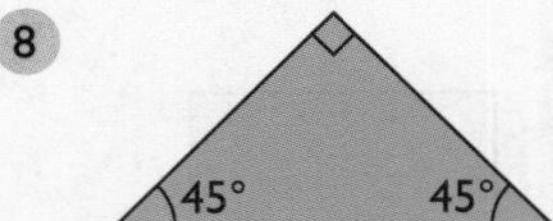

10 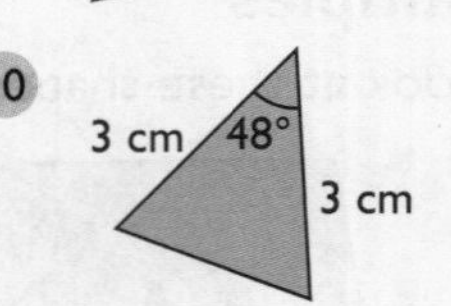

Are these statements true or false?

11 Isosceles triangles have three sides that are equal lengths.

12 Regular polygons can have some angles that are different from others.

13 Squares always have more lines of symmetry than triangles.

14 Right-angled triangles have one pair of perpendicular sides.

15 Triangles always have three acute angles.

Set C

1 Copy and complete the table:

	Pairs of parallel sides	Lines of symmetry	Number of obtuse angles
Equilateral triangle			
Rectangle			
Regular octagon			
Rhombus			

Name all the quadrilaterals that could be described using the sentences below:

2 All sides are the same length.

3 It has 2 pairs of parallel sides but no lines of symmetry.

4 It has 2 acute angles and no parallel sides.

5 It has at least one pair of perpendicular sides.

6 Write two similarities and two differences about the two shapes below.

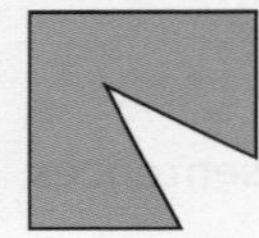

Identify the type of triangle from the pieces of information. Explain your answers.

7 The three angles are 54°, 72° and 54°.

8 The three sides are 8 m, 6 m and 12 m.

9 Two sides are 7 cm and the angle between them is 60°.

Are these statements true or false? Explain your answers.

10 The diagonals of quadrilaterals always cross at right angles.

11 Regular heptagons have fewer pairs of parallel sides than regular hexagons.

12 All polygons with equal length sides are regular polygons.

I can classify and compare 2D shapes based on their features.     

Circles

You need to know the names for different parts of a circle — let's take a look at some of the examples below...

Examples

Label the circumference, radius and diameter of this circle:

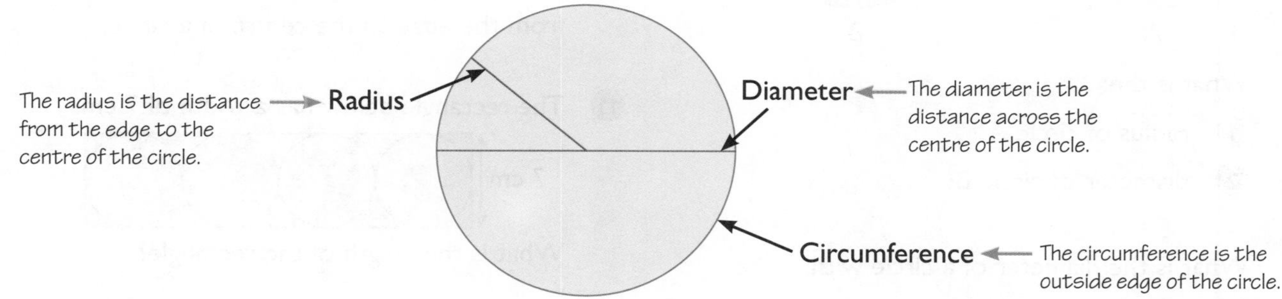
The radius is the distance from the edge to the centre of the circle.
Radius
Diameter
The diameter is the distance across the centre of the circle.
Circumference
The circumference is the outside edge of the circle.

A vinyl record has a radius of 15 cm. What is the diameter of the vinyl record?

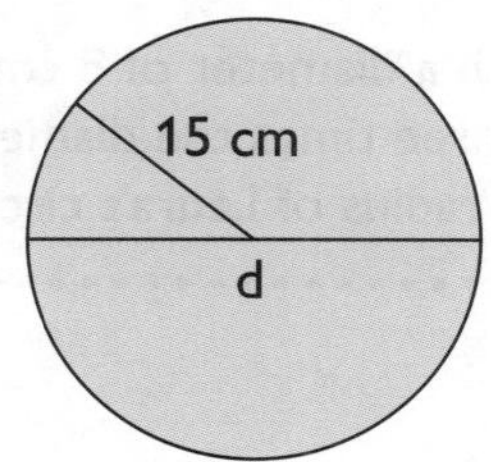
15 cm
d

15 cm × 2 = 30 cm ← The diameter is twice the radius.

diameter = **30 cm**

VINYL

Set A

1. For each letter in the circles below, decide if it is pointing to the circumference, diameter or radius.

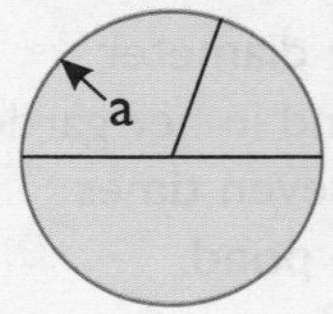
a
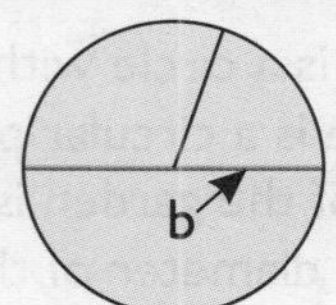
b
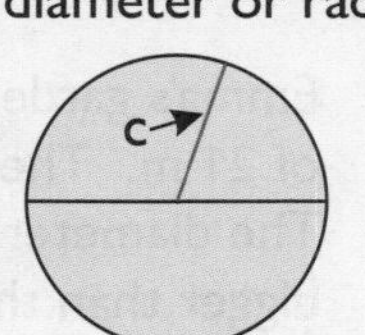
c

Measure the diameter and radius of these circles.

2.

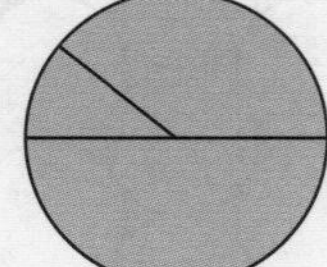

3.

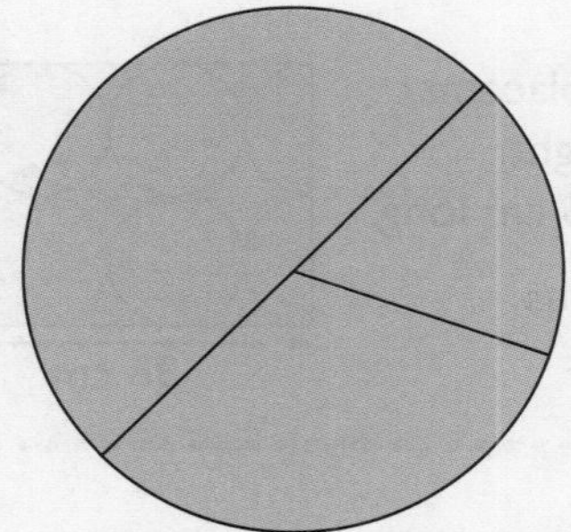

What is the diameter of a circle with:

4. a radius of 3 cm?
5. a radius of 7 cm?
6. a radius of 10 m?

What is the radius of a circle with:

7. a diameter of 8 cm?
8. a diameter of 14 cm?
9. a diameter of 30 m?

10. Freda has a circular swimming pool with a radius of 6 m. What is the diameter of her swimming pool?

11. A circular coffee table has a diameter of 80 cm. What is the radius of the coffee table?

12. A 5p coin has a diameter of 18 mm. What is the radius of a 5p coin?

Set B

Look at the circles below:

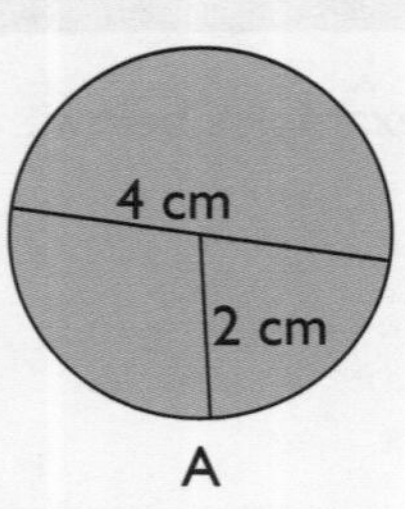

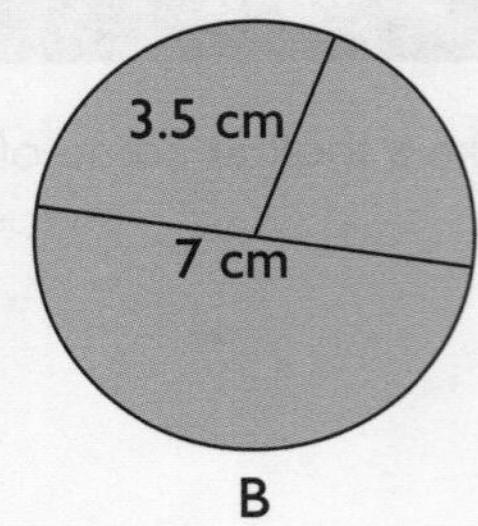

What is the:

1. radius of circle A?
2. diameter of circle B?

What is the diameter of a circle with:

3. a radius of 19 cm?
4. a radius of 31 m?

What is the radius of a circle with:

5. a diameter of 46 cm?
6. a diameter of 74 m?

Answer true or false:

7. The circumference is the outside edge of a shape.
8. The diameter of a circle is always smaller than the radius.
9. The radius of a circle is half the diameter.
10. The diameter measures the distance from the edge to the centre of a circle.

11. The rectangle below has a width of 7 cm.

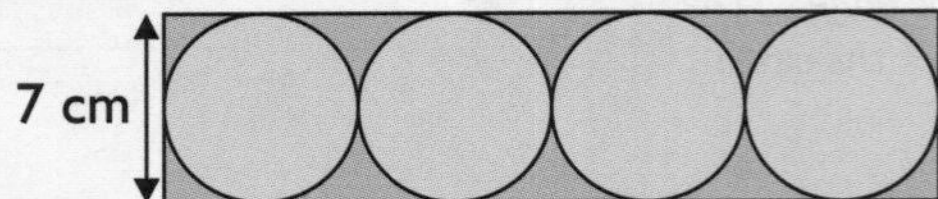

What is the length of the rectangle?

12. The radius of a small circular plate is 9 cm. The radius of a large circular plate is twice as big. What is the diameter of the large plate?

13. Ben draws a circle with a diameter of 8 cm. Laura draws a circle three times the diameter of Ben's. What is the radius of Laura's circle?

Set C

1. Sketch the diagram below and write the names of the different parts of the circle in the boxes.

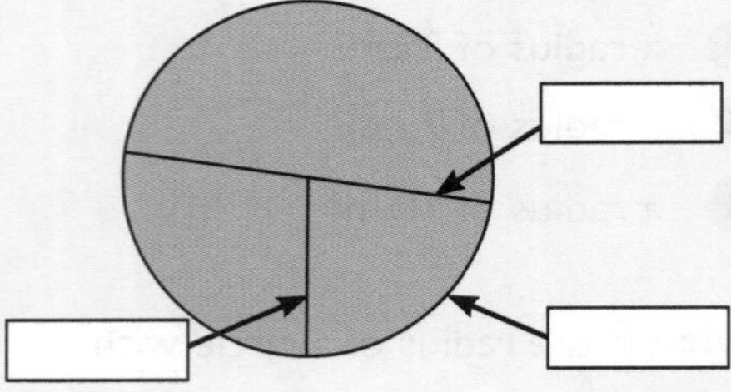

What is the diameter of a circle with:

2. a radius of 6.5 cm?
3. a radius of 17.3 m?
4. a radius of 41.9 cm?

What is the radius of a circle with:

5. a diameter of 19 cm?
6. a diameter of 32.6 cm?
7. a diameter of 55.2 m?

8. The radius of a target's bullseye is 2.5 cm. The radius of the target is six times as big. What is the diameter of the target?

9. Emma's garden is a circle with a diameter of 21 m. There is a circular pond in her garden. The diameter of the garden is seven times bigger than the diameter of the pond. What is the radius of the pond?

10. In the diagram on the right each small circle has a radius of 2.1 cm.

    What is the diameter of the large circle?

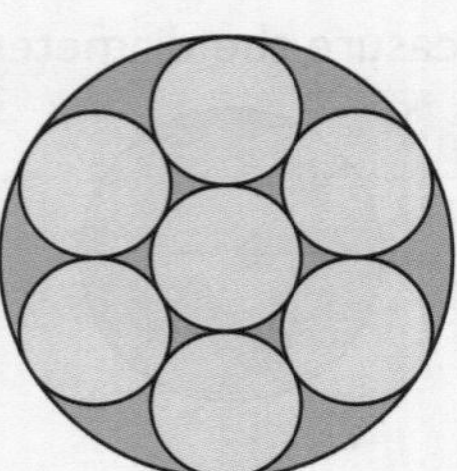

11. The pattern on a placemat is shown on the right. The placemat is 36 cm long.

    Work out the radius of each blue circle.

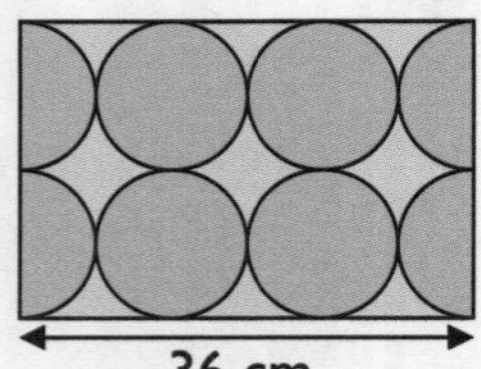

I can name different parts of a circle and I know that the diameter is twice the radius.

3D Shapes

This page gives you a chance to brush up on your 3D shape knowledge. Make sure you know the names of the different 3D shapes and what they look like — you won't always be shown a diagram.

Example

How many more vertices does shape A have than shape B?

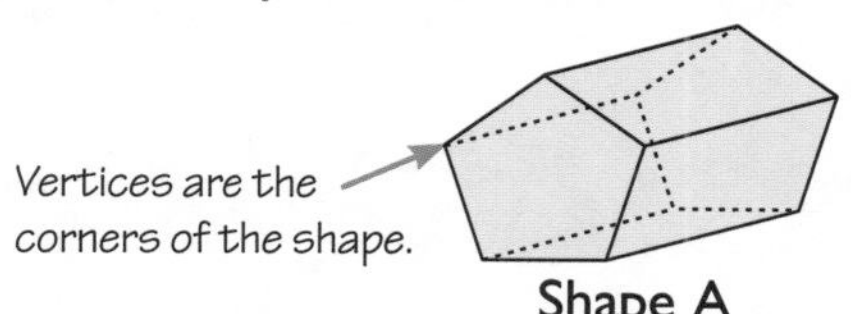

Shape A

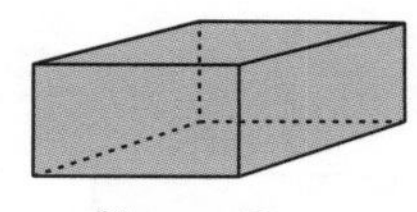
Shape B

Shape A has 10 vertices and shape B has 8 vertices.

So shape A has 10 – 8 = **2 more vertices.**

Set A

Look at the shapes below.

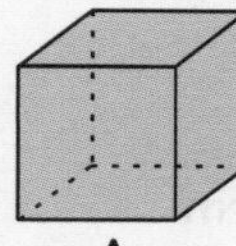
A

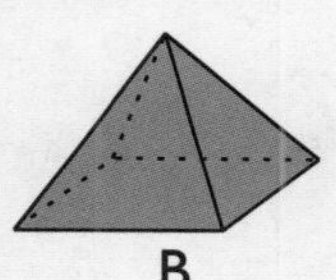
B

Which shape has more:

1. faces?
2. edges?
3. vertices?

Three 3D shapes are shown below.

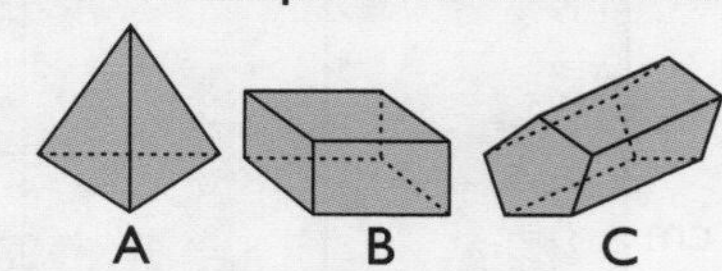

4. Order the shapes from most to least number of faces.
5. What would the order be if you compared the number of edges instead of faces?

Which of these shapes match the descriptions below?

cube	triangular prism
cuboid	tetrahedron

6. This shape has 6 identical faces.
7. This shape has 9 edges.
8. This shape has fewer than 6 vertices.

Set B

Name each shape:

1. "I have 6 faces. They are all the same shape but not all the same size."
2. "I have 5 faces. Two of them are triangles and the others are rectangles."
3. "I have one curved face, no corners and no edges."

Look at the 3D shapes below.

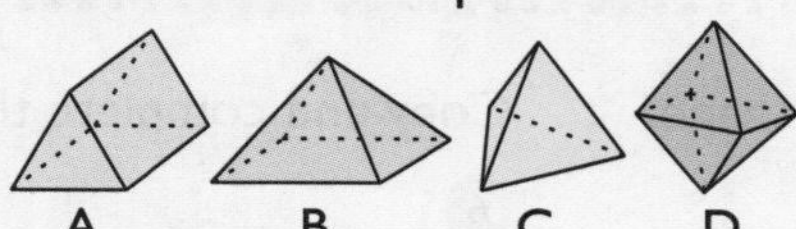

Which shape has:

4. more vertices than faces?
5. twice as many edges as vertices?
6. two more edges than faces?

Find the missing numbers in the sentences below:

7. A cuboid has ☐ more edges than a tetrahedron.
8. Triangular prisms and square based pyramids both have ☐ faces.
9. A cube has ☐ more faces than a cone.

Set C

Name each shape:

1. "I have 8 faces, 2 are regular hexagons and the others are rectangles."
2. "I have 8 vertices and all my faces are equal."
3. "I have 5 faces and only one of them is a square."
4. "I have 0 vertices and 2 circular faces."

Here are the names of four shapes:

cuboid	triangular prism
hemisphere	tetrahedron

5. Put the shapes in order from least to most vertices.
6. Which shape has the most triangular faces?
7. Name any shapes which have more then 6 edges.

True or false?
Explain your answers.

8. A hemisphere has more circular faces than a cone.
9. A hexagonal prism has fewer vertices than a cuboid.
10. Octagonal prisms have 15 more edges than triangular prisms.

I can recognise, describe and compare 3D shapes.

Making 3D Shapes

Nets are patterns that can be cut and folded to make 3D shapes.
Each face of the shape matches up with part of the net.

Examples

Draw an accurate net for the cuboid below:

2 cm
3 cm
2 cm

There are lots of different ways to draw the net of a cuboid. You might want to draw a quick sketch before you start:

Then use a ruler to help you draw the net accurately.

2 cm
2 cm
2 cm
2 cm
2 cm
2 cm
3 cm
3 cm
2 cm
2 cm
2 cm
2 cm
2 cm
2 cm

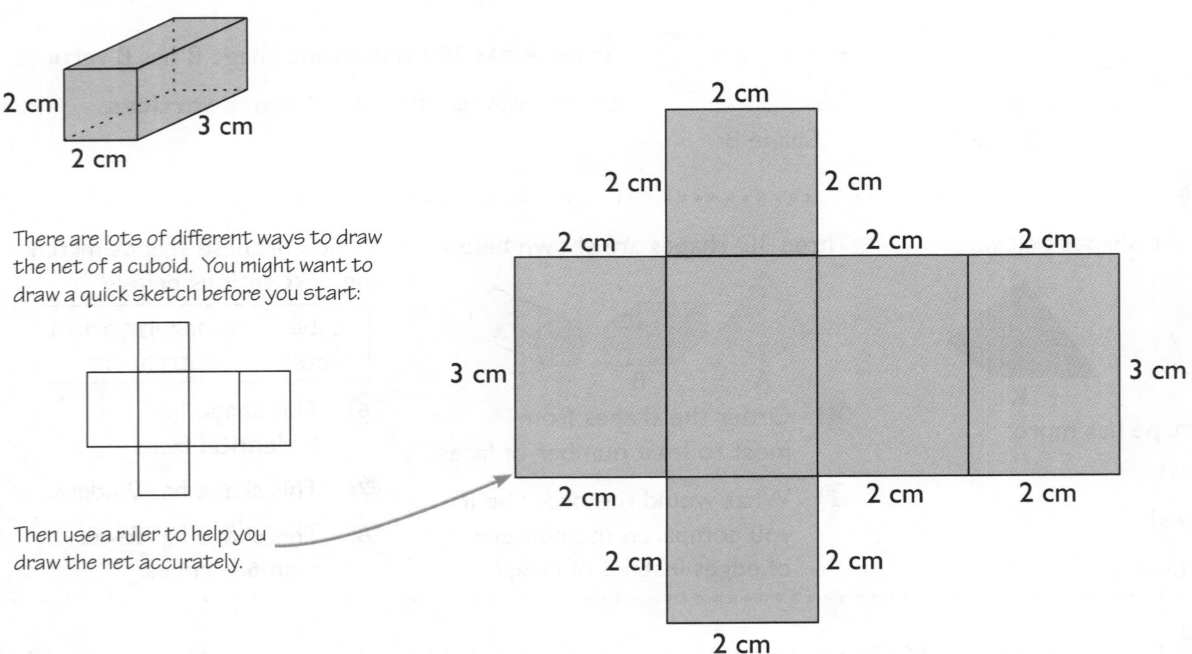

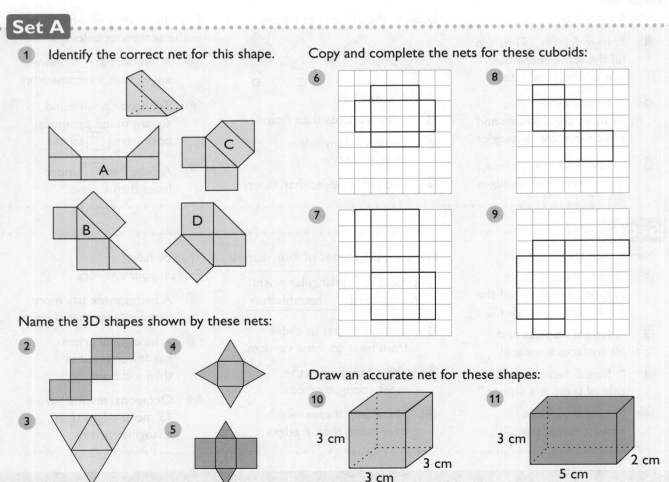

Set A

1. Identify the correct net for this shape.

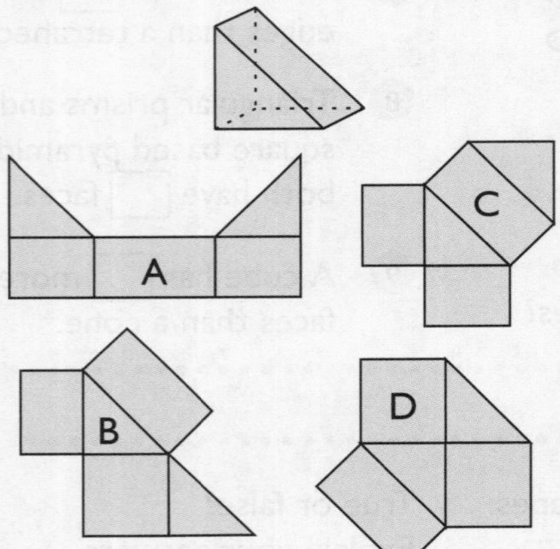

A
B
C
D

Name the 3D shapes shown by these nets:

2.

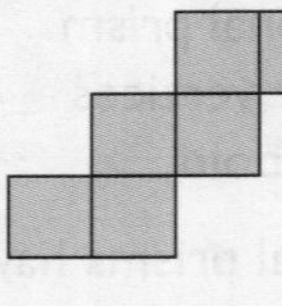

3.

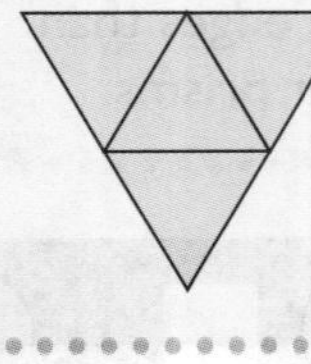

4.

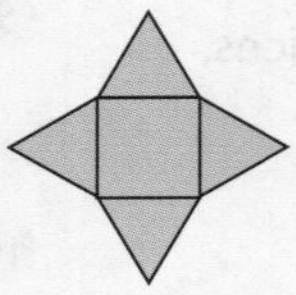

5.

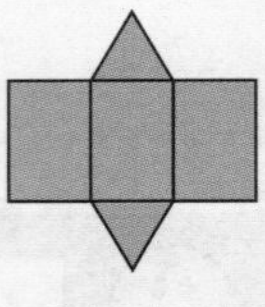

Copy and complete the nets for these cuboids:

6.

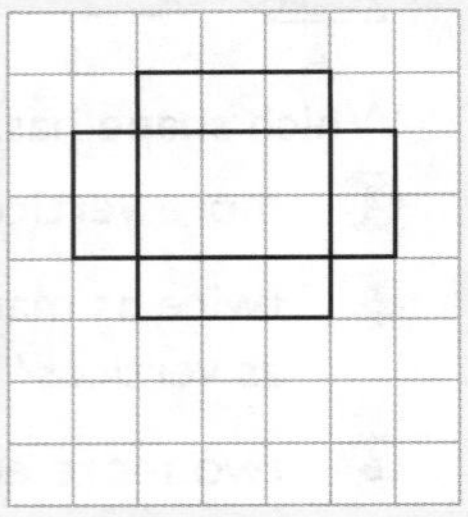

7.

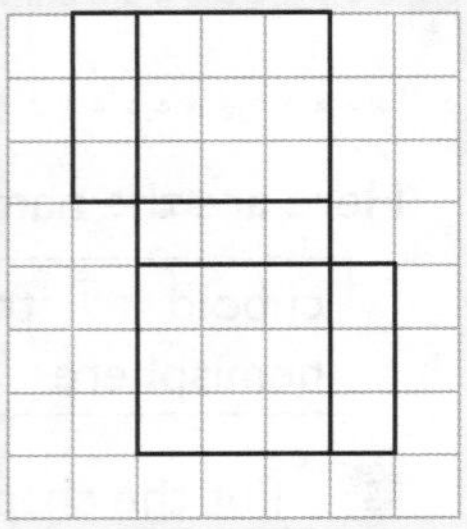

8.

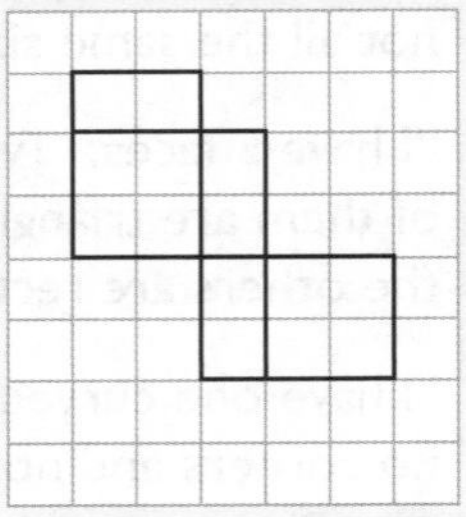

9.

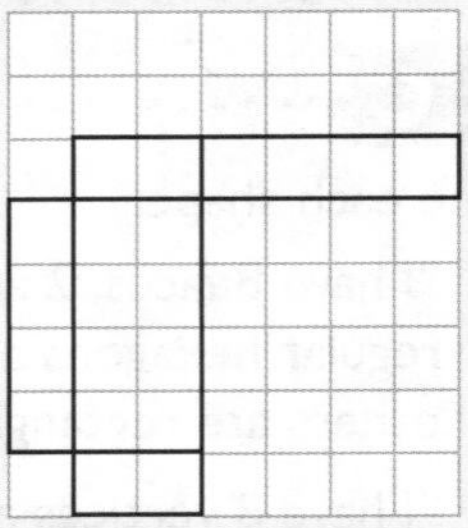

Draw an accurate net for these shapes:

10.

3 cm
3 cm
3 cm

11.

3 cm
2 cm
5 cm

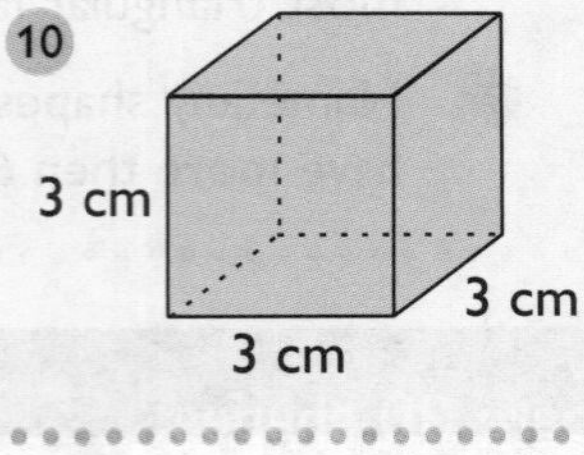

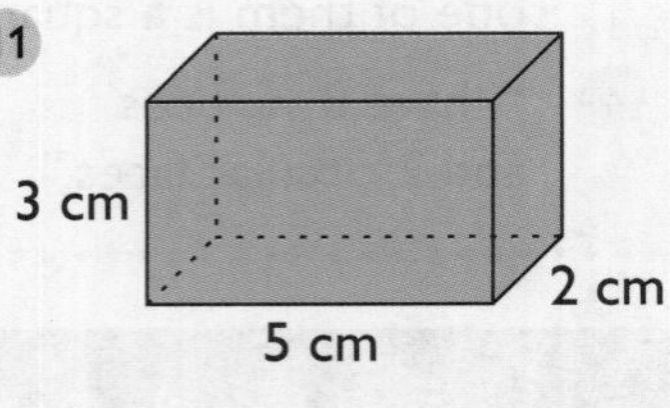

Set B

1 Write the letter of all the correct nets for this shape.

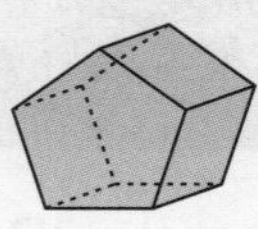

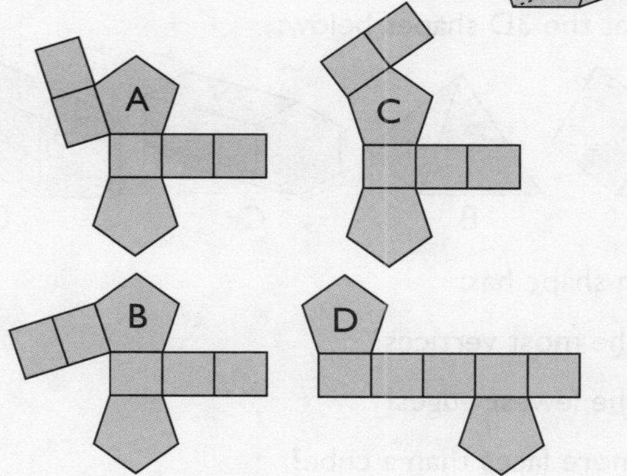

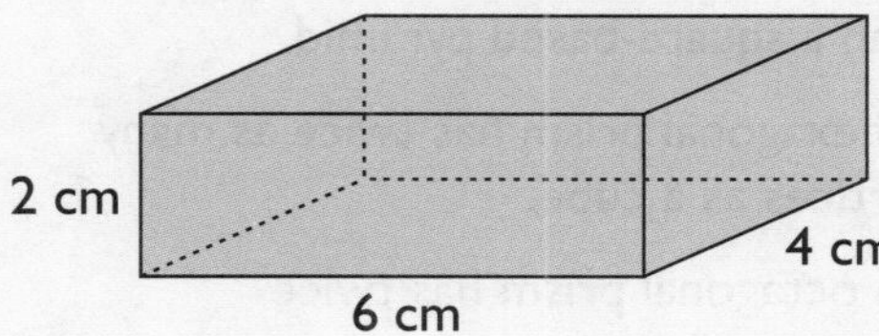

2 Accurately draw two different nets for the cuboid below.

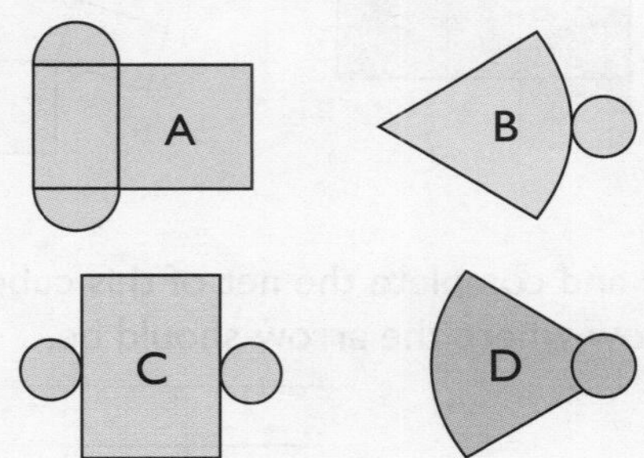

Use isometric paper to accurately draw the 3D shapes made from these nets:

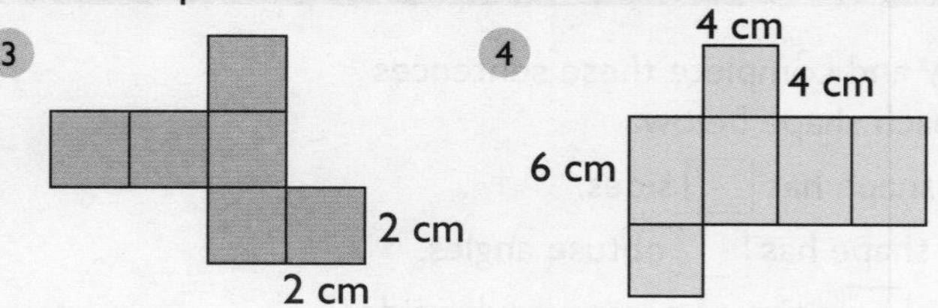

Accurately draw nets for these prisms:

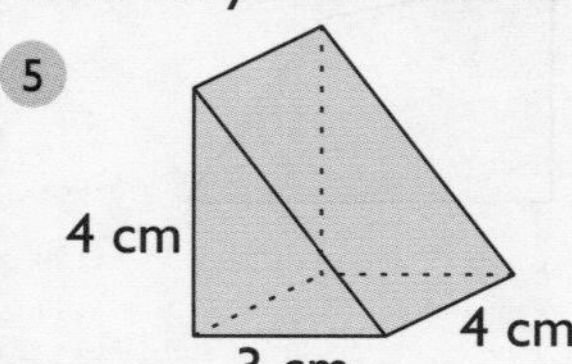

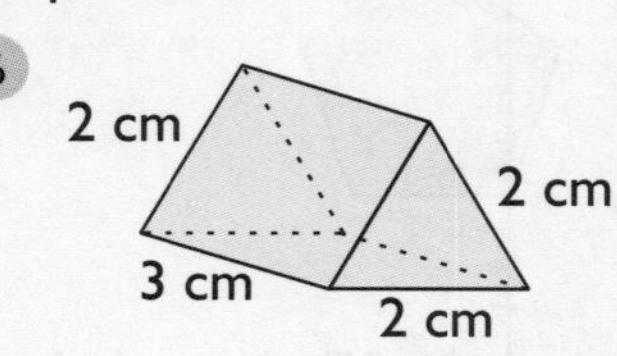

7 Copy and shade in the net to make a correct net of the prism below.

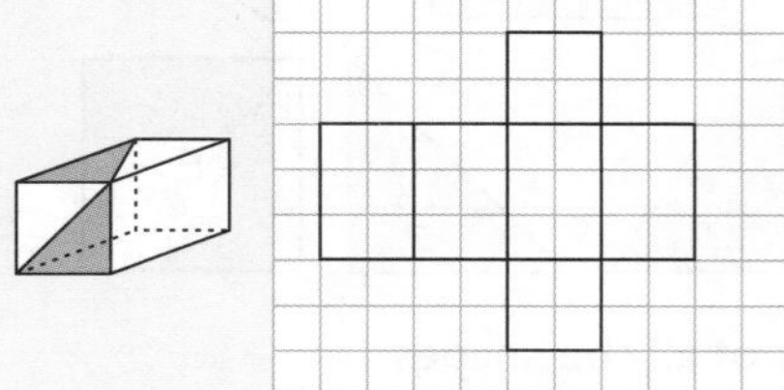

Set C

Look at the four nets below:

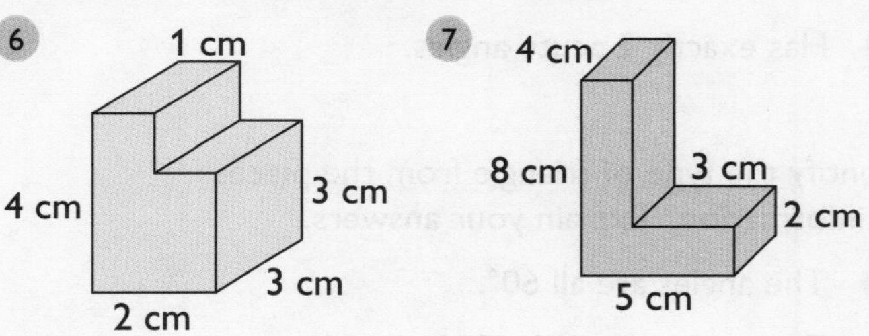

Which net will fold up to make:

1 a cone?

2 a cylinder?

Accurately draw nets for the 3D shapes being described below.

3 A cube with side length 4 cm.

4 A cuboid with side lengths of 5 cm, 1 cm and 4 cm.

5 A square-based pyramid where the square face is 3 cm long and the triangular faces have a 3 cm base and 4 cm height.

Accurately draw nets for these shapes:

6
1 cm
4 cm
3 cm
3 cm
2 cm

7
4 cm
8 cm
3 cm
2 cm
5 cm

Noah has drawn a net for the cuboid on the left.

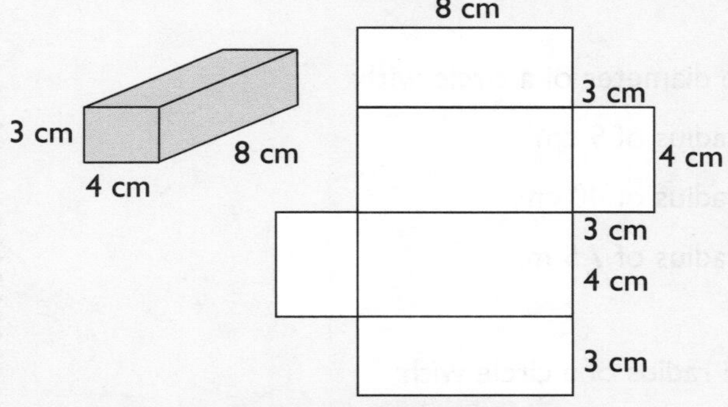

8 Explain how you know he has drawn the net incorrectly.

9 Draw a correct net for the cuboid.

I can draw and use nets of 3D shapes.

Geometry — Review 3

Copy and complete these sentences for each shape below:

The shape has ☐ sides.

This shape has ☐ obtuse angles.

It has ☐ pairs of perpendicular sides.

1 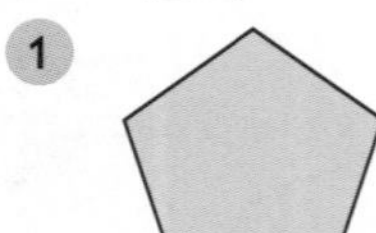

2 

Look at the 2D shapes below:

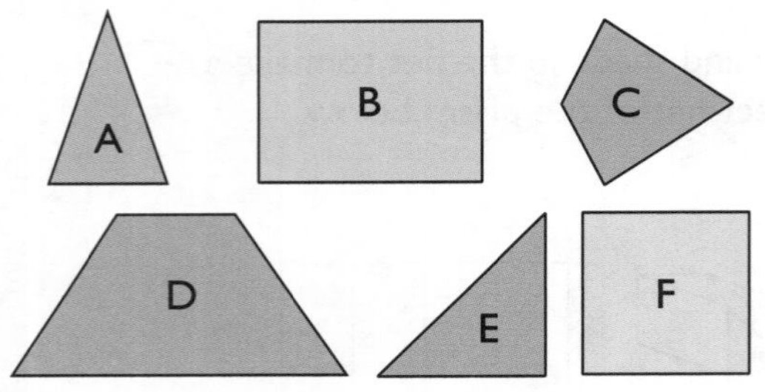

Write the letters of all the shapes that match these descriptions:

3 Is an irregular polygon.

4 Has more than one line of symmetry.

5 Has no pairs of parallel sides.

6 Has exactly 2 acute angles.

Identify the type of triangle from the pieces of information. Explain your answers.

7 The angles are all 60°.

8 The angles are 15°, 135° and 30°.

9 Two sides are 8 cm with a 50° angle between them.

Find the diameter of a circle with:

10 a radius of 9 cm.

11 a radius of 40 cm.

12 a radius of 7.5 m.

Find the radius of a circle with:

13 a diameter of 30 m.

14 a diameter of 9 cm.

15 a diameter of 23 m.

Look at the 3D shapes below:

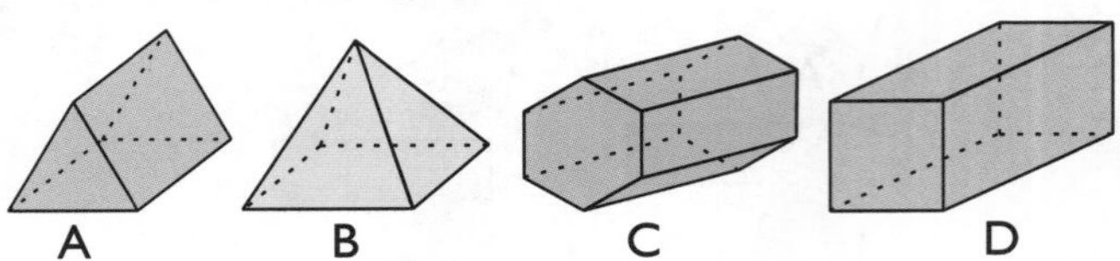

Which shape has:

16 the most vertices?

17 the fewest edges?

18 more faces than a cube?

19 twice as many vertices as a tetrahedron?

True or false? Explain your answers.

20 A tetrahedron has more triangular faces than a square-based pyramid.

21 A hexagonal prism has twice as many vertices as a cube.

22 An octagonal prism has twice as many edges as a cuboid.

Name the shapes shown by these nets.

23 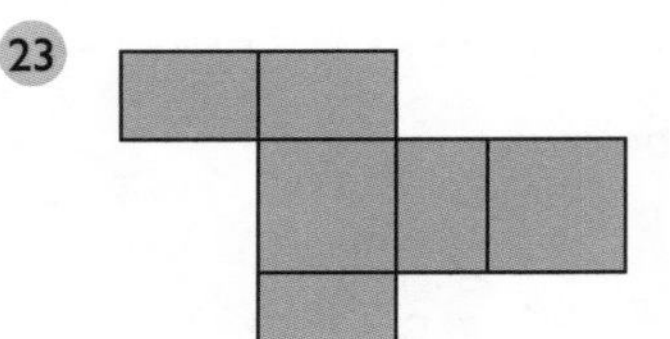

24 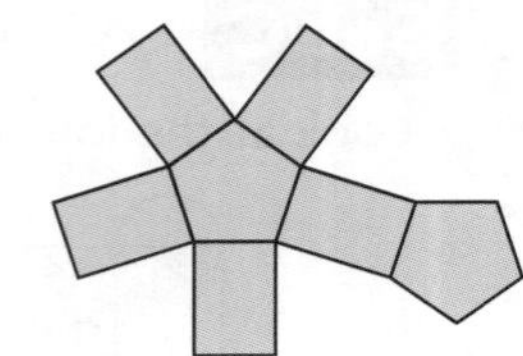

25 Copy and complete the net of this cube to show where the arrow should be.

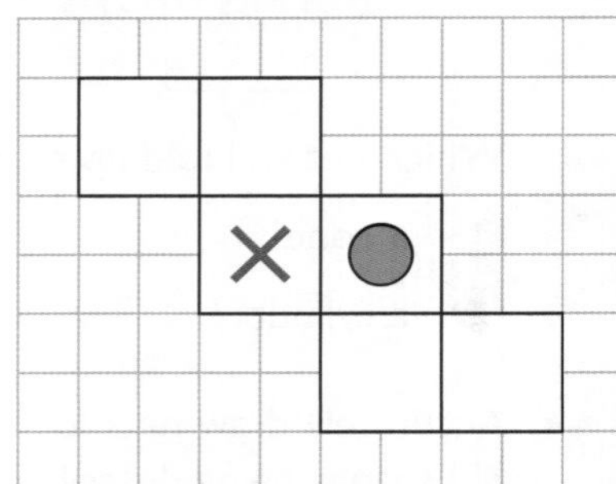

Accurately draw the nets for the shapes below.

26 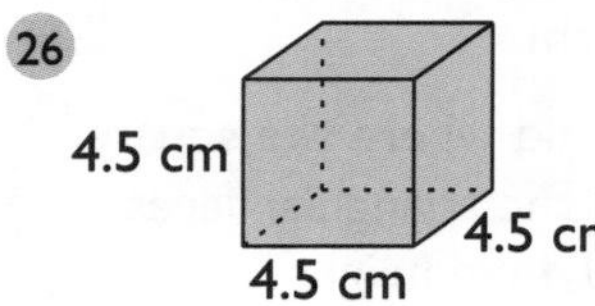

27 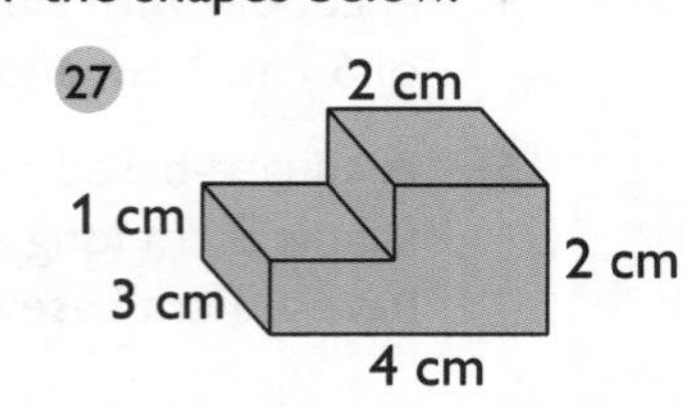

Good stuff — if you managed to do all those questions then you've cracked it!

Coordinates — 1

You already know about coordinates and grids, but you might not have seen grids with four quadrants before. On these pages you'll practise using four quadrant grids and finding points that have negative coordinates.

Examples

Use the grid on the right to answer these questions.

What point on the grid has coordinates (–3, 2)?

The point with coordinates (–3, 2) is **point A**.

Go along the x-axis to –3 then go up till you get to 2 on the y-axis.

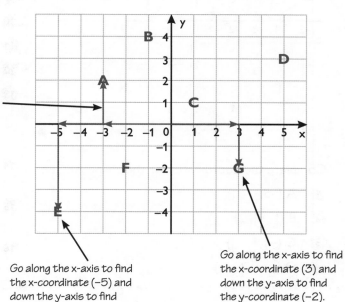

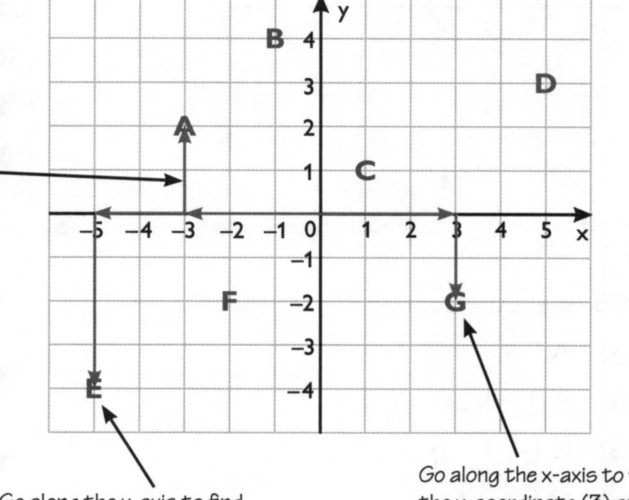

What are the coordinates of point E?

The coordinates of point E are **(–5, –4)**.

Go along the x-axis to find the x-coordinate (–5) and down the y-axis to find the y-coordinate (–4).

What are the coordinates of point G?

The coordinates of point G are **(3, –2)**.

Go along the x-axis to find the x-coordinate (3) and down the y-axis to find the y-coordinate (–2).

Set A

Look at the grid below.

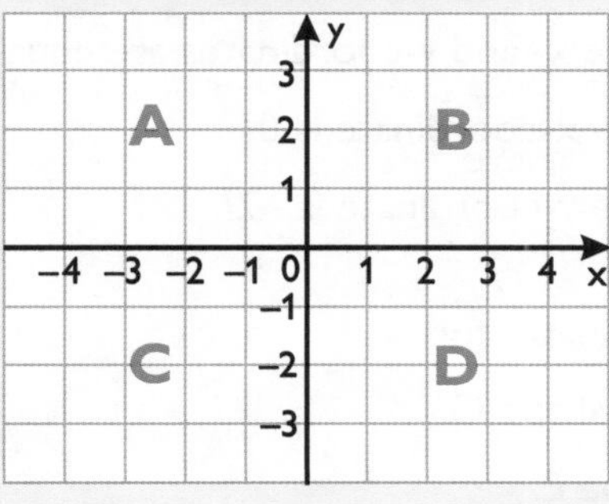

For each of the coordinates below, decide if they are in quadrant A, B, C or D.

1. (–2, –3)
2. (3, –1)
3. (–4, 2)
4. (2, 1)
5. (3, 3)
6. (4, –2)
7. (–1, –1)
8. (–3, 2)

Look at the grid below.

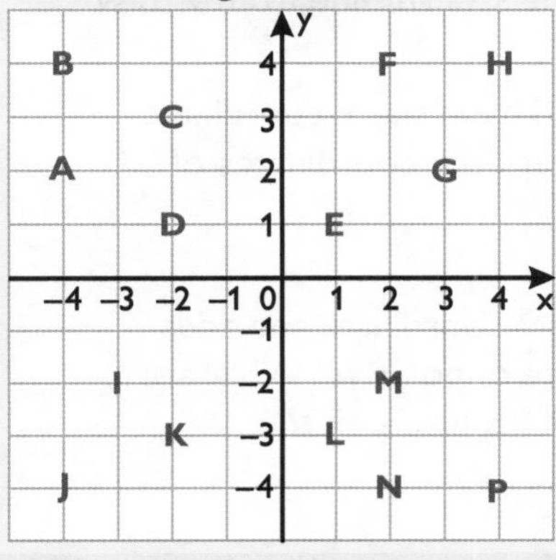

What is the x-coordinate of:

9. point A?
10. point F?
11. point I?

What is the y-coordinate of:

12. point D?
13. point J?
14. point L?

Which point has coordinates:

15. (–4, 4)
16. (–2, 3)

Complete the coordinates for:

17. point G (3, ☐)
18. point K (☐, –3)
19. point M (☐, ☐)
20. point N (☐, ☐)

Set B

Look at the grid below.

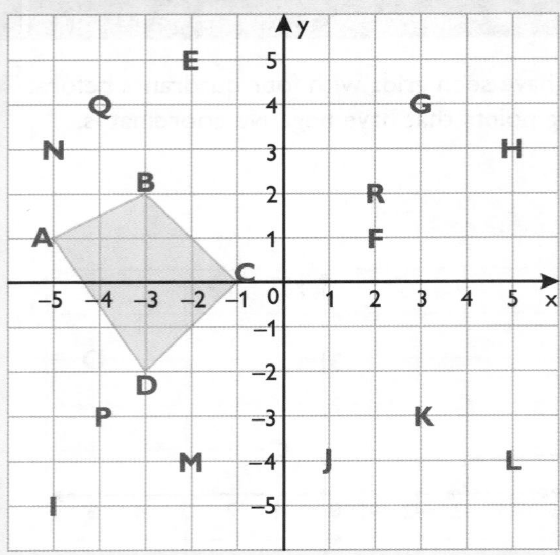

Complete the coordinates for the shape ABCD:

1. A (–5, ☐)
2. B (☐, 2)
3. C (–1, ☐)
4. D (☐, ☐)

Look at the grid on the left.

5. Which point has the coordinates (5, 3)?
6. Which point has the coordinates (–2, 5)?
7. What are the coordinates of point N?
8. What are the coordinates of point E?
9. Which points have a positive x-coordinate?
10. Which points have a negative y-coordinate?
11. Which points have an x-coordinate of 3?
12. Which points have a y-coordinate of –4?
13. Write down all the points where the x-coordinate and y-coordinate are equal.
14. Point S is 2 squares left and 1 square down from point L. What are the coordinates of point S?
15. Point T is 3 squares right and 3 squares up from point B. What are the coordinates of point T?
16. Point U is 5 squares left and 3 squares up from point J. What are the coordinates of point U?

Set C

Look at the grid below.

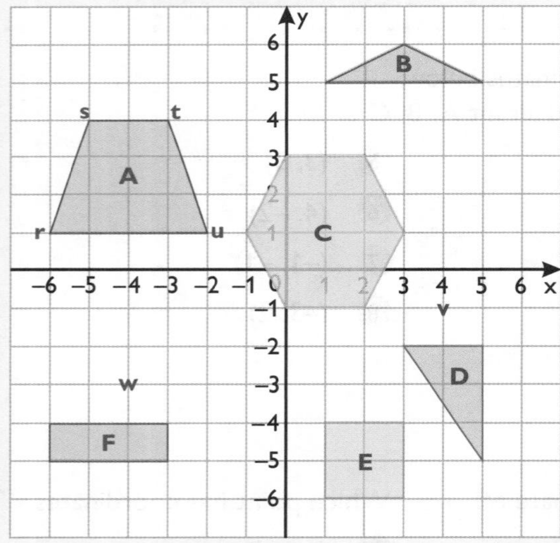

The vertices of shape A are labelled r, s, t and u. Find the coordinates of the vertices:

1. r (☐, ☐)
2. s (☐, ☐)
3. t (☐, ☐)
4. u (☐, ☐)

Which shape has:

5. a vertex with the coordinates (3, –2)?
6. negative x- and y-coordinates for all of its vertices?
7. a vertex where the x- and y-coordinates are equal?
8. vertices where the x-coordinate is 0?
9. vertices where the y-coordinate is –2?

Write down the coordinates for:

10. all the vertices of shape C.
11. the centre of shape E.
12. the point where the diagonals of shape A cross.
13. the midpoint of the straight line from v to w.
14. Maxine subtracts 8 from the x-coordinate of point v. What are the coordinates of her new point?
15. Tim adds 3 to the x-coordinate and adds 7 to the y-coordinate of point w. What are the coordinates of his new point?

I can describe position using coordinates.     

Coordinates — 2

You can plot points on a coordinate grid and join them up to make lines and shapes. You can also find missing coordinates using the properties of a shape. Have a look at these examples to see how it's done.

Examples

Plot the coordinates (–2, –1), (1, 1), (3, –1), (2, –4) and (–1, –4) on the grid and join up the points to create a pentagon.

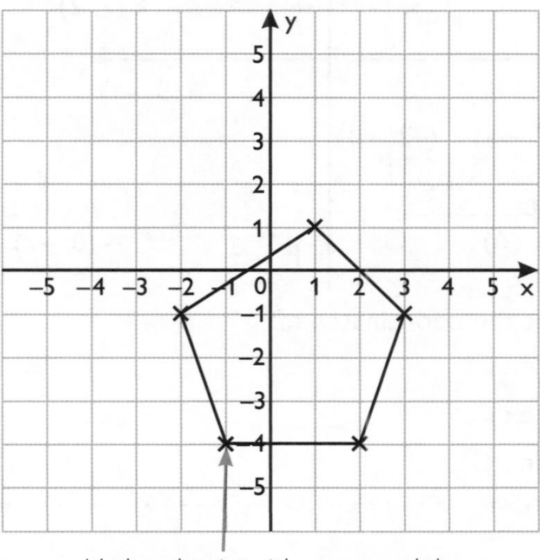

Mark each point with a cross and then join each point with a straight line.

A parallelogram is drawn on the grid below. What are the coordinates of point A?

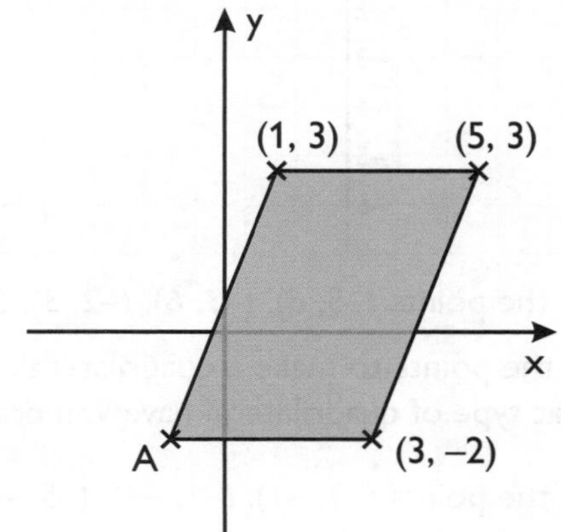

To get from (5, 3) to (1, 3) you subtract 4 from the x-coordinate and keep the y-coordinate the same. Do the same from (3, –2) to find the coordinates of A.

Coordinates of point A = (3 – 4, –2) = **(–1, –2)**

Set A

On a blank copy of the grid above:

1. Put a cross at point (–5, 4) and label it A.
2. Put a cross at point (1, 2) and label it B.
3. Join points A and B together with a straight line.
4. Put a cross at point (2, 5) and label it C.
5. Put a cross at point (–4, 2) and label it D.
6. Join points C and D together with a straight line.
7. At what point does line AB cross line CD?
8. Plot the following 3 points:
   E (2, –1), F (1, –4) and G (3, –4).
9. Join points E, F and G with straight lines to make a triangle. What type of triangle have you drawn?
10. Plot the following 3 points:
    H (–5, –2), I (–5, –5) and J (–2, –2).
11. Point K is plotted so that points H, I, J and K can be joined to make a square. What are the coordinates of point K?

Work out the coordinates of the missing corners on these shapes:

12.

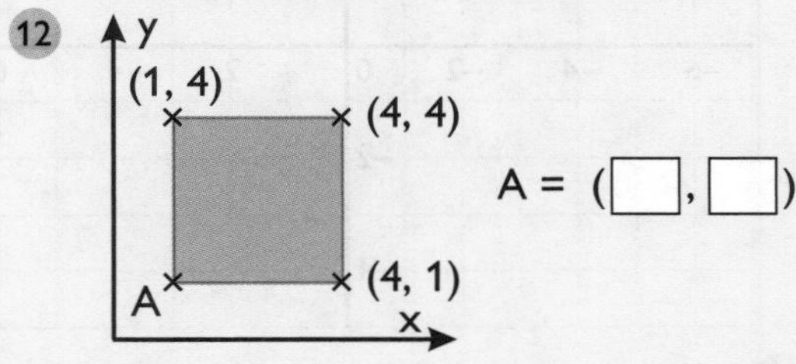

A = (☐, ☐)

13.

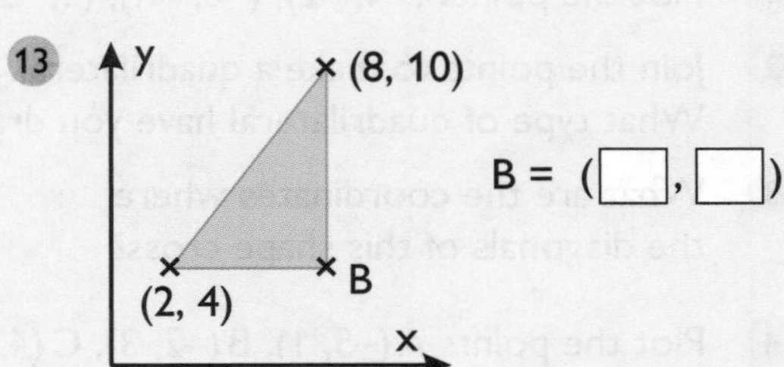

B = (☐, ☐)

14.

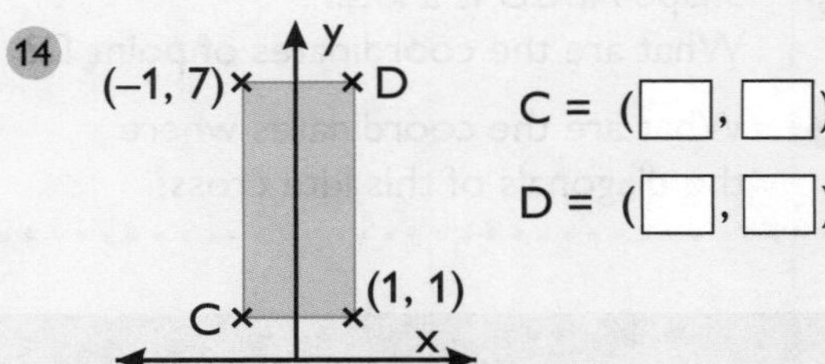

C = (☐, ☐)

D = (☐, ☐)

Set B

Copy out the grid below:

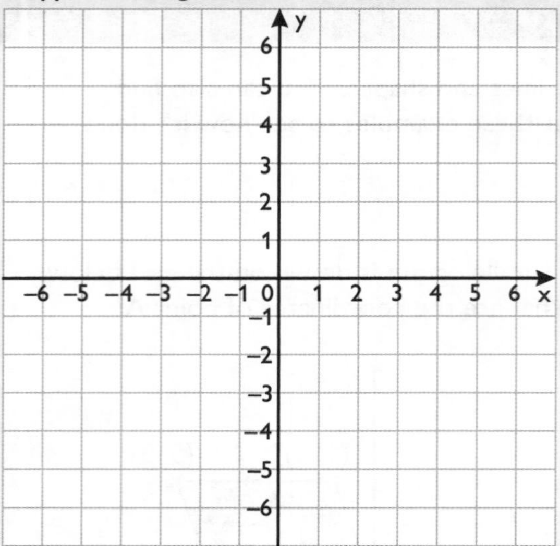

1. Plot the points (–5, 6), (–3, 6), (–2, 3), (–5, 4).
2. Join the points to make a quadrilateral. What type of quadrilateral have you drawn?
3. Plot the points (–2, –1), (–1, –4), (–5, –5).
4. Join the points to make a triangle. What type of triangle have you drawn?
5. Plot the points A (5, –6), B (2, –6) and C (5, 4).
6. Shape ABCD is a rectangle. What are the coordinates of vertex D?

A rectangle, parallelogram and isosceles triangle are drawn on the axes below.

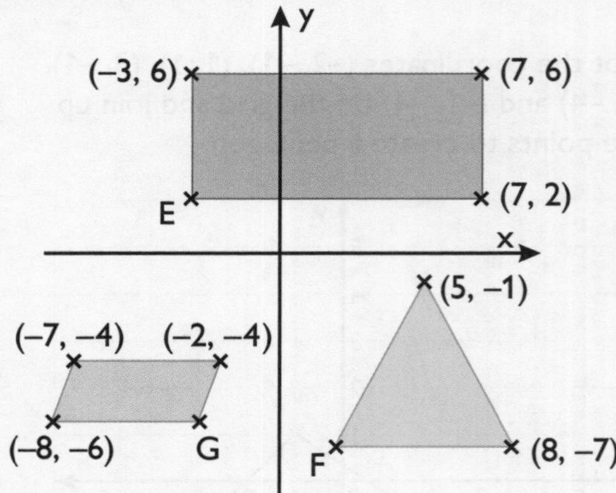

Work out the coordinates of:

7. vertex E
8. vertex F
9. vertex G

Set C

Copy out the grid below:

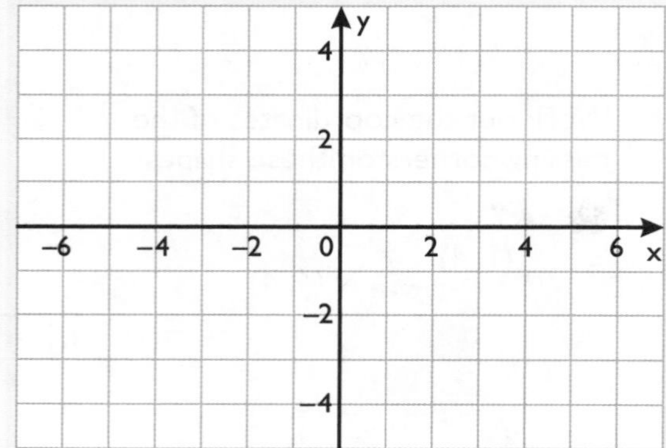

1. Plot the points (–4, –2), (–6, –4), (4, –2), (2, –4).
2. Join the points to make a quadrilateral. What type of quadrilateral have you drawn?
3. What are the coordinates where the diagonals of this shape cross?
4. Plot the points A (–5, 1), B (–2, 3), C (4, 1).
5. Shape ABCD is a kite. What are the coordinates of point D?
6. What are the coordinates where the diagonals of this kite cross?
7. Three vertices of a rectangle have the coordinates (11, –5), (7, –5) and (11, 0). What are the coordinates of the final corner?
8. A parallelogram is drawn on the axes below.

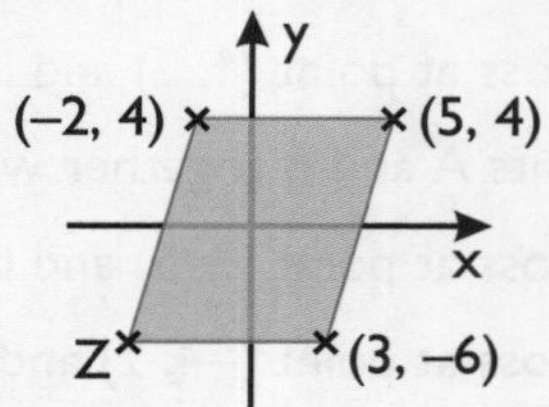

Work out the coordinates of vertex Z.

Six identical triangles are drawn on the axes below. Work out the coordinates of:

9. vertex A
10. vertex B
11. vertex C
12. vertex D
13. vertex E
14. vertex F

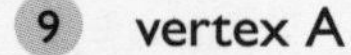
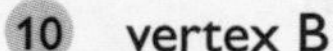
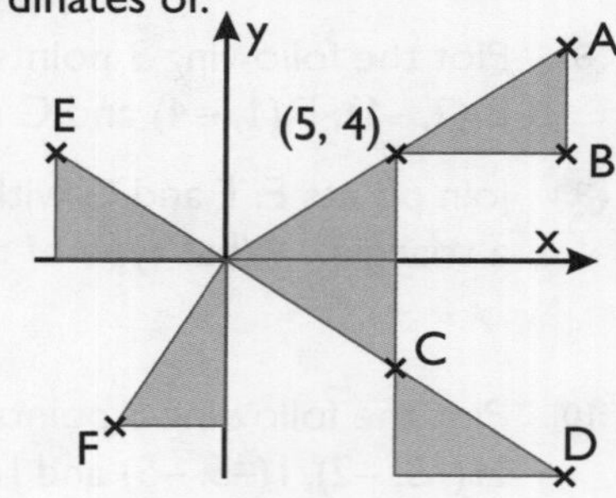

I can plot points and draw shapes using coordinates.

Reflection

You'll have seen reflection before, but here you'll use the axes of a coordinate grid as the mirror lines.

Examples

Reflect shape A in the y-axis. Label the shape B.

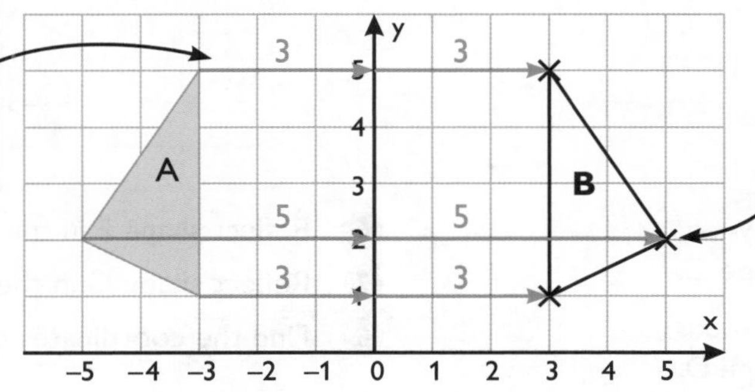

Use the y-axis as a mirror line. For each point count the number of squares to the y-axis. Then count the same number of squares on the other side of the y-axis.
Plot each point of the reflected shape, then join them with straight lines.
A
B

Reflect shape C in the x-axis. Label the shape D.

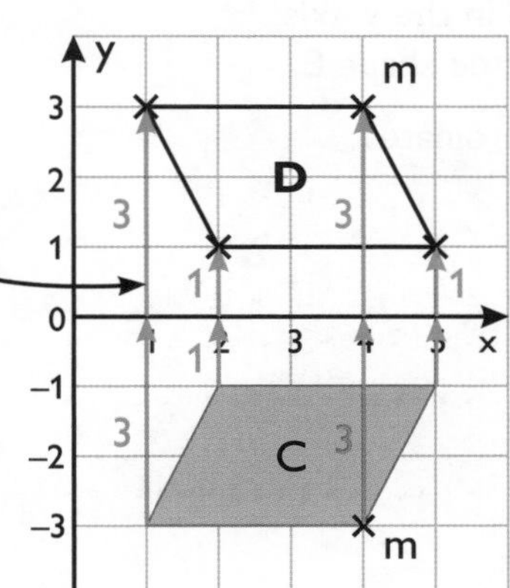

What are the coordinates of point m on shape D?

The coordinates of point m on shape D = **(4, 3)**.

Set A

1. Copy and complete the grid to show shape A reflected in the y-axis.

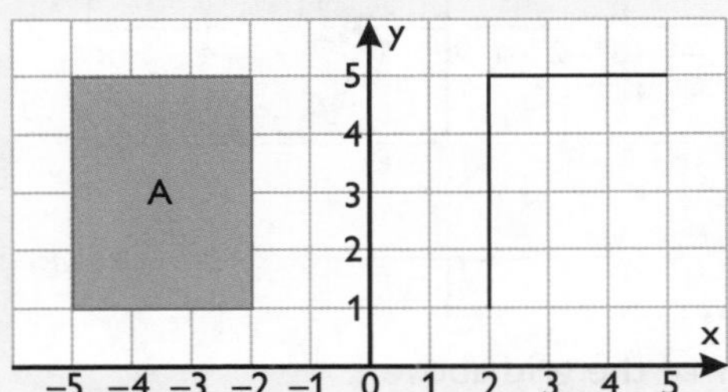

2. Copy the grid and reflect shape B in the x-axis.

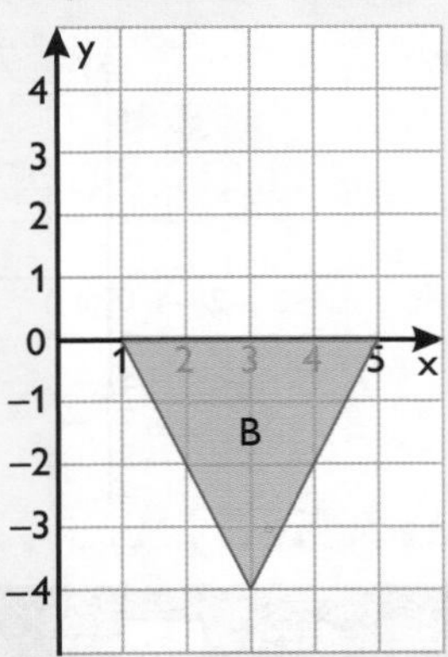

Copy the grid below:

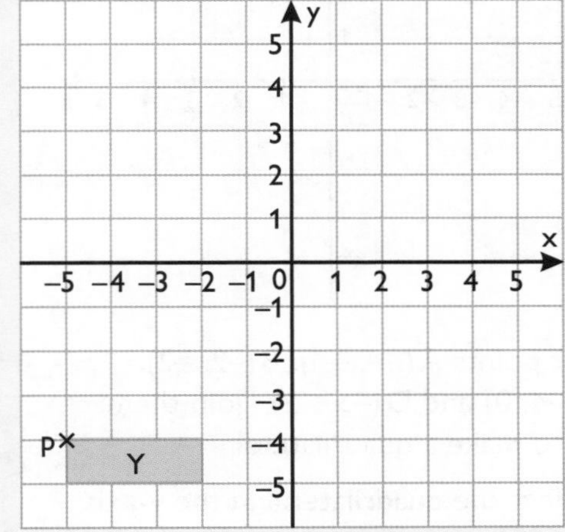

3. Reflect shape Y in the x-axis. Label the reflected shape Z.
4. Find the coordinates of vertex p on shape Z.
5. Draw a right-angled triangle with vertices at A (1, 3), B (1, 1) and C (4, 1).
6. Reflect the triangle you have drawn in the y-axis.
7. What are the coordinates of vertices A, B and C on the reflected shape?

Set B

Copy the grid below:

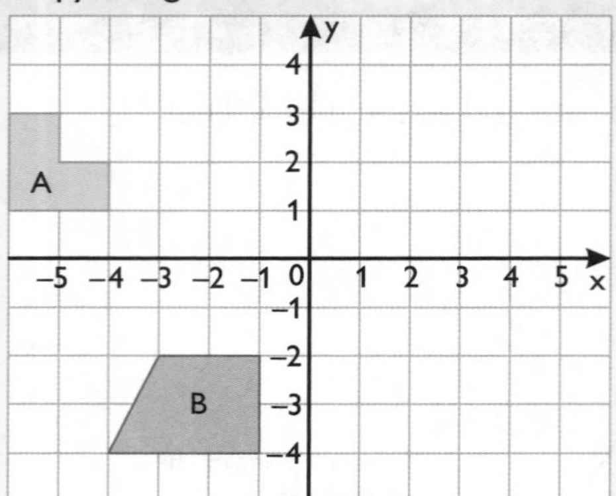

1. Reflect shape A in the y-axis. Label the reflected shape C.
2. Reflect shape B in the x-axis. Label the reflected shape D.
3. Reflect shape B in the y-axis. Label the reflected shape E.

Write down the coordinates of all the vertices of:

4. shape C
5. shape E

Copy the grid below:

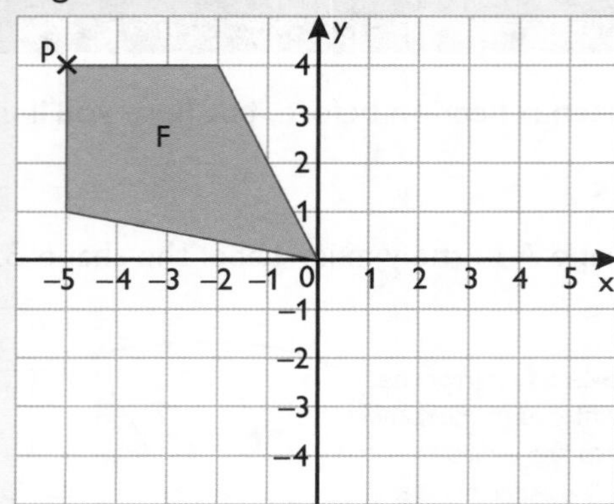

6. Reflect shape F in the y-axis. Label this shape G.
7. Reflect shape G in the x-axis. Label this shape H.
8. Find the coordinates of vertex p on shape H.

Copy the grid on the right:

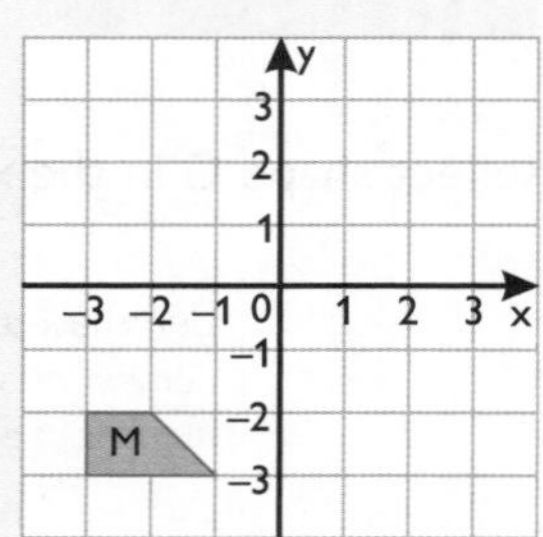

9. Shape M is reflected in one of the axes. One of the vertices on the reflected shape has coordinates (−3, 2). Perform the reflection.

Set C

Copy the grid below:

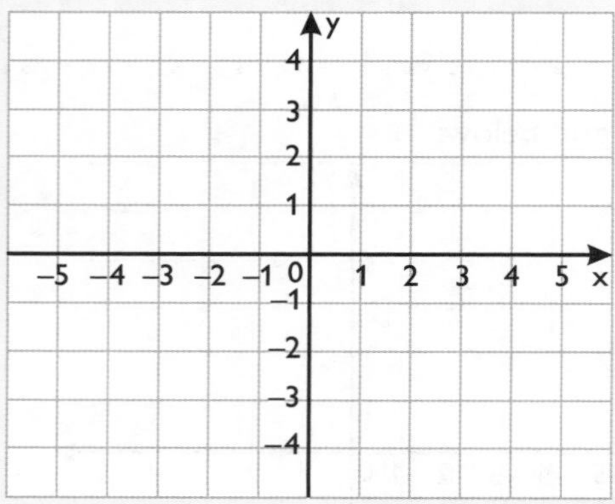

1. Plot points A (−4, −4), B (−2, −2), C (−4, 0) and D (−5, −2). Join them up to make a quadrilateral.
2. Reflect the quadrilateral in the y-axis.
3. Find the coordinates of point B on the reflected shape. What do you notice?
4. Reflect both of the shapes you have drawn in the x-axis.
5. Find the coordinates of point B on these reflected shapes. What do you notice?

Look at the grid below.

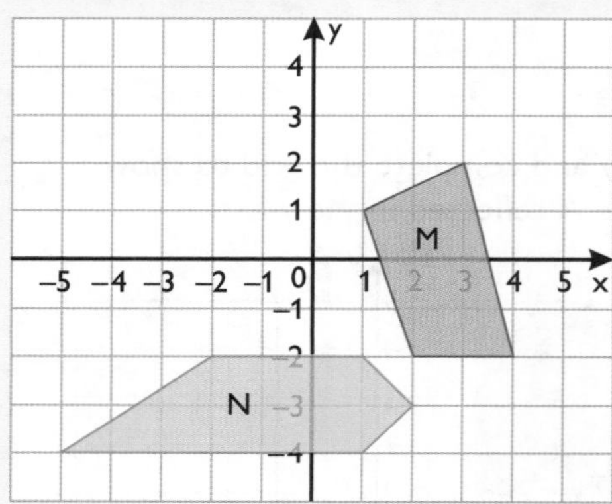

On a copy of the grid above:

6. Draw the reflection of shape M in the x-axis.
7. Draw the reflection of shape N in the y-axis.

Copy the grid on the right.

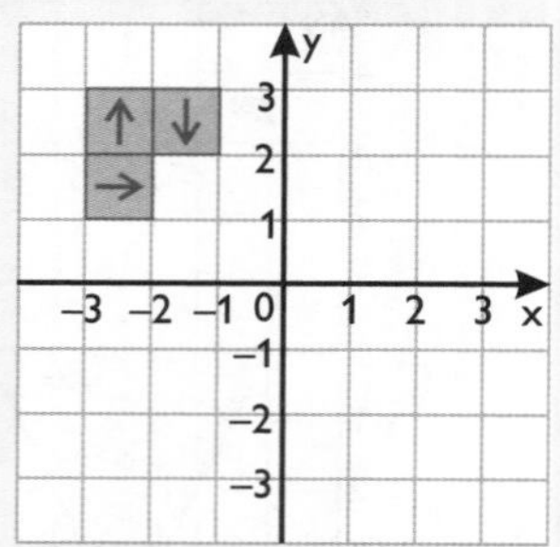

8. Reflect the shape with arrows in the x-axis.
9. Reflect both of the shapes on your grid in the y-axis.

I can reflect shapes in the x- and y-axes.      

Translation

Translating a shape on a coordinate grid just means sliding it from one place to another.

Examples

Translate shape A 6 units left and 5 units down. Label this shape B.

Translate each point one at a time. From each point count 6 units left and 5 units down and draw a cross.

Join up the plotted points with straight lines and label the shape B.

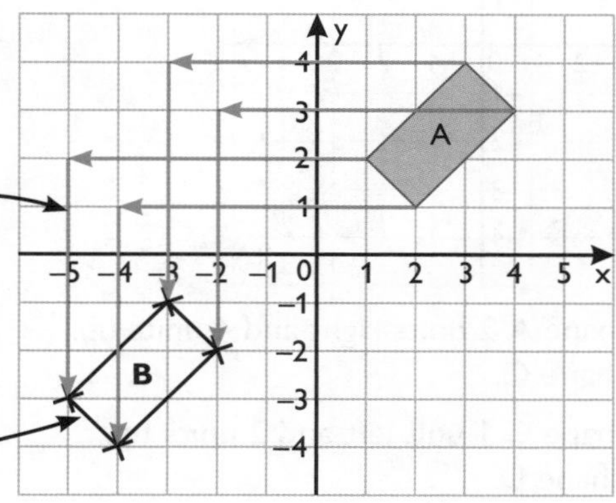

Translate shape C –5 units horizontally and +4 units vertically. Label this shape D.

–5 units horizontally means move the shape 5 units to the left. +4 units vertically means move the shape 4 units up.

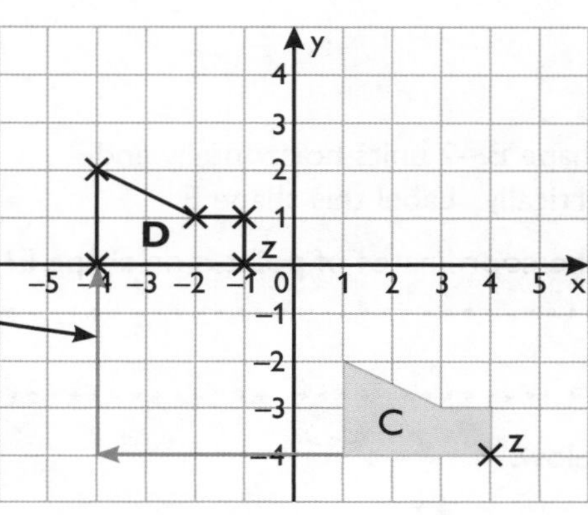

What are the coordinates of point z on shape D?

The coordinates of point z on shape D = **(–1, 0)**.

Set A

Look at the shapes on the grid below.

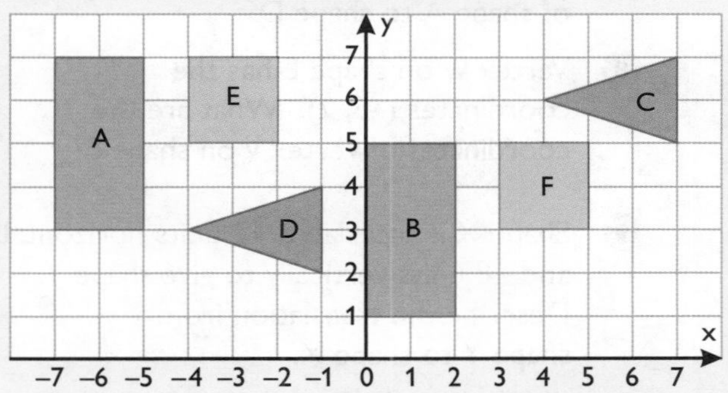

Complete these sentences to describe the translations:

1. Shape A has been translated ☐ units right and ☐ units down to shape B.
2. Shape C has been translated ☐ units left and ☐ units down to shape D.
3. Shape D has been translated ☐ units right and ☐ units up to shape C.
4. Shape E has been translated 7 units ☐ and 2 units ☐ to shape F.

Copy the grid below:

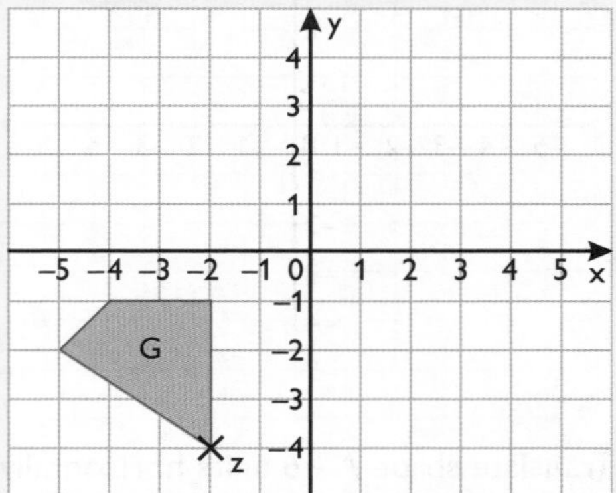

5. Translate shape G 4 units up. Label this shape H.
6. Translate shape G 6 units to the right. Label this shape I.
7. Translate shape G 5 units to the right and 3 units up. Label this shape J.

What are the coordinates of vertex z on:

8. shape H?
9. shape J?

Set B

Copy the grid below:

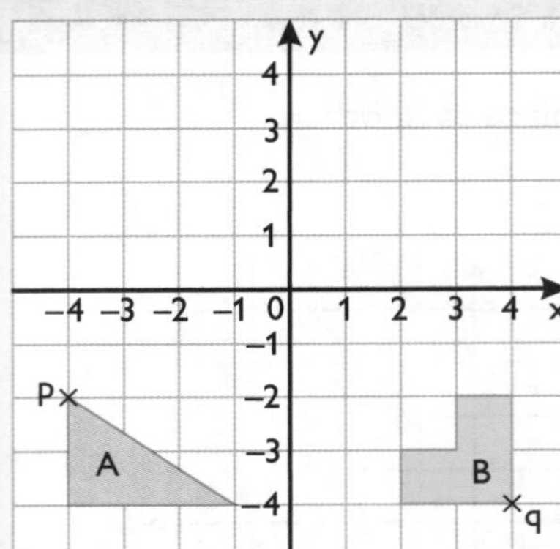

1 Translate shape A 2 units right and 4 units up. Label the shape C.

2 Translate shape C 1 unit left and 2 units up. Label this shape D.

What are the coordinates of vertex p on:

3 shape C?

4 shape D?

5 Translate shape B –2 units horizontally and +5 units vertically. Label this shape E.

6 What are the coordinates of point q on shape E?

Look at the grid below:

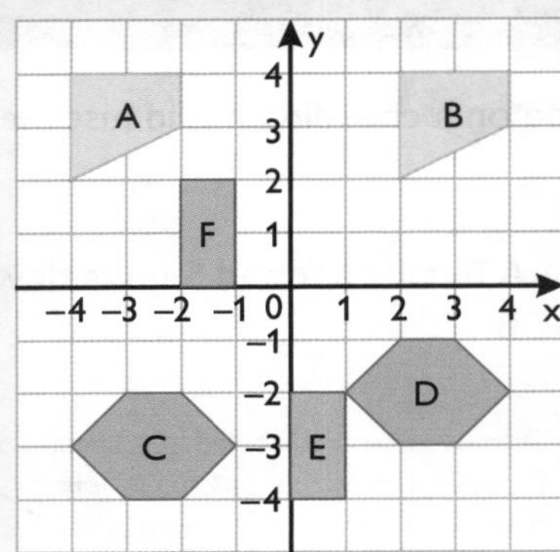

Describe the translation from:

7 shape A to shape B.

8 shape C to shape D.

9 shape E to shape F.

10 The coordinates of vertex x on shape R are (–5, 4). Shape R is translated +6 units horizontally and –8 units vertically to give shape S. What are the coordinates of vertex x on shape S?

Set C

Copy the grid below:

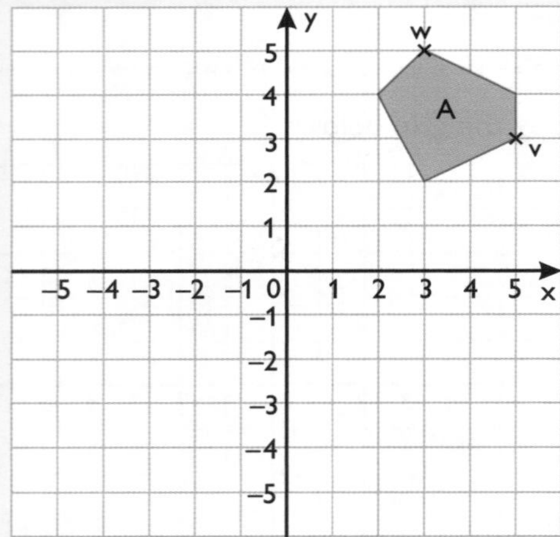

1 Translate shape A –6 units horizontally and –4 units vertically. Label this shape B.

2 Translate shape B +4 units horizontally and –3 units vertically. Label this shape C.

3 Describe the translation from shape A to shape C.

What are the coordinates of:

4 vertex w in shape B?

5 vertex v in shape C?

Shapes D and E are translations of shape A.

6 Draw shape D where the coordinates of vertex v are (–3, –4).

7 Describe the translation of shape A to shape D.

8 Vertex w on shape E has the coordinates (–5, 2). What are the coordinates of vertex v on shape E?

9 Shape X is translated +7 units horizontally and –8 units vertically to give shape Y. Describe the translation from shape Y to shape X.

10 Vertex p on shape M has coordinates (3, –2). After a translation of shape M, the coordinates of vertex p are (–10, 8). Describe the translation.

11 Vertex q on shape R has coordinates (a, b) = (–1, 5). Shape R is translated to Shape S, and the new coordinates of vertex q are (a + 9, b – 4). What are the coordinates of vertex q on Shape S?

I can translate shapes on a coordinate grid.     

Geometry — Review 4

Look at the grid below:

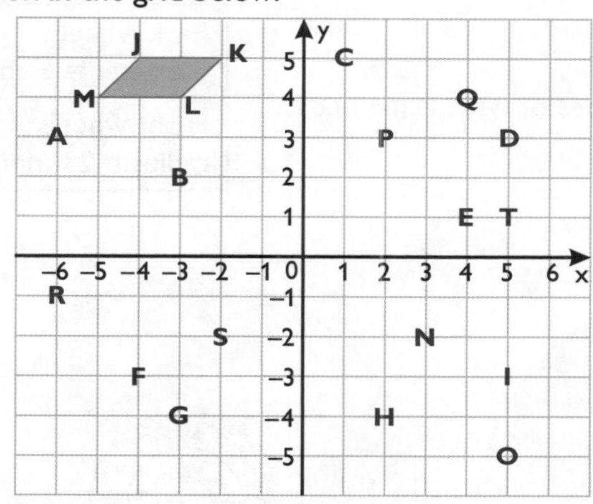

Write down the coordinates of:

1. point B
2. point D
3. point G
4. the vertices of shape JKLM

Which point has the coordinates:

5. (1, 5)?
6. (5, –5)?
7. (–6, –1)?
8. (3, –2)?

9. Which two points have an x-coordinate of 2?
10. Which two points have a y-coordinate of –2?

Copy the grid below:

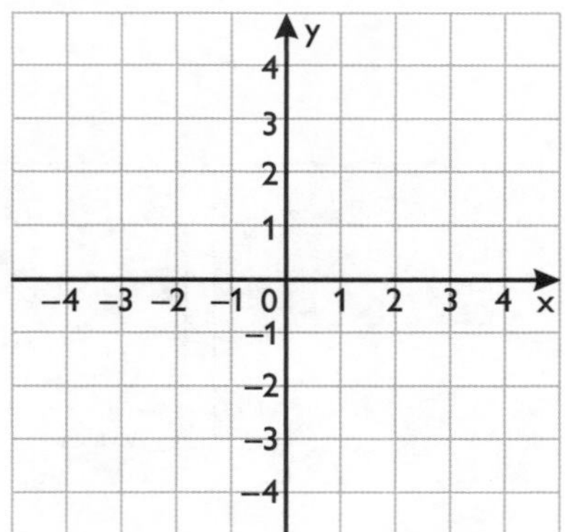

11. Plot points A (–2, 4), B (–3, 2), C (1, 2) and D (2, 4). Join them up to make a quadrilateral.
12. What type of quadrilateral have you drawn?

13. An isosceles triangle is drawn on the axis on the right. The top angle is the same as angle A. What are the coordinates of vertex A?

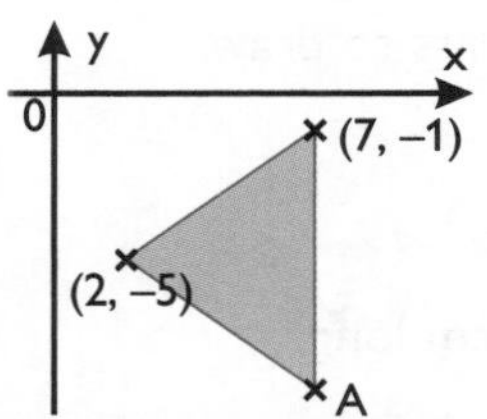

Copy the grid below:

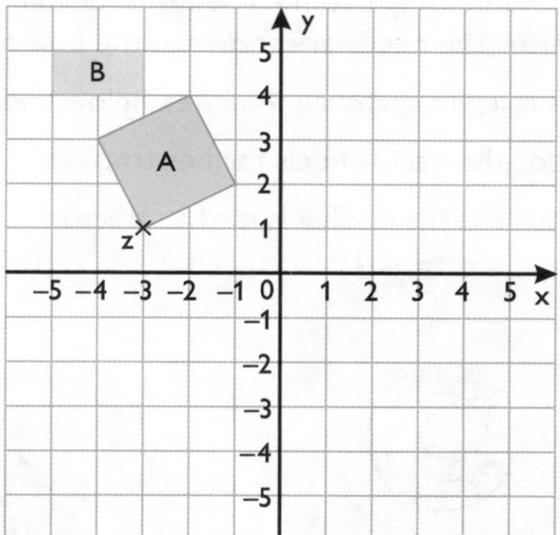

14. Reflect shape B in the x-axis. Label this shape C.
15. Reflect shape A in the y-axis. Label this shape D.
16. Reflect shape D in the x-axis. Label this shape E.
17. Find the coordinates of vertex z on shape D.
18. Find the coordinates of vertex z on shape E.

Copy the grid below:

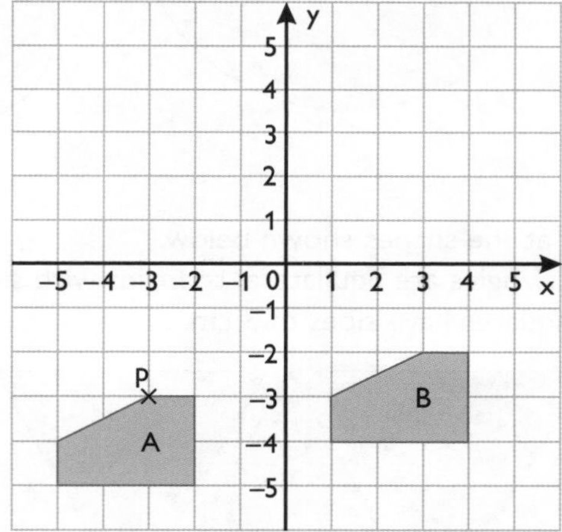

19. Describe the translation of shape A to shape B.
20. Translate shape A 7 units right and 8 units up. Label this shape C.
21. What are the coordinates of point p on shape C?
22. Translate shape C –5 units horizontally and –3 units vertically. Label this shape D.
23. Shape A is translated so that the coordinates of vertex p are (1, 1). Describe this translation.

24. Vertex y on shape T has coordinates (–4, 3). After a translation of shape T, the coordinates of vertex y are (9, –9). Describe the translation.

Phew, that rounds up all you need to know about coordinate grids — nicely done!

Geometry — Challenges

Esme wants to get some new tyres for her toy tractor.
The sizes she needs are shown in the box on the right.

Back wheels:
diameter = 6 cm

Front wheels:
radius = 23 mm

Use a ruler to measure the tyres below and decide which types of tyres Esme needs:

a) for the back wheels for her tractor.

b) for the front wheels for her tractor.

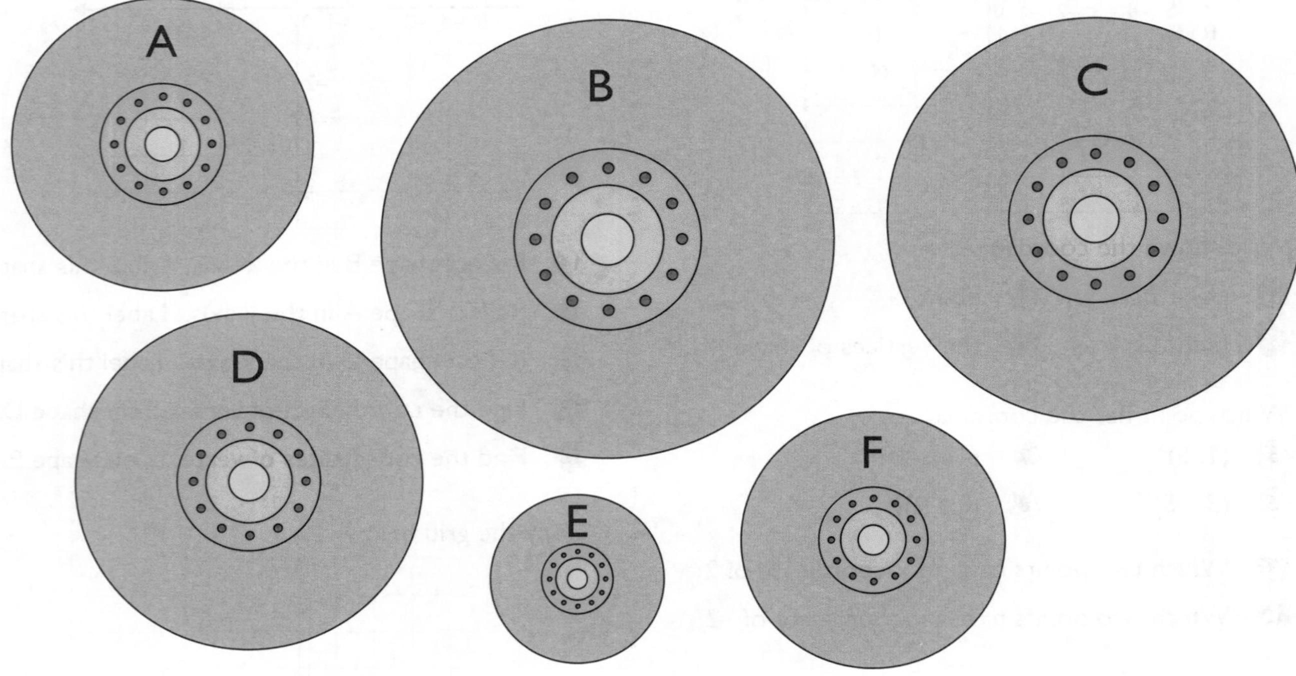

Look at the shapes shown below.
The triangles are equilateral triangles with sides of 3 cm.
The squares have sides of 3 cm.

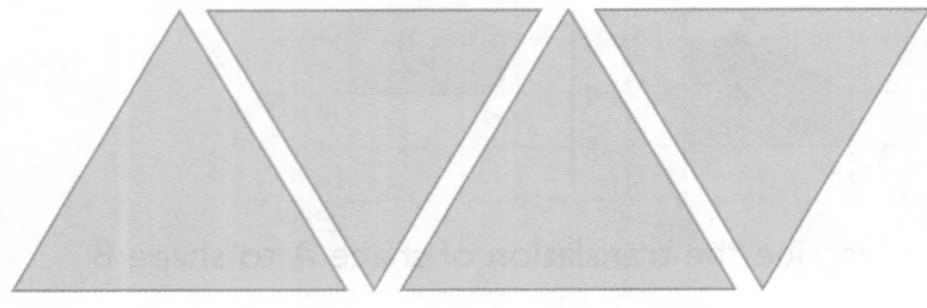

There are four shapes whose nets can be made using any combination of the shapes above.

a) Three of these shapes have a name that you know — what are they?

b) Draw the nets of all four shapes you can make, using the measurements given above.

Mrs Skelton is describing a triangle that she wants her class to draw.

- One angle in the triangle is 52°.
- The smallest angle is 60° smaller than the largest angle.
- The side between the smallest and largest angles is 6 cm long.

a) Draw the triangle that Mrs Skelton is describing.

b) Write your own instructions for drawing a quadrilateral by giving some angle sizes and side lengths. Can a friend draw the shape from your instructions?

4 The coastguard uses a coordinate grid to represent an area of the sea.
Each square on the grid represents 1 square mile.
The compass shows the directions of North, South, East and West.
The coastguard's base is located at the origin (0, 0) on the grid.

a) When the coastguard goes on patrol they go to points A to H in order then back to base.
Write instructions for the coastguard's patrol route. The first instruction is given below:

- Go 8 miles East and 3 miles North to get to point A.

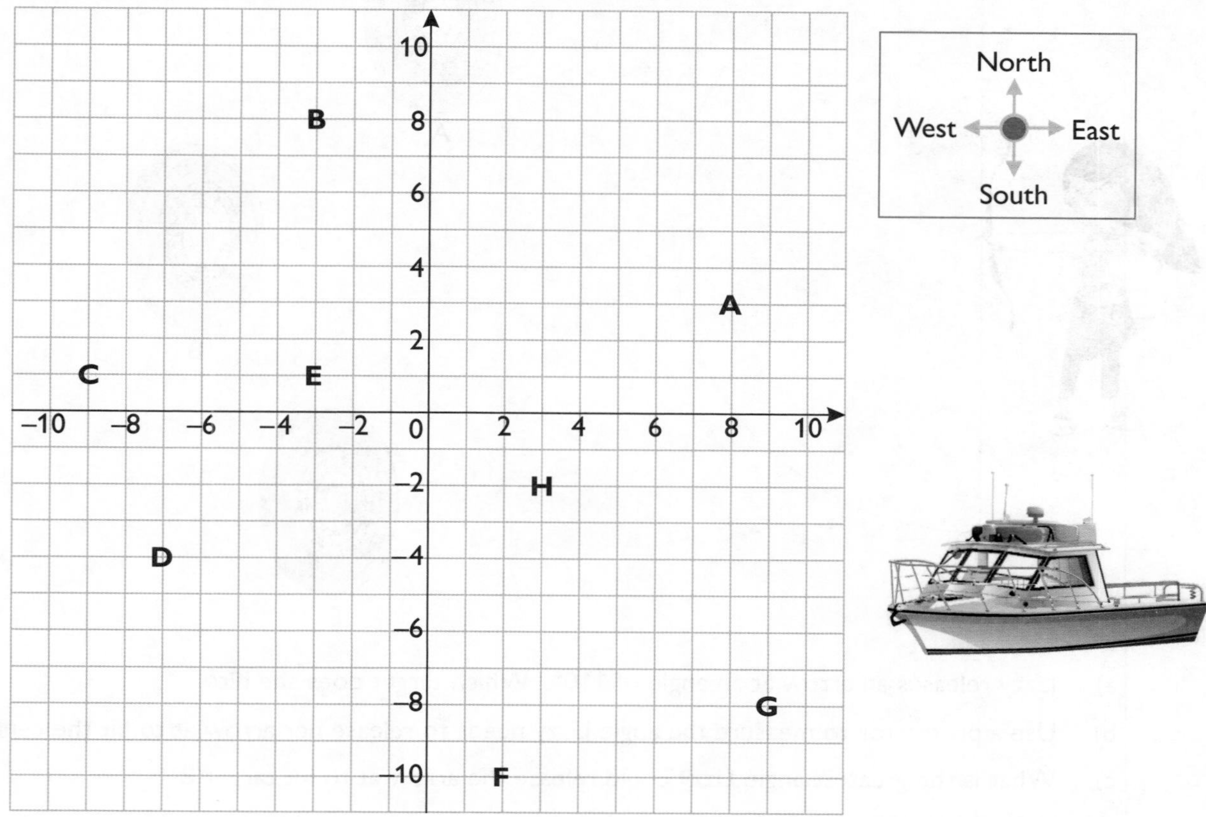

b) At point C, the coastguard gets a call for help from the point halfway between points H and G.
Write an instruction to direct the coastguard from point C to the call for help.

c) Write your own set of instructions for a different route starting and ending at the origin.
Give your instructions to a friend and see if they can mark all your points on the grid.

5 Oliver has drawn the four cube nets below.

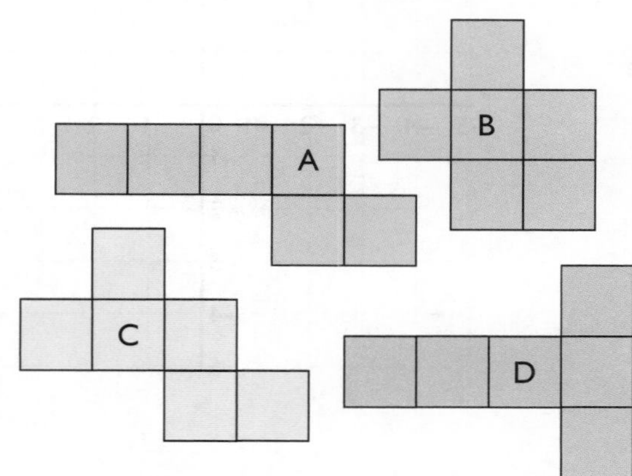

a) Two of the nets do not fold to make a cube. Which two are incorrect?

b) Oliver's teacher tells him there are 11 different ways to make a cube net.
Draw the 9 other nets for a cube.

Make sure your nets are all different — some nets might look different but they're really just reflections or rotations of each other.

c) How many different nets can you draw for:

(i) a tetrahedron?

(ii) a square-based pyramid where the triangle faces are equilateral triangles?

6 Lizzy is taking part in an archery competition.
When she releases the arrow it flies in a straight line.

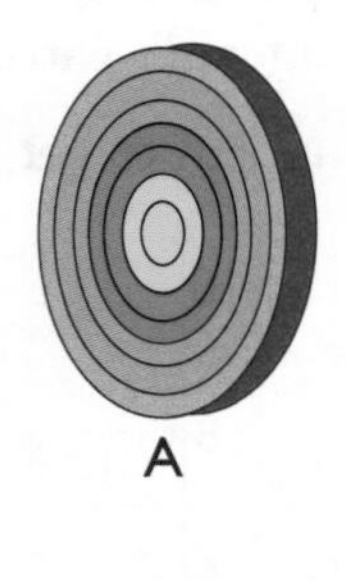
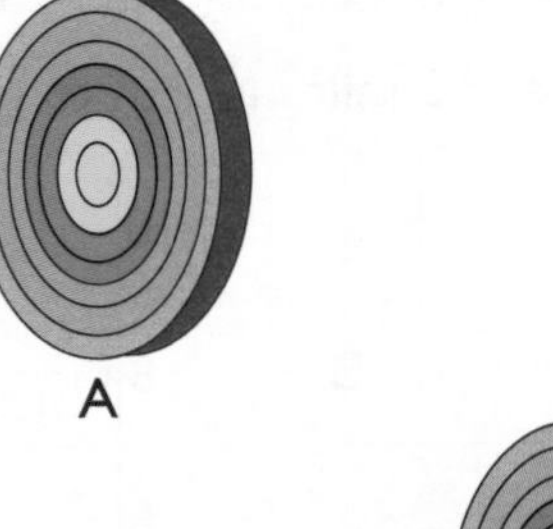
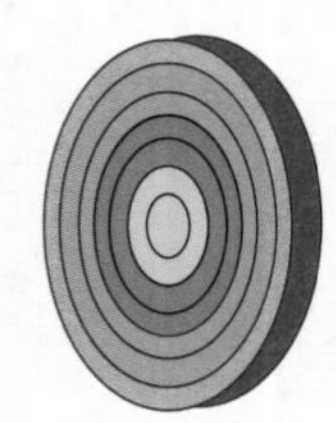
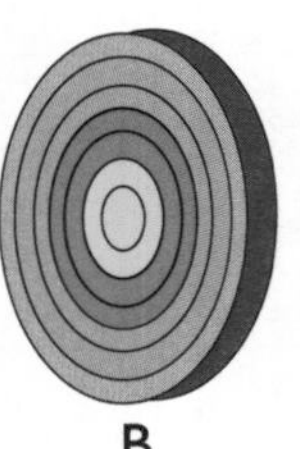

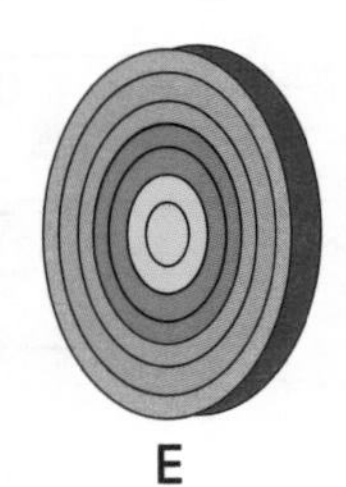

180°

0°

A B C D E F

a) Lizzy releases an arrow at an angle of 110°. Which target does she hit?

b) Use a protractor to measure the angle Lizzy needs to release her arrow at to hit the centre of target D.

c) What is the greatest angle Lizzy could release the arrow at to hit target B?

d) What is the range of angles Lizzy could release the arrow at to hit target F?

7 Use the grid on the right to help you answer these puzzles.

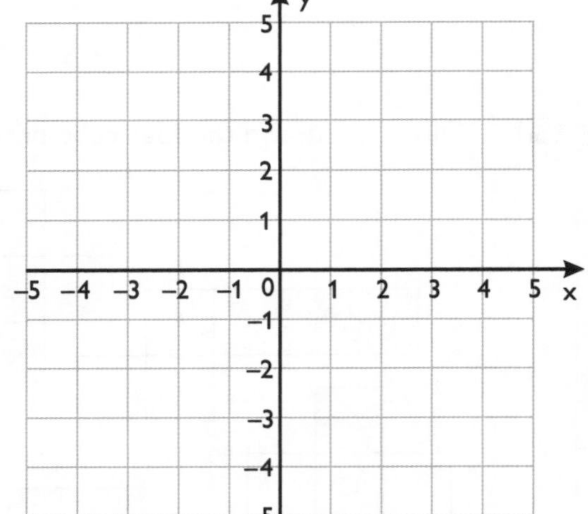

a) Two vertices of an isosceles triangle are drawn at (–2, 4) and (4, 4). Find all the possible coordinates on the grid for the third vertex of the triangle.

There are 12 to find in total.

b) How can you draw a shape on the grid so that if you reflect it in the x- and y-axis you get the same shape you started with in the same position?

c) Choose a point with a positive x- and y-coordinate.

Write down the new coordinates and describe what you notice after you:

(i) reflect your point in the x-axis.

(ii) reflect your point in the y-axis.

(iii) reflect your point in the x-axis and then in the y-axis.

Challenges complete — well done for finishing those off, they were no walk in the park!

Solving Problems with Line Graphs — 1

Line graphs are a great way to show how two things are connected.
You can plot and read off line graphs to convert between units of money and measures.

Examples

Becky is visiting Denmark, and needs to exchange some British pounds for Danish kroner (kr). Her bank uses the graph on the right to work out the exchange rate.

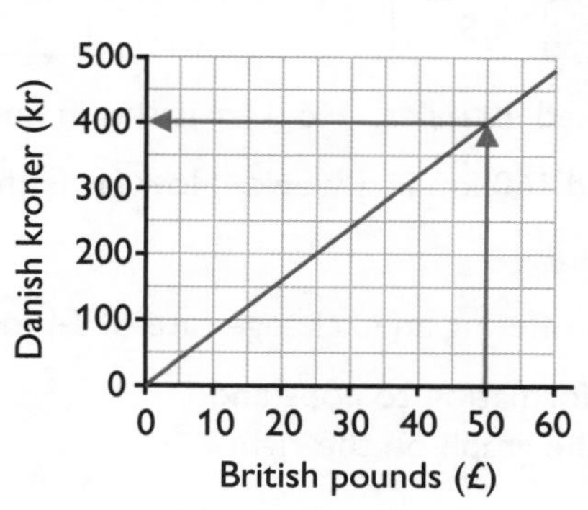

How many Danish kroner will Becky get for £50?

Draw a vertical line up from £50 on the horizontal axis to the red line.

Then draw a line across to the vertical axis to get the answer: £50 = **400 kr**

How many British pounds would Becky have to exchange to get 1000 kr?

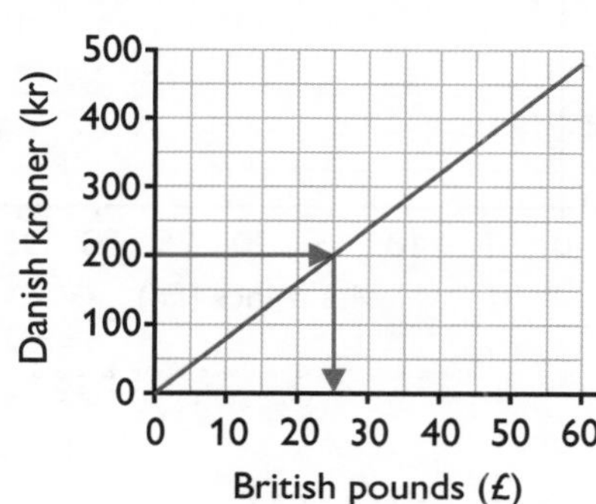

1000 kr isn't on the graph so use a smaller conversion and scale up. Draw a line across from 200 kr on the vertical axis to the red line.

Then draw a line down to the horizontal axis to find 200 kr = £25.

1000 kr = 200 kr × 5
So 1000 kr = £25 × 5 = **£125**

Set A

The graph on the right shows the exchange rate between British pounds (£) and US dollars ($).

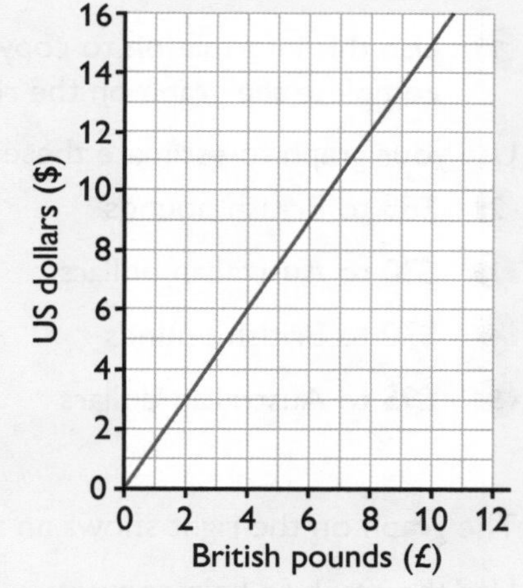

Use the graph to find these amounts in US dollars:

1. £8
2. £4
3. £10
4. £5

Use the graph to find these amounts in British pounds:

5. $3
6. $9
7. Use your answer to question 6 to convert $90 to British pounds.

The table below shows approximate conversions between centimetres and inches.

Centimetres	5	10	20
Inches	2	4	8

8. Use the information in the table to copy and complete the conversion graph on the right.

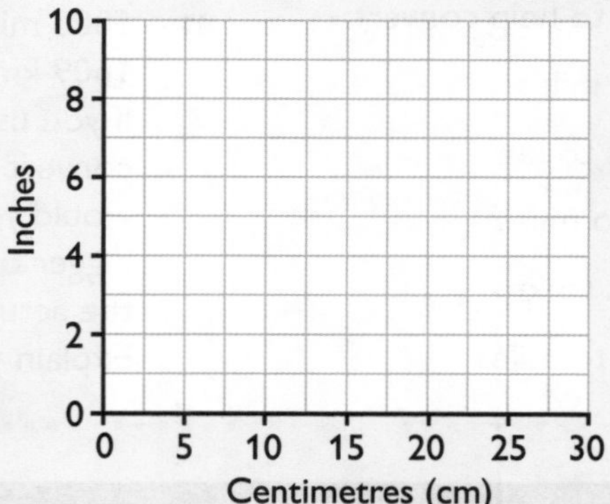

Use your graph to convert:

9. 25 cm to inches
10. 6 inches to cm
11. 12.5 cm to inches
12. 3 inches to cm

Set B

1 Four walking routes are shown in the table below. Use the graph on the right to copy and complete the table to show the route lengths in km and miles.

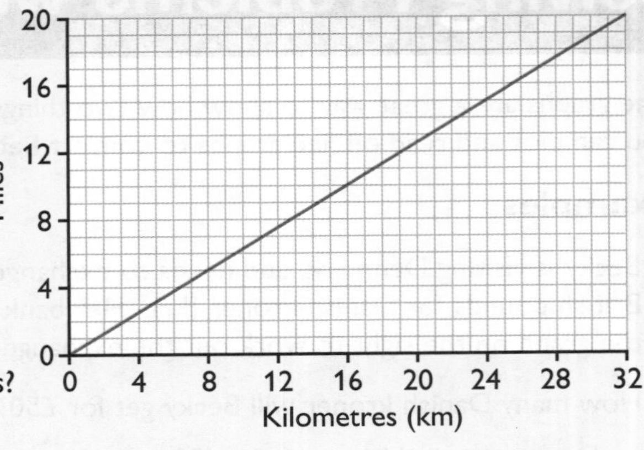

Route	A	B	C	D
Kilometres		16		12
Miles	5		15	

2 Nancy walked 40 miles. How far is this in km?

3 Fred walked 160 km in a week. How far is this in miles?

A travel agent is offering an exchange rate of £4 for 5 Swiss francs.

4 Use this information to copy and complete the graph on the right.

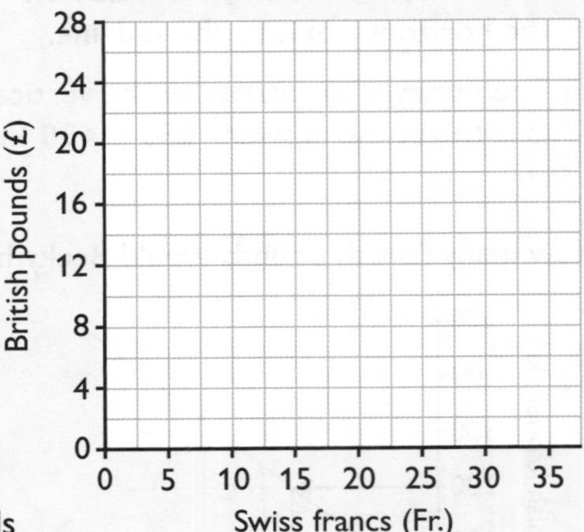

Use your graph to convert the following amounts:

5 £8 to Swiss francs

6 £24 to Swiss francs

7 15 Fr. to British pounds

8 £14 to Swiss francs

9 32.50 Fr. to British pounds

Use values from your graph to help you convert these amounts:

10 £40 to Swiss francs

11 £120 to Swiss francs

12 250 Fr. to British pounds

13 3000 Fr. to British pounds

Set C

Charlie exchanges £100 in British pounds, for $170 in Australian dollars.

1 Use this information to copy and complete the graph on the right.

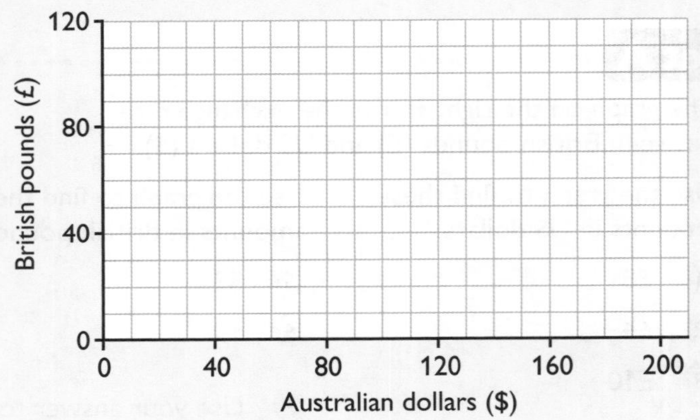

Use your graph to estimate these conversions:

2 $85 to British pounds

3 £30 to Australian dollars

4 $70 to British pounds

5 £95 to Australian dollars

The graph on the right shows an approximate conversion between miles and kilometres.

Use the graph to help convert:

6 80 km to miles

7 200 miles to km

8 800 km to miles

9 120 miles to km

10 4000 km to miles

11 1000 miles is equal to 1609 km to the nearest km. If you use the graph to convert 1000 miles to km, would your answer be bigger or smaller than the actual value? Explain your answer.

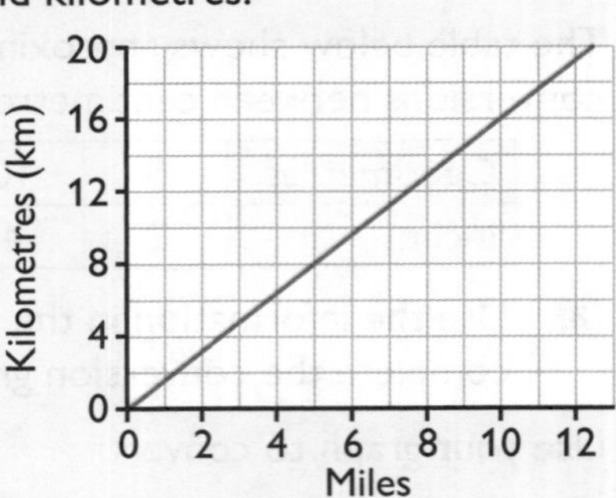

I can solve conversion problems with line graphs.

Solving Problems with Line Graphs — 2

If you want to understand a line graph, you need to be sure what each axis is showing. Always check this out first, before you try to do anything else with the graph.

Examples

One day Stevie walked 1250 m. She recorded her height above sea level at 5 points and drew a line graph to show her journey.

At the end of the walk, she is 20 m higher than at the start. Complete the graph to show this.

At the start of the walk, Stevie is 30 m above sea level.

She finishes 30 + 20 = **50 m** above sea level, after walking **1250 m**.

Plot a point up from 1250 m and across from 50 m, then connect this point to the end of the graph with a straight line.

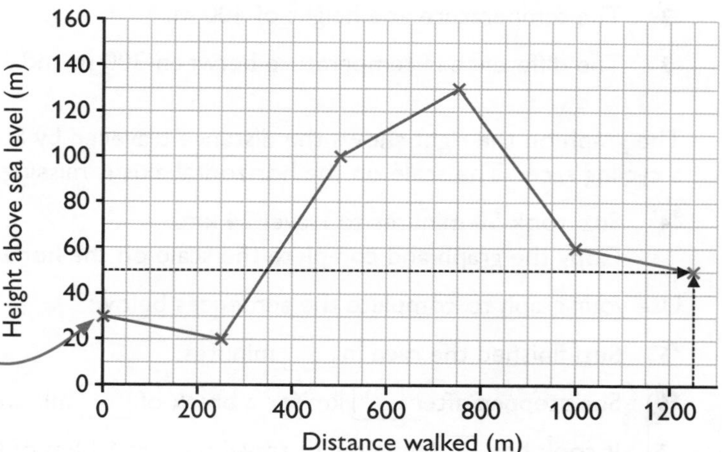

What is the difference in height between the highest and lowest points that Stevie recorded?

The highest point is at 130 m, and the lowest point is at 20 m.

So the difference in height is 130 m – 20 m = **110 m**

Set A

Rowan's fitness app measures her heart rate and the number of steps taken during a run. Four of these measurements are shown on the graph on the right.

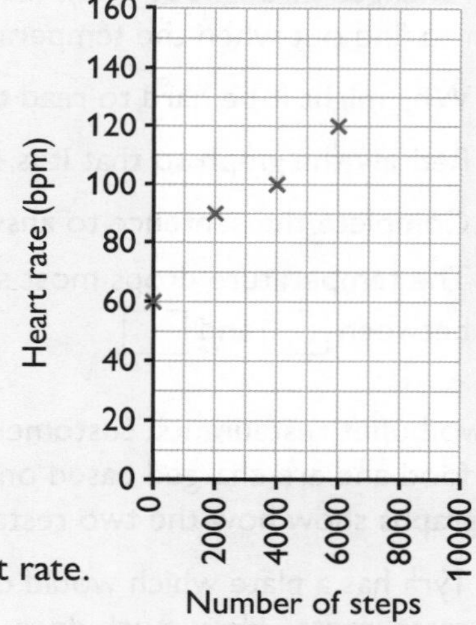

1. Copy the graph.
2. After 8000 steps, Rowan's heart rate was 150 beats per minute (bpm). Plot this point on the graph.
3. Rowan stops after 10 000 steps. Her heart rate is 160 bpm. Plot this point on the graph.
4. Join the points with straight lines to complete the graph.
5. After how many steps was Rowan's heart rate 100 bpm?
6. Find the difference between her highest and lowest recorded heart rate.

The graph on the right shows how the temperature inside a fridge changed over a period of 20 minutes. The fridge door had been left open, but it was shut when the temperature was 11 °C.

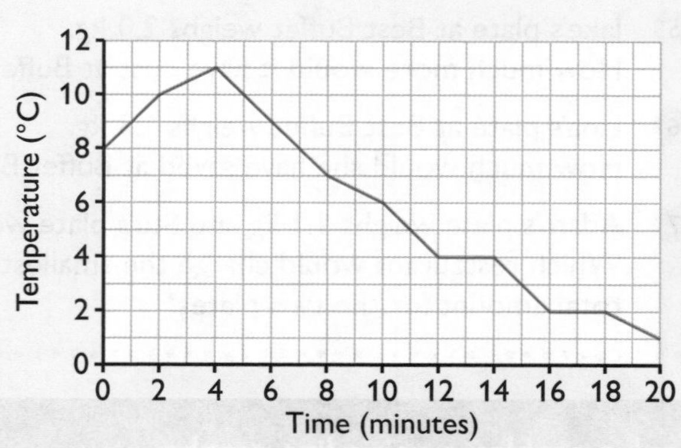

7. How many minutes after timing started was the fridge door shut?
8. What was the temperature inside the fridge 10 minutes after the door was shut?
9. How long does it take after the door was shut for the temperature to drop to 2 °C?

Set B

Dane records the temperature at different heights as he climbs up a mountain:

Height climbed (m)	0	200	500	800	900
Temperature (°C)	13	12	9	3	2

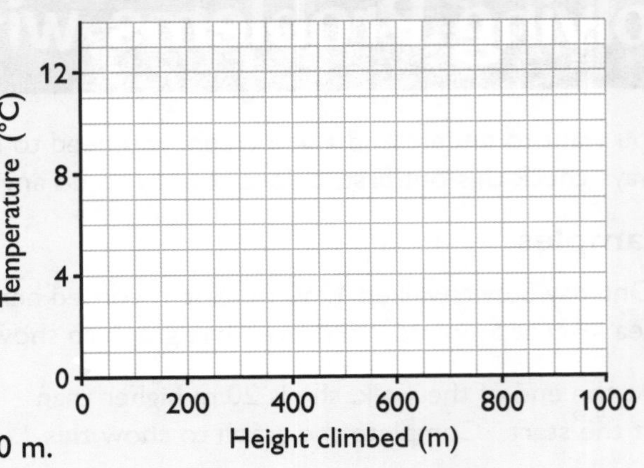

1. Copy the axes shown on the right, then plot the data in Dane's table as a line graph.

Use the graph to estimate the following:

2. The temperature at a height of 400 m.
3. The difference in temperature between 300 m and 750 m.

The graph on the right shows the distance travelled by Suzi during a cycling race. The scale on the horizontal axis is missing.

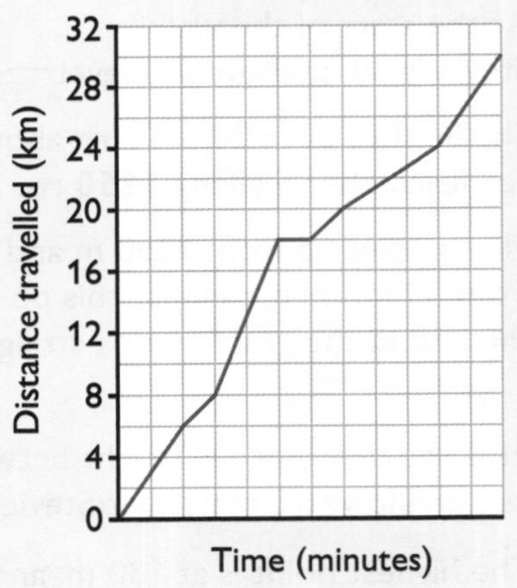

4. Suzi took 50 minutes to travel 24 km. Copy the graph and complete the scale on the horizontal axis.

Use your graph to complete the sentences below:

5. Suzi finished the race in ☐ minutes.
6. She stopped after ☐ km for a break of ☐ minutes.
7. It took her ☐ minutes to travel the last 10 km of the race.
8. Suzi travelled ☐ km in the last 5 minutes of the race.

Set C

The graph on the right shows how the temperature in a room changes throughout a day. Lauren wants to use this graph to find out when the temperature drops most sharply.

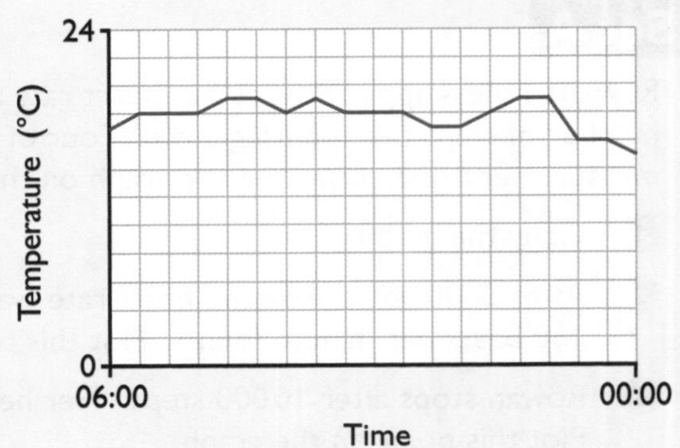

1. Why might it be hard to read this off the graph shown?
2. Redraw the graph so that it is easier to read.
3. Complete the sentence to answer Lauren's question:
   The temperature drops most sharply between ☐ and ☐.

At two buffet restaurants, customers fill their plates with food and are charged based on the weight of their plate. The graphs show how the two restaurants charge customers.

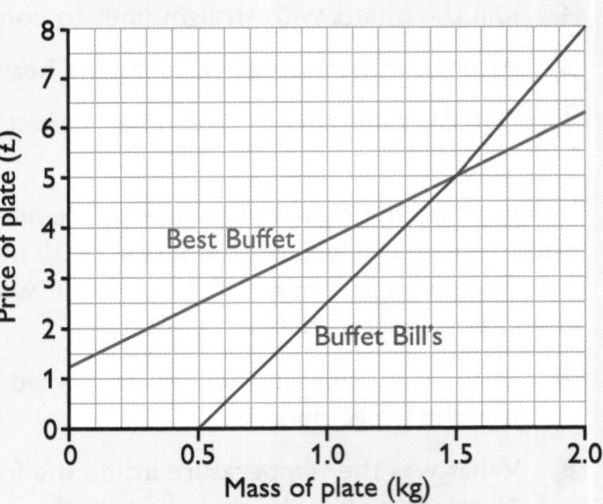

4. Tyra has a plate which would cost the same in both restaurants. How much does Tyra's plate weigh?
5. Jake's plate at Best Buffet weighs 2.0 kg. How much more would it have cost at Buffet Bill's?
6. Lina's plate at Best Buffet weighs 1.3 kg. How much would she have saved at Buffet Bill's?
7. Adam's plate weighs 1.1 kg and Stu's plate weighs 1.9 kg. Which restaurant would charge the smallest total amount for the two plates?

I can solve problems using line graphs.

Statistics — Review 1

The graph below can be used to convert between pints and gallons.

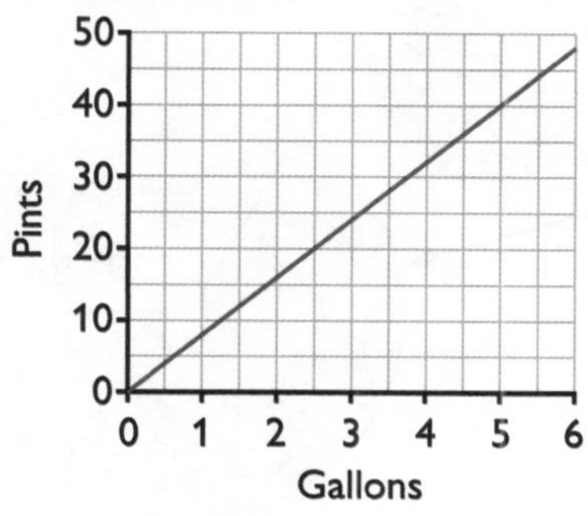

Use the graph to convert:

1 5 gallons to pints.

2 20 pints to gallons.

3 10 gallons to pints.

4 1 gallon to pints.

The graph below can be used to convert between British pounds (£) and Japanese yen (¥).

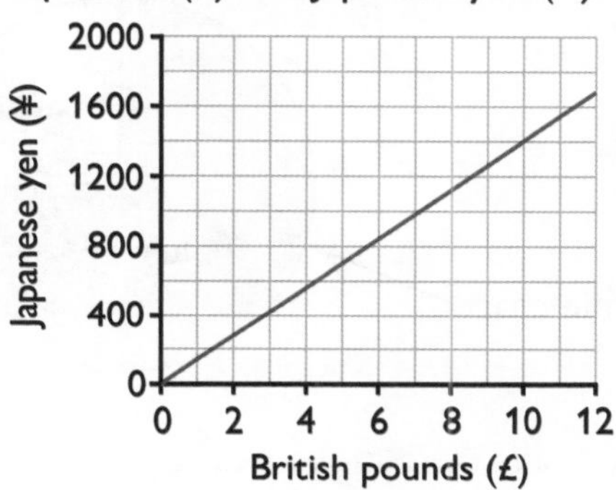

Use the graph to help you convert:

5 £10 to yen.

6 ¥700 to pounds.

7 ¥7000 to pounds.

8 £100 to yen.

3 metres is approximately equal to 10 feet.

9 Use this information to copy and complete the conversion graph below.

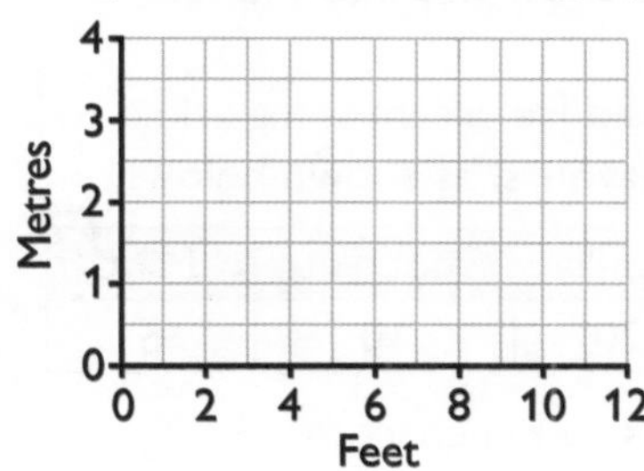

Use the graph to convert:

10 8 feet to metres, to the nearest 0.5 m.

11 1.75 metres to feet, to the nearest whole foot.

Anji measures the depth of the sea at 1 metre intervals from the shore. She records her first five measurements on the graph below:

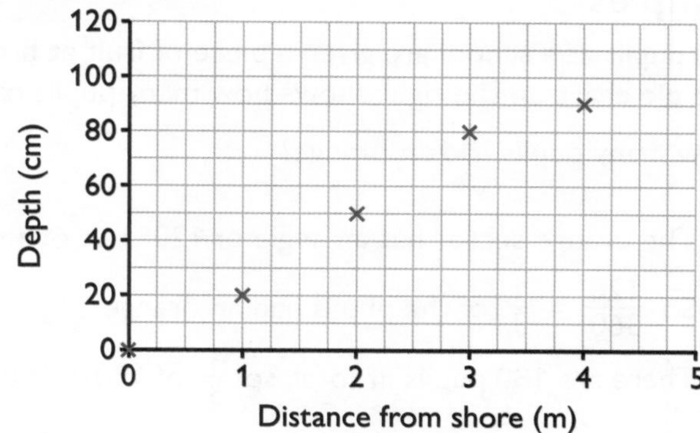

12 5 m from the shore, the water is 110 cm deep. Make a copy of the graph and plot this point.

13 Draw straight lines between the points to complete the graph.

Use your completed graph to find or estimate the depth at the following distances from the shore:

14 3 m

15 2 m

16 3.5 m

17 4.25 m

Estimate how far from the shore you'll be when the depth is:

18 10 cm

19 0.4 m

Two friends play a 90 second computer game. Their points totals during the game are shown below:

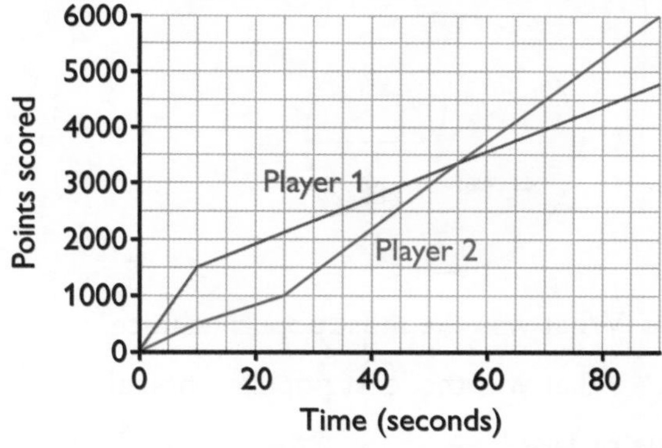

20 What was their points total after 10 seconds?

21 How much time had passed when the two players had equal points (greater than 0)?

22 How many more points did Player 2 have than Player 1 by the end of the game?

23 Estimate how much longer Player 2 took to score 2000 points than Player 1.

Good going on these graphs — a fantastic effort!

Pie Charts

Pie charts are a handy way to show proportions — each sector of the pie chart makes up a fraction of the total. Drawing a pie chart will put your arithmetic and angle drawing skills to the test.

Examples

180 pupils at a school are given a piece of fruit at break time. The pie chart on the right shows how many pupils had each type of fruit.

How many pupils had an orange?

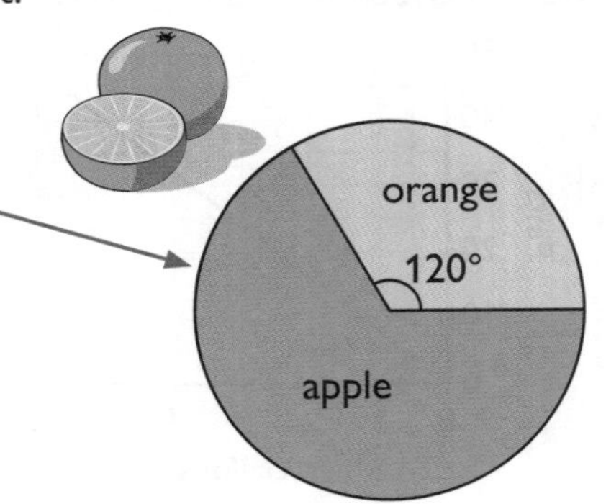

The orange sector has an angle of 120° out of a total of 360°.

So $\frac{120}{360} = \frac{1}{3}$ of the pupils had an orange.

There are 180 pupils in total, so $\frac{1}{3}$ of 180 = 180 ÷ 3 = **60 pupils** had an orange.

The angles of all the sectors in a pie chart always add up to 360°.

On a different day, 45 pupils had a banana and 135 had a plum. Draw a pie chart to show this information.

It helps to make a table to calculate the sector angles:

	Banana	Plum	Total
Number	45	135	180
Sector angle	45 × 2° = **90°**	135 × 2° = **270°**	360°

Divide 360° by the total: 360° ÷ 180 = 2°. So 2° represents one pupil.

Multiply the number of pupils by 2° to find each sector angle.

Now you've found the angles you can use a protractor to draw your pie chart. Remember to label each sector.

Set A

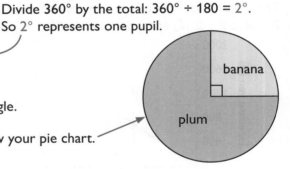

The pie chart below shows the breakfast choices of guests in a hotel.

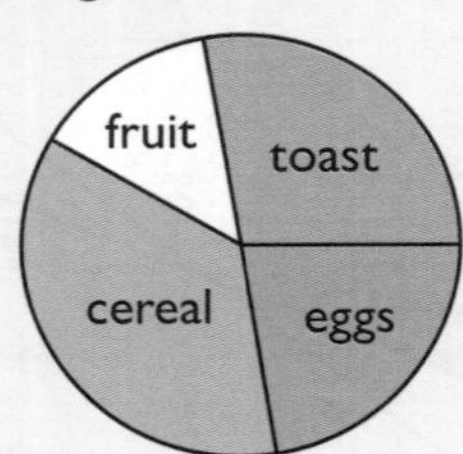

1. What was the most popular choice?
2. What was the least popular choice?

True or false?

3. Eggs were more popular than toast.
4. Half of the guests chose cereal or fruit.

The guests also chose between tea or coffee, as shown in the pie chart on the right:

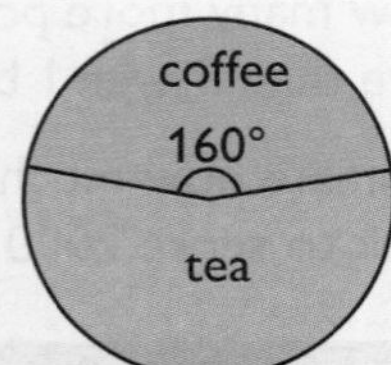

5. What is the angle of the 'tea' sector?

80 people were asked whether they liked ice cream. The results are shown in the table below:

	Yes	No	Total
Number of people	60	20	80
Sector angle	270°		360°

6. Work out the sector angle for the people who said 'No'.
7. Draw a pie chart to show this information.

36 of the people who liked ice cream were asked to choose between three flavours, as shown below:

	Vanilla	Chocolate	Mint
Number of people	20	10	6

Sally wants to show this in a pie chart. Find the missing numbers:

8. 360° ÷ 36 = ☐°, so ☐° represents one person.
9. 'Vanilla' sector angle = 20 × ☐° = ☐°
10. 'Chocolate' sector angle = 10 × ☐° = ☐°
11. 'Mint' sector angle = 6 × ☐° = ☐°

Set B

A pack of cake candles contains three different colours, as shown by the pie chart below.

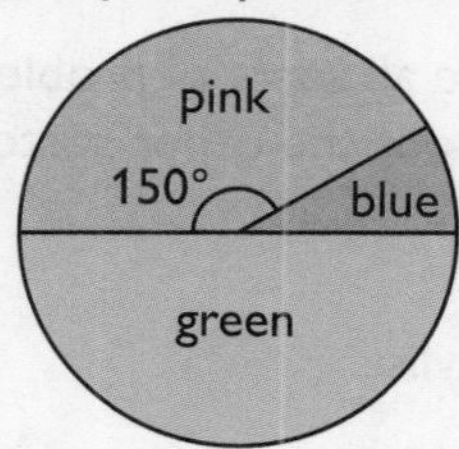

1. Which colour is the most common?
2. What is the angle of the 'blue' sector?
3. What percentage of the candles are green?
4. What fraction of the candles are pink?

There are 60 candles in the pack and 10 of them are broken.

5. Copy and complete the table to work out the sector angles for a pie chart showing this data.

	Broken	Not broken
Number	10	
Sector angle	60°	

6. Use the table to draw a pie chart.

At the end of a game show, contestants choose one of the envelopes A, B, C or D. The choices made by 20 contestants are shown in the pie chart below:

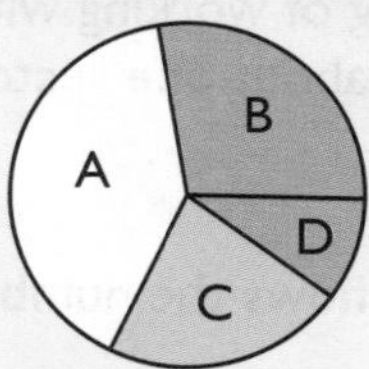

7. Work out the angle of the pie chart that represents one person.
8. 8 people chose envelope A. What is the sector angle for envelope A?
9. The sector angle for envelope D is 36°. How many people chose envelope D?

18 of the contestants won some money. The amount they won is shown in the table below.

	£1000	£100	£1
Number of people	4	6	8
Sector angle			

10. Work out the sector angle for each amount.
11. Draw a pie chart to show this data.

Set C

The pie chart on the right shows the hair colours of 36 members of a choir.

Blond 100°, Brown, Grey 60°

1. Put the hair colours in order, starting with the most common.
2. What angle of the pie chart represents one person?

What fraction of the choir members have:

3. grey hair?
4. blond hair?
5. brown hair?
6. The table below shows the eye colours of people in the choir. Complete the table and use it to draw a pie chart showing this information.

Eye colour	Brown	Blue	Green	Hazel
No. of people	10	15	9	2
Sector angle				

The two pie charts below show the hand that Year 6 girls and boys use to write.

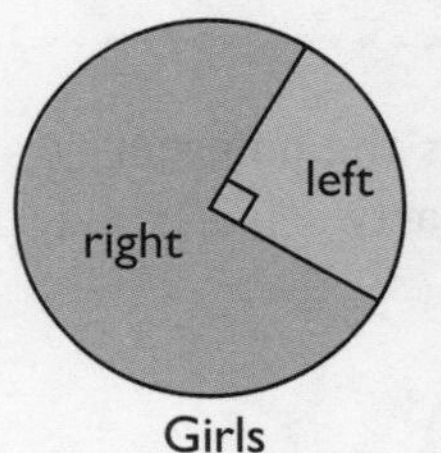

Girls

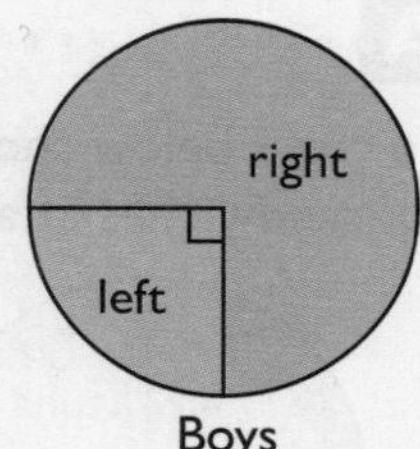

Boys

There are four more girls than boys in Year 6. Decide whether these statements are true or false. Explain your answers.

7. The same number of boys and girls write with their left hand.
8. A quarter of all Year 6 children write with their left hand.
9. More boys than girls write with their right hand.
10. Riya collects red, white and blue buttons. Half of her buttons are red. She has three times as many white as blue buttons. Draw a pie chart to show this information.

I can draw and use pie charts.      

Solving Problems with Pie Charts

Once you've got the hang of working with pie charts, you will be able to solve all sorts of problems. You can use information about one sector of the chart to work things out about the other sectors.

Examples

The pie chart below shows the number of each type of song on Anet's playlist.

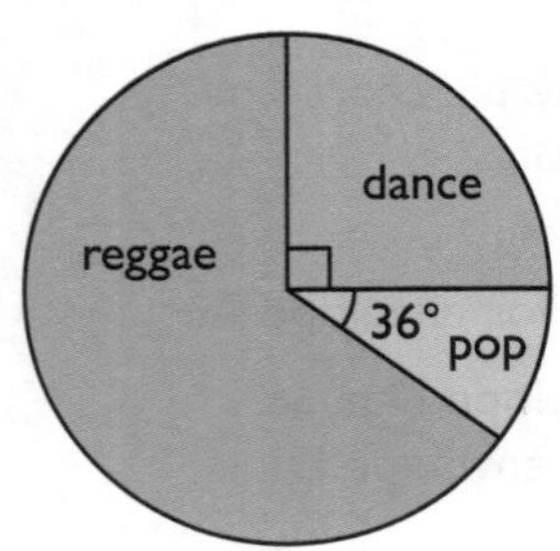

If there are 44 pop songs, work out the number of dance songs.

Pop songs make up $\frac{36}{360} = \frac{1}{10}$ of the playlist.

So the total number of songs must be 44 × 10 = 440 songs

Of these, $\frac{1}{4}$ are dance songs.

So there are 440 ÷ 4 = **110 dance songs**

The pie chart below shows the number of each type of song on Beena's playlist.
There are 90 songs on the playlist in total.

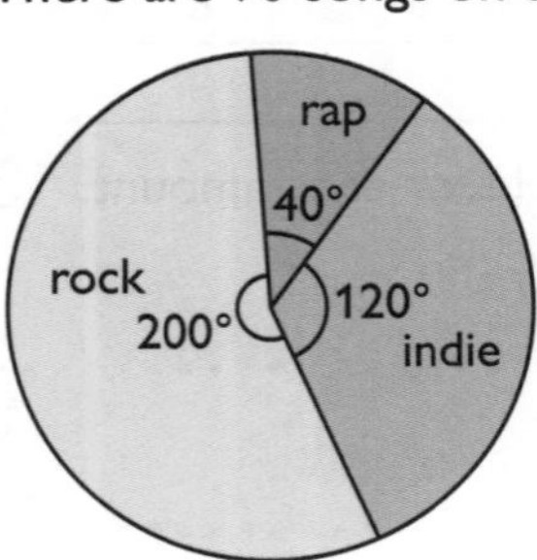

How many more rock songs than indie songs are there on her playlist?

The difference between rock and indie is 200° – 120° = 80°.

80° makes up $\frac{80}{360} = \frac{2}{9}$ of the pie chart.

So there are $\frac{2}{9}$ of 90 = 90 ÷ 9 × 2
= 10 × 2 = **20** more rock songs than indie songs.

You could also find the number of rock songs (50) and indie songs (30), then find the difference.

Set A

The pie chart below shows the different types of sandwiches at a party.

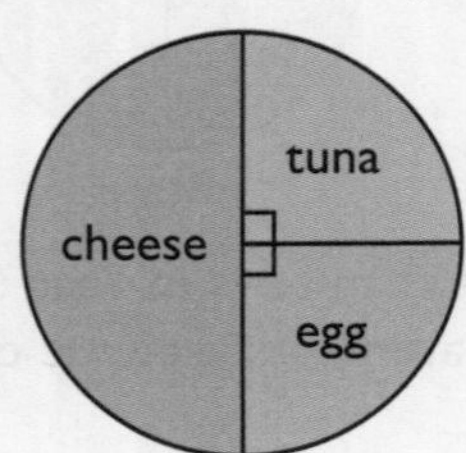

There are 12 cheese sandwiches.

1. How many sandwiches are there in total?
2. How many egg sandwiches are there?

Half of the tuna sandwiches also have cucumber.

3. How many tuna and cucumber sandwiches are there?
4. What would the sector angle for tuna and cucumber sandwiches be?

One third of the egg sandwiches also have cress.

5. How many egg and cress sandwiches are there?
6. What would the sector angle for egg and cress sandwiches be?

This pie chart below shows how many green, blue, red and white cars are parked in a car park. There are 160 cars in total. How many cars are:

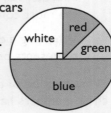

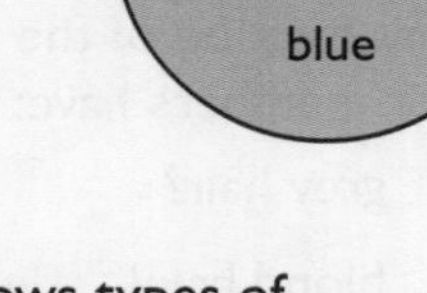

7. blue?
8. green?

The pie chart below shows types of drinks cans sold by a vending machine.

12 cans of juice were sold. How many:

9. cans were sold in total?
10. cans of cola were sold?
11. cans of lemonade were sold?

Set B

Some pupils from Years 4, 5 and 6 are in a school play. The pie chart below shows the proportion of the cast from each year.

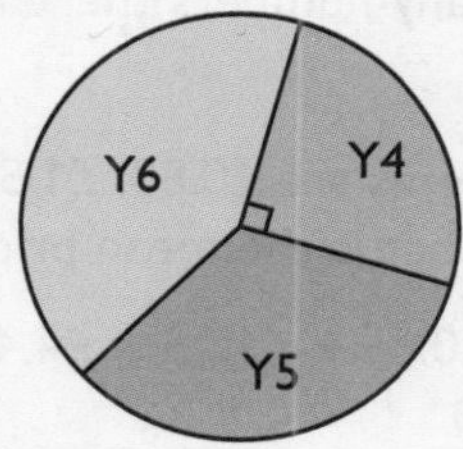

There are five pupils from Year 4 in the cast.

1. How many pupils are in the cast in total?
2. 30% of the cast are in Year 5. How many Year 5 pupils are in the cast?
3. How many Year 6 pupils are in the cast?
4. Jan finished in the top 3 places of gymnastics competitions 40 times. The pie chart on the right shows how often she finished 1st, 2nd and 3rd.

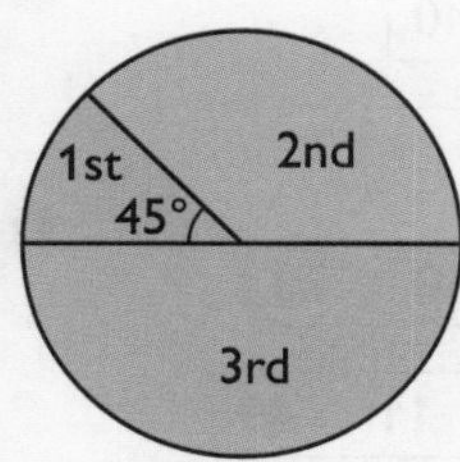

How many times did Jan finish in each place?

5. Chen asked people in his town if they like reality TV. The results are shown in the pie chart on the right.

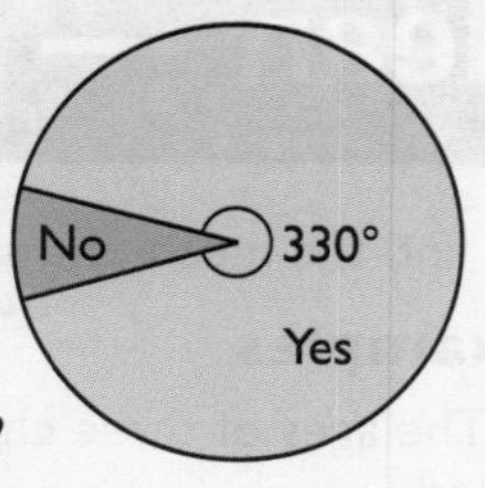

6 people said 'No'. How many people said 'Yes'?

The two pie charts below show the number of cones and lollies sold by an ice-cream van one weekend.

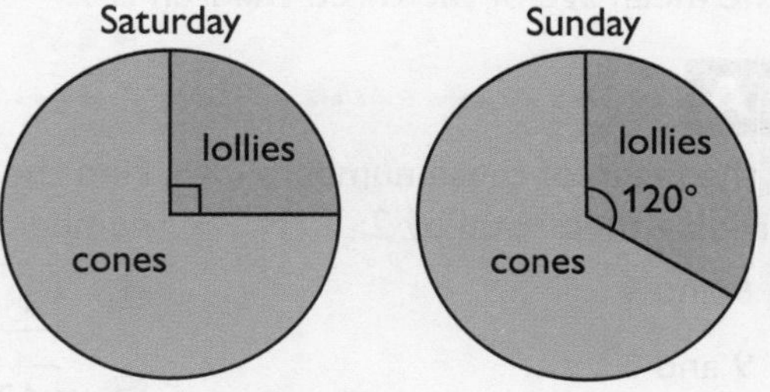

The same number of lollies were sold each day.

6. On which day were more cones sold? Explain your answer.

There were 300 cones sold on Saturday.

7. How many lollies were sold on Saturday?
8. How many cones were sold on Sunday?

Set C

Boxes A and B contain the same number of biscuits. The type of biscuits in each box is shown in the pie charts below:

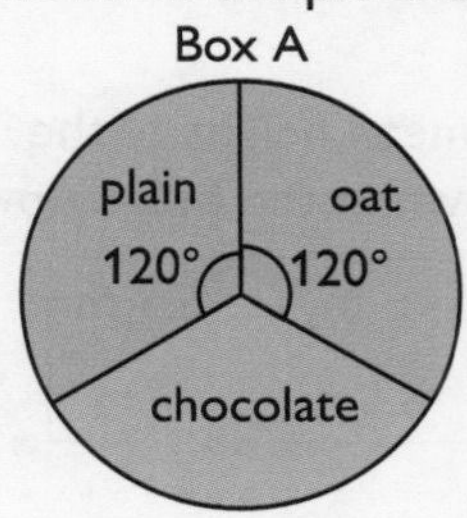

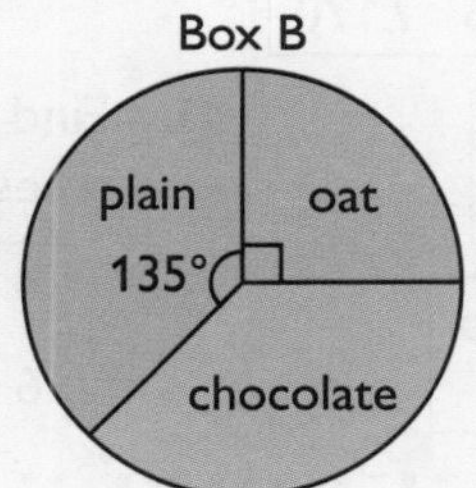

There are 16 plain biscuits in Box A.

1. How many biscuits are in Box A in total?
2. How many oat biscuits are in Box B?
3. How many more chocolate biscuits are in Box B than Box A?

Wes spent £180 on clothes, food and travel in a week. The pie chart on the right shows how he spent the money.

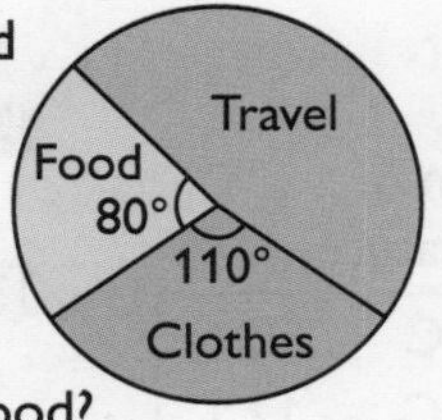

4. How much more did he spend on clothes than on food?

A money jar contains three types of silver coin: 10p, 20p and 50p. The pie chart on the right shows the number of each type of coin in the money jar.

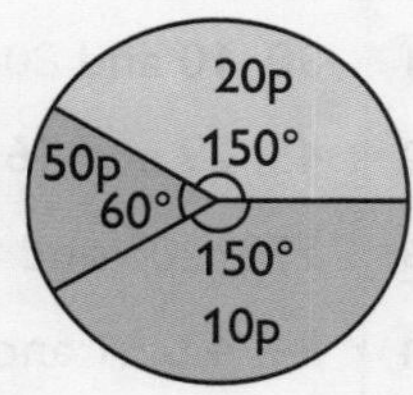

The 50p coins in the jar have a total value of £4.

5. How many coins are in the jar in total?
6. How many 10p coins are in the jar?
7. How much money is in the jar in total?
8. The ingredients in two different bowls of muesli are shown in the pie charts below:

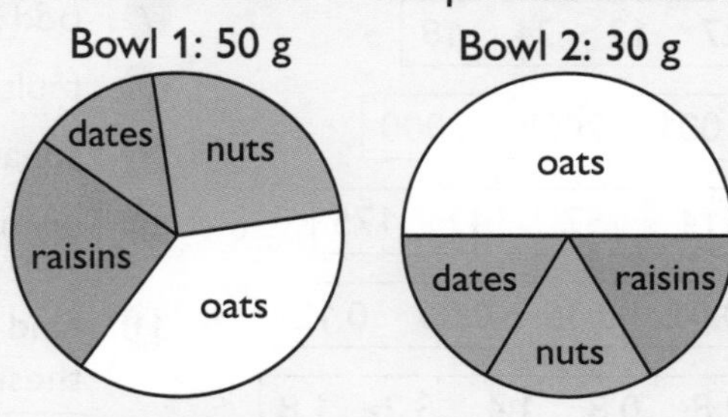

Estimate how many more grams of raisins are in bowl 1 than bowl 2. Explain your answer.

I can solve problems involving pie charts.

Mean — 1

To find the mean of a set of numbers, just add them up and divide by how many numbers there are.

Examples

The ages of three children are 8, 8 and 11.
What is their mean age?

8 + 8 + 11 = 27
27 ÷ 3 = **9**
So the mean age of the three children is **9**.

The prices of four items are £0.80, £1.50, £0.85 and £1.25. What is the mean price?

£0.80 + £1.50 + £0.85 + £1.25 = £4.40
£4.40 ÷ 4 = **£1.10**
So the mean price is **£1.10**.

Set A

Find the mean of these numbers by dividing their total by 2:

1. 6 and 4
2. 9 and 13
3. 42 and 40

Find the mean of these numbers by dividing their totals by 3:

4. 3, 8 and 10
5. 7, 11 and 15

Find the mean of the numbers in each box:

6. 1 10 13
7. 13 13 40
8. 1 6 8 9
9. 10 20 30 20
10. 5 9 6 11 19

11. A plumber has 3 pieces of pipe measuring 2 m, 3 m and 7 m. What is their mean length?
12. Three sisters are 6, 14 and 16 years old. What is their mean age?
13. On Nadiya's last four shopping trips she spent £10, £22, £28 and £40. What is the mean amount she spent each trip?

Set B

Find the mean of these numbers:

1. 30, 10 and 80
2. 45, 29 and 16
3. 220, 205 and 145
4. 34, 42, 51 and 33
5. 130, 250, 320 and 180
6. 1000, 1200, 2100 and 3700
7. 7, 23, 16, 19, 18 and 13

Find the mean of the prices in each box:

8. £11 £12 £20 £29
9. £115 £130 £145 £170
10. £1500 £4300 £600 £2400
11. 45p 52p 88p £1.03 £1.12

12. Rico babysits two 6 year olds and three 11 year olds. What is the mean age of the children he babysits?
13. Find the mean height of the trees shown in the box below.

4 m	6 m	6.5 m
6 m	6.5 m	7 m

Set C

Find the mean of these numbers:

1. 27 12 34 19
2. 1001 2002 3000
3. 114 157 142 175
4. 0.01 0.05 0.06 0.12
5. 2.8 0.8 1.4 3.2 1.8
6. –5 –6 20 –2 9 –1

Find the mean of the first five:

7. odd numbers
8. multiples of five
9. square numbers
10. prime numbers
11. Find the mean of these temperatures:

–3°C	–5°C	10°C
5°C	–1°C	12°C

The weights of 3 girls and 3 boys are shown in the table below.

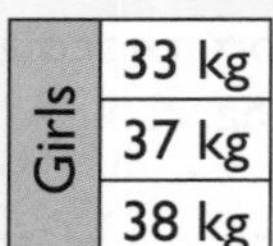

Girls	Boys
33 kg	36 kg
37 kg	41 kg
38 kg	43 kg

12. What is the mean weight of all the children?
13. How much heavier is the mean weight of the boys than the girls?

I can calculate the mean.

Mean — 2

As well as being able to calculate the mean, you need to understand what it actually tells you.

Examples

Four school classes have a mean class size of 28.
How many pupils are there in total?

Mean = total number of pupils ÷ 4 = 28,
so total = 28 × 4 = **112 pupils**.

Three school bags have a mean mass of 2 kg.
Two of the bags weigh 1.1 kg and 1.8 kg.
How much does the third school bag weigh?

Total mass = 2 × 3 = 6 kg
6 – 1.1 – 1.8 = 3.1
So the third school bag weighs **3.1 kg**.

Set A

Work out the mean number of runs scored by these cricketers:

1. Total runs = 40
   Games = 8
2. Total runs = 200
   Games = 5
3. Total runs = 150
   Games = 3
4. Total runs = 500
   Games = 10
5. The mean age of two people is 20. What is their total age?
6. Peter has 10 packs of sweets. The mean number of sweets in each pack is 12. How many sweets does he have in total?
7. Amir has 7 buttons, with a mean mass of 5 g. What is the total mass of the buttons?

Find the missing values:

8. mean = 7
   values: 5, 8 and ☐
9. mean = 11
   values: 10, ☐ and 12
10. mean = 15
    values: 11, 15 and ☐
11. mean = 3
    values: 2, 2, 3 and ☐

Set B

1. Five lambs have a total weight of 65 kg. What is the mean weight of the lambs?
2. Four friends have a mean height of 130 cm. What is their total height?
3. The mean number of pupils in a class is 30. There are 360 pupils in the school. How many classes are there?

Sally got a mean mark of 14 on 5 science tests.

4. How many marks did Sally get in total?
5. Four of her marks were 12, 10, 14 and 18. What mark did she get on the other test?
6. On the sixth test, Sally got 15 marks. Will this make her mean mark higher or lower?

Find the missing amounts:

7. 28 m, 14 m, 19 m, ☐ m
   (mean = 20 m)
8. £10, £25, £32, £48, £☐
   (mean = £40)
9. 1040 ml, 950 ml, ☐ ml
   (mean = 1800 ml)
10. 0.8 kg, 1.9 kg, ☐ kg
    (mean = 1.3 kg)

Set C

Find the missing amounts:

1. 350 m, 470 m, 220 m, ☐ m
   (mean = 290 m)
2. 128 ml, 114 ml, 119 ml, ☐ ml
   (mean = 117 ml)
3. 4.5 g, 7.4 g, 2.1 g, 4.7 g, ☐ g
   (mean = 4 g)
4. £3.50, £4.20, £2.90, £☐
   (mean = £3.80)
5. Jack runs 100 m five times and his mean time is 12 s. His first 4 times were: 12.8 s, 12.2 s, 11.5 s, 11.7 s. What was his fifth time?
6. Five apples have a mean mass of 85 g. An orange is added, and the mean mass drops to 80 g. What is the mass of the orange?

The mean length of 8 pencils is 10 cm. When a blue and a red pencil are added, the mean length goes up to 11 cm.

7. Find the total length of the blue and red pencils.
8. The red pencil is 4 cm longer than the blue pencil. Work out the length of the red and blue pencils.

I can calculate and interpret the mean.

Statistics — Review 2

Flo the florist makes bunches of flowers. The pie chart below shows how many of each type of flower she uses in each bunch.

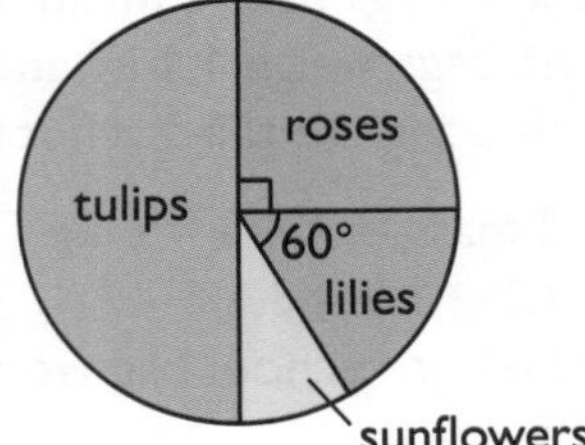

1. What type of flower does Flo use most?
2. What percentage of the bunch is made of tulips?
3. What fraction of the bunch is made of lilies?
4. What is the angle of the 'sunflowers' sector?

The number of each type of nut in a bag of mixed nuts is recorded in the table below.

	brazil	cashew	peanut	Total
Number	15	45	120	180
Sector angle				360°

5. What angle represents 1 nut on the pie chart?
6. Copy and complete the table above to find the angles for each sector of the pie chart.
7. Draw a pie chart to show this information.

The pie chart below shows the different types of tree in a forest.

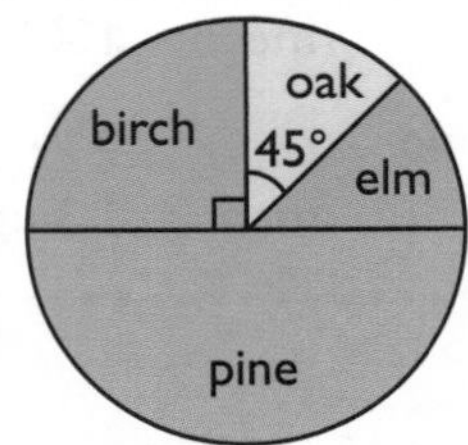

There are 560 trees in the forest in total. How many trees are:

8. pine?
9. birch?
10. oak?
11. elm?

Two more forests have exactly the same pie chart as the one above.

12. In one of the forests, there are 190 elm trees. How many pine trees are there?
13. In the other forest there are 200 birch trees. How many more pines than elms are there?

The number of minutes spent on music, news and chat on two different radio shows are shown on these pie charts.

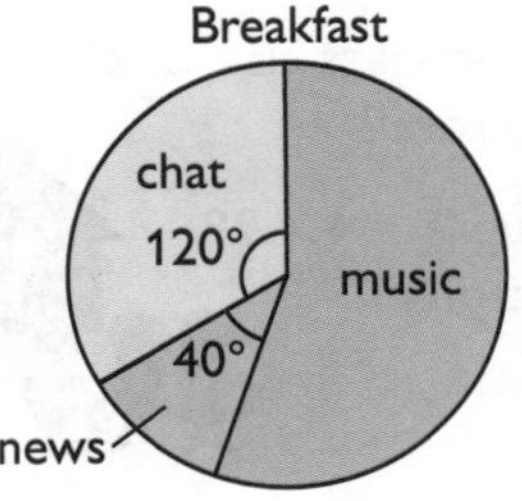

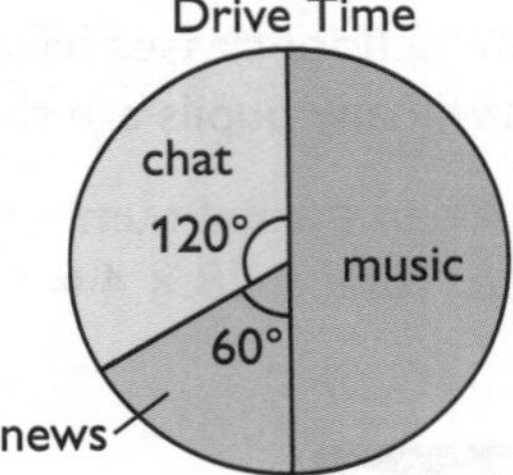

There are 10 minutes of news on the Breakfast show. There are 20 minutes of chat on the Drive Time show.

14. How many minutes of news are on the Drive Time show?
15. How many minutes long is the Drive Time show?
16. How many minutes long is the Breakfast show?
17. How many more minutes of chat are on the Breakfast Show than the Drive Time show?
18. How many minutes of music are played in total over both shows?

Find the mean of:

19. 5, 7 and 9
20. 12, 15 and 21
21. 8, 7, 11 and 18
22. 20, 10, 40, 60 and 10
23. 47, 38, 34 and 41
24. 250, 180, 160 and 210
25. 1500, 1900 and 3200
26. 0.7, 1.3, 2.9 and 3.1
27. 45, 78, 64, 79 and 34
28. –2, –9, 4, 5, 6 and 8

29. The heights of six teachers are shown below:

155 cm	164 cm	180 cm
162 cm	175 cm	160 cm

What is the mean height of the six teachers?

The mean age of the five members of a band is 33.

30. What is the total age of the band?
31. Four of the members have ages of 25, 27, 30 and 33. How old is the fifth member?

The mean number of spots on ten ladybirds is 4.3.

32. What is the total number of spots on the ladybirds?
33. There are six ladybirds with 2 spots, and three ladybirds with 7 spots. How many spots does the last ladybird have?

There were some mean questions in there — but you got through it like a piece of pie!

Statistics — Challenges

a) Which of the statements A-E below are true for this pie chart?

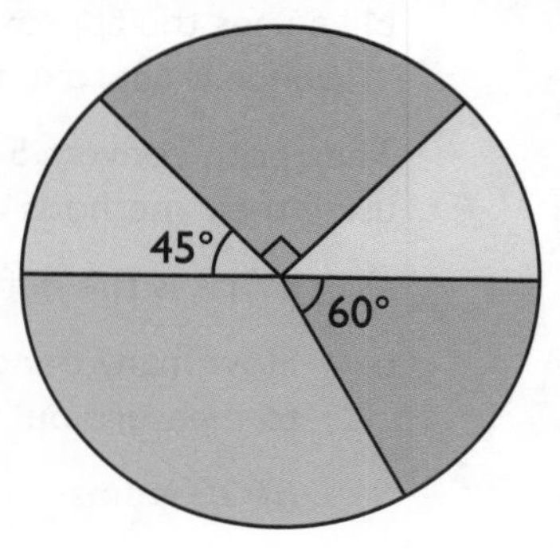

A: The biggest sector makes up a quarter of the chart.

B: Two of the sectors are the same size.

C: The smallest sector is 10% of the chart.

D: The two smallest sectors make up 25% of the chart.

E: The two biggest sectors make up half of the chart.

b) Complete the table of values below which have been used to make the pie chart.

	green	purple	yellow	red	blue
Number		150			

Lola is travelling through Europe on the train.

She is travelling from Croatia to Hungary, and wants to change her money from Croatian kuna (kn) into Hungarian forints (Ft).

The graphs below show the exchange rate between each of these currencies and euros.

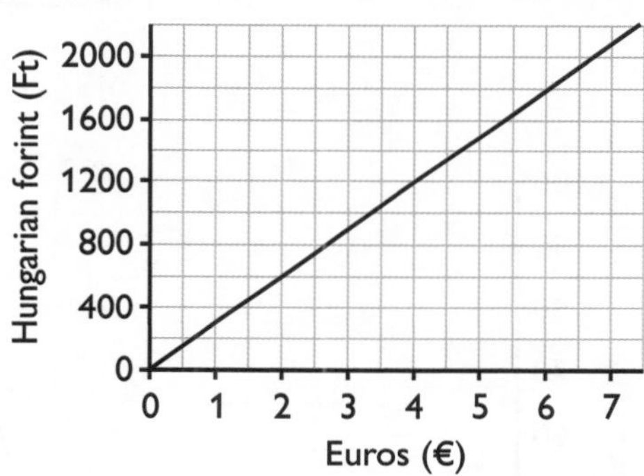

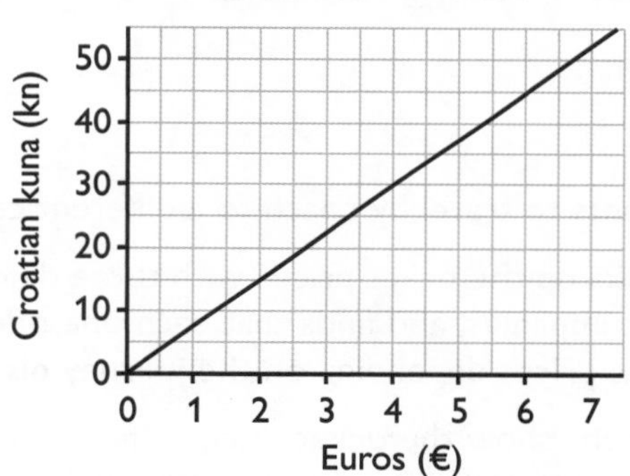

a) Lola has 30 kn. Use the graphs to work out how much this will be in Hungarian forints.

b) Use your answer to part a) to plot a new graph for Lola to convert kuna to forints.

c) Now try some conversions of your own:

- Choose an amount of Hungarian forint and use your graph, or the graphs above, to convert it to Croatian kuna.
- Tell a friend the amount in Croatian kuna and see if they can convert it into Hungarian forint.

Did they get the same amount you started with?

Libby has to take tests in Maths, English, Science, History and Music. Each test is out of 100.

Libby's parents have promised her a present if she gets a mean test score of at least 90.

Here are her results so far:

Maths: 75 English: 80 Science: 85
History: ? Music: ?

Will Priti be able to get a present? Explain your answer.

4 Kim and Mike use a different method to convert between grams and ounces.

Kim uses the conversion graph on the right.

Mike uses the approximation:
"1 ounce is approximately equal to 28 grams."

They both convert 5 ounces of flour to grams using their methods and measure out that amount.

a) What is the difference in the amount of flour they measure out?

b) How many ounces of flour would they need to measure out for the difference to be:

(i) 20 grams?

(ii) 100 grams?

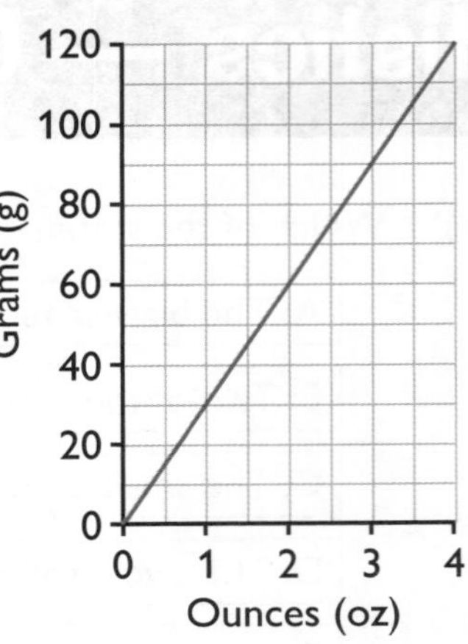

5 Six friends are hoping to be selected for the school's maths quiz team.

They each take an entry test, and get a combined points total of 180. The pie chart on the right shows how the points are shared.

The teacher selects four of the friends for the team. Their mean score in the test was 35.

Who was selected for the team?

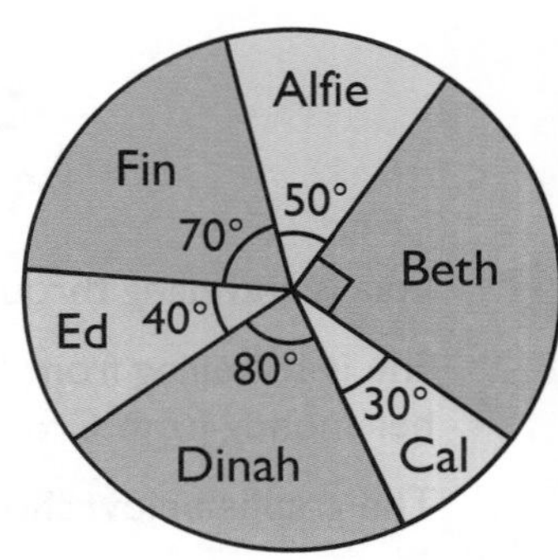

6 Judy wants to travel by coach to a different city.

She looks up the ticket prices with three different coach companies, and finds that each one offers different prices depending on the journey distance.

The graphs show the ticket prices offered by each company, but Judy is not sure which graph matches which company.

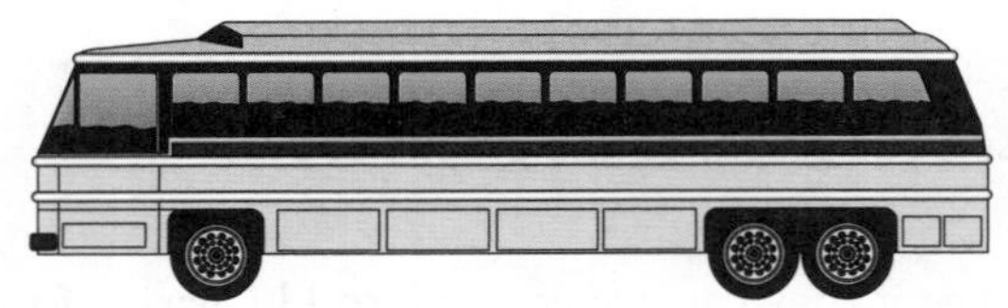

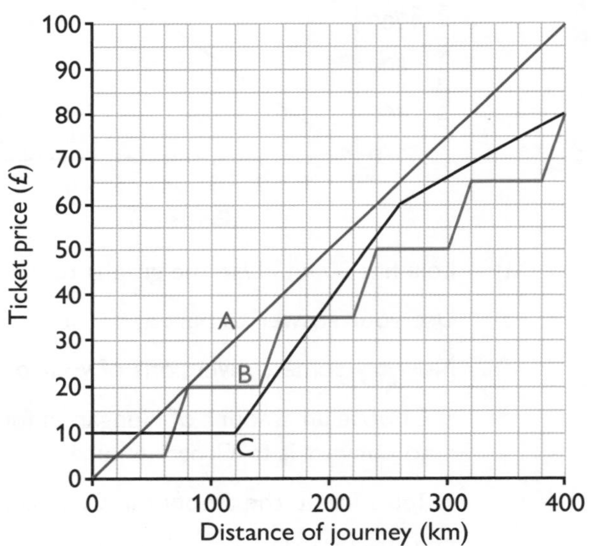

a) Use the information below to match each company to graph A, B and C.

With SlowCoach, you'll pay the same amount whether your journey is 80 km or 120 km.	CoachPotato charge up to £30 less than Coach-to-Coast for a ticket.

b) Find the cost of a 220 km journey with each company.

c) Estimate the range of journey distances where company C is the cheapest.

A big 'well done' to you for tackling those tricky tasks!

Glossary and Index

acute angle	An angle that measures less than 90°. It is smaller than a right angle. p135-136
area	The area of a shape is the amount of surface it covers. p106-111
axis/axes	The horizontal axis is the line that goes across a graph or chart from the origin. The vertical axis is the line that goes up and/or down from the origin. Axes is the word for more than one axis. p143-150
BODMAS	The order that you do things in a calculation. It stands for Brackets, Division, Multiplication, Addition and Subtraction. p33-34
capacity	The amount something can hold when it's full. Capacity is usually measured in litres or millilitres. p101
circumference	The distance around the edge of a circle. (The perimeter of a circle.) p137-138
common factor	Factors that two or more numbers share. p31
common multiple	Multiples that two or more numbers share. For example, multiples of 3 are 3, 6, 9, 12, 15... Multiples of 5 are 5, 10, 15... 15 is a common multiple of 3 and 5. p32
conversion graph	A line graph that lets you convert between different units. For example, from kilometres to miles, or miles to kilometres. p155-156
coordinates	Tell you the position of a point from the origin. They're always written in the same way, for example, (3, 4). The first number gives the position on the x-axis and the second number gives the position on the y-axis. p143-148
cubic centimetre, cm^3	A unit for measuring volume. A cube with edges 1 cm long. p113-116
decimal places	The places in a number to the right of the decimal point. For example, the number 4.56 has 2 decimal places. p57-58
degrees, °	The unit used to measure angles. p120-133
denominator	The bottom number of a fraction. p47
diagonal	A diagonal line is the line joining two corners that aren't next to each other in a shape. People also say 'a diagonal line' to mean a sloping line (not horizontal or vertical). p135-136
diameter	The distance across a circle, passing through the centre. p137-138
enlargement	An enlargement is where a shape gets bigger using a scale factor. p78-79
equation	A mathematical statement with one or more missing numbers represented by symbols or letters. For example, 5X + 2Y = 7. p91-94
equivalent fractions	Fractions which are written differently but are equal to each other. For example, $\frac{3}{6}$ and $\frac{1}{2}$. p47
estimate	An estimate is a sensible guess at the answer. You can use rounding to help you estimate answers. p37-38

Glossary and Index

exterior angle	An angle between the side of a shape and a line extended from the next side. p124
face	A side of a solid shape. Faces can be flat, as on cubes. They can also be curved, as on cylinders. p139
factor	A whole number that divides exactly into another whole number. For example, the factors of 6 are 1, 2, 3 and 6. p31
formula	A formula tells you how to work out one quantity when you know a different quantity. For example, you can work out the total number of legs in a group of ants by using the formula: Total number of legs = number of ants × 6. p85-87
horizontal	Going across. Shelves and table tops are horizontal. p149-150
hundredth	The second digit to the right of the decimal point. One hundredth is written 0.01 or $\frac{1}{100}$. p57-58
improper fraction	A fraction with a numerator bigger than its denominator, for example, $\frac{9}{7}$. p48-52
interior angle	An angle inside a shape between two adjacent sides. p124
irregular polygon	In an irregular polygon, not all sides are of equal length and not all of the angles are equal. p135-136
kilogram, kg	A unit for measuring mass. 1 kilogram = 1000 grams. p101
kite	A quadrilateral with two pairs of equal sides and one pair of equal angles. p122-123
length	A measure of how long or how far something is. Length is usually measured in millimetres, centimetres, metres or kilometres. p99-100
line graph	A graph with points that are joined by lines. p155-158
line of symmetry	If you put a mirror on the line of symmetry, it looks like you can see the whole shape. It's the same thing as a mirror line. p135-136
litre, l	A unit for measuring volume or capacity. 1 litre = 1000 millilitres. Orange juice often comes in 1 litre cartons. p101
mass	Mass is what most people mean when they say 'weight'. Mass is usually measured in kilograms or grams. p101
mean	One kind of average. To work out the mean, you add up all the values then divide by the total number of values. p164-165
mixed number	A mixed number has a whole-number part and a fraction part, for example, $3\frac{1}{2}$. p48-52
multiple	Multiples are the numbers in a times table. For example, the multiples of 4 are 4, 8, 12, 16... p32

Glossary and Index

negative	Negative numbers are numbers below 0. For example, –1 or –10. p4
net	A 2D shape that will fold up to make a 3D shape. p140-141
numerator	The top number of a fraction. p47
obtuse angle	An angle that measures more than 90° but less than 180°. It is between one and two right angles. p135-136
ordering	Putting in order. For example, to order 3, 1 and 2 from smallest to largest, start with the smallest, then the next smallest: 1, 2, 3. p6, p48
origin	Where the two axes of a graph meet. It has the coordinates (0, 0). p143-144
parallel	Parallel lines are always the same distance apart. They will never meet or cross. p135-136
parallelogram	A quadrilateral with two pairs of parallel sides opposite each other. p108-109
partition	Split a number up. You can partition numbers in many ways. For example, 173 = 100 + 70 + 3 or 173 = 150 + 20 + 3. p13-14
perimeter	The distance around the outside of a 2D shape. p110-111
perpendicular	Lines that meet each other at right angles (or would meet at right angles if you extended them) are perpendicular. p135-136
pie chart	A circular chart that shows things as proportions. The angles of the sectors in a pie chart add up to 360°. p160-163
place value	A digit's value in a number depends on its position in the number. Each position has a different place value. For example, the value of 2 in 827 is 2 tens. p2
polygon	Any flat shape with straight sides. p132-133, p135-136
powers of 10	Numbers that are a 10 followed by just zeros: 10, 100, 1000, 10 000, 100 000 and 1 000 000 are powers of 10. p57-58
proportion	Another word for fraction. For example, 1 in every 4 is the same as $\frac{1}{4}$. p73
protractor	You can use a protractor to measure angles. p128-133
quadrant	Each quarter of a grid. There are 4 quadrants altogether. p143-144
quadrilateral	A flat shape with four straight sides. p122-123, p130-131, p135-136
radius	The distance from the centre of a circle to the edge. p137-138
ratio	A ratio is one way of comparing amounts. For example, if there are three apples and two oranges in a bowl, the ratio of apples to oranges is 3 to 2, written 3:2. p74

Glossary and Index

rectangle	A quadrilateral with two pairs of equal sides and four right angles. p110-111
reflection	The image of a shape shown by a mirror across a mirror line. p147-148
regular polygon	In a regular polygon, all the sides are equal lengths and all the angles are the same. p124, p135-136
remainder	What's left over when you divide. For example, 7 ÷ 2 = 3 remainder 1. p29
right angle	A quarter turn, or 90°. p135-136
rounding	Finding a nearby number that's similar, but easier to use in calculations. For example, 27 rounded to the nearest 10 is 30. p7, p36
scale factor	The number each side of a shape is multiplied by in an enlargement. p78-79
sequence	A list of numbers. There is a rule or pattern that links each number to the one before. For example, 3, 6, 9, 12... is a sequence. p88-89
simplifying	Simplifying fractions means finding an equivalent fraction with the smallest possible denominator. For example, $\frac{8}{10}$ simplifies to $\frac{4}{5}$. p47
square centimetre, cm^2	A unit for measuring area. A square with sides 1 cm long. p106-111
tenth	The first digit after the decimal point. One tenth is written 0.1 or $\frac{1}{10}$. p57-58
term	Each number in a number sequence. For example, in the sequence 0, 2, 4, 6, 8, there are 5 terms. p88-89
thousandth	The third digit after the decimal point. One thousandth is written as 0.001 or $\frac{1}{1000}$. p57-58
translation	When a shape moves from one place to another without rotating or flipping. p149-150
vertex/vertices	A vertex is a corner. Vertices is the word for corners. p139
vertical	Going straight up and down. Walls and flag poles are vertical. p149-150
vertically opposite angles	Pairs of angles made when two lines cross. Vertically opposite angles are equal. p125-126
volume	The volume of a shape is the amount of space it takes up. p113-116

M6PB21